D0792855

scratching
the surface

canadian

anti-racist

feminist

thought

edited by

ENAKSHI DUA and ANGELA ROBERTSON

women's
P R E S S

To our mothers and grandmothers.

CATALOGUING IN PUBLICATION DATA

Main entry under title:

Scratching the surface : Canadian, anti-racist, feminist thought

Includes bibliographical references and index.
ISBN 0-88961-230-7

1. Minority women – Canada – Social conditions. 2. Sex discrimination against women – Canada. 3. Racism – Canada. 4. Canada – Race relations. 5. Feminist theory – Canada. I. Dua, Enakshi, 1958– . II. Robertson, Angela, 1967– .

HQ1453.S385 1999   305.48'8'00971   C99-931319-3

Cover art: LauraLee Harris' *Return*
Cover design and interior layout: Heather Guylar
Editor: Ann Decter
Assistant copy editor: Alexis Nicols
Proofreader: Alexis Nicols
Indexer: Martha Ayim

Published by Women's Press, 180 Bloor St. W. # 801, Toronto, Ontario M5S 2V6
www.womenspress.ca

All rights reserved. No part of this book may be used or reproduced in any manner whatsoever without written permission except in the case of brief quotations embodied in critical articles and reviews. For information address Women's Press.

This book was produced by the collective effort of Women's Press.

Women's Press gratefully acknowledges the support received for its publishing program from the Ontario Arts Council and the Canada Council for the Arts.

Printed and bound in Canada.

THE CANADA COUNCIL   LE CONSEIL DES ARTS
FOR THE ARTS   DU CANADA
SINCE 1957   DEPUIS 1957

4 5 2005

Contents

Acknowledgements

A project on anti-racist feminist thought is truly a collective project. We would like to begin by acknowledging all of the women who have worked as anti-racist feminists. This book could not have been written without their on-going efforts to challenge racism and sexism.

One of the joys of working on this collection has been that it gave us the opportunity to spend countless hours in conversations, as we sought to define the contours of this project. In this process, many women helped define and shape the collection. We thank the Social Issues Committee at Women's Press for their ideas and assistance when we began the project. We thank Beverly Bain, Janice Drakich, Dionne Falconer, Punam Kholsa, Mona Oikawa, M. Noubesse Philip, Joanne St. Lewis, Chandra Mohanty, Douglas Stewart, and Penni Stewart for their efforts to contribute to the collection, and Fay Blaney, Sharon McIvor, and Winnie Ng for their efforts to participate in the roundtable discussion on anti-racist feminism. Other women contributed in different ways. Conversations with Pramilla Aggarwal, Dionne Brand, Dionne Falconer, Maureen FitzGerald, Patricia Monture, and Theresa Nahanee helped us identify contributors. Others assisted us with thinking through difficult ideas and moments, particularly Sedef Arat-Koc, Beverly Bain, Abigail Bakan, Linda Carty, Tania Das Gupta, Dionne Falconer, Punam Khosla, Penni Stewart, and Alissa Trotz. Dionne Falconer's assistance in organizing the round table was invaluable, as was Pat Murphy's expert assistance in editing a chapter. We also thank our friends and family who have sustained us throughout this process.

The staff at Women's Press have been truly supportive and committed to this project. Special thanks to Ann Decter for her advice and editorial skills — they were invaluable. Martha Ayim for her patience with a project that she must have wondered if it would ever end. Martha Ayim and Terry Guerriero for scrapping together funds for different pieces. Heather Guylar's many efforts to get us to press.

We thank all the authors, their conversations and writing have made this an unforgettable project. We also thank them for their patience and commitment in seeing this through to the end.

Canadian Anti-Racist Feminist Thought: Scratching the Surface of Racism

ENAKSHI DUA

Recently, a twelve-year old friend asked his parents if I was Canadian or Indian. After discussing the question for a couple of minutes, one of his parents, jokingly referring to childhood years spent in the United States, replied that I was neither — I was American. While this excursion into national identity drew humorously on notions of hybridity, fluidity, and dislocation, it also illuminates the structures that organize race and gender in Canada. As anti-racist feminists have pointed out, the social and political definitions of who is defined as Canadian reflect the race and gender underpinnings of Canadian society. Underlying this question is the image of a Canadian as someone who is white. This stereotype works to determine who belongs to Canada, who is from elsewhere, who is a hyphenated-Canadian, and who is normal.

The question of whether a person of colour is a Canadian hides the complex history through which Canada became a white settler society. As, historically, the notion of who could be legally eligible for Canadian citizenship was tied to race, skin colour became a central (though not the only) marker of who could belong to the Canadian national formation. In the words of John A. Macdonald, Canada was to be a "white man's country." Today, the stereotype of who is and is not a Canadian works to reinforce the historical process by which indigenous, mixed race, African-Canadians, Asian-Canadians, Arab-Canadians, and others[1] have been marginalized from Canadian society, as it obscures the history of colonialism, settlement, immigration, and citizenship policies that ensured the racialization and gendering of twentieth century Canada. Both the historical and the contemporary locations that women of colour occupy in Canadian society have been shaped by multifaceted racialized, classed, and gendered processes that made Canada into a white settler society.

Since the arrival of Europeans, Canadian anti-racist feminists have been actively engaged in deconstructing race and gender relations. Contained within their efforts is a distinct way of understanding gender, race, and society. Foremost, anti-racist feminists have concentrated on analyzing the forces that have shaped the historically specific pattern of racialization in Canada. It is their focus on the process of racialization which differentiates their writing from other kinds of feminist theorizing.[2] This body of thought illustrates the process by which racialization produces differences among women, challenging the idea that a com-

7

mon experience with gender exists. In addition, by bringing an analysis of race to feminist theorizing, this work offers a different feminist epistemology — a distinctive method of analyzing gender, nation, state, economy, and society.

In 1968, Dr. Carrie Best, the publisher of the newspaper, *The Clarion*, articulated the perspective of anti-racist feminists:

> Canadian society is a white society. Its legislators are white. Its judges are white; its teachers are almost universally white; its police are white; its executives are white; its newsmen are white; its real estate agents are white; its landlords are white; its school board administrators, its mayors and alderman, its bankers, its armed forces, and its Prime Minister are white. They support and perpetuate the institutions and customs that make Canada what it is. Thus they are racists. If you are a liberal, middle-class white, the word 'racist' has a very concrete and narrow definition. Apartheid is racist. Segregation is racist. The political, social and economic systems which enslave human beings, which deny them their identities, their freedom, their dignity and their future are all racist systems. This definition is good as far as it goes but it only begins to scratch the surface of racism (Carrie Best 1968, quoted in Backhouse 1998).

Canadian anti-racist feminist thought has been scratching the surface of Canadian society, exposing the dynamics of racism.

ANTI-RACIST FEMINIST THOUGHT:
CONNECTING RACE AND GENDER

In several national contexts, the past two decades have witnessed efforts to trace those bodies of feminist writing that theorize the connections between race and gender (in the United States, hooks 1981; Patricia Hill Collins 1990; in Britain see Mirza 1997). Those who have undertaken such projects have done so with very different intentions. For some, like Hill Collins (1990), given the historical marginalization of anti-racist writing within feminist theory, the underlying purpose is to make visible the ideas of anti-racist feminists. For others, such efforts arise out of the challenge to develop an integrative feminist theory, one which combines racism with gender and class in analyzing oppression (Ramazanglu 1989; Stasiulis 1990). Finally for others, theorizing interconnections comes out of the desire to make racism as central as gender inequality in feminist theorizing (Carby 1986; hooks 1981, 1984, 1989; Parmar and Amos 1982, 1984; Hill Collins 1990).

Within Canadian feminist literature, a collection of writing exists which we have labelled anti-racist feminist thought. Notably, these writers have often been excluded from Canadian feminist historiographies. While this body of thought is part of the history of Canadian feminist theorizing, to date, there has been little documentation of the work and ideas of these writers (for an exception, see Bristow 1994). In particular, the writings of those who wrote on race and gender before the 1960s have been unrecorded. Such omissions in feminist historiography are especially problematic as the vast majority of those who are part of this body of work are women of colour. The failure to record anti-racist feminist work has facilitated the impression that women of colour have been historically absent from feminist and anti-racist theorizing and organizing.

Not only has there been little documentation of this body of work, but an analysis of its underlying epistemological and ontological assumptions is also missing (for an exception, see Stasiulis 1990). As Canadian anti-racist feminist thought is premised on offering a different epistemological and ontological approach to the study of gender, the failure to undertake such an analysis makes it difficult to assess the usefulness of its central tenet: that an analysis of race needs to be integrated into feminist theorizing.

Evaluating a distinct body of thought involves delineating its parameters. However, defining what constitutes anti-racist feminist thought is a contentious task. While anti-racist feminist thought is generally defined as an attempt to theorize the interconnections between race, class, and gender, there are different interpretations on how to go about this. As the vast majority of those who write on these topics are women of colour, there are those who would narrow this body of work to the writings of "Black feminists" (for example, Hill Collins 1990; in Canada see Stasiulis 1990, 282). For others, anti-racist thought is the body of literature that positions the lives and experiences of women of colour as the starting point for a feminist analysis (Brand 1988; Dua 1992; Agnew 1996). And for some, anti-racist thought is the body of literature that examines the "multiplicity of experiences" (Stasiulis 1990; Khayatt 1995).

For a number of reasons, I have deliberately chosen the term anti-racist thought as opposed to Black feminist thought. Not all of those who write on the interconnections of race, class, and gender are women of colour. I want to be inclusive of these writers. I also want to reflect the historical specificity of naming. The term "Black feminist thought" comes out of the United States or Britain, where such naming reflects very different histories. In Canada, for a variety of reasons, the term has much less resonance.[3] Most importantly, I did not employ the label "Black feminist thought" in order to avoid essentialist assumptions while examining this literature. Too often, both sympathetic and critical reviews of such bodies of work assume that writers put forward their ideas because they are racialized and gendered beings (see for example, Jhappan 1996). While who we are clearly reflects how we write, such an approach shifts attention from the ideas and debates that are crucial for the study of interconnections. Theoretical and epistemological differences over how to integrate the study of race and gender, over the primacy of race, gender or class, and over the importance of a standpoint epistemology are reduced to the "race" of the writer. Given these concerns, I have defined anti-racist feminist thought as a body of writing that attempts to integrate the way race and gender function together in structuring social inequality.

The history of Canadian anti-racist feminist work can be traced through three phases of development, which I have identified as first, second, and third wave.

Since the nineteenth century, anti-racist feminists have pointed to the importance of racism, and questioned a universal politics of gender. Hill Collins has suggested that in the case of the United States, contemporary Black feminist thought stems from Black women's increasing willingness to strive for gender equality within African-American organizations (1990, 8). I would suggest that in Canada, anti-racist feminism stems from women of colour's willingness to strive for equality within a racialized society and feminist movement. These writers have consistently illustrated how the workings of race and gender need to be located in a particular history — the history of a post-colonial, white settler formation. Significantly, in each phase writers have focused on similar questions, and offered remarkably similar epistemological approaches to the interconnections of race and gender.

Despite a long legacy of illustrating the ways in which a racialized society impacted on women of colour, two significant epistemological differences have recently emerged among anti-racist feminists. The first is what to prioritize in the study of interconnections. As Satzewich (1998) notes, there are considerable differences among writers about how to conceptualize the interrelationship between race and gender: "there are class approaches to race and gender, gender approaches to race and class, and race approaches to class and gender" (Satzewich 1998, 41). Secondly, anti-racist feminist writers are divided between employing a reformulated political economy approach or a standpoint methodology.

These epistemological differences have led to important debates among anti-racist writers, such as, what are the implications of employing the term women of colour? While the term arises from an attempt to disrupt the universalist and essentialist notion of gender in Canadian feminist theorizing, does it replace the concept of a woman with an equally universalist and essentialist concept of a woman of colour? Does it homogenize experiences of racism? Does it hide class difference? Does the acknowledgement of a diversity of experiences with racism mean that we need to identify different kinds of racism? Does analyzing a women of colour outsider-within status allow for different insights? Does a standpoint epistemology challenge simplistic accounts of identity and inequality, or replace these accounts with an essentialist one?

Given the extensive size and richness of the literature, the following survey will only focus on key writers and debates. While I have placed writers into different categories for analytical purposes, I would like to point out that, as with all categories, there is slippage.[4]

THE FIRST WAVE, 1850-1970:
A FORGOTTEN AND UNRECORDED HISTORY

Given the scarcity of documentation, it is difficult to delineate the ideas of first wave anti-racist feminists. Until recently, feminist historians neglected the writings of anti-racist feminists. As Iacovetta and Valverde (1992, xiv) have noted, Canadian women's history has been characterized by a strong preoccupation with articulate, white, middle-class women.[5] This orientation has placed significant limits on our ability to explore anti-racist feminist ideas in this period, as there is little documentation of their writings.[6] Moreover, as the majority of anti-racist writers have been women of colour, such omissions make it appear as if women of colour were politically inactive in this period. For example, Agnew has suggested that women of colour "were victimised by white Canadian culture and by men of their own communities. But there was no ideological or organizational base that could help them identify their oppression or assert their rights" (1996, 42). Finally, the emphasis on the ideas of white, middle-class women in this period has meant that we have little information on ways in which first wave feminists promoted a racialized nation-state.

Recently, a small number of feminist historians have taken up the task of documenting the lives of anti-racist feminists (see Bristow 1994; Miller and Chuchryk 1996). Given the neglect of women of colour in feminist historiography, much of this work has focused on documenting the multifaceted ways in which women of colour have challenged the racial, gender, and class oppression in Canadian society. Such work is clearly needed and important, for as Bristow suggests, the exclusion of women of colour from the pages of mainstream and feminist Canadian history reflects the process by which racism is denied, the process by which a past is hidden (1994, 3). However, much of the work has focused on documenting the political activities of these women, rather than exploring their social and political ideas.

This literature has successfully documented that women of colour have a long history of political resistance. As Carrie Best stated, "Long before there was a Women's Liberation Movement as such, the Black female was involved in a death struggle for herself and her family" (quoted in Hamilton 1993, 200). Moreover, much of their resistance was directed at disrupting the set of political, social, and economic processes that racialized Canada.

This rich history of resistance began with the arrival of Europeans. Since contact, First Nation women fought the marginalization of indigenous peoples through activities that ranged from negotiating treaties to organizing armed resistance to the appropriation of indigenous lands (Bourgeault 1988; Dickason 1992). The Metis, born of First Nations women, articulated the legacy of resistance by putting forward a vision of Rupert's land which simultaneously challenged the structures of the emerging white settler nation-state and offered an anti-colonial, anti-racist alternative (Dickason 1992). Payment (1996), using oral histories and Metis accounts of resistance, has demonstrated that Metis women were not only active agents in the Metis Rebellion, but after the decimation of the adult male population, played a vital role in the reconstruction of the community through continuing the demands for lands, political representation in governments, and favourable economic policies.

Black and Asian-Canadian women were also politically active. From the early days of their migration, these women have challenged racism, sexism, and classism in Canada and the world economy. South Asian women such as Bhikaiji

Rustom Cama were active in supporting the Ghadar and other anti-racist organizations which organized systematic legal and political challenges to Canadian immigration, settlement, labour, and citizenship laws. Black women like Mary Ann Shadd wrote extensively about racism, sexism, and universal suffrage (Bristow 1994). Other Black women challenged the racist practices of employers and white workers by working to organize unions like the Brotherhood of Black Porters (Brand 1988; Calliste 1987). During internment, Japanese-Canadian women challenged the government's dispersal and deportation policies (Adachi 1976; Kitagawa 1985; Kogawa 1981). Women of colour also worked to provide the educational and social services that were denied to their communities (Chinese Canadian National Council, Women's Book Committee 1992; Hamilton 1993; Cooper 1994).

While we need to more thoroughly document and analyze the ideas of these women, we can see that a particular discursive understanding of how to constitute feminist anti-racist praxis arises from this history of resistance. Challenging racism became the starting point for these women's activism, and was linked to challenging the legal and social process through which a white settler society was being constructed. Harriet Tubman's words "We're rooted here, and they can't pull us up" (quoted in Bristow 1993, 145) resonated for other women of colour. The most important issues for these women were treaties, immigration policies, settlement policies, and access to democratic rights. Issues of gender equality, both within Canadian society and within communities of colour, are glaringly missing. This emphasis on racism as the starting point for a gender and class analysis would continue to be a characteristic of the second and third wave anti-racist feminist thought.

The focus on racism as a starting point clearly marginalized these women from the organized women's movement. Not only did mainstream feminist organizations fail to identify racism as an issue for feminist mobilizing, but as Valverde (1992) has illustrated, their claims for gender equality were often premised on the project of making Canada white. The leaders of these organizations perpetuated the prevailing racist stereotypes of women of colour as either victims or as barbaric. As Valverde notes, for mainstream feminists, women of colour were "never active subjects of a cross-cultural gender-based feminism" (1992, 6). Moreover, as the goals of many women's organizations in this period centred around female (meaning white female) suffrage rather than universal suffrage, women of colour were clearly excluded. A host of laws and practices, ranging from the *Indian Act* to citizenship, naturalization, immigration, and voter registration acts disqualified First Nation people and Asians from voting (Bolaria and Li 1988). Given the racialized politics of first wave feminists, women of colour chose to organize within communities of colour.

This is not to imply that these women had an equal place in the anti-racist struggles, or that their position was not gendered. Bristow's (1993, 1994) and Hamilton's (1993, 1994) studies suggest that Black communities were characterized by ideologies of Black womanhood, where gendering made Black women responsible for the social and moral welfare of the community (see also Chinese

Canadian National Council, Women's Book Committee 1992). As Dua (forthcoming) illustrates, the gendering of South Asian women paralleled that of white women in this period, for while white women were gendered as mothers of the nation, South Asian women were gendered as mothers of "their communities" (Dua, forthcoming).

In the context of racism, the social and political meaning that women of colour made of such gendering was not uniform. Bristow argues that the ideologies of motherhood and womanhood allowed Black women to transcend the socially imposed limits of race, class, and gender (1993, 146). Her study of Black women involved in the Hour-a-Day Club, illustrates how the identity of being a mother became the basis for political activism. Other studies suggest that for some women, such gendering did impose limits. While Payment (1996) shows that Metis women were active in the Metis Rebellion, she also suggests that they were gendered as wives and mothers, a process that often lead to unhappiness (see also Nipp 1983). Despite the different meanings women brought to being gendered, it is clear that these women shared an understanding of the importance of racism in their lives. In their particular historical moment, with its own particular modes of domination, there was no necessary connection between racism and sexism, either theoretically or in praxis.

THE SECOND WAVE, 1970-1990:
MAKING CANADIAN RACISM VISIBLE

By the mid-1980s a definite body of literature had emerged in sociology, political science, history, and women's studies that clearly focused on the interconnections between race and gender. Several changes in Canadian society created an intellectual climate which allowed for such work to emerge within Canadian academia. Anti-racist challenges to the Canadian women's movement combined with a growing number of women of colour in academic institutions challenged the failure of Canadian academics to deal with the complex interconnections between racism and sexism. That similar challenges to hegemonic academic discourse were taking place in American and British academia legitimized Canadian struggles, as activists and scholars across national boundaries supported the development of a new body of scholarly thought within the Canadian academy.

The second wave of Canadian anti-racist thought was located in connecting women of colour's activism to the way in which scholars analyzed Canadian society. The 1970s witnessed several anti-racist feminist initiatives throughout Canada (see Carty 1993). These initiatives included challenging the racism of the police, challenging discriminatory immigration policies (especially towards domestic workers), organizing those sectors in which women of colour were concentrated, challenging racism within the women's movement (Cayenne 1989; Thornhill 1989; Gabriel and Scott 1993; Gottlieb 1993), creating a shelter movement to provide women of colour with a space safe from both male violence and racism (Kohli 1993), and challenging what Spivak (1991) has called epistemic violence.

Believing that political activism needed a discursive voice, the Canadian anti-racist feminist movement linked the struggles taking place in the streets, workplaces, and within the halls of state organizations to the ways in which knowledge of Canadian society was created. Many of the emerging scholars were actively involved in the anti-racist feminist initiatives that were taking place in the 1980s. As a result, anti-racist feminists who had access to universities tied political activism to theorizing the ways in which women of colour experienced society.

The project of linking anti-racist activism to scholarly thought began with deconstructing the discursive understanding of race in Canadian society. Himani Bannerji (1988) argued that the most difficult aspect of talking about racism in Canada was that it was so common sense — so embedded in everyday life. She pointed out that because racism was embedded in the diffused cultural practices of Canadian society it was erased. As a result "there were gaps and silences, that people like us were never present...and this happens in a country with the history of a settler colonial state and economy, where 'reserves' exist in large numbers for indigenous peoples, where a working class is still being created through racist immigration policies and the segmentation of the labour market and where a U.S. dependent capitalism has long ago entered an imperialist phase" (1987, 10-11).

Roxana Ng (1989) located the erasure of racism in the Eurocentrism of Canadian society. She suggested that because Canadian society was based on a European lens, Eurocentric ideas were employed to construct the idea of the nation, motherhood, and morality. She further pointed out that such a lens rendered immigrant women outsiders. As she noted, in everyday language the expression "immigrant woman" is used to refer to Canadian-born women of colour, women who do not speak English well, and immigrant women from the Third World. Such linguistic structures make those who are white (including those who are not Canadian-born) appear as native, while women of colour (including First Nations women) appear as outsiders (Ng 1988). As a result of such a common sense understanding of the social world, Bannerji (1988) and Ng (1988, 1989) argued that challenging racism and sexism required challenging the very foundations of Canadian society — whiteness.

The third cornerstone of anti-racist thought in this period was its identification with a socialist-feminist project. For many of these writers, socialist feminism allowed for a focus on how institutions organize and maintain gender and racial relations, particularly through colonialism, state, labour markets, and other institutions. As a result, several writers have pointed out that the Canadian state continues to be the crucial institution in organizing and maintaining racial and gender inequalities. Carty and Brand (1988) noted that the category of a visible minority woman was a creation of the Canadian state. Other writers have documented the ways in which immigration policies construct racial inequalities by admitting "Third World immigrants only to fill specific gaps in the labour force which could not be filled otherwise" (Law Union of Canada 1981, 235). Estable (1988) and others illustrated that in addition to having a racial bias, immigration policies have also been gendered. They documented that given the structure of these policies, women enter Canada as dependents, as part of the family package that men are allowed to bring. The consequence of this legal status is that immigrant women are denied language training and employment assistance programs (Go 1987; Paredes 1989; Boyd 1990). In addition, these policies construct patriarchal relations as they work to make immigrant women financially and legally dependent on their husbands, even in cases of abusive relationships (Giles 1987).

The concern with state, immigration, and citizenship had come to a head in 1976, when two domestic women from Jamaica were threatened with deportation. The case epitomized the links between immigration policies and the labour market. As a result, the focus on institutions led anti-racist feminist writers to analyze how work has been racialized and gendered in Canada. This work began by analyzing the implications of the racialized organization of domestic work in Canada (Leah and Morgan 1979; Brand 1988; Silvera 1983; Calliste 1989). As Arat-Koc has argued, "while emphasising domesticity and motherhood as ideal roles for white women, dominant ideologies and institutions have no problems accepting women of colour as workers first and foremost even when this worker status is achieved at the expense of separation from family and children" (1992, 236).

Other writers have focused on the racial and gender characteristics of the Canadian labour force. As several writers noted, in both the past and the present, women of colour have higher rates of labour force participation than their white counterparts (Das Gupta 1989; Ng and Estable 1989). Das Gupta (1989) pointed out that immigrant women are concentrated on the lowest rungs of Canadian society — farm work, paid domestic work, textile, garment, rubber, chemical and other manufacturing industries as labourers, performing the most monotonous tasks and being paid the lowest wages (see also Aggarwal 1989).

Anti-racist feminists asked how it was that women of colour were concentrated in poorly-paid sectors of the labour force. This question again took writers back to the role of the Canadian state in organizing racism and sexism. In a study of state-sponsored employment programs for immigrant women, Ng (1986) found that rather than assisting immigrant women in locating jobs for which they had training, counsellors systematically channelled immigrant women into jobs located in poorly paid sectors. Dionne Brand's (1988) study locates the role of the state in the framework of a capitalist society. As she illustrated, Canadian capitalist development has historically been juxtaposed with the super-exploitation of Black women and men.

The focus on working within a socialist feminist tradition has implications for anti-racist feminist writing in this period. While noting the personal ways in which women of colour experience their social world, the second wave of anti-racist feminist thought has been primarily concerned with using the personal to analyze the political — particularly the workings of the Canadian state and economy. This literature underemphasizes issues of identity, social and cultural difference, and identity politics. Also underemphasized are issues of sexism in communities of colour, domestic violence, sexuality, and homophobia. Instead, the concern with state and economy led writers to be sensitive to the analysis of systemic discrimination, the ways in which Canadian social institutions perpetuate racism and sexism. However, as anti-racist feminists turned their attention to explaining why, in addition to organizing class and gender inequality, Canadian social institutions organized racial inequality, several writers would break from a socialist feminist framework.

THE THIRD WAVE, 1990-1999: THEORIZING RACIAL DIFFERENCES IN AN INCREASINGLY FRAGMENTED WORLD

By the end of the 1980s Canadian anti-racist feminist thought represented a new way of feminist theorizing, a project of integrating race and gender that offered exciting possibilities for feminist thinking and organizing. In the next decade, anti-racist writers built on this scholarship. The recognition that Canadian social institutions perpetuate racism would lead several writers to reject the epistemology underlying socialist feminist and Canadian political economy traditions. As a consequence, in the past decade two different epistemological approaches to the study of race and gender have emerged. The literature in this period can be categorized as having three broad parameters: interrogating mainstream feminist theory and praxis for the ways in which it perpetuated racism, raising epistemological questions of how to theorize the interconnection between race and gender, and continuing to document how racial differences are created between women.

The third wave of anti-racist feminist writing has concentrated on interrogating mainstream feminism, both theory and praxis, for its role in perpetuating racial difference between women. Several writers illustrated the ways in which middle-class women's standpoint historically came to configure the contours of liberal, radical, and socialist-feminist theory (Dua 1992; Mukerjee 1992; Simms 1992; Monture-Okanee 1992; 1995; Agnew 1996). These writers pointed out that women of colour's experiences with all aspects of gender — femininity, sexuality, marriage, family, and work — varied substantially from that of middle-class, white women. Such differences raised the question of whether a universal experience with gender exists (Mukerjee 1992; Monture-Okaneee 1992). This led others to argue that by marginalizing the study of race in feminist analyses, mainstream feminists continue to marginalize women of colour from feminist organizations (Simms 1992; Bannerji 1995). Writers also noted that underlying the feminist movement has been a commitment to a racialized nation-state, a commitment that has contributed to positioning women differentially within the political economy. As Valverde (1991) has illustrated, first wave feminists' commitment to a racialized bourgeois project contributed to the social construction of white femininity, masculinity, and the nation. Echoing what anti-racist feminists had been advocating since the nineteenth century, these writers suggested that an inclusive feminist movement required feminists to come to terms with the multifaceted processes through which racialization has taken place.

Ironically, despite an increasing awareness of the ways in which mainstream feminist praxis created divisions among women, transforming feminist organizations and theory was not an easy task. Attempts to alter shelters, crisis lines, immigrant women's services, and cultural institutions were met with resistance and hostility, struggles that often were well-covered by Canadian newspapers (for a report of such cases see CAYENNE 1988; Kohli 1993; Crean 1991; Gabriel and Scott 1993; Agnew 1996). While efforts to make the National Action Committee on the Status of Women (NAC) inclusive resulted in the election of two women of colour as presidents, this was accompanied by a loss of support. As Beverley Bains, who worked for NAC during these years, stated: "we do hear from some white women their perception that suddenly Black women's or non-white women's issues are becoming important. These women...are not seeing the connections between Black women and white women's issues" (quoted in Gottlieb 1993, 382). The result of such resistance has been to entrench coalition and identity politics within these organizations (Bannerji 1995; Robertson, in this book).

Anti-racist feminist academics found it equally difficult to challenge the pedagogical paradigms and canons of various disciplines, including feminist theory (Carty 1991; Bannerji, et al. 1995; Das Gupta 1996; Millar 1993). As many writers have repeatedly pointed out, most disciplines, including women's studies, have largely ignored anti-racist feminist thought (Mukherjee 1992; Carty 1993; Stevenson 1992, 1995; Jhappan 1996). Carty noted, despite the call for more inclusive writing, most feminist work continues to be written as if racial differences do not exist between women. She asked, "Why is Canadian feminist scholarship still not representative of the racial-ethnic diversity in Canadian society?" (1993, 9-10).

Anti-racist feminists tied their critique of feminist praxis to an analysis of the ways in which Canadian academia constructed knowledge about race. Starting from the perspective that the social relations of production of knowledge in institutional settings privilege perspectives that encompass systematic ideological stances, several writers argued that canons of various disciplines worked to maintain the ideological frameworks through which racial differences among women are maintained (Bannerji 1995; Monture-Okanee 1995; LaRocque 1996). These writers pointed out that when it came to racialization, it was not only conservative and liberal frameworks that contributed to a discursive understanding of race. Importantly, critical paradigms, particularly the Canadian political economy approach[7] and socialist feminist analysis, also perpetuated the discursive understanding of race. Stasiulis (1990), Kobayashi and Peake (1994), and Stasiulis and Crease (1996) have pointed out that both of these paradigms are marred by theoretical limitations which make the interconnections between racism and sexism invisible (see also Bannerji 1995; Monture-Angus 1995). The recognition that critical paradigms worked to obscure the interconnections between race, class, and gender led anti-racist writers to call for either a reformulation of existing paradigms (Stasiulis 1998; Stasiulis and Crease 1996), or for new paradigms (Bannerji 1995; Henry, et al. 1995).

Coming out of this critique is the second parameter of anti-racist feminist thought in this period: the project of developing methodologies for the study of race and gender. In undertaking this, anti-racist writers have employed two very different strategies. For some, this requires a reformulation of the tradition of Canadian political economy (Stasiulis 1998; Stasiulis and Crease 1996). Stasiulis and Crease have argued that "understanding the multiple and contradictory intersections of race, class, gender and sexuality in local and international contexts, is central to developing a more adequate political economy" (1996, 5). Others, such as Bannerji (1995) and Henry et al. (1995), have called for new paradigms with which to analyze Canadian society. Bannerji stated: "Concepts such as capital, class, imperialism, etc., are thus considered as totalizing, abstract 'master narratives,' and untenable bases for political subjectivity since they are arrived at rationally and analytically, moving beyond the concreteness of immediate experience" (1995, 73).

Given these different projects, it is not surprising that anti-racist feminists have put forward two very different approaches to the study of race and gender-- one approach located in a standpoint epistemology and another approach located in a reformulation of Canadian political economy. These two approaches offer two very different epistemological frameworks for how to integrate race into a gender and class analysis. Moreover, such differences lead to differences on several key questions: whether the focus should be on the differences between white women and women of colour; how to analyze class differences between women of colour; and how to theorize the role of race in Canadian society.

For those writers who called for a new paradigm to analyze Canadian society, many, if not most, have turned to a standpoint epistemology (Brand 1988; Carty 1992; Nourbese Philip 1992; Bannerji 1995). While these feminists do not draw on the Canadian tradition of political economy, significantly they draw on Third World marxist writers, such as Marcus Garvey, Walter Rodney, and Franz Fanon (for example, Brand 1988; Carty 1988; Bannerji 1995). As Paul Gilroy (1982, 277) has noted, for over one hundred years, Black marxist theorists have been engaged in a critical dialogue with marxism, in which they have challenged the simplistic reduction of race to class.

The clearest exposition of this approach has been put forward by Himani Bannerji in *Thinking Through* (1995). Bannerji begins by identifying an epistemological site in which a new paradigm can be formulated. As she asked: "Where are we to turn? Where are we to find interpretive frameworks and methods that are more than alternative and would go beyond inclusion? How can we gain insight into the social relations and culture of advanced capitalism which allows for direct representation and a revolutionary political agency?" (1995, 63). The answer to this question was to begin with the lived experiences of women of colour: "once again I must begin from myself. From my body as a political signifier" (1995, 61).

For Bannerji, the strength of turning to the "experience" of women of colour is not located in a reductionist notion of subjugated knowledge. In contrast to Harstock (1983) and Hill Collins (1990),[8] Bannerji rejects the idea that those who are oppressed "know" their oppression. Drawing on marxist theories of class mobilization, she points out that "since political subjectivities are articulated within a given political and ideological environment, and self-identities are fraught with contradictory possibilities...then there is no guarantee that there is only one form of politics of identity which will emerge, or that it will avoid the formulation of 'identity and community versus structures and class'. Victims and subjects of capital do not automatically become socialists. Misery does not automatically produce communism, and desire for change born of suffering does not spontaneously know 'what is to be done?' to end oppression" (1995, 35).

For Bannerji and others (for example, Brand 1988; Carty 1992; Nourbese Philip 1992), the strength of employing a standpoint methodology is located in women of colour's "outsider-within" status. Anticipating Homi Bhabha's concept of a "third space," these writers have pointed out that women of colour occupy a structural position within the Canadian political economy which overlaps the margins of race, gender, and class. They argue that by tracing how women of colour are positioned within Canadian society, we can simultaneously trace how race, class, and gender have been constituted in Canadian history. As Bannerji states: "For this reason, an adequate description of the smallest racist incident leaves room for reference or contextualization to slavery, colonization, imperialism; exploitation of surplus value and construction of the labour market through gender, 'race' and ethnicity; nation-states to organize and facilitate these processes and practices; and concomitant reifying forms of consciousness" (1995, 84).

The strength of a standpoint epistemology is that it allows for a more sophisticated understanding of the ways in which the discourse of race shaped the contingent character of colonialism, imperialism, and capitalism. Underlying this approach is the premise that racialized regimes of power and knowledge were as important in determining the historical specific path of Canadian colonial and capitalist development as was the imperative for profits. Acknowledging these regimes "allows us to create a knowledge which shows how the social relations and forms come into being in and through each other, to show how a mode of production is an historically and socially concrete formation" (Bannerji 1995, 84).

The use of a standpoint methodology has not been without criticisms (Stasiulis 1990; Khayatt 1995; Jhappan 1996). Several writers have pointed out that women's experiences with racialization vary according to class location, the different ways different groups have been racialized, sexuality, and personal history (Mahtani 1995; Ahmad 1995). This led Jhappan (1996) to question whether a standpoint methodology replaced "gender essentialism" with an equally problematic "race essentialism." Others noted that an additional danger in such a methodology was that it did not allow for the fluid character of social identities. As Khayatt pointed out "the formation of my identity includes my class, my colour, my ethnicity, my sexuality, and my religion.... Rigid definitions of race and ethnicity which do not account for the fluidity of categories are not useful in that they mask differences of class and location. They fail to respect individual identities or to take into account lived experiences" (1995, 10).

The degree to which experiences with racism among women of colour are shared raises important methodological issues regarding how to integrate a race, gender, and class analyses, whether the aim of anti-racist feminism should be to explain differences between white women and women of colour and whether a standpoint approach conflates race and class. Similar concerns have led others, such as Stasiulis (1990), Khayatt (1995), and Stasiulis and Crease (1996), to reformulate the Canadian political economy approach. For these writers the advantage of working within the framework of political economy is that it allows for an epistemology which would focus on the "inevitable intrusions of capitalist relations within the construction of intersecting forms of oppression" (Stasiulis 1990, 294).

The clearest exposition of this approach has been put forward by Stasiulis (1990) in *Theorising Connections*. Referring mainly to the work of second wave writers, Stasiulis questioned the analytical use of skin colour as a demarkation of racism. She argues that such an approach limited the study of race, class, and gender to an "implicit Black/white dichotomy that is frequently assumed to structure the racist and gendered oppression of women" (290). She suggests that such a dichotomy poses a number of limitations: it fails to deal with other "immigrant" women; it links racism to skin colour rather than structural location of the particular groups of women in concrete social relations; it ignores different kinds of racism — especially those built on language, religion and other cultural markers; and it treats women of colour as a homogenous category, thereby failing to account for the fact that women of colour are located in a variety of class positions. She concludes that "Black feminism" does not allow for the task of understanding the complex processes through which race, class, and gender are constructed for specific groups of racial and ethnic-minority women. In contrast, Stasiulis advocates an epistemology that focuses on "the structural location of particular groups of women in concrete and historically specific social relations and to the accompanying discourses that aid in the processes of denigration, subordination, and exploitation" (1990, 290). Through this, anti-racist feminism is better able to produce "a more complex mapping of oppression, inequality and resistance" (Stasiulis 1994, 6).

These two approaches offer very different ways of studying the interconnections between race and gender. Importantly, they differ on what should constitute the subject of study, on what central question needs to be investigated. For those who employ a standpoint methodology, the central question is: how are racial differences between women created and maintained? For those who work within the broad framework of political economy, the central question is to explain how women come into and experience multiple locations and identities. These are two different, but not contradictory, questions.

The two approaches also adopt very different implicit epistemological assumptions on how to theorize racism. For those who work within a political economy epistemology it is crucial to study racism as relational and contradictory (Stasiulis and Crease 1996, 8.) These writers posit racism as a phenomena which differs according to one's structural location. Drawing on the early work of Stuart Hall (1980), these writers see racism as having multiple meanings and expressions. Hall (1980) argued that as individuals differentially articulate and experience racist ideas, the study of racism required focusing on how the experience and articulation of racism is tied to an individual's structural location.

In contrast, those who employ a standpoint epistemology conceptualize race, racism, racialization and social structures differently. For them it is not sufficient to focus on how the process of racialization creates differences among women, for such a focus leaves the systems of oppression unexplained, raising the danger of taking them for granted. As Bannerji states: "But why is racism still at the level of being named rather than an integral part of the economic analysis?... How fundamental a role 'ethnicity' and 'race' have played as organizational and administrative categories of both the economy and the state" (1995, 77).

Drawing from the later work of Stuart Hall (1992) and other critical race theorists (for example Rattansi 1992), these writers conceptualize race as discourse, which is constituted in multiple ways, through knowledge, culture, the imperatives of imperialism and capitalism, as well as through power and agency. For these writers, the discourse of race becomes the starting point for analyzing institutional mechanisms that locate women in differential positions and social relations. Moreover, it is through discursive operations that racialized structures are created. As Bannerji states: "When delinking from its history as a white settler colony and its present as an imperialist capitalist state which continues to import labour on the basis of ethnicity, race and class — creating class on its own terrain — the Canadian economy becomes an abstraction. The erasure of the factors 'race', racism and continual immigration prevents an adequate understanding of the Canadian economy" (1995, 77). This does not deny that such discursive operations are not historically contingent, that they operate through different signifiers (language, immigration status) and differently for different groups of racialized women (including white women), and vary according to class location. It does suggest that the discourse of race is as "foundational" to the creation and maintenance of the Canadian political economy as are capitalist relations and patriarchy.

While these two approaches adopt different approaches to the study of racism, I would point out that again these writers are asking different questions. For those who work within a standpoint epistemology, the central question is to show how the discourse of race shapes and maintains a racialized political economy. For those who work within the broad framework of political economy, the central question is to explain how the process of racialization differentiates between women, according to race, ethnicity, class, and sexuality. Again, these are not incompatible questions. One way to evaluate these two approaches is to study the social construction of the discourse of race in Canada, and how this has created racial differences among women. This leads to the third parameter of anti-racist feminist writing in this period, studies which examine the impact of a discourse of race on women of colour.

Drawing on the anti-racist work in the second wave, writers have continued to document the ways in which Canadian "culture" and institutions create and maintain racial differences. Nourbese Philip (1992) pointed out that culture is the central mechanism through which the whiteness is asserted. Through cultural images in stories, narratives, and photographs, Canadians are divided into a normalized group and "others." Others illustrated the prevalence of racialized images of femininities: the dutiful Asian or Islamic wife and daughter, the happy and grateful female immigrant worker, the sexually available First Nation woman, the controlling Black mother, the unassimilated immigrant women unable to adequately socialize her children, the ignorant and oppressed third world women (see for examples, Douglas 1988; Hoodfar 1993; James and Shadd 1994; Bannerji 1995). Hoodfar (1993) points out that these images lead to psychological and socio-economic consequences for women of colour, who must work harder to establish themselves as thinking, rational, legitimate members of society.

Others pointed out that these notions were tied to the maintenance of white hegemony. Brand (1988), Hoodfar (1993), and Bannerji (1995) point out that these images are located in imperial regimes of power — as the racialization of colonized women legitimated colonial and capitalist domination. Dua (forthcoming) illustrates how the racialization of South-Asian Canadian women normalized white femininity and masculinity, and allowed for the construction of a Canadian national identity. The hegemonic role of "culture" in reproducing racism has led to several struggles over the access that people of colour have to Canadian cultural institutions and over cultural appropriation — struggles over who has the power to define whom, and when, and how (Crean 1991; Nourbese Philip 1992; Gabriel and Scott 1993; Henry 1995).

Another focus of the research has been to continue to elaborate on the ways in which employment practices reproduce racialized labour markets. Statistical analyses suggested that the colour of one's skin translated into advantage or discrimination in the labour market. Li (1998), employing 1991 census data, found that the Canadian economy places a market value on skin colour, such that people of colour suffer an income penalty while white Canadians receive an income premium. This did not imply that women of colour are positioned similarily within income and occupational structures. Boyd, employing 1986 data, illustrated the "split" character of women of colour's labour force participation — that women of colour occupy both some of the better jobs in Canadian society as well as many of the poorly paid jobs in Canadian society (Boyd 1992). Moreover, Boyd (1992) demonstrated that, in 1986, the effect of being foreign-born, a member of a visible minority group or female was accumulative, such that foreign-born women of colour received the lowest wages and salaries of all workers (Boyd 1992). The implications for such differential location with the labour market remains to be explored. Others noted that gender-based equity policies failed to include women of colour, reproducing racial difference between women (Stasiulis 1989; Boyd 1992; Joanne St. Lewis 1997).

Writers also elaborated on how state policies produce racial differences. While postwar immigration policies have tied immigration to labour market needs, these policies have incorporated Canadian state and public concerns that "new" immigrants do not alter the "foundations" of Canada (Stafford 1992). These policies continue to deny some categories of migrants, such as domestic workers, rights such as residency and family unification (Arat-Koc 1992; Bakan and Stasiulis 1997). Importantly, Arat-Koc (1992) pointed to the connections between immigration policies and contemporary concerns with citizenship; she argued that the discourse of the good and bad immigrant was tied to ambiguities of who deserves to be a citizen of Canada.

For First Nation women, the impact of dominant culture in maintaining race and gender became a divisive issue, leading to radically different positions on the issue of First Nations self-government. Most writers have illustrated that the Department of Indian Affairs, empowered by a number of legislative *Acts*, placed indigenous women in subordinate positions, in First Nations communities as well as in Canadian society (see McIvor and Stevenson, in this collection). However, given the entrenchment of patriarchal relations, First Nation women differed on how to view self-government. The Native Women's Association of Canada argued that given the entrenchment of male power in First Nation communities, self-government would not allow First Nation women to deal with sexism and violence. Rather, the Canadian *Charter* offered First Nation women the most influential mechanism with which to challenge gender inequality within First Nation communities (Nahanee 1997). In contrast, Monture-Angus (1995) and Turpel (1989-90, 1990) point out that not only are these gender (and other) inequalities the consequence of European discourses and social patterns, these discourses are continually being reproduced through the legal apparatus. Given these conditions, Monture-Angus (1995) and Turpel (1990) argue that it is only through "traditional" gender, social, and legal practices that differences within First Nations communities can be eradicated.

This body of work does point to the importance of discourses of race for how women of colour are positioned within Canadian society. These writers illustrate the ways in which notions of insiders and outsiders are crucial for the production of racial differences. They also suggest that these notions have an impact on how an individual is economically and socially located within Canadian society. On the other hand, they tell us little about the processes through which these ideas came to be hegemonic in the Canadian context. In contrast to the United States and Britain, where critical race and postcolonial theorists have documented the contingent and multifaceted connections between the discourse of race and the social organization of class and gender (see Stepan 1990: Guillaumin 1995; Stoler 1995; McClintock 1996), in Canada such work is just beginning (see Creese 1988-89; Satzewich 1989).

SYNTHESIZING CANADIAN ANTI-RACIST FEMINIST THOUGHT

Despite the diversity and richness of Canadian anti-racist feminist thought, much of this work remains fragmented, as many writers have often focused on a particular aspect of state, nation, economy, society, or culture. There is no synthesis of the processes through which racialization has taken place in Canada. The purpose of this book is to bring together writers to undertake a critical analysis of Canadian history and Canadian institutions and to interrogate the ways in which the nation-state and its institutions racialize, gender, and class women of colour.

This collection examines the social construction of race and gender from the eighteenth century to the present. It is organized into sections that broadly analyze the ways in which the historically contingent process of racialization has shaped Canadian colonialism, capitalist development, the Canadian state, patriarchy, and other social institutions. The purpose is to illustrate how this process of racialization has shaped and continues to shape women of colour's experience of gender, class, and racism. Many of the authors have engaged in new research: the ways in which gender is organized in First Nation communities, how sexism is organized in communities of colour, how the discourse of race organized the institution of the family, the implication of recent changes in immigration policies, and the impact of globalization on women of colour.

Part I deals with the ways in which projects of colonialism positioned white women and women of colour. Linda Carty argues that gender played a central role in both legitimizing imperialism as well as in facilitating imperial relations. As she illustrates, Western feminists played an important role in perpetuating the racialized discourse of colonized women as the "Other." Winona Stevenson demonstrates the importance of the discourse of the colonized woman as the "Other" in legitimizing French and British colonialism in Canada. She shows that the European ideology of womanhood offered a powerful justification for legitimizing colonialism. Moreover, this ideology was employed to reconstruct familial and gender relations along patriarchal lines.

Part II covers the history of capitalist development in Canada and the ways in which this history has impacted women of colour. Dionne Brand examines the ways in which colonialism interacted with capitalism to organize racially gendered labour markets. Ronnie Leah examines the history of the Canadian trade union movement, illustrating the relationship between the labour movement and women of colour as a contradictory one. The labour movement has more often been framed by racism and sexism than by solidarity and inclusion, and as a result, reinforced racial and gender differences in the labour market. Christina Gabriel examines the ways in which the recent phase of economic restructuring has impacted women of colour. As she points out, economic restructuring has been accompanied by neo-liberal policy responses — which exacerbate the economic and social vulnerability of women of colour within the labour market. This social vulnerability has translated into higher rates of unemployment, underemployment and lower earnings for women of colour and Aboriginal women than their non-visible counterparts.

Part III focuses on the ways in which Canadian state policies create and maintain racial and gender inequality. Sharon McIvor examines the ways in which post-Confederation policies continue to regulate gender relations within First Nation communities. She argues that the consequence of such policies is to make marriage a tool in the oppression of First Nation women. Tania Das Gupta examines multicultural policies, through a case study of consultation meetings. She shows that state managers reduce the demand for an anti-racist agenda to cultural retention. Not only does such a discourse allow state managers to construct immigrant women as victims of their own communities, it co-opts anti-racist initiatives. As a result, Das Gupta concludes that immigrant women have taken an active role in reproducing their own subordination. Sedef Arat-Koc examines the ways in which Canadian immigration has been racialized and gendered. She points out that while the post-1960s policies are seen as non-discriminatory, these policies continue to structure race and gender inequality. In addition, she examines the changes in immigration and settlement policies in the 1990s, pointing out that changes in language training, criteria regarding knowledge of official languages and measures against the family class accompanied by the introduction of a modern "head" tax will further disadvantage women of colour in immigration and settlement.

Part IV focuses on interconnections between racism and patriarchy in the lives of women of colour. I question why it is that white women and women of colour experience the institution of the nuclear family in radically different ways, arguing that these differences are located in the institution of the nuclear family itself, as the nuclear family has been tied to the reproduction of a white settler society. As a result, state policies have encouraged white women to participate in nuclear familial patterns, while discouraging or preventing women of colour's participation in familial relations. Himani Bannerji explores the ways in which sexism in communities of colour is maintained through state structures. She points out that the concept of a "community of colour" is not a natural consequence, but the product of complex forces, the result of being collectively marked out as different by the majority, an othering that implies racism, ethnicization, and homogenization. Bannerji argues that essentialized cultural identities are inherently classed and gendered, and suggests that "traditional" communities and the "modern" Canadian state have worked in remarkably similar ways.

Part V looks at the ways institutions work to reinforce racism in the lives of women of colour. Sherene Razack examines the ways in which the law is racialized in Canada. Linda Gardner and Carolyn Egan examine the racism in health care in Canada as well as the ways in which feminists have challenged state regulation of reproduction. They illustrate that coalitions can offer effective ways for challenging state policies. We conclude with a discussion of feminist anti-racist organizing. Angela Robertson assesses the successes and failures of the Canadian anti-racist feminist movement in the last ten years.

In bringing together this collection, we have attempted to be comprehensive, but several questions remain to be investigated. Notably, we found that there is little work in Canada on many issues, particularly on the intersections of sexuality with race and gender, homophobia in communities of colour, and domestic violence against women of colour. We note our lack of writing with a sustained focus on women who have migrated from the Middle-East.

With this collection we bring to readers Canadian anti-racist feminist analyses of the making of race and gender in Canada. In many ways, these analyses document Canadian society, pushing us to rethink Canadian society from the standpoint of women who have been racialized as dangerous, as alien, as hyphenated Canadians. We hope this collection will enable scholars and students to focus on Canadian society through such a lens, the lens of those who are struggling to go beyond the surface of racism.

NOTES

1. Hereafter I will use the term "women of colour" to refer to indigenous, mixed race, African-Canadians, Asian-Canadians, Arab-Canadians, and Central and South American-Canadians.

2. Hereafter, I will use the term "mainstream feminism" to refer to liberal, radical, and socialist feminist paradigms.

3. In Canada, there is little consensus among anti-racist feminist writers of how to name those groups that have been marginalized by racialization. Writers have employed several different terms: immigrant women (Ng 1987; Das Gupta 1988), women of colour (Dua 1992), non-white women (Bannerji 1995), women from Africa, Asia and the Caribbean (Agnew 1996) and racialized women (Kobayashi and Peake 1994).

4. For example, by categorising anti-racist feminist writing into three distinct periods, I am able to trace its development over time. However, these categories obscure the reality that these periods overlap and are not discrete.

5. The paucity in Canadian documentation of anti-racist feminist writing starkly contrasts the documentation established in the United States and Britain. In both of these countries, feminist historians have documented the writings on nineteenth century anti-racist feminists (for examples see hooks 1981, 1985, 1988; Ware 1992; Burton 1994; Jayawardena 1995).

6. In addition, the lack of documentation makes it difficult to trace the ways in which the writings of first wave anti-racist feminists influenced writers in the second and third wave. Further research is needed to flesh out the continuity in Canadian anti-racist feminist thought.

7. By the Canadian political economy approach, I refer to the analyses of the development of Canadian capitalism and state (see for examples, Laxer 1973, 1989; Naylor 1975; Panich 1994). While it is beyond the scope of this chapter to document the ideas within Canadian political economy, for my purposes, I would like to draw attention to two of its characteristics. First, because of its focus on Canada's peripheral position within British and American capitalist development, the Canadian tradition of political economy has underemphasized the role Canada has played in facilitating imperialist and neo-imperialist expansion. Second, is the reduction of race to class. Bolaria and Li (1988), for example, argue that the Canadian capitalist class' "functional" need for a reserve army of labour explains the emergence and persistence of racism. For Bolaria and Li, it is the process of accumulation that has led to racialized immigration policies, discourses, and practices.

8. Both Harstock (1983) and Hill Collins (1992) have argued that oppressed subjects possess subjugated knowledge. Hill Collins argues that underlying a standpoint epistemology is the idea that conditions in the wider political economy not only shape women of colour's subordination but also their resistance. Located in this resistance is the knowledge through which both radical theories and strategies can be constructed. For Hill Collins, this subjugated knowledge is the starting point for feminist theorizing on race and gender (1992, 10).

REFERENCES

Adachi, Ken. *The Enemy that Never Was*. Toronto: McClelland and Stewart, 1976.

Agnew, Vijay. *Resisting Discrimination: Women from Asia, Africa, and the Caribbean and the Women's Movement in Canada*. Toronto: University of Toronto Press, 1996.

Aggarwal, Pramila. "Business as Usual in the Factory." *Resources for Feminine Research/Documentation sur la recherche feministe*, vol. 16, no. 1 (1987): 42-4.

Ahmad, Fawzia. "Reflections of an African Woman." *Canadian Woman Studies*, vol. 14, no. 2 (1995): 25-8.

Amos, Valerie, and Pratibha Parmar. "Challenging Imperial Feminism." *Feminist Review*, vol. 17 (1984): 3-19.

Andrew, Caroline, and Sandra Rodgers. *Women and the Canadian State/Les Femmes et l'etat Canadien*. Montreal and Kingston: McGill-Queen's University Press, 1997.

Arat-Koc, Sedef. "Immigration Policies, Migrant Domestic Workers and the Definition of Citizenship in Canada." In *Deconstructing a Nation: Immigration, Multiculturalism and Racism in '90s Canada*, ed. Vic Satzewich. Saskatoon: University of Saskatchewan Press, 1992

Bacchi, Carol. *Liberation Deferred? The Ideas of the English-Canadian Suffragists, 1877-1918*. Toronto: University of Toronto Press, 1983.

Backhouse, Constance. "'I Was Unable to Identify with Topsy': Carrie Best's Struggle Against Racial Segregation in Nova Scotia, 1942." *Atlantis*, vol. 22, no. 2 (Spring/Summer 1998): 16-27.

Bakkan, Abigail, and D. Stasiulis. *Not in the Family: Foreign Domestic Workers in Canada*. Toronto: University of Toronto Press, 1997.

Bannerji, Himani. "Introducing Racism: Notes Towards an Anti-Racist Feminism." *Resources for Feminine Research/Documentation sur la recherche feministe*, vol. 16, no. 1 (1987): 10-13.
———.*Thinking Through: Essays on Feminism, Marxism, and Anti-Racism*. Toronto: Women's Press, 1995.

Bolaria B. Singh, and Peter S. Lee, eds. *Racial Oppression in Canada*. Toronto: Garamond Press, 1988.

Bourgeault, Ron. "Race and Class under Mercantilism: Indigenous People in Nineteenth-Century Canada." In *Racial Oppression In Canada*, eds. Singh Bolaria and Peter Li. Toronto: Garamond Press, 1988.
———. "Race, Class, and Gender." In *Racism in Canada*, ed. Ormond McKague. Saskatoon: Fifth House Publishers, 1991.

Boyd, Monica. "Gender, Visible Minority and Immigrant Earnings Inequality: Reassessing an Employment Equity Premise." In *Deconstructing a Nation: Immigration, Multiculturalism and Racism in '90s Canada*, ed. Vic Satzewich. Saskatoon: University of Saskatchewan Press, 1992.
———. "Immigrant Women: Language, Socio-economic Inequalities and Policy Issues." In *Ethnic Demography: Canadian Immigrant, Racial, and Cultural Variations*, eds. S. Halli, F. Trovato, and L. Driedger. Ottawa: Carleton University Press, 1990.

Brand, Dionne. "Black Women in Toronto: Gender, Race, and Class." *Fireweed* (Summer/Fall 1984): 26-43.

Brand, Dionne, and Krisantha Sri Bhaggiya Datta. *Rivers Have Sources, Trees Have Roots: Speaking Of Racism*. Toronto: Cross-Cultural Communication Centre, 1986.

Brand, Dionne. *A Conceptual Analysis of How Gender Roles Are Racially Constructed: Black Women*. Master's Thesis, University of Toronto, 1988.

Bristow, Peggy, ed. *We're Rooted Here and They Can't Pull Us Up: Essays in African Canadian Women's History*. Toronto: University of Toronto Press, 1994.
———. "Introduction." In *We're Rooted Here and They Can't Pull Us Up: Essays in African Canadian Women's History*, ed. Peggy Bristow. Toronto: University of Toronto Press, 1994.
———. "'Whatever you raise in the ground you can sell it in Chatham': Black Women in Buxton." In *We're Rooted Here and They Can't Pull Us Up: Essays in African Canadian Women's History*, ed. Peggy Bristow. Toronto: University of Toronto Press, 1994.
———. "The Hour-A-Day Study Club." In *And Still We Rise: Feminist Political Mobilizing in Contemporary Canada*, ed. Linda Carty. Toronto: Women's Press, 1997.

Burton, Antoinette. *Burden's of History: British Feminists, Indian Women, and Imperial Culture, 1865-1915*. Chapel Hill: University of North Carolina Press, 1994.

Calliste, Agnes. "Canada's Immigration Policy and Domestics from the Caribbean: The Second Domestic Scheme." In *Race, Class, and Gender: Bonds and Barriers*, eds. J. Vorst, et al. Toronto: Between The Lines Press, 1989.

Carby, Hazel. "White Woman Listen! Black Feminism and the Boundaries of Sisterhood." In *The Empire Strikes Back: Race and Racism in 70s Britain*. London: Centre for Contemporary Culture Studies, 1986.

Carter, Sarah. "First Nations Women of Prairie Canada in the Early Reserve Years, the 1870s to the 1920s: A Preliminary Inquiry." In *Women of the First Nations: Power, Wisdom and Strength*, eds. Christine Miller and Patricia Churchryk. Winnipeg: University of Manitoba Press, 1996.

Carty, Linda. "Black Women in Academia: A Statement from the Periphery." In *Unsettling Relations: The University as a Site of Feminist Struggles*, H. Bannerji, et al. Toronto: Women's Press, 1991.

———. "Combining Our Efforts: Making Feminism Relevant." In *And Still We Rise: Feminist Political Mobilizing in Contemporary Canada*, ed. Linda Carty. Toronto: Women's Press, 1997.

Carty, Linda, and Dionne Brand. "'Visible Minority' Women: A Creation of the Canadian State." *Resources for Feminist Research*, vol. 17, no. 3 (1989): 39-40.

Cayenne. "Racism and International Women's Day in Toronto." *Cayenne*, vol. 12, nos. 2/3 (1986): 25-45.

Collins, Patricia Hill. *Black Feminist Thought: Knowledge, Consciousness, and the Politics of Empowerment*. New York and London: Routledge, 1991.

Cooper, A. "Black Women and Work in Nineteenth-Century Canada." In *We're Rooted Here and They Can't Pull Us Up: Essays in African Canadian Women's history*, ed. Peggy Bristow. Toronto: University of Toronto Press, 1994.

Crean, Susan. "Taking the Missionary Position." In *Racism in Canada*, ed. Ormond McKague. Saskatoon: Fifth House Publishers, 1991.

Creese, Gillian. "Exclusion of Solidarity? Vancouver Workers Confront the 'Oriental Problem.'" *BC Studies*, no. 80 (Winter 1988-89): 24-51.

Creese, Gillian, and Daiva Stasiulis. "Introduction: Intersections of Gender, Race, Class and Sexuality." In *Studies in Political Economy*, vol. 51 (Fall 1996): 15-64.

Das Gupta, Tania. "Unravelling the Web of History." *Resources for Feminine Research/Documentation sur la recherche feministe*, vol. 16, no. 1 (1987): 13-15.

———. *Learning from Our History: Community Development by Immigrant Women in Ontario 1958-1986*. Toronto: Cross-Cultural Communication Centre, 1986.

———. "Involving Immigrant Women: A Case of Participatory Research." *Canadian Woman Studies*, vol. 8 (1987): 14-15.

Dickason, Olive Patricia. *Canada's First Nations: A History of Founding Peoples from Earliest Times*. Toronto: McClelland and Stewart, 1993.

Douglas, Debbie. "Young Black Women Speak." *Resources for Feminist Research*, vol. 16, no. 1 (1989): 23-8.

Dua, Enakshi. "The Hindu Woman's Question: Canadian Nation-Building and the Social Construction of Gender for South Asian Women." In *Canadian Reader on Anti-Racism*, eds. George Dei and Agnes Calliste. Toronto: University of Toronto Press, forthcoming.

———. "Racism or Gender: Understanding Oppression of South-Asian Canadian Women." *Canadian Women's Studies*, vol. 13, no. 1 (1992): 6-10.

Estable, Alma. "Immigration Policy and Regulations." *Resources for Feminine Research/Documentation sur la recherche feministe*, vol. 16, no. 1 (1987): 28-9.

Fanon, Franz. *Black Skin, White Masks*. New York: Grove Press, 1986.

Gabriel, Chris, and Katherine Scott. "Women's Press at Twenty: The Politics of Feminist Publishing." In *And Still We Rise: Feminist Political Mobilizing in Contemporary Canada*, ed. Linda Carty. Toronto: Women's Press, 1997.

Giles, Winona. "Language Rights are Women's Rights: Discrimination Against Immigrant Women in Canadian Language Training Policies." In *Resources for Feminine Research/Documentation sur la recherche feministe*, vol. 17, no. 3 (1988): 13-15.

Gilroy, Paul. "Steppin' out of Babylon: Race, Class and Autonomy." in *The Empire Strikes Back: Race and Racism in 70s Britain*. London: Hutchinson, The Centre For Contemporary Studies 1982.

Go, Amy Teng-Teng. *Discussion Paper on E.S.L. Funding for Submission to the OCASI Board Of Directors*. Toronto: OCASI, 1987.

Gottlieb, Amy. "What about Us? Organizing Inclusively in the National Action Committee on the Status of Women." In *And Still We Rise: Feminist Political Mobilizing in Contemporary Canada*, ed. Linda Carty. Toronto: Women's Press, 1997.

Guillaumin, C. *Racism, Sexism, Power and Ideology*. London: Routledge, 1995.

Hall, Stuart. "Racism and Reaction." In *Five Views of Multi-Racial Britain*. London: Commission for Racial Equality, 1978.

Hall, Stuart. "New Ethnicities." In *'Race', Culture and Difference*, eds. James Donald and Ali Rattansi. London: Sage, 1941.

Hamilton, Sylvia. "Naming Names, Naming Ourselves: A Survey of Early Black Women in Nova Scotia." In *We're Rooted Here And They Can't Pull Us Up: Essays in African Canadian Women's History*, ed. Peggy Bristow. Toronto: University of Toronto Press, 1994.

Hamilton, Sylvia. "The Women at the Well: African Baptist Women Organize." In *And Still We Rise: Feminist Political Mobilizing in Contemporary Canada*, ed. Linda Carty. Toronto: Women's Press, 1993.

Harstock, Nancy. "The Feminist Standpoint: Developing the Ground for a Specifically Feminist Historical Materialism." In *Discovering Reality*, ed. Sandra Harding. Boston: D. Reidel, 1983.

Henry, Frances, C. Tator, W. Mattis, and T. Rees. *The Colour of Democracy: Racism in Canadian Society*. Toronto: Harcourt Brace, 1995.

Hoodfar, Homa. "The Veil in Their Minds and on Our Heads: The Persistence of Colonial Images of Muslim Women." *Resources for Feminine Research/Documentation sur la recherche feministe*, vol. 22, nos. 3/4 (1993): 5-19.

hooks, bell. *Ain't I a Woman: Black Woman and Feminism*. Boston: South End Press, 1981.

———. *From Margin to Center*. Boston: South End Press, 1984.

Talking Back: Thinking Feminist, Thinking Black. Boston: South End Press, 1989.

Iacovetta, Franca, and Mariana Valverde. "Introduction." In *Gender Conflicts*, eds. Franca Iacovetta and Mariana Valverde. Toronto: University of Toronto Press, 1992.

James, Carl E., and Adrienne Shadd. *Talking About Difference: Encounters in Culture, Language and Identity*. Toronto: Between The Lines, 1994.

Jayawardena, Kumari. *The White Woman's Other Burden: Western Women and South Asia During British Rule*. London: Routledge, 1995.

Jhappan, Radha. "Post-Modern Race and Gender Essentialism or a Post-Mortem of Scholarship." *Studies in Political Economy*, vol. 51, (Fall 1996): 15-64.

Khayatt, Didi. "The Boundaries of Identity at the Intersections of Race and Gender." *Canadian Woman Studies*, vol. 14, no. 2 (1994): 6-14.

Kitagawa, Muriel. *This Is My Own: Letters to Wes and Other Writings on Japanese Canadians, 1941-1948*. Vancouver: Talon, 1981.

Kobayashi, Audrey, and Linda Peake. "Unnatural Discourse, 'Race' and Gender in Geography." *Gender, Place and Culture*, vol. 1, no. 2 (1994): 225-43.

Kohli, Rita. "Power or Empowerment: Questions of Agency in the Shelter Movement." In *And Still We Rise: Feminist Political Mobilizing in Contemporary Canada*. Toronto: Women's Press, 1993.

Kogawa, Joy. *Obasan*. Toronto: Lester and Orpen Denneys, 1981.

LaRocque, Emma. "The Colonization of a Native Woman Scholar." In *Women of the First Nations: Power, Wisdom and Strength*, eds. Christine Miller and Patricia Churchryk. Winnipeg: University of Manitoba Press, 1997.

Law Union of Canada. *Immigrant Women's Handbook*. Montreal: Black Rose, 1981.

Laxer, Gordon. *Open for Business: The Routes of Foreign Ownership in Canada*. Toronto: Oxford University Press, 1989.

Laxer, Robert. *(Canada) Limited: The Political Economy of Dependency*. Toronto: McClelland and Stewart, 1973.

Leah, Ronnie, and Gwen Morgan. "Immigrant Women Fight Back: The Case of the Seven Jamaican Women." *Resources for Feminist Research*, vol. 8, no. 3 (1979): 23-4.

Li, Peter S. "The Economics of Brain Drain: Recruitment of Skilled Labour to Canada, 1954-1986." In *Deconstructing a Nation: Immigration, Multiculturalism and Racism in '90s Canada*, ed. Vic Satzewich. Saskatoon: University of Saskatchewan, 1992.

———. "The Market Value and Social Value of Race." In *Racism and Social Inequality in Canada: Concepts, Controversies and Strategies of Resistance*, ed. Vic Satzewich. Toronto: Thompson Educational Publishing, 1998.

Mahtani, Minelle. "Polarity versus Plurality: Confessions of an Ambivalent Woman of Colour." *Canadian Woman Studies*, vol. 14, no. 2 (1994): 14-18.

McClintock, Anne. *Imperial Leather: Race, Gender and Sexuality in the Colonial Conquest*. London: Routledge, 1995.

McIvor, Sharon. "Self-Government and Aboriginal Women." In *Scratching the Surface: Canadian Anti-Racist Feminist Thought*, eds. Enakshi Dua and Angela Robertson. Toronto: Women's Press, 1999.

Miles, Robert. *Racism*. London: Routledge, 1989.

Mirza, Heidi Safia. *Black British Feminism*. London and New York: Routledge, 1997.

Monture-Angus, Patricia. *Thunder in My Soul: A Mohawk Woman Speaks*. Halifax: Fernwood, 1995.

Monture-Okanee, Patricia. "The Violence We Women Do: A First Nations View." In *Challenging Times: The Women's Movement in Canada and the United states*. Montreal and Kingston: McGill-Queen's Press, 1992.

Mukherjee, Arun. "A House Divided: Women of Colour and American Feminist Theory." In *Challenging Times: The Women's Movement in Canada and the United States*, eds. Constance Backhouse and David Flaherty. Montreal and Kingston: McGill-Queen's University Press, 1992.

Nahanee, Theresa. "Indian Women, Sex Equality, and the Charter." In *Women and the Canadian State*, eds. C. Andrews and S. Rodgers. Kingston: McGill-Queen's University Press, 1997.

Naylor, Tom. *The History of Canadian Business, 1867-1914*. 2nd ed. Toronto: McClelland and Stewart, 1975.

Ng, Roxana, and Alma Estable. "Immigrant Women in the Labour Force: An Overview of Present Knowledge and Research Gaps." *Resources for Feminine Research/Documentation sur la recherche feministe*, vol. 16, no. 1 (1987): 29-34.

Ng, Roxana. "Immigrant Women in Canada: A Socially Constructed Category." *Resources for Feminist Research*, vol. 15, no. 1 (1986): 13-14.
———. *The Politics of Community Service*. Toronto: Garamond, 1988a.
———. "Immigrant Women and Institutionalized Racism." In *Changing Patterns: Women in Canada*, eds. S. Burt, L. Code, and L. Dorney. Toronto: McClelland and Stewart, 1988b.
Nip, Dora. *Canada-Bound: An Exploratory Study of Pioneer Chinese Women in Western Canada*. Master's thesis, University of Toronto, 1983.
Nourbese Philip, Marlene. "Distortions and Liberal Intentions: Pandering to the Unwitting Subtleties of Racism." In *Racism in Canada*, ed. Ormond McKague. Saskatoon: Fifth House Publishers, 1991.
———. *Frontiers: Essays and Writings on Racism and Culture*. Stratford: The Mercury Press, 1992.
Panich, Leo. *The Canadian State: Political Economy and Political Power*. Toronto: University of Toronto Press, 1977.
Paredes, Milagros. "Immigrant Women and Second-Language Education." *Resources for Feminist Research*, vol. 16, no. 1 (1989): 23-8.
Parmar, Pratibha. "Gender, Race, and Class: Asian Women in Resistance." In *The Empire Strikes Back: Race and Racism in 70s Britain*. London: Hutchinson, The Centre For Contemporary Studies 1985.
Payment, Diane. "La Vie En Rose?" In *Women of the First Nations: Power, Wisdom and Strength*, eds. Christine Miller and Patricia Churchryk. Winnipeg: University of Manitoba Press, 1996.
Ramazanaglu, Caroline. *Feminism and the Contradictions of Oppression*. London: Routledge, 1989.
Rattansi, Ali. "Changing the Subject? Racism, Culture and Education." In *'Race', Culture and Difference*, eds. James Donald and Ali Rattansi. London: Sage, 1992.
Razack, Sherene. *Looking White People in the Eye*. Toronto: University of Toronto Press, 1998.
Roberts, Barbara. "Ladies, Women and the State: Managing Female Immigration, 1880-1920." In *Community Organization and the Canadian State*, eds. R. Ng, G. Walker, and J. Muller. Toronto: Garamond, 1990.
Robertson, Angela. "Continuing on the Ground: Feminists of Colour Discuss Organizing." In *Scratching the Surface: Canadian Anti-Racist Feminist Thought*, eds. Enakshi Dua and Angela Robertson. Toronto: Women's Press, 1999.
Satzewich, Vic. "Racisms: The Reactions to Chinese Migrants in Canada at the Turn of the Century." *International Sociology*, vol. 4, no. 3: 321-27.
———. ed. *Racism and Social Inequality in Canada*. Toronto: Thompson Educational Press Inc., 1998.
Shepard, Bruce. "Plain Racism: The Reaction Against Oklahoma Black Immigration to the Canadian Plains." In *Racism in Canada*, ed. Ormond McKague. Saskatoon: Fifth House Publishers, 1991.
Silvera, Makeda. *Silenced*. Toronto: Williams-Wallace, 1983.
Simms, Glenda. "Beyond The White Veil." In *Challenging Times: The Women's Movement in Canada and the United States*, eds. Constance Backhouse and David Flaherty. Montreal and Kingston: McGill-Queen's Press, 1992.
Spivak, Gaytri. "Can the Subaltern Speak." In *Marxism and the Interpretations of Culture*, eds. C. Nelson and L. Grossberg. London: MacMillan, 1988.
St. Lewis, Joanne. "The Entire Women: Immigrant and Visible Minority Women." In *Women and the Canadian State*, eds. Caroline Andrew and Sandra Rodgers. Kingston: McGill-Queen's Press, 1997.
Stafford, James. "The Impact of the New Immigration Policy on Racism in Canada." In *Deconstructing a Nation: Immigration, Multiculturalism and Racism in '90s Canada*, ed. Vic Satzewich. Saskatoon: University of Saskatchewan, 1992.
Stasiulis, Daiva and Radha Jhappan. "The Fractious Politics of a Settler Society: Canada." In *Unsettling Settler Societies*, eds. Daiva Stasiulis and Nira Yuval-Davis. London: Sage, 1995.
Stasiulis, Daiva, "Theorizing Connections: Gender, Race, Ethnicity, and Class." In *Race and Ethnic Relations in Canada*, ed. Peter Li. Toronto: Oxford University Press, 1990.
Stepan, Nancy. "Race and Gender: The Role of Anatomy in Science." In *The Anatomy of Racism*, ed. David Goldberg. Minneapolis: University of Minnesota Press, 1990.
Stevenson, Winona. "Colonialism and First Nations Women in Canada." In *Scratching the Surface: Canadian Anti-Racist Feminist Thought*, eds. Enakshi Dua and Angela Robertson. Toronto: Women's Press, 1999.
Stoler, Ann Laura. *Race and the Education of Desire*. Durham: Duke University Press, 1995.
Thornhill, Esmerelda. "Focus on Black Women." In *Race, Class, and Gender: Bonds and Barriers*, eds. J. Vorst, et al. Toronto: Between The Lines Press, 1989.
Turpel, Mary Ellen. "Aboriginal People and the Canadian Charter: Interpretive Monopolies, Cultural Differences." *Canadian Human Rights Yearbook*, vol. 6, no. 3 (1989-90): 3-45.
———. "Women on the Rekindling of Spirit at the Wake for the Meech Lake Accord." *Queen's Law Journal*, vol. 15 (nd): 345-59.
Valverde, Mariana. *The Age of Light, Soap and Water: Moral Reform in English Canada, 1885-*

1925. Toronto: McClelland and Stewart
Press, 1991.

———. "'When the Mother of the Race is Free': Race, Reproduction, and Sexuality in First-Wave
Feminism." In *Gender Conflicts*, eds. Franca Iacovetta and Mariana Valverde. Toronto:
University of Toronto Press, 1992.

Walker, James W. *"Race," Rights and the Law in the Supreme Court of Canada: Historical Case
Studies*. Waterloo: The Osgoode Society for Canadian Legal History and Wilfred Laurier
University Press, 1997.

Ware, Vron. *Beyond the Pale: White Women, Racism and History*. London: Verso, 1992.

Wotherspoon, Terry. "From Assimilation to Self-government: Towards a Political Economy of Canada's
Aboriginal Policies." In *Deconstructing a Nation: Immigration, Multiculturalism and Racism in
'90s Canada*, ed. Vic Satzewich. Saskatoon: University of Saskatchewan Press, 1992.

The Women's Book Committee, Chinese Canadian National Council. *Jin Guo: Voices of Chinese
Canadian Women*. Toronto: Women's Press, 1992.

PART I

COLONIALISM AND THE HISTORICAL CONSTRUCTION OF GENDER

CHAPTER ONE

The Discourse of Empire and the Social Construction of Gender

LINDA CARTY

When feminists of colour talk about gender, colonialism, and imperialism in academic discourse, we implicitly acknowledge the impact of Empire on the depth of the meaning of gender in this context.

First, we see how the Other is socially constructed out of beliefs of white superiority. Second, we see a narrative of gender advanced by white women, one that follows a similar organizing principle, built on hierarchy. And finally, we see how racism weaves itself into white relations of rule, becomes part of the fabric of ideas reflecting the social needs and aspirations of the dominant race, sex, class, and culture, bestowing a taken-for-granted character to all its creations. Unearned white privilege — the product of pillage during the creation of Empire — becomes the standard by which all else is judged.

This essay outlines the imperial context out of which Euro-American and Euro-Canadian feminism emerged, and examines Empire's legacy in academic feminist discourse today, at the close of the twentieth century. It is an old story, but well worth repeating, because so much in feminist theory today, so much in postmodernism, merely attempts to dismiss as "essentialist" any discussion of the connections between the social construction of knowledge and the identities and locations of those framing the discourse. What follows here is an analysis of how the specifics of the domination and subordination inherent in colonialism and imperialism shape feminist praxis very differently for their subjects. Questions of experience, history, culture, and identity are necessarily in the foreground of this analysis.

THE CONSTRUCTION OF THE OTHER
AND THE CREATION OF EMPIRE

The island nation of England, along with France, Spain, Portugal, and the Netherlands, began to colonize most of what is now called the "Third World" back in the sixteenth century. For those European nations, gaining possession of colonies played a central role in the development of capitalism from its mercantile to its industrial phase. The colonies provided the raw materials that formed the industrial base for the trade and commerce that led to modern capitalism.

In the case of England, colonization was propelled by the Atlantic slave trade. That trade gave England an economic edge over its European rivals, by allowing it to develop its sugar and cotton industries, two pillars of its industrial revolution. The "West Indian" islands, an end point of the Atlantic slave trade, contributed significantly to that industrial revolution and creation of Empire. As Eric Williams writes:

> The West Indian islands became the hub of the British Empire, of immense importance to the grandeur and prosperity of England. It was the Negro slaves who made these sugar colonies the most precious colonies ever recorded in the whole annals of imperialism.[2]

The wealth England drained from its many colonies put it well ahead of its competitors. England's highly unequal trade policies with the colonies simultaneously ensured its wealth as it guaranteed their impoverishment. In India, for example, in the early 1800s, the British imposed a 73 percent duty on Indian cotton imported into England, while it levied a mere 3.5 percent on English cottons imported into India. India's value to England can, like the value of the islands of the West Indies, be traced through the records of the British East India Company, which collected revenue in India for the British Treasury. In 1857 alone, the Company collected £15.7 million in land revenue and almost half as much in taxes and customs duties.[3]

By the late eighteenth century, England, one of the smallest countries in Europe, would "own" and rule most of the world. Empire was to a large extent made possible through the English mercantile and planter class, which, in the early seventeenth century, was quick to substitute sugar for tobacco when the latter became unprofitable. As sugar production expanded so did its demands for labour, until that demand exceeded the supply. As Cedric Robinson points out,

> Having already decimated those aboriginal populations they had encountered in the West Indies, the English mercantile and planter bourgeoisie found it necessary and expedient to expand their Irish (and homeland) strategy to West Africa. As they did so, the scale of their enterprise grew beyond anything seen in English history.[4]

England's Atlantic slave trade, based on the buying and selling of Africans for forced labour, drew its model from earlier forms of slavery elsewhere. Slavery as an economic phenomenon did not arise from racism. The belief that whites are superior to Blacks, however, is a consequence of slavery.[5]

English contact with Africans would add another layer to the social construction of the Other. The first had been laid down with contact, through Cristóbal Colón in his encounters with Aboriginal peoples, and by the freelancers and *conquistadores* who followed in his wake. Constructing the Other would give legitimacy to the belief in white superiority and its "civilizing" mission.

The Other, as used here, refers not to race *per se* — a phenomenon which did not emerge in European social thought until the late eighteenth century[6] — but to a system of stratification based on skin colour and exemplified through

England's positioning of its inhabitants in relation to those of the colonies, particularly in relation to the Africans.[7]

Hence, the Africans whether in Africa, the West Indies, or the Americas, were perceived very differently than the white, colonial subjects of Canada and Australia, for example, who, though at moments in history were seen as being different from the English, were seen to be different primarily on the grounds of social class (and also inherently, though differently, inferior). This is not to say that, prior to the enslavement of the Africans, other peoples were not characterized as Other and thus inferior. Indeed, in Europe, the Irish and Jews were defined as such, to name just two.[8] However, the characterization of Africans as Other was particularly pejorative, and assigned cultural and economic characteristics which designated the Africans as extremely backward.

All sorts of analyses tried to sort out how to differentiate between Africans. Some tried to explain differences in skin colour, while others tried to explain differences in physical attributes. All were bent on justifying the claim that Africans were inferior.[9]

The mission to "civilize" the Africans would also prove critical in constructing them as Other. Discussions of what to do about these "heathens" and "pagans" run parallel to those about their skin colour. The discourse on colour and Christianity was itself part of legitimating English (in fact European) colonial expansion into Africa in the nineteenth century. Yet, we know that the discourse on the inferiority of the colonized, a discourse based on skin colour and representations of the colonized as Other, were not limited to the Africans, but extended to the peoples of today's India, Pakistan, Sri Lanka, Bangladesh, and to the peoples of the Orient[10] and Indigenous peoples of the "Americas."

THE INTERPLAY OF GENDER AND RACE:
WOMEN AS COLONIZER AND COLONIZED

Much has been written about the creation of the British Empire and the belief in inherent cultural, national, and imperial superiority that obtained from it. The belief in one's inherent superiority was not limited to the British ruling class of the time, but was the pride of all the United Kingdom of Great Britain and Ireland.[11] Nor was it limited to British men, though the very nature of colonialism, with its impetus in seizure, ownership, and exploitation, was particularly patriarchal. Indeed, women from the United Kingdom who went to the colonies, either on their own or as wives of colonial administrators, took it as their mission — indeed, their burden — to save the unfortunate women of those colonies.[12]

The mission would go a long way toward shaping British women's outlook on their own lives. Throughout the colonies, they saw themselves as crusaders for the Empire and served as the maternal counterparts of British patriarchs. Together with their men, they carried out the exploitation and subordination of the resources and peoples of the colonies. They were full, if not equal, participants in the creation of white supremacy. They then set themselves up as helpers of women of colour. During the Victorian era, middle-class British feminists saw Indian women, including Indian feminists, as helpless and needing to be saved from their own backwardness, a condition born of a backward culture. It was up to British women to save the women of India.

White women played an instrumental role in maintaining the racist relations of rule put in place by their men, the colonial administrators. Whether white women or men were more responsible for racial tension in the colonies is of no interest here. What is of interest are the relations of domination and subordination that made the colonizers superior and turned the colonized into the Other. Race and gender were inextricable. One case that brings the impossibility of disentangling them sharply into focus is the colonial government of India's 1883 attempt to remove a racially discriminatory clause from the *Indian Penal Code.* While European civil servants had the right to exercise criminal jurisdiction over native subjects living in certain areas, the Indian civil servants had no such right over the Europeans. The bill to remove the clause, the *Ilbert Bill,* caused a near riot in the country as white men and women alike spoke and wrote in vehement opposition to the *Bill.* The opposition focused on the prestige and security of the "pure and defenceless" white woman of India.[13] Wherever this white woman went in the colonies, she went as the symbol of purity and defencelessness, even as her primary role there was to aid in the defilement and exploitation of the colonized, and in particular, of colonized women.

British women in the colonies were often simultaneously resistant to and complicit with the policies and practices of imperial administrators. Many, including Flora Shaw (the first colonial writer for *The Times* of London, later Lady Lugard and subsequently a Dame of the British Empire) and Beatrice Webb (a Fabian socialist renowned as an advocate for the poor in London) consciously took up very active roles in promoting imperialism and its elitist ideology of the "natural" superiority of the "British race" and its consequent entitlement to dominate others.[14] Such women did much to spread the discourse of imperialism, using its ideological imperatives to justify women's subordinate role in the domestic arena while supporting the Empire's domination of other peoples.

The Empire's feminists might be women, but they were *British* women, and therefore deserving of the rights they fought for. Their own oppression taught them nothing about the universal condition of women under patriarchy. On the contrary, they aligned themselves with men of the Empire. Their preoccupation with, and support for the belief in, the superiority of the British "race" and its Empire kept them from imagining any other relationship with colonized women.

Why should gender be so integral to Empire? Many women imperialists protested the inequality between the sexes while at the same time espousing the extension of Empire as Britain's paternal responsibility.[15] Such women clearly understood how they were oppressed as women. Frequently, across the Empire, they talked and wrote about enslaved and colonized women as the Other, to emphasize their own argument of the inequality of the sexes. Distinguishing themselves from enslaved and, later, from colonized women, soon became part of how some women of the Empire's ruling and middle classes won respect from the men who ruled it and, even more critically, an underpinning of the fight for women's suffrage. In *A Vindication of the Rights of Woman,* Mary Wollstonecraft in 1792, makes no fewer than eighty references to *slavery* as an analogy for the condition of the white, middle-class women whose rights she was championing.[16] In keeping with the language of Empire and in accordance with its received beliefs, she casts Africans as an homogeneous and inferior group. Her conviction was that white, middle-class women were superior to slaves and should, therefore, not be treated as slaves.[17]

LEGITIMIZING THE OTHER IN COLONIALIST DISCOURSE

Wherever the colonisers went in the colonies, they deemed non-Europeans backward and inferior. The structures of domination — the policies and practices of colonial institutions — that white hegemony guaranteed resulted in the near erasure of the histories and cultural identities of the colonized. Dominant discourse — received wisdom — offers many examples of how differences are at once marshalled and flattened, ultimately reducing others to the homogenized Other.

Historically, those who rule have always used categories to control the ruled. When the British ruled what is now known as Nigeria, for example, they systematically distinguished between two of the largest groups, the Ibos and the Yorubas, in the southern part of the country. The former were deemed to be more capable intellectually and thus sophisticated (read: less resistant and easier to work with). Similarly, in what is now India, Bangladesh, and Pakistan, the British also stratified the population into different "races," equating some with Africans and others with whites. The distinctions worked to convince the women of the local elites that the British were not practising racial discrimination against them.

Such categorizations found their way into colonialist discourse, which attempted to draw distinctions while at the same time making links between the many Other(s) in the colonies. This was often a strategic move on the part of the British ruling elite. The following statement by Sir Harry Johnston, the first Commissioner of British Central Africa, exemplifies the colonialist thinking on the Other's presumed inferiority to the British and the presumed distinctions between the Others which made their future hopeless. He wrote in 1894:

> On the whole I think the admixture of yellow that the negro requires should come from India, and that Eastern Africa and British Central Africa should become the America of the Hindu. The mixture of the two races would give the Indian the physical development which he lacks, and he in turn would transmit to his half negro offspring the industry, ambition, and aspiration towards a civilized life which the negro so markedly lacks.[18]

Empire ruled the waves and its discourse ruled academic and social thought, granting legitimacy to British rule and superiority. The discussions ranged from the subtle to the oftentimes absurd, but never failed to expose how racism is born of ignorance. We see examples of this as early as the seventeenth century in English travelogues. Samuel Purchas in *Purchas His Pilgrimage*, 1613, outlines the various theories of skin colour, beginning with classical thought:

> Now if any would looke that wee should here in our discourse of the Negro's assigne some cause of that their black colour: I answere, that I cannot well answere this question, as being in it selfe difficult, and made more by the variety of answeres, that others giue hereunto. Some alledge the heat of this Torrid Region, proceeding from the direct beames of the Sunne; And why then shoulde all the West Indies which stretch from the one Tropike to the other, haue no other people?...why should Africa yeeld white people in Melinde? Some...attribute it to the drynesse of the earth: ...as though Niger were here dryed up.... Why then are the Portugalls Children and Generations white, or *Mulatos* at most, that is tawnie, in *St. Thomez* and other places amongst them? Some ascribe it (as Herodotus) to the blacknessse of the Parents sperme or seede; And how made they the search to know the colour thereof, which if it hath (a thing by others denyed), by what reason should it imprint this colour on the skinne?[19]

Well over two centuries later, we find that colonists' pejorative beliefs about the natives of the colonies and the social construction of them as the Other have been passed on successfully to European women. Hence, when European women travel to the colonies, they speak of the peoples there much as their male predecessors did. Mary Kingsley, whom some have written of as an anti-colonialist, compares French and British colonialism in her account of her travels to West Africa in the early 1890s:

> I confess I am not an enthusiast on civilising the African. My idea is that the French method of dealing with Africa is the best at present. Get as much of the continent as possible down on the map as yours, make your flag wherever you go as sacred a thing to the native...then when you have done this, you may abandon the French plan and gradually develop the trade in an English manner.[20]

It is true that Kingsley is not without her contradictions. On one occasion, for example, she writes that, "unlike others," she does not see the African as an undeveloped white man any more than she sees a rabbit as an undeveloped hare. For some, such sentiment is taken as anti-colonialist. Nonetheless, as the bulk of her writings show, she was no less a defender of Empire than were the men of the dominant race and class, and she was certainly no more knowledgeable about African civilizations, about which she notes:

> ...they are notably deficient in all mechanical arts: they have never made, unless under white direction and instruction, a single fourteenth rate piece of cloth, pottery, a tool or machine, house, road, bridge, picture or statue...a written language of their own construction they none of them possess.[21]

Like Wollstonecraft before her, Kingsley shares the beliefs of her male counterparts. She claims this about the peoples of Africa:

> The mental condition of the lower forms of both races (Bantu and Negro)
> seems very near the other great borderline that separates man from the
> anthropoid apes, and I believe that if we had the material, or rather if we
> could understand it, we should find little or no gap existing in mental
> evolution in this old, undisturbed continent of Africa.[22]

Historically, Empire's discourse has served to legitimize the racist beliefs
and practices that precipitated the social construction of the Other. Thus, while
it is true that the First Wave of feminism in the United States emerged out of
the mid-nineteenth century movement to abolish slavery in that country, that
feminism also found itself deeply mired in racism.[23]

At the time, the history of Black people in the West was largely one of being
made into commodities, a history of being the property of white slave-plantation
owners. Africans on the continent who had not been enslaved — indeed, all peoples of colour — were nevertheless seen as backward and often as less human
than whites. At the same time, patriarchy had made all women subordinate in the
relations of gender.

When white women began to fight against patriarchal oppression, they capitalized on white privilege and located themselves as being superior to Black women
and other women of colour. Patriarchy took on such racial significance in the
struggle for women's suffrage in the United States that white feminists of the time
argued that, as they were superior to Black men, the franchise should first be
extended to white women. It should be no surprise that these white feminists did
not conceive of Black and other women of colour as deserving of the rights white
women ought to have.

WESTERN FEMINIST DISCOURSE AND THE ERASING
OF THIRD WORLD WOMEN'S MULTIPLE SUBJECTIVITIES

That women share patriarchal oppression has never precluded the fundamental
political differences amongst women. Such differences appear most sharply when
we analyze the discourse of gender, where Third World women find their multiple subjectivities stroked out by the pens of white feminists.

Third World women, whether in advanced capitalist states or in the former colonies, find themselves cast to the periphery of Western (also known as liberal) feminist
theory, where they are positioned as a monolith, pitied as passive, dismissed as tradition-bound. The discourse mirrors that of the Empire (where Third World women
can be seen only as naive and tradition-bound subjects) and of global capitalism.
Once the former colonies became inserted into capitalism's international division of
labour, Third World women became the world's cheapest source of labour.

The rapid advance of technologically driven monopoly capitalism led, by
the time of the Second World War, to the end of the Empire's need for colonies.
The changes in capitalism brought to the fore new challenges to the

marginalization and super-exploitation of Third World peoples in the relations of capitalist production. One key challenge was the Black civil rights struggle in the U.S. The feminism of the 1960s emerged, like its forerunner in the nineteenth century, out of that Black struggle against racism.[24]

And the feminism of the 1960s, like that of the nineteenth century, couched its discourse in anti-racist and anti-imperialist terms. Not long after, however, the feminist movement became co-opted by middle-class, white women who opposed capitalism's further privatization of the family, privatization that relegated them to domestic labour in the household. Their liberal agenda, devoid of an analysis of race and class, marks white, Western feminism to this day. In voicing their objections to capitalism's patriarchal dictates on what they themselves ought to be doing with their lives, Western feminists have overlooked much of women's history. In much of the world women have always worked outside the immediate confines of the home — most often in agriculture — as well as within it. All less-privileged women in advanced capitalist societies — specifically, most Black women, women of colour, and white, working-class women — had to work out-side the home to survive and still must do so. Yet Western feminism focused on domestic life as the site of women's oppression.

Western feminism deemed the structure of the family household oppressive for most white, middle-class women. Yet the very factors of race and class that afforded them the privilege of objecting to it created a very different structure for the Black family and for other families of colour (and, of course, for many white, working-class families as well). Even as capitalist patriarchy afforded men in Black and other families of colour more power than it afforded the women, its racism and anti-working-class character prevented the men from earning a "fam-ily" wage. The women did not have the "privilege" of being materially dependent on the men. For Black people and people of colour, the family served as protec-tion against, and a central source of resistance to, racist oppression.

Ironically, as white, middle-class women fought for the right to engage in wage labour outside the home and to escape domestic labour, many women of colour, having no access to other waged work, laboured — and still do labour — in the homes of privileged, white women and in other similar service jobs such as domestic work in hospitals and hotels. The conditions of privileged, white wom-en's lives were — and are — directly linked to the absence of privilege in other women's lives. When Betty Friedan published *The Feminine Mystique* in 1963,[25] advocating that wage work liberated women, she, like many of her privileged, white sisters, was referring to high-paying, influential careers. Friedan feminists failed to recognize that most women working outside of the home worked — and still do work — in menial, minimum-wage jobs that could not — and still cannot — liberate them from dependence on men nor from other forms of patriarchal domination.

Friedan feminists, however, did not shrink from universalizing their experi-ences. That the discourse of feminism should exclude Black women and women of colour is hardly a small oversight. On the contrary, it reflects a comprehension of a social world where whites were — and are — superior. Western feminists continue to claim that feminism aims to "empower" women, all the while ignoring the glaring differences between their lives and those of most of the world's women.

Race and class have never been central to Western feminism's discourse of gender. Challenges to the discourse have come from the margin, from "Third World" women, who are seen to be uniform in their thinking and experiences, from "minority" women (when they are most of the women of the world), from the thought-to-be-homogenized Other. Western feminists — white, middle-class feminists — on the other hand, position themselves in ways that imply they are "non-traditional" and quite varied in their experiences and goals.[26] Such positioning, with its social constructions deemed to be the only legitimate referents, erases the class, race, and ethnicity of "Third World" women, removing all traces of their multiple subjectivities.

That such feminism distorts social reality is not new, nor is Third World feminists' demand that white feminists acknowledge racism as the organizing principle of the relationships between white and Third World women. Constructions of gender for white women and Third World women — including, but not limited to, women's role in domestic labour in the family — have always been different because they have been determined by race and class privilege. This cuts to the heart of the meaning of womanhood itself.

Sojourner Truth stripped bare the racial and class framework of womanhood one hundred and fifty years ago at the National Convention on Women's Rights in the United States when in response to a man's objection to women's suffrage because women were so dependent on men, she declared:

> That man over there says women need to be helped into carriages, and lifted over ditches, and to have the best place everywhere. Nobody ever helps me into carriages, and lifted over ditches, or over mud-puddles, or gives me any best place! And aint I a woman? Look at me! Look at my arm! I have ploughed, and planted, and gathered into barns, and no man could head me! And aint I a woman? I could work as much and eat as much as a man — when I could get it — and bear the lash as well! And aint I a woman? I have born thirteen children, and seen most all sold off to slavery, and when I cried with my mother's grief, none but Jesus heard me! And aint I a woman?[27]

The imperial practices of racism and sexism and racist sexism that Truth spoke out against continue as discursive colonialism in Western, hegemonic, feminist discourse.

Postmodern feminism would have us believe that there are no fundamental differences which separate women. Yet it cannot account for the divisions between "white" and "Black," between "traditional" and "modern," between "Western" and "Third World," between "advanced" and "backward" because it has no way of recognizing, never mind analyzing, the economic and social forces that gave rise to these divisions and how those forces shaped — and still shape — the lives of most women.

The connections between race, class, and gender in the lives of Third World women cannot be over-stressed. Nor can the need for Third World feminism to integrate these multiple subjectivities into feminist discourse be overstated, even as Western feminism denies them. "Globalization" — the latest phase of colonialism — seeks to carve out the ideal conditions for the ever-greater accumulation of capital and the ever-wider and ever-broader thrust of its reach. That is the point of free trade agreements and of the Multilateral Agreement on Investment. Whatever guise globalization wears, it depends on an ever-ready, ever-disposable pool of cheap labour around the world. That pool is brimming with Third World women, brimming with women of colour.

That holds true not just for the Third World itself, the former colonies, the old outposts of Empire. In London, New York, and Toronto we find Third World women holding the same kinds of jobs. Received wisdom still holds that Black women are eminently suitable for employment as maids and nurses aides, that Filipinas make good nannies, that other Asian women have the most nimble fingers, making them the best suited for electronic assembly.

Institutionalized discrimination subordinates Third World women, consigns them to the bottom of the hierarchy of capitalist social relations, and then legitimizes that position, which, in turn, secures the hegemony of white women in the world of work for women.[28] Third World women understand that their experiences are determined by racism and by class. From the bid to privatize water in Nelspruit, South Africa, to the maquiladoras/industrial parks of Mexico, they understand the power and influence of capital, they know full well the reach of transnational corporations. Far from being passive or deterministic about their plight, Third World women deploy many strategies of resistance in the workplace and in their communities. Indeed, their refusal to suffer passively often results in the State relying on repression, in the hope of crushing resistance.

Western feminist discourse takes into account how capital organizes and exploits white, middle-class women but generally overlooks the exploitation of white, working-class women and almost always ignores entirely the super-exploitation of Third World women. In the 1970s and 1980s, a plethora of works by Western feminists did begin to look at women's subordination in the household, in education, and in the workplace,[29] the three central arenas of capitalist reproduction of gender inequalities. Few, if any, of these works acknowledged Third World women at all.

That, too, is hardly a small oversight. Advanced capitalist states in the West have always systematically regulated immigrant labour and have always done so according to gender. One example can be found in the boom following the Second World War when Britain, the United States, and Canada made haste to relax their immigration policies to allow more immigrants of colour from Asia, Africa, and the Caribbean. They did not do this to make their societies more colourful or more diverse; the precise intent was to bring cheap labour to capital.[30] Immigration became an issue of serious political contention in those countries when some opposition politicians objected to the influx of Third World peoples. By the 1980s, as the economies of the metropole slid into recession, immigrants became targets of racist attacks both from the State and xenophobic elements in the general population.

In Canada, in 1955, the federal government initiated the *Domestic Workers Scheme,* a policy to bring Caribbean women to Canada to work in the homes of prosperous whites. Though the scheme officially ended in the late 1960s, the federal government continued to allow Caribbean women into the country because of the unspoken but nonetheless recognized need for their labour. Today, as Black women move out of domestic work in private homes, the profession is no less racialized and the jobs are being filled by Filipina and North and East African women. Similarly, Third World women who immigrated to Britain in the 1950s and 1960s found the only jobs available to them in a racialized labour market were in domestic and factory work. In the United States, Third World women have fared no better.

Peoples of the Third World, particularly Third World women, have been at the core of the labour force in Britain, the United States, and Canada — three leading western capitalist states — for well over four decades. Capitalism finds it strategic to exploit these workers' sex, race, and class — multiple subjectivities which make their labour power the cheapest in the market place — in order to extract maximum profits. This held true under colonialism, and it holds true today under globalization. Western feminism's collapsing of Third World women's multiple subjectivities into the amorphous category "gender," its ignorance of Third World women's contributions to past and present capitalist development — in short, its repetition of the discourse of Empire — is racist in its effect, whatever its designs may be.

From the plantations of Empire past to the factories of Empire present, in the home and in the community, Third World women have abundant experience in struggle. Third Wave feminism, that ever-expanding collection of works by, about, and for Third World women, is far more than a reaction to the discourse of Empire. Together with the handful of white women who are prepared to move beyond liberalism, neo- or otherwise, Third World feminists — whether in the hinterland or in the metropole — are forging the first fully *emancipatory* politics of feminism.

NOTES

1.   Here the term "Third World" refers to these countries of the South which comprise the periphery in the context of global capitalism. Their populations, people of colour, are the most exploited in the relations of capitalist production, hence, the countries/regions remain the poorest in the world. Later in this essay, the term refers to the peoples of those countries both at home as well as in the advanced capitalist world.
2.   Eric Williams, *Capitalism and Slavery* (New York: Capricorn Books, G. P. Putnam's Sons, 1966), 52.
3.   J. Liddle and R. Joshi, *Daughters of Independence* (London: Zed Books, 1986), 24-5.
4.   Cedric J. Robinson, *Black Marxism* (London: Zed Books, 1983), 161.
5.   Eric Williams, 7.

6.   This is when "race" enters European science and is given precise meaning. As British sociologist Robert Miles states, "...the sense of difference embodied in European representations of the Other became interpreted as a difference of 'race,' that is, as a primarily *biological* and *natural* difference which was inherent and unalterable. Moreover, the supposed difference was presented as scientific (that is, objective) fact"; Robert Miles, *Racism* (London: Routledge, 1989), 31. Later, "race" would become a category for assigning privilege.
7.   Wherever "race" is used in this essay it is used as a social construct, not as a fact of science.
8.   See for example, L. P. Curtis, *Apes and Angels: The Irishman in Victorian Caricature* (Washington: The Smithsonian Institution Press, 1971); G. L. Mosse, *Toward the Final Solution: A History of European Racism* (London: Dent and Sons, 1978). Such beliefs live on in present-day discrimination against the Irish living in England and in anti-Semitism and anti-immigrant beliefs.
9.   For details on the academic debate on the differences amongst Africans and what they meant, see P. D. Curtin, *The Image of Africa: British Ideas and Action, 1780-1850* (London: Macmillian, 1965); D. B. Davis, *Slavery and Human Progress* (New York: Oxford University Press, 1984); W. J. Jordan, *White Over Black: American Attitudes Toward the Negro, 1550-1812* (Chapel Hill: University of North Carolina Press, 1968); and S. Joshi and S. Carter, *Race and Class,* vol. 25, no. 3: 53-70.
10. See Talal Asad, ed., *Anthropology and the Colonial Encounter* (New York: Humanities Press, 1973); Cedric J. Robinson, *Black Marxism* (London: Zed Books, 1983); Edward W. Said, *Orientalism* (Harmondsworth: Penguin, 1985); R. Kabbani, *Europe's Myth of Orient: Devise and Rule* (London: Macmillian, 1986).
11. "Great Britain" itself is the product of conquest and colonization. The first official use of "Great Britain" came in 1604 with the crowning of James I as "King of Great Britain" though the English Parliament would not proclaim the Act of Union with Scotland until 1707. Wales had been the subject of repeated English invasions and Welsh resistance was defeated in the fourteenth century. England first invaded Ireland in the twelfth century. Following renewed resistance, the Irish proclaimed the Irish Free State in 1922 (later to become the Republic of Ireland), and the United Kingdom of Great Britain and Ireland became the United Kingdom of Great Britain and Northern Ireland.
12. Antoinette M. Burton, "The White Woman's Burden: British Feminists and the Indian Woman, 1865-1915," in *Western Women and Imperialism*, eds. N. Chaudhuri and M. Strobel (Bloomington: Indiana University Press, 1992), 137-57.
13. Mrinalini Sinha, "Chathams, Pitts, and Gladstones in Petticoats: The Politics of Gender and Race in the Ilbert Bill Controversy, 1883-1884," in *Western Women and Imperialism,* 98-116.
14. Flora Shaw (1852-1929) who became Colonial Editor of *The Times* during the 1890s was a vehement promoter of imperialism. See Helen Callaway and Dorothy O. Helly, "Crusader for Empire: Flora Shaw/Lady Lugard," in N. Chaudhuri and M. Strobel, 79-97. It's worth noting that, for the most part, women became "British" once they went to the Empire. At home, they tended strongly to call themselves "English," or "Scots," and so on.
15. Callaway and Helly, in Chaudhuri and Strobel, 79-97.
16. Mary Wollstonecraft, *A Vindication of the Rights of Woman,* 2nd ed., ed. Carol Poston (New York: W. W. Norton, 1988).
17. In the past, imperial historians blamed white women's arrival in the colonies for the supposed breakdown in race relations. Such is the nature of patriarchy. However, recently, some women historians have tried to give a more balanced view by writing laudable accounts of white women's role in colonialism. There are many such revisionist accounts of the role of Mary Wollstonecraft amongst others. For insight into some of this equally unbalanced history, see Jane Haggis, "Gendering Colonisation or Colonising Gender? Recent Women's Studies Approaches to White Women and the History of British Colonialism," *Women's Studies International Forum,* vol. 13, nos. 1 & 2 (1990).
18. Quoted in Cedric J. Robinson, *Black Marxism* (London: Zed Books, 1983), 131.
19. Lynda E. Bosse, "'The Getting of a Lawful Race': Racial Discourse in Early Modern England and the Unrepresentable Black Woman," in *Women, "Race," and Writing in the Early Modern Period,* eds. Margo Hendricks and Patricia Parker (London & New York: Routledge, 1994), 42-3.
20. Mary Kingsley as quoted in Sara Mills, *Discourses of Difference: An Analysis of Women's Travel Writing and Colonialism* (London and New York: Routledge, 1991), 159.
21. Mary Kingsley as quoted in Sara Mills, 160.
22. Mary Kingsley as quoted in Sara Mills, 160.
23. For just one of the many works on this point, see Angela Y. Davis, *Women, Race and Class* (New York: Random House, 1981). Various works on women in the early birth control and eugenics movements also explore this point in depth.
24. See Paula Giddings, *When and Where I Enter: The Impact of Black Women on Race and Sex in America* (New York: William Morrow, 1984); Sara Evans, *Personal Politics: The Roots of Women's Liberation in the Civil Rights Movement and the New Left* (New York: Vintage, 1979);

and G. Hull, P. Scott, and B. Smith, *But Some of Us Are Brave* (New York: The Feminist Press, 1982).

25. Betty Friedan, *The Feminine Mystique* (New York: W. W. Norton Company, 1963).

26. For a nice explication of this problematical construction and some of its implications, see Chandra Talpade Mohanty, "Under Western Eyes: Feminist Scholarship and Colonial Discourses," in *Third World Women and the Politics of Feminism*, eds. Mohanty, et al. (Bloomington & Indianapolis: Indiana University Press, 1991), 51-80.

27. J. Lowenberg and R. Bogin, eds., *Black Women in Nineteenth Century American Life* (Pennsylvania: Pennsylvania State University Press, 1978), 235.

28. See Stuart Hall, "Race, Articulation and Societies Structured in Dominance," in *Sociological Theories, Race and Colonialism* (UNESCO, 1981) for a cogent analysis of how racism, under specific historical conditions, manages to accomplish a set of ideological, political, and economic practices which subordinate certain groups in society.

29. For a sample of these, see: Ann Oakley, *The Sociology of Housework* (Bath: Martin Robinson, 1974); also by Oakley, *Woman's Work: The Housewife Past and Present* (New York: Vintage Books, 1976); Maxine Molyneux, "Beyond the Domestic Labour Debate," *New Left Review* (July/August 1979); Barbara Ehrenreich and Deirdre English, "Microbes and the Manufacture of Housework," in *For Her Own Good: 150 Years of the Experts' Advice to Women* (New York: Anchor/Double Day, 1978); Veronica Beechey, "Some Notes on Female Wage Labour," *Capital and Class*, no. 3 (1977); P. Phillips and Erin Phillips, *Women and Work: Inequality in the Labour Market* (Toronto: James Lorimer & Co., 1983); P. Armstrong and Hugh Armstrong, *The Double Ghetto: Canadian Women and Their Segregated Work* (Toronto: McClelland & Stewart, 1984); H. J. Maroney and M. Luxton, eds., *Feminism and Political Economy: Women's Work, Women's Struggles* (Toronto: Methuen, 1987).

30. See: Margaret Prescod-Roberts and Norma Steele, *Bringing It All Back Home* (London: Falling Wall Press, 1980); S. Castles and G. Kosack, *Immigrant Workers and Class Structure in Western Europe* (London: Oxford University Press, 1973); Nancy Foner, "Women, Work and Migration: Jamaicans in London," *New Community*, vol. 5, nos. 1-2 (Summer 1976); Annie Phizacklea and Robert Miles, *Labour and Racism* (London: Routledge and Kegan Paul, 1980); Pratibha Parmar, "Gender, Race and Class: Asian Women in Resistance," in *The Empire Strikes Back* (Birmingham: Centre for Contemporary Cultural Studies, University of Birmingham, 1982); Nathan Glazer and Ken Young, eds., *Ethnic Pluralism and Public Policy: Achieving Equality in the US and Britain* (Lexington, Mass.: D. C. Heath, 1983); Cynthia Enloe, "The Growth of the State and Ethnic Mobilization: The American Experience," *Ethnic and Racial Studies*, vol. 4, no. 2 (1981); Dionne Brand & Krisantha Sri Bhaggiyadatta, *Rivers Have Sources, Trees Have Roots: Speaking of Racism* (Toronto: Cross Cultural Communication Centre, 1986); Makeda Silvera, *Silenced* (Toronto: Williams-Wallace Publishers, 1983); B. Singh Bolaria and Peter S. Li, *Racial Oppression in Canada*, 2nd ed. (Toronto: Garamond Press, 1988).

CHAPTER TWO

Colonialism and
First Nations Women in Canada

WINONA STEVENSON

T he colonization of First Nations Peoples by Western European nations and later by Canada, has had a number of phases, each with its own set of overlapping economic, social, political, and legal agendas.[1] Mercantilists wanted our furs, missionaries wanted our souls, colonial governments, and later Canada, wanted our lands. Five hundred years later colonialist wants are still unsatiated — First Nations Peoples across present-day Canada continue struggling to protect their natural resources (lumber, minerals, and water), to protect their traditional ways of life from missionary incursions, currently in the form of Protestant fundamentalism; and to reclaim stolen lands and self-government jurisdictions.

In each phase of colonialism relationships are imposed to facilitate the agendas and goals of colonial agencies. Rationalization(s) supporting colonial relations and agendas are created through a variety of strategies which depend primarily on the ability of colonial agents to manipulate public perceptions. The manner in which colonial agents represented Aboriginal Peoples were primarily the result of their need to convince themselves and other members of their societies that their agendas were righteous. Imaging, through visual and other forms of representation, also served, and still serves, those in power to rationalize or explain socio-economic inequities.

The intent of this chapter is to provide a brief overview of the historic colonization of First Nations women from contact to the end of the early reserve era.[2] More specifically, it will describe the goals and rationalizations of colonial agencies; demonstrate how colonial agencies manipulated public perceptions of First Nations women to rationalize their subjugation; and describe the process by which the Victorian patriarchy was imposed on First Nations women and societies through federal legislation.[3] This chapter is intended as an outline history; as such, it draws heavily from existing studies on various aspects of Aboriginal women's history.

CHRONOLOGY OF COLONIAL RELATIONS

The colonization of Aboriginal Canada began at first contact and continues in the present.[4] The current socio-economic, political, legal, and socio-cultural conditions of Aboriginal Peoples in Canada are a direct result of Canada's

49

historic and contemporary colonial heritage (Royal Commission on Aboriginal Peoples, 1996).

There can be no doubt that our colonization falls into the classical model of Third World colonization. Classical colonialism occurs when:

> metropolitan nations incorporate new territories or peoples through processes that are essentially involuntary, such as war, conquest, capture, and other forms of force or manipulation (Blauner 1987, 150).

Classical colonialism is distinguished by economic exploitation, forced entry, and cultural imperialism through the imposition of new institutions and ways of thought.

What differentiates our experience from those in the Third World is the fact that we, like Australian, New Zealand, American and other Indigenous Peoples, are minority populations in our own lands. To identify our shared experience, the concept of Fourth World is useful. Noel Dick describes the shared characteristics of Fourth World communities as follows:

> they are minority populations that have no hope of ever prevailing in their respective national societies on the basis of numbers; they are recognized as different from other segments of the national population by virtue of their Aboriginal or indigenous status; they tend to suffer from a lack of political power, economic subjugation, and social and cultural stigmatization...and finally, minority indigenous peoples are located within nation-states that make little or no provision for the exercise of rights beyond those provided by legislatures in the form of citizenship. Aboriginal peoples' claims for special rights fly in the face of this charter premise of the nation-state (Dick 1985, 236-7).

The colonization of First Nations Peoples in present-day Canada was not a monolithic process. It occurred in simultaneous, overlapping, and spatially distinct waves of different European imperial regimes. Given the nature of Canada's colonial heritage, there were roughly four periods of Indian-White relations: French colonial, English colonial, late pre-Confederation, and post-Confederation.[5]

French–First Nations Relations

The classical colonial era began with John Cabot's 1497 visit to the eastern seaboard and St. Lawrence Seaway.[6] Following his return home, news of the great seaboard fisheries in the New World drew fishermen from France, Britain, and Portugal. From then until the end of the sixteenth century colonial efforts were confined to the cod fishery, whaling industry, and casual fur trading.

During the sixteenth century, the French had no intention of establishing colonial settlements, they were only interested in the New World as a source of wealth to help finance wartime activities at home. Encounters between Aboriginal Peoples and Europeans were intermittent — European fishermen arrived seasonally to harvest, then returned home with their catches. Where Aboriginal knowledge and skills were required, relations between the two peoples were strained but amiable. For example, Europeans embarking on sea mammal hunting required Aboriginal expertise which, in turn, required them to accept and adopt many Aboriginal practices and to enter into personal associations (Dickason 1992). However, where Aboriginal knowledge and skills were not needed by Europeans in pursuit of economic profit, as in the coastal fisheries, relations were strained and often violent. The extermination of the entire Beothuk Nation of present-day Newfoundland is a case in point.

The Beothuk of Newfoundland were a fishing, hunting, and gathering people whose annual subsistence round encompassed the entire island. As the coastal fisheries grew in importance they attracted more fishermen; soon temporary fish camps turned into permanent villages and inland agricultural settlements sprung up. Increasingly, the Beothuk were dispossessed of their seasonal coastal fisheries, inland fisheries, and hunting territories. Conflicts over access to dwindling resources resulted in Beothuk raiding and European retaliation. In many instances, European onslaughts against Beothuk communities were outright slaughter. Massacres, combined with starvation and newly introduced European diseases, quickly resulted in the extermination of the entire Beothuk nation. The last living Beothuk was Shawnadithit who was in her early twenties when she succumbed to tuberculosis in 1829 (Pastore 1987; Marshall 1988a,b; Upton 1977; Howley 1915).

Throughout the 1500s the fisheries grew in economic importance but by the end of the century insatiable European fashion demands for beaver felt hats stimulated the fur trade. The fur trade soon took on major economic importance to French, English, and Dutch merchants which exacerbated existing imperial rivalries on the eastern seaboard, instigated inland exploration, and spurred the creation of permanent French colonies.

Early French colonial policy towards Aboriginal Peoples was shaped by two influential ideologies — mercantilism and Roman Catholicism (Frideres 1998, 15). Initially only a handful of merchants emigrated to New France and they were totally dependent on Aboriginal Peoples for subsistence, survival, and fur gathering skills. In order to secure Indian trade partners, fur traders entered into already existing Aboriginal trade networks and alliance systems which were quite unlike any they were used to. In most Aboriginal societies trade was more than an economic venture — trade was facilitated through diplomatic relationships which included personal, social, political, and military obligations (Dickason 1992). These alliances were cemented through marriage, adoption, and ceremony. Interracial marriages unsanctioned by church ceremony followed Indigenous rites and became known as *mariages à la façon du pays*, or "marriage according to the custom of the country." Marriages between French fur traders and Aboriginal women were initially common practice and, for a short time, became French policy (Dickason 1985).

Winning the trade loyalties of Aboriginal Peoples were essential to the ability of the French to lay colonial claims in North America. From the beginning, the French Crown tied the fur trade to colonial expansion, first by securing Aboriginal Peoples as military allies through trade; second by granting merchants trade monopolies on the condition that some of their profits be used to help establish permanent colonies; and third by promoting interracial marriage as a means to create French nationals to populate its North American colonies (Ray 1996; Dickason 1992).

Permanent settlements began in the early seventeenth century but were characterized by a shortage of marriageable French women. Europe was still recovering from the Black Death and the emigration of French women was discouraged. In order to create an overseas French population, the Crown encouraged marriage between its sons and Aboriginal women. The French policy to turn Aboriginal Peoples into French citizens was called "Frenchification." Samuel de Champlain promoted this policy among Aboriginal Peoples in his oft-cited proclamation to the Huron chiefs, "Our young men will marry your daughters, and we shall be one people" (cited in Dickason 1992, 167). The French church approved this policy on the condition that the brides were Roman Catholic converts.

The French Crown relied on the Roman Catholic missionaries to convert Aboriginal Peoples on the grounds that Christian conversion and French "civilizing" influences would make them more loyal and stronger allies. One of the missionary priorities was to regularize interracial marriages according to Christian practices and to facilitate their work they convinced the colonial authorities to offer official incentives. In 1680 Versaille allocated 50 livres each as dowries to French and Aboriginal women marrying French men. Funds were also allocated for the education of Aboriginal girls to prepare them for marriage which the Ursulines had been providing since they arrived in 1639 (Dickason 1992; Ray 1996). The overall objective of the program was the creation of a settled and farming mixed-blood population that was culturally French yet possessing the physical strength, knowledge, and skills of their mothers' people.

By the turn of the sixteenth century the "Frenchification" program was announced a dismal failure. In far too many instances mixed families did not produce a sedentary farming population. French men preferred fur trading over farming and Aboriginal lifestyles over French, and Aboriginal women rejected the confining yolk that settlement life imposed. Colonial authorities were baffled by the resistance to settlement life and at their apparent "blindness" towards the benefits of "civilization." Colonial authorities reversed their earlier opinions on the grounds that interracial marriages were producing a people embodying the worst traits of both parentages. Despite official denouncements, frontier marriages continued unabated outside the watchful eyes of the colonies and eventually produced a new syncretic society, the Great Lakes Metis (J. S. H. Brown 1987; Dickason 1985; Peterson 1978).

The Frenchification policy also failed because the focus of the fur trade moved inland to the beaver-rich regions of the upper Great Lakes in the mid-1600s. Despite French colonial attempts to contain colonists in New France, hundreds of French men slipped away to the Old Northwest where they married into Aboriginal communities, profited as fur traders, and gained freedom from

French authority and rule. French officials outlawed uncontrolled trade activities outside the boundaries of New France which forced these *coureur du bois*, or "runners of the woods," to trade their furs among the Americans or smuggle them to Europe (Ray 1996; Dickason 1992, 1985). French neglect of the wealth in furs in the Old Northwest opened the door for English incursions.

"[P]acification and reconciliation" through Indigenous alliance systems were the foundations for French Indian policy throughout the seventeenth century (Jaenen 1991, 27). The primary objectives were conversion to Catholicism and the eventual assimilation of Aboriginal Peoples into French civil and commercial life through incorporation, rather than by force or extinguishment of Aboriginal title. This policy required French authorities to restrict settlement to the lower St. Lawrence Valley, allowing only small fur trade and military posts in First Nations territories beyond. Within New France a number of mission reserves were established, but beyond its boundaries First Nations self-determination and territorial rights were respected (Jaenen 1991).

English–First Nations Relations

The English entered present-day Canada on two fronts: the eastern seaboard colonies of New England and Hudson's Bay in the far Northwest. Relations between Aboriginal Peoples and English colonists to the south of New France were negative almost from the start. Unlike the French, the English fur trade on the eastern seaboard was inconsequential in light of the rush for agricultural settlement.[7] Aboriginal survival skills in New England were only required when English colonists first arrived. Once established, the English colonists expanded by pushing into coveted Aboriginal lands by force. Driven by land lust and exonerated by manifest destiny ideology, English colonists waged war on Aboriginal communities. Local colonization companies, established by English Royal Charters throughout the seventeenth century, were often given carte blanche permission to:

> collect troops and wage wars on the barbarians, and to pursue them even beyond the limits of their province and if God shall grant it, to vanquish and captivate them; and the captive put to death (Charles I, cited in Frideres 1998, 16).

The English followed a policy of expediency — when ignoring Aboriginal Peoples was no longer feasible in their rush for land, they annihilated them or pushed them onto small, isolated, and marginal tracts of land. English colonials on the eastern seaboard maintained that "a 'savage' could never validly exercise sovereignty" which only organized states, and some added Christian states, could assert (Dickason 1992, 177). This was the case until imperial warfare forced the English to follow the lead of their French enemies and seek military support from First Nations.

Relations with First Nations came under imperial authority, and from 1745 onward the English adopted a series of policies to regulate trade, protect Indian lands from encroachment, and secure military allies through the distribution of gifts (Tobias 1991). In 1755, the Indian Department was officially established under imperial military authority.

In the far Northwest, English-Indian relations developed differently than on the eastern seaboard, primarily because English interests in the north were in the fur trade rather than in settlement. In 1670, Prince Rupert, cousin of King Charles II, along with other wealthy English merchants founded the Hudson's Bay Company (HBC) and received a Royal Charter granting them exclusive trade rights to a vast region encompassing all the land draining into the Hudson's Bay. The region, named Rupert's Land, covered "roughly one-third of Native Canada" (Ray 1996, 70).

The Governors of the HBC were only interested in establishing trade relations with First Nations Peoples. Unlike their English cousins and the French to the south, the HBC directors had no intention of establishing farming colonies or converting First Nations people to Christianity. The HBC realized all too well that Christian conversion and its concomitant "civilization" would divert First Nations Peoples away from trapping, provisioning, and seasonal wage labour, and toward sedentary farming, with disastrous effects on the trade. Farming settlements undermined the trade. They transformed the landscape, placed added pressures on valuable resources, and imposed "impractical" Christian sensitivities and norms on fur trade society. To protect its economic interests, the HBC prohibited European women and missionaries from entering Rupert's Land (Stevenson 1988; Van Kirk 1987).

Fur traders depended on the traditional lifestyles and skills of First Nations people for fur production, especially the knowledge, skills, and familial comforts of First Nations women. Initially, the distant HBC directors tried to restrict fraternizing between its servants and local First Nations women but the policy proved impractical. The Company could neither control the social needs of its servants nor avoid Cree and Assiniboine trade relations protocol which required kinship ties (Ray 1996; Dickason 1992; Van Kirk 1987, 1980; J. S. H. Brown 1976). By the end of the seventeenth century, a large mixed-blood population had grown up around HBC posts and among First Nations communities.

Initially the fur trade was characterized by mutual exchange and interdependency. As the fur trade became increasingly entrenched, however, the balance of power shifted. Ron Bourgeault (1991) describes how the patriarchy and the commodification of First Nation resources and labour introduced by the fur trade slowly destroyed egalitarian or communal relations between First Nations men and women. As the fur trade expanded in Western Canada, female labour power and sexuality were commodified and male private property introduced. In some instances, Aboriginal women benefited materially from their roles as intermediaries between their peoples and fur traders, but many more were exploited and abused (Bourgeault 1991; Van Kirk 1987).

Following the conquest of New France, Montreal-based merchants increasingly challenged the HBC dominance in Rupert's Land which resulted in violent trade wars from 1765 until the HBC reasserted its monopoly in 1820 (Ray 1996, 93). While Aboriginal fur producers and provisioners profited by the competition, overall it had long-lasting disastrous effects — over-hunting, gluts in the market, declining prices, and more over-hunting. The increase in frontier violence against Aboriginal women was also a prominent feature of the competition era (Bourgeault 1991; Van Kirk 1980). As the fur trade expanded further inland, traders depended less on the skills of Aboriginal women and increasingly disregarded them as marriage partners in favour of their more amenable mixed-blood daughters. The daughters of mixed unions were generally fair complexioned and when raised in mixed company were more acculturated to European norms and expectations. They were also bilingual and heirs to their mothers' skills. French Metis and English "daughters of the country" were the preferred marriage partners until the arrival of missionaries and Euro-Canadian settler populations exacerbated already existing racial tensions (Van Kirk 1987, 1980).

COLONIAL REPRESENTATIONS OF FIRST NATIONS WOMEN

Smandych and Lee stress that any attempt to explain aspects of "the relationship linking law, colonialism and gender relations in post-contact societies" needs to address issues raised in recent feminist and Native ethnohistorical studies (1995, 29). In an effort to explain the rationales behind the subjugation of First Nations women, scholars have paid special attention to how stereotypical images of Aboriginal women were historically constructed. European colonialists arrived on our shores with predetermined ideas of appropriate female behaviour and status which served as their lens for "understanding" the behaviour and status of Aboriginal women.

Recent studies demonstrate that the ideal condition of women in Western European society served as an index of "civilization" (Shoemaker 1995; Acoose 1995; Smith 1987; Weist 1983; Smits 1982; Fee 1973). According to this index, how a society treated its women indicated its place on the social evolutionary scale. The status and condition of European women represented the pinnacle of civilization, the result of a "long and painful evolutionary struggle away from nature" (Fee 1973, 24) and a "victory of self-discipline over instinct" (Cominos 1963, 219).

The European ideal of womanhood, or the "cult of true womanhood," revolved around female domesticity (Riley 1986). The appropriate position of women was confinement to the household where they were enjoined to subordinate their wills to their fathers, husbands, or nearest appropriate male relative, and to direct their energies to the efficient management of the resources their men provided. The ideal woman was characterized by the virtues of piety, purity, submissiveness, and domesticity (Weist 1983). She was defined as a nurturer, providing "selfless, gentle, benign, and humane" support for her family. She was further burdened with the responsibility of socializing her children, of transmitting the cultural disciplines, morals, and values of her society to the next generation (M. Young 1980, 98). By the nineteenth century, the ideal woman emerged as the prime symbol of civility and represented female emancipation at its peak (Riley 1986).

The European ideal of womanhood was projected on Aboriginal societies throughout the colonized world where it functioned as "the single most important criterion for contrasting savagism with civility" (Smits 1982, 298). Victorian morality was the severe standard against which Aboriginal women were judged. They were ultimately found wanting because almost everything about their being — their appearance, their social, economic, political, and spiritual positions, activities, and authority — was a violent affront to the European ideal. Compared to European women, Aboriginal women appeared "antithetical to the presumed natural condition of women" (Weist 1983, 39).

 Confronted by women who were almost the exact counter-image of their own culture's ideal, initially caused much confusion in the minds of early European observers in present-day Canada. Where European women were fragile and weak, Aboriginal women were hard-working and strong; where European women were confined to affairs of the household, Aboriginal women were economically independent and actively involved in the public sphere; where European women were chaste and dependent on men, Aboriginal women had considerable personal autonomy and independence — they controlled their own sexuality, had the right to divorce, and owned the products of their labour (Leacock 1980; Grumet 1980; Devens 1992; J. Brown 1975).

In the early phases of the Western fur trade, many of the traits that set Aboriginal women apart from European women were valued by European men. A number of studies demonstrate that European men soon became dependent on the traditional hunting, gathering, and manufacturing skills of Aboriginal women for their personal survival, and on their abilities as interpreters, cultural mediators, and guides to further the trade (Van Kirk 1996, 1980; J. S. H. Brown 1980). Many fur traders were intimately associated with Aboriginal women and learned much about traditional societies, but their documented perceptions strongly reflect their Western European sensitivities and biases. Samuel Hearne commented during a journey among the Northern Dene in the 1770s:

> Ask a Northern Indian, what is beauty? He will answer, a broad, flat face, small eyes, high cheekbones...a low forehead, a large broad chin, a clumsy hook-nose, a tawny hide, and breasts handing down to the belt. Those beauties are greatly heightened, or at least rendered more valuable, when the possessor is capable of dressing all kinds of skins, converting them into the different parts of their clothing, and able to carry eight to ten score stone in summer, or haul a much greater weight in winter (cited in Van Kirk 1980, 10).[8]

Fur traders were shocked by the physical strength of Aboriginal women, by their clothing and beautifying styles, marriage and child-rearing practices, and by what they perceived as the drudgery of Aboriginal women's lives. In their ideal world, women were frail, dependent on men, and incapable of labourious tasks. In contrast, Aboriginal women made substantial contributions through small animal hunting, fishing, and gathering, and among some First Nations were full-time horticulturalists. When big game hunting failed, women were the sole providers for their families and communities. Furthermore, the economic contributions they made translated into considerable personal autonomy since women were generally responsible for distributing the products of their labour and were owners of the household (Bourgeault 1991; Etienne and Leacock 1980; Van Kirk 1980; Anderson 1992).

The cumulative affect of all this was that Aboriginal women were understood and represented in ambiguous and contradictory terms — the "noble savagess" (Princess) or the "ignoble savagess" (Squaw Drudge).[9] The former is the archetypal Indian Princess, "a Pocahontas type who was virginal," "childlike, naturally innocent," beautiful, helper and mate to European men, and inclined to civilization and Christian conversion (Smith 1987, 65). Her antithesis, the Squaw Drudge, is characterized as a "squat, haggard, papoose-lugging drudge who toiled endlessly," who "lived a most unfortunate, brutal life," and "fought enemies with a vengeance and thirst for blood unmatched by any man" (Smith 1987, 65). In contrast to her noble sister, the Squaw Drudge is also sexually licentious, ugly, beast of burden, and slave to men (Weist 1983; Acoose 1995).

This binary classification has its roots in the patriarchal Victorian virgin-whore dichotomy. However, colonialist imperatives, supported by racist ideology, intensified the binary imaging of Aboriginal women. In the minds of European men, the perceived condition of First Nations women was understood as an inevitable condition of their savagery. Unlike European women, Aboriginal women faced a "peculiar kind of sexism...grounded in the pernicious and ever-present ideologies of racism" (Albers 1983, 15). Also unlike European women, their burden was even more severe — to be "good" they had to defy their own people, exile themselves from them, and transform into the European ideal (Green 1990, 18). Their nobility as "princesses" or their savagery as "squaw drudges" were defined in terms of their relationship to or with European men. Images of Aboriginal women, initially ambivalent and contradictory, became unambiguously negative and unidimensional when missionaries arrived on the scene.

Missionary activity in present-day Canada occurred in two waves. French imperial expansion in the southeast was as much a religious as it was an economic venture. Consequently, Catholic missionaries primarily from the Sulpician and Jesuit orders, accompanied fur traders into First Nations territories. The HBC in Rupert's Land prohibited missionary intrusions for the first 150 years of its occupation. By the turn of the eighteenth century, however, the HBC was under increasing attack from philanthropic and missionary societies for failing to open the West for settlement and forsaking its moral obligation to introduce First Nation Peoples to the "benefits" of Christianity and "civilization." Under threat of losing its exclusive license to trade, the HBC begrudgingly facilitated the establishment of the Selkirk (Red River) colony in present-day southern Manitoba and cautiously permitted missionaries entry. The Catholic Oblates were summoned to contain the Metis challenge to HBC authority;[10] Anglicans and Presbyterians were brought in to look after the souls of retired and active company men and their families; and in 1840 Methodists were permitted to establish missions outside the confines of the Red River colony (Stevenson 1988).

Missionaries in the field waged a violent war against paganism. Their weapons were Eurocentric beliefs in their own cultural superiority, biblical injunction, and the pen. Many were prolific writers of adventure stories, autobiographical texts, journals, reports, and a plethora of correspondence. As vanguards of Western civilization they had a powerful influence on public opinions about Aboriginal peoples and on the development of federal Indian policies.

More than any other colonial agency missionaries represented the condition of Aboriginal women in fatalistic and derogatory terms. Missionaries found no redeeming qualities; in their indigenous form Aboriginal women had no value (Carter 1984). While many fur traders viewed Aboriginal women multidimensionally, missionaries could only see the debased "savage." Missionaries condemned almost everything about First Nations ways of life that appeared to challenge or violate "civilized" Christian norms. However, they were especially damning of those aspects of Aboriginal women's lives and characters that appeared to blatantly transgress the European "ideal woman" construct. Vivid descriptions of Aboriginal women as exploited, overworked drudges, abused, misused, dirty, haggard, resigned, and beaten abound in missionary literature (Devens 1992; Carter 1984; Leacock 1980; E. R. Young 1893; McLean 1889; Jones 1861; West 1823). Missionaries generally believed that "mutual love and sympathy" in Aboriginal family life "was unknown in their pagan state" (E. R. Young 1893, 63). Whereas civilized people "pampered their women; savage people mistreated them" (Smith 1987, 66). At best, Aboriginal women were pitied and their wretched state was blamed on the savagism of their men. Images of Aboriginal women created by men like the Reverend Egerton Ryerson Young, a Methodist missionary among Lake Winnipeg Cree and Saulteaux Peoples from 1868 to 1876, reflect their Eurocentric biases:

> This was one of the sad aspects of paganism which I often had to witness as I travelled among those bands that had not, up to that time, accepted the Gospel. When these poor women get old and feeble, very sad and deplorable is their condition. When able to toil and slave, *they are tolerated as necessary Evils.* When aged and weak, they are shamefully neglected, and, often, put out of existence (E. R. Young 1893, 48, emphasis added).

Young was a popular and prolific writer of frontier adventure stories based on his experiences among First Nations Peoples. His representations of First Nations Peoples reached a huge audience. Speaking from personal experience, Janice Acoose reminds us that the negative images created in the past have an enduring quality that has dramatically impacted First Nation women's history and life:

> Such representations create very powerful images that perpetuate stereotypes, and perhaps more importantly, foster dangerous attitudes that affect human relations and inform institutional ideology (1995, 39-40).

Missionaries directly attacked those aspects of Aboriginal women's lives and characters that exemplified their personal autonomy and independence. More specifically, they assailed the lack of patriarchal family structures, complementarity in gender relations, female authority in the household, polygamy, the rights of both sexes to divorce, sexual freedom outside of marriage, and female ownership of and control over lands, resources, and produce (Anderson 1992; Carter 1984; Weist 1983; Smits 1982; Leacock 1981, 1980).

As early as the 1650s, Jesuit missionaries among the Montagnais and Naskapi of present-day Quebec attempted to restructure their society by introducing the European family organization complete with male authority, female fidelity, and the elimination of the right of divorce (Leacock 1980). Successive waves of missionaries continued this cultural transformation program but found that patriarchal family structures were difficult to impose. One of the reasons for this was that in many Aboriginal societies women controlled the produce of their own labour and had a high degree of control over the products of men's labour. Among the Cree, Ojibway, and Algonquian Peoples, for example, women controlled the distribution of meat; "once the men reported the kill, it became the woman's property" to butcher, process, and distribute as they saw fit (Devens 1992, 11). Among those tribes who followed matrilineal descent and matrifocal residence patterns, like the Iroquois, female heads of families ruled the households and were in charge of allocating work and distributing all goods and foods produced by their families — from the garden, hunting, trapping, fishing, as well as manufactured goods (Montour 1987; Rothenberg 1980; J. Brown 1975). Female authority over the home and garden was in direct opposition to the Christian, patriarchal family structure and male-dominated agriculture. In Aboriginal terms, women's ability to distribute the foods and goods produced by their families among the community is evidence of their autonomy and authority in household matters (Bourgeault 1991; Etienne and Leacock 1980). It also reinforced a "sense of interdependence among the households" (Devens 1992, 12).

Divorce, polygamy, and sexual freedom were a major "source of horror" to missionaries (Nock 1988, 55; Devens 1992; Buffalohead 1983; Leacock 1980). According to Jesuit LeJeune, who worked among the Montagnais-Naskapi of Quebec in the seventeenth century, the "inconsistency of marriages and the facility with which they divorce each other, are a great obstacle to the Faith of Jesus Christ" (cited in Leacock 1980, 30). Two centuries later, Methodist missionary Reverend Young, among the Cree of Northern Manitoba, stressed that one of his most "perplexing and trying duties" was "reorganizing, on a Christian basis, the families of once heathen polygamists" (E. R. Young 1893, 217).

While missionaries recognized that their cultural replacement programs would be difficult to impose, they did not anticipate vehement resistance from Aboriginal women, especially as they were accustomed to female submissiveness.

FEMALE RESISTANCE TO CHRISTIAN CONVERSION

Most scholars agree that Aboriginal women were judged harshly by colonial observers because they posed an affront to Victorian ideals of womanhood. More recent studies, however, suggest another significant factor — in many instances Aboriginal women resisted Christian conversion and its concomitant social imperatives. This resistance was effective enough to compel missionaries, as agents of social change, to seek the coercive backing of the state.

Numerous studies and first-hand accounts demonstrate that Christian missionaries were most successful among Aboriginal societies experiencing severe socio-economic stress. Spiritual doubts and vacuums resulting from settlement pressures, economic and environmental stress, dislocation and depopulation by disease and warfare, combined to leave Aboriginal Peoples vulnerable to Christian conversion (Axtell 1988; Grant 1984; McDougall 1895). Other studies demonstrate that colonial pressures affected Aboriginal men and women differently (Devens 1992; Anderson 1992; Bourgeault 1991; Leacock 1980). The patriarchal structure of colonial agencies, especially the fur trade, demanded closer relations and negotiations with Aboriginal men than with women. As Aboriginal men were increasingly drawn into European circles, they grew more receptive to introduced practices and values that promised better success in dealing with outsiders. Because men interacted more closely with Europeans, through various economic and political transactions, they realized early the advantages of cultivating relationships with missionaries who could provide access to new forms of spiritual and mundane power. Thus, one of the first segments of Aboriginal societies to convert were men in search of new forms of power to enhance or replace Aboriginal sources outmoded or undermined by newly introduced European germs, ideas, and technologies (Devens 1992; Anderson 1992; Grant 1984; Leacock 1980).[11]

Carol Devens' study of Ojibway, Cree, and Montagnais responses to missionary activities in the Great Lakes region demonstrates that when missionary intrusions affected women and men differently, or unevenly, Aboriginal responses divided along gender lines. She claims that, in general, men favoured Christian accommodation because of its promising benefits, while women tended to resist and reject it. Aboriginal women tenaciously maintained their cultural values, norms, roles, and behaviours, resisting Christian conversion until conditions left them little choice. This was because they had far more to lose by converting to Christianity than their male counterparts did (Devens 1992; Rothenberg 1980).

While European missionaries represented Aboriginal women's lot in life in super-negative terms, they also provide evidence that Aboriginal women had far more personal freedom, independence, and security than Western European women. As recent studies demonstrate, one of the many ironies of the Christian-Aboriginal encounter was that Aboriginal women had far more personal autonomy and self-determination than their "emancipated" European counterparts (Devens 1992; Smith 1987; Lurie 1972). As such, they had little or nothing to gain by converting to Christianity until external pressures became intolerable.

The work of the late Eleanor Leacock into seventeenth century Jesuit mission records provides fascinating insights into the female conversion process used on the Montagnais-Naskapi of Quebec and into female resistance. Missionaries first had to convince men of the righteousness of the patriarchy, especially male domination and the principle of punishment. Once converted, a handful of Montagnais men were encouraged to forcefully impose their newly acquired authority on women and children who suffered terrible psychological and physical pain at their hands. Some of the punishments LeJeune's neophytes subjected their women to included withholding food, public and private beatings, head-shearing, and incarcerations. Women resisted covertly by sabotaging neophyte men's work, and overtly by physically fighting back and running away (Leacock 1981, 1980).

Aboriginal women resisted marital monogamy because polygamy was both practical and preferred (Leacock 1980; Devens 1992). Warfare and the dangers of male occupations reduced the number of marriageable men; polygamy ensured that all women desiring marriage could acquire it. Men's acceptance of Christianity removed the possibility of marriage for many women, leaving them "to a life of social and economic uncertainty" (Devens 1992, 27). Polygamy was also preferred by women because household chores could be shared among co-wives, which allowed for more leisure and independent time. It also ensured that women, by virtue of their numbers, controlled the household (Devens 1992). Monogamy, on the other hand, created a large pool of poverty-struck, over-worked, single-parent, female-headed families (Leacock 1980; E. R. Young 1893). One of the ways women resisted monogamy was by assuming "illicit" relations with their "husbands." Numerous accounts of illegitimate children being born to mature women singled by monogamy, divorce, or widowhood testify that women remained sexually active.[12]

Missionaries were least successful in their attempts to prevent divorce. Women refused to give up their right to divorce spouses "who were poor or lazy hunters or otherwise...inadequate as mates" (Devens 1992, 26). The threat of divorce also allowed women to maintain control over the household and served as insurance against mistreatment by their husbands.

Women in horticultural societies refused to give up control over agriculture—production, distribution, and the land. It wasn't so much that women were afraid of losing authority or power over their households, rather, they feared male mismanagement. Men were not learned in the skills or sacred ceremonies associated with agriculture and were less sensitive to the needs of the community because they were often absent on hunting and diplomatic missions (LaFramboise 1990; Montour 1987; Smits 1982; Rothenberg 1980; Grumet 1980; J. Brown 1975). Women in coastal areas and inland regions where fishing made up the primary subsistence base also maintained their roles in the fisheries and control over the distribution of fish and other products (Fiske 1987; Klein 1976).

Many Aboriginal women resisted Christian marriage to maintain control over access to resources and the right to distribute the products of family labour. Tlingit women in Northern British Columbia, for example, handled all family wealth and managed trade activities. When urged to "legitimate" their marriages they resisted on the grounds that they refused to hand over their "purse strings" to their husbands (Klein 1976, 173). During the Pacific maritime fur trade Tlingit and other coastal women maintained control over the products of their labour — "fresh and dried fish, ducks, shellfish, berries, and shoots" — by trading directly with European merchants (Littlefield 1987, 181; Klein 1976). When missionaries attempted to replace communal access-ownership with patriarchal private property, women most vehemently refused to hand it over. Placing men in charge of land and agriculture was central to the missionary enterprise but women held fast — some even they went so far as to publicly humiliate and ridicule their men for trying to farm (Rothenberg 1980).

Among the most telling evidence of Aboriginal women's resistance to cultural transformation was their reluctance to send their daughters to mission schools. Records indicate that boys greatly outnumbered girls at mission schools (Devens 1992; Nock 1988). The public reason was that girls were needed at home more than boys were. Privately, mothers resisted the mission education of their daughters in an effort to protect and hide them from missionary influences, especially during their early formative years (Devens 1992). Mission schools posed a threat to the socialization of their children and to the cultural integrity of the community.

The imposition of the nuclear family system which undermined extended family matrifocal living patterns was also resisted by Aboriginal women. Traditional living arrangements reduced women's workload, safeguarded against family violence, and facilitated the sharing of provisions and goods. The transition to single-family dwellings was accompanied by minor acts of resistance like refusing to take up household chores (Rothenberg 1980, 78). Indian agents reported that women resisted "any progress towards modernization" and were "a hindrance to the advancement of men" (Carter 1996a, 162). The reality was that women preferred traditional airy and clean tents over dark, dirt-floored cabins, plus there was always a great shortage of household maintenance supplies.

Methodist missionary John Sinclair reported in 1867 that inland (Bush) Cree women "deliberately discouraged Home Guard women" at the Hudson's Bay Company trading posts and the Rossville mission from collaborating with missionaries. Local Cree women, he claimed, "refused to cooperate in the manufacture of handiwork" for sale in England, at the urging of their inland sisters. According to Sinclair:

> The minds of the women are so much prejudiced by our country ladies [bush Cree women] that they care little of doing any work for us, or for anyone else whom they know is sending home work to England (cited in Devens 1992, 56).

It is conceivable that inland Cree women were aware that handicrafts made by Home Guard Cree women were being sold in England to help finance the mission.

The historical evidence demonstrates that when Aboriginal women were faced with losing personal autonomy and power, they resisted. They resisted the patriarchy because it threatened to undermine their socio-economic autonomy and because it threatened the socio-cultural cohesion of their communities. Studies on Aboriginal women's resistance strategies against colonial domination are recent and few but what they tell us so far is that women developed resistance tactics ranging from overt violence to covert symbolic acts. Cursory studies of Aboriginal resistance indicate that "it was women who have formed the very core of indigenous resistance to genocide and colonization since the first moment of conflict between Indians and invaders" (Jaimes 1992, 311). That women were the primary caregivers for children and keepers of the home compelled them to maintain traditional values, norms, and belief systems. The strength and tenacity of female resistance to colonial intrusion is well known among Aboriginal Peoples — as the old Cheyenne proverb goes, "A nation is not conquered until the hearts of its women are on the ground."

MISSIONARY AND STATE STRATEGIES AND COLLABORATION
Pre- to Post-Confederation Indian-White Relations

As the moral vanguards and defenders of Victorian civilization, missionaries pursued female conversion with zealous fervour. Punishments of women and children by neophyte converts, for reasons and in forms previously unknown in most Aboriginal societies, were introduced and encouraged by missionaries. Eleanor Leacock documents numerous accounts in which missionaries encouraged neophyte Montagnais-Naskapi men to coerce female conformity to European Christian practices. Women were deprived of food, humiliated, tied to posts in the centre of the village and publicly whipped (Leacock 1980, 32-5). One of Leacock's sources, Bartholemy Vimont, recorded that on one occasion, after neophytes beat a young woman for talking to a suitor against her parent's wishes, her Christian relatives proclaimed:

> We are taught that God loves obedience. We see the French practicing it; they have such a regard for that virtue that, if any one of them fail in it, he is punished.... This is the first punishment by beating that we have inflicted upon anyone of our Nation. We are resolved to continue it, if any one among us should be disobedient (cited in Leacock 1980, 35).

However, Aboriginal responses to missionary conversion efforts were not uniform. They ranged from "zealous dedication, through formal conversion, that might well involve backsliding, to indifference, and finally to hostility" (Leacock 1980, 36). The relative degree of conversion also depended on a wide range of exacting factors, from individual inclination to socio-economic stress (Axtell 1988; Grant 1984).

Over time, the resolve of many Aboriginal women tempered and many converted. However, female conversion was often superficial and did not immediately result in their cultural transformation into prototypes of the Victorian Christian ideal (Devens 1992). It is also clear that the public act of conversion by women may have been a form of resistance to divert missionaries' attentions away from themselves (Scott 1990; Devens 1992; Leacock 1980).

Finding their efforts frustrated by the tenacity of Aboriginal women, missionaries solicited outside support from home missionary societies, philanthropic organizations, the public at large, and the federal government. The missionary lobby was extensive because Aboriginal resistance was not the only challenge they faced — they also had to contend with bleeding-heart liberals and primitivists who mourned the decline of the noble savage. However, the urgent nature of their task, combined with Christian zeal and the need to rationalize their vocation, prohibited missionaries from acknowledging, let alone lamenting, the loss of noble Aboriginal traits. They were cultural imperialists — all Aboriginal characteristics incompatible with Christianity had to be destroyed.

To garner support for the mission enterprise, missionary literature employed what Gerald Berreman calls "impressionistic management" (1962). Missionaries wrote to please their readers and to elicit public and government support. In their attempts to persuade readers of the righteousness of their vocation missionaries capitalized on negative stereotypes — they had to convince their readers of the savage wretchedness of Aboriginal life. Since the condition of women "was the single most important criterion for contrasting savagism with civility" (Smits 1982, 298), missionaries represented Aboriginal women's lives and characters in the most negative light. If anything could touch the hearts of philanthropists and good Christians, it was "woman as victim."

Missionary representations of the degraded condition of women served an even larger object — they provided the ideological rationale for colonial conquest, dispossession, and cultural genocide. As Sarah Carter points out in her study of missionary literature, by "proving the inferiority of the Indian, the missionaries provided justification for the appropriation of their land" and convinced their readers "that there was every justification and, indeed, a great need to transfer the future of the Indians and their lands into more capable hands" (1984, 41, 40). Expounding on the righteous triumph of civilization over savagery, missionaries also provided relief to those experiencing guilt or "personal anxieties about the destruction of Indian societ[ies]" (Smits 1982, 281).

Rayna Green demonstrates further that colonial representations of the ignoble Squaw Drudge, and all she stands for, reduce Aboriginal women to powerless and depersonalized objects of scorn. Like her male counterpart, the Bloodthirsty Savage, she can be easily destroyed without reference to her humanity and "her physical removal can be understood as necessary to the progress of civilization" (Green 1990, 20-1).

The fact that Aboriginal women resisted Christian conversion provided missionaries with even more justification to employ coercive conversion tactics and to solicit support from the state. Since missionary goals for Aboriginal peoples differed little from the goals established by the Canadian Indian Department, these two powerful colonial agencies combined their forces — missionaries provided the ideological rationale for government to develop and employ coercive cultural transformation strategies.

Following the fall of New France and Pontiac's resistance against the terms of the 1763 Treaty of Paris which opened Indian territory in the Old Northwest for settlement, the British imperial government assumed responsibility for the administration of Indian Affairs until 1860, when it was transferred to the United Canadas. British Indian policy was based on a set of principles outlined in the Royal Proclamation, namely: that a line separating Indian territory from British territory be established; that only the Crown could acquire First Nations lands; and that the acquisition of First Nations lands must take the form of a formal agreement (treaty) and must be agreed upon by the majority of the Nation (Jaenen 1991; Milloy 1991).

The War of 1812 ended imperial rivalries in British North America and the need for First Nations Peoples as military allies. From then on, First Nations relations with the British shifted from allies to wards of the state. Settlement pressures demanded Indian removal and containment which prompted a series of land cession treaties and the establishment of Indian Reserves for the "protection, civilization, and assimilation" of First Nations Peoples and their lands (Tobias 1991, 127). Indian Reserves in Canada can best be conceptualized as "internal colonies" within Canada — originally intended as social laboratories to prepare First Nations people for coping with Europeans. Following 1815, missionary-state collaboration and interdependence was consolidated (Frideres 1998, 3; Jaenen 1991). In 1830, administration of Indian Affairs was removed from military authority and became a branch of the public service. No official Indian policy existed for First Nations in Rupert's Land and points further west and north until Confederation in 1867.

THE STATUTORY SUBJUGATION OF FIRST NATIONS WOMEN

From 1850 on, colonial legislatures, and later the Federal Government of Canada, imposed a series of regulations intended to enforce the patriarchy and coerce Aboriginal women to conform to the regiments and edicts demanded by local missionaries and Indian agents in present-day eastern Canada. The development and implementation of these regulations is especially significant because most remained in effect until 1951, others were not repealed until 1985. The last six generations of First Nations women in Canada have suffered under, or at least been impacted by, the paternalistic imposition of Euro-Canadian, patriarchal social institutions (Acoose 1995; Medicine 1993; Montour 1987; Van Kirk 1987; Sanders 1984; Jamieson 1978, 1986).

The authority under which the Federal government based its coercive powers was the 1867 *British North America Act*. Section 91(24) of the *BNA Act* gave the Federal Government of Canada exclusive jurisdiction over the administration of Indians and lands reserved for Indians. The first legislation passed under this authority in 1868 consolidated all previous colonial regulations concerning

Indian status, lands, and revenues, and established the bureaucratic organization of the Indian Department (Lyon 1985). In 1876 the *Indian Act* was passed, which extended the powers of the state and imposed even more stringent regulations affecting Indian life and lands. From then on, the process of statutory female subjugation was intensified as regulations were passed which discriminately undermined the traditional roles, authority, and autonomy of Aboriginal women. Almost every aspect of women's lives was directly impacted by the *Indian Act*.

Following the transfer of Rupert's Land from the HBC to Canada, the federal government extended its authority over Western Canada through a series of Treaties with First Nations from 1870 to 1921. These treaties, combined with the imposition of the 1876 *Indian Act* on Western First Nations, strongly demonstrate that the federal government's primary concern was to clear the land for newly arriving settler populations. Recent studies on the impact of the transition to reserve life on First Nations women show that once under the thumbs of federal agents and local missionaries, the roles and conditions of women dramatically altered (Carter 1997, 1996a,b). First Nations poverty, unemployment, ill-health, and malnutrition resulting from the extinction of the buffalo and the collapse of the fur trade were exacerbated by competition from new settlers over access to declining resources. In an effort to facilitate Euro-Canadian settlement, legitimize repressive measures against First Nations Peoples, and justify the unprecedented level of First Nations poverty, the federal government and its agents — the national press and the missionaries who supported them — constructed and "promoted a cluster of negative images of Aboriginal women" (Carter 1997, 160). According to recent studies by Sarah Carter, the central rationalization supporting the new repressive programs were "images of Aboriginal women as dissolute, dangerous, and sinister, in comparison to their fragile and vulnerable pure-white counterparts" (Carter 1997, 159).

The morality of Aboriginal women and their skills as mothers and homemakers were constantly disparaged by government officials. Indian agents and inspectors, like missionaries, reported that women were indifferent and neglectful parents, that they "wilfully refused to apply their lessons in house wifery," and by their nature had an "immoral and corrupting" influence on White men (Carter 1997, 162; 1996a, 65; 1997, 186). By conveniently ignoring the systemic causes of the appalling conditions of poverty on Indian reserves, and the horrendous frontier violence perpetrated against First Nations women by government agents, the state created an image that blamed First Nations women for their lot in life and justified state intervention (Carter 1997).

Missionaries provided the state with (mis)information about the lives and conditions of Aboriginal people that justified the colonial enterprise and sanctioned, or authorized, the wholesale attack on Aboriginal cultures. Not only did missionaries provide the ideological rationale for the subjugation of Aboriginal Peoples, they also had direct input into the development of federal Indian policies and regulations (Deven 1992; Cole 1990; Nock 1988; Fiske 1987; Grant 1984; Fisher 1983).

The statutory subjugation of First Nations women did not occur in isolation from that of First Nations men. The repressive measures against both were concerted and those experienced by First Nations men were just as severe and debilitating. For the purposes of this paper, however, the focus of the following discussion is on those regulations imposed by the *Indian Act* of 1876 and amendments directed against First Nations women.[13]

Perhaps the most oppressive and controversial legal manoeuvre of the colonial, and later federal, government was to usurp the right to determine who was, and who was not, an "Indian." The first definition was passed by the lower Canada legislature in 1850 for the purpose of Indian administration, but it wasn't until 1869 that definition by patrilineage was imposed (Canada, SPC 1850, c.41; Canada, SC 1869, c.6).[14] According to the 1869 definition, a person was defined an "Indian" if their father or husband was a registered Indian. It established that "Indian women marrying other than an Indian shall cease to be an Indian within the meaning of this Act, nor shall the children issue of such marriage be considered Indians" (Canada House of Commons 1869, 83). The 1876 consolidated *Indian Act* defined "Indian" as follows:

> the term "Indian" means *First.* Any male person of Indian blood reputed to belong to a particular band; *Secondly.* Any child of such person; *Thirdly.* Any woman who is or was lawfully married to such person (Canada, SC 1876, c.18, s. 3(3)).

By the stroke of a pen First Nations women and their children could be denied their birth right as First Nation citizens, depending on whom they married — if born registered Indians, they could only remain "Indian" if they married a registered Indian man or never married at all. If they married anyone else — Euro-Canadian, Metis, or non-status Indian men — they were struck from the Indian register which denied them whatever protections and rights the *Indian Act* offered. However, women marrying-out were able to retain their Band or First Nation membership which entitled them Band annuities or revenues (Jamieson 1978, 61). Additionally, if First Nations women married First Nations men from a different Band, they and their children were arbitrarily transferred to their husband's Band.

First Nation responses to the membership provisions of the 1869 *Indian Act* were immediate. In 1872 the Grand Council of Ontario and Quebec Indians sent letters of protest on behalf of the Six Nations First Nation of Brantford, Ontario, demanding that the provision be amended,

> so that Indian women may have the privilege of marrying when and whom they please; without subjecting themselves to exclusion or expulsion of their tribes and the consequent loss of property and rights (cited in Jamieson 1978, 31-2).

During the Treaty No. 1 negotiations at the Stone Fort in Manitoba, Saulteaux First Nation leaders strongly opposed the exclusionary definition of "Indian":

I should not feel happy if I was to mess with some of my children that are around me — those children we call the Half-breed — those that have been born of our women of Indian blood. We wish that they be counted with us, and have their share of what you have promised. We wish you to accept our demands (cited in Morris 1880, 41).

Like Iroquois leaders, prairie First Nations leaders opposed federal regulations which categorized and defined membership because it went against traditional family structures.

The immediate and long-term effect of this provision was to reduce the number of status Indians the government was responsible for,[15] impose the European patrilineage system, and elevate the power and authority of men at the expense of women. Traditional lineage systems, many of which followed the female line (matrilineage), were unilaterally replaced by patriarchal lineage, and Indian women were penalized for marrying outside their First Nations. In contrast, First Nations men could marry whomever they chose without ever losing either their status or Band membership. In addition, their wives — be they First Nations, Metis, or Euro-Canadian — automatically acquired their husband's Indian status and membership, as did any children issue of such marriages. The result was a major disruption of traditional kinship systems, matrilineal descent patterns, and matrilocal, post-marital residency patterns. Furthermore, it embodied and imposed the principle that Indian women and their children, like European women and their children, would be subject to their fathers and husbands.

In 1951 this regulation was amended, making it even more stringent by denying women who married-out their First Nation/Band membership. Under law, she in fact ceased to be an "Indian," denied protection and benefits under the *Indian Act* and her First Nations membership. The loss of First Nations membership meant, in tangible terms, that women lost the right to live on-reserve free from taxation or liens; be buried on-reserve; receive their fair share of First Nation annuities, revenues, and any on-reserve services like health and education. (Canada, SC 1951, c.29). In more intangible terms, it meant they lost the right to live on traditional lands, participate in First Nations local activities (cultural, social, economic, spiritual), and raise their children in the traditional extended family system. They were legally stripped of their identity and forced to make their way, as best they could, in an alien society. This regulation remained in effect until the *Indian Act* was revised in 1985 by Bill C-31.[16]

The primary goal of the federal government's Indian policy was the destruction of tribal organization, cultural transformation, and the eventual assimilation of all First Nation Peoples into the Canadian mainstream body politic (Tobias 1983). The thrust of the official "civilization" policy was initially formalized in 1857 when legislation was passed to facilitate the "gradual destruction of the tribal organization." This legislation, aptly entitled *An Act to Encourage the Gradual Civilization of the Indians in This Province, and to Amend Laws Respecting Indians* determined that an Indian could not be accorded the rights and privileges of Canadian citizenship until he met certain criterion that proved he was "civilized" (Canada, SPC 1857, c.26). The criterion included the ability to read and write in either French or English, freedom from debts, and sound moral character attested to by a local clergyman. If the candidate passed a three-year probationary period, during which his behaviour was closely monitored, he was granted Canadian citizenship. The process was called enfranchisement and it was viewed as the means to facilitate the acquisition of real property and its concomitant social values — individualism and material accumulation — which were considered a necessary prerequisite for civil rights and citizenship.

At first glance, the enfranchisement regulations appear rather liberal and somewhat benevolent because it entitled enfranchised Indians the rights and privileges of Canadian citizenship. However, on their part, enfranchised individuals were required to give up the protections and rights accorded them under the treaties, and their First Nation membership (Canada, SPC 1857, c.26; Canada, SC 1869, c.6; Canada, SC 1876, c.18). While First Nations women who married non-Indian men were accorded Canadian citizenship (albeit by default), enfranchisement differed. Subjective standards and criterion were imposed that had to be met and women had no choice in the matter.

Between the passage of the consolidated *Indian Act* in 1876 and the revised *Indian Act* of 1951 there were basically two means by which a First Nations person could be enfranchised — voluntarily or involuntarily — both of which came with prescribed criterion. Any Indian man or unmarried Indian woman over the age of twenty-one years could, with the consent of their Band, voluntarily enfranchise if their application was supported by a report from the local Indian agent verifying they had attained a "degree of civilization" that qualified them to become proprietors of land in fee simple. This was met if the applicant demonstrated a level of integrity, morality, and sobriety determined on-the-spot according to the subjective standards of the local Indian agent (Canada, SC 1876, c.18, s.86). To encourage First Nations people who met the requirements to enfranchise, the colonial authorities initially offered incentives in the form of fee simple grants from reserve lands.

The impact of this provision on First Nations women was severe. First Nations men were given the unilateral authority to enfranchise their dependents — wives and children (Canada, SC 1876, c.18, s.86; Canada, SC 1918, c.26, s.6(2)). Women's legal status as First Nation citizens could be unilaterally and irrevocably stolen by federal legislation that allowed their fathers or husbands to make decisions on their behalf. This regulation was a major affront to women's autonomy — women had no recourse if their fathers or husbands "sold" them out of status. It also seriously undermined the matrilineal descent rule of many tribes by giving men authority to decide whether or not their families would retain First Nation membership. The voluntary enfranchisement provisions remained in effect until 1985.

The federal government realized quickly, however, that First Nations Peoples were not easily enticed to gain Canadian citizenship through enfranchisement. Between 1876 and 1918 only 102 First Nation individuals across Canada voluntarily enfranchised (Jamieson 1978). The reality was that First Nations Peoples were unwilling to open their reserves to fee simple ownership, to give up the protections and benefits afforded under the *Indian Act*, treaties, and First Nations membership, to deny their cultural heritage, separate from family and friends, and assimilate into Canadian mainstream society.

To facilitate assimilation, the *Indian Act* also provided for compulsory or involuntary enfranchisement. Any First Nations individual who lived in a foreign country for five simultaneous years could lose their First Nations membership and be denied the right to return home (Canada, SC 1876, c.18, s.3a). In addition, any First Nations individual who received a university degree,

> or who may be admitted in any Province of the Dominion to practice law either as an Advocate or as a Barrister or Counsellor or Solicitor or Attorney or to be a Notary Public, or who may enter Holy Orders or who may be licensed by any denomination of Christians as a Minister of the Gospel, shall *ipso facto* become and be enfranchised under this Act (Canada, SC 1876, c.18, s.86(1)).

While it is presently unknown how many individuals lost their Band membership as a result of these two compulsory enfranchisement provisions, they clearly demonstrate the federal government's desire to reduce First Nation populations. They also demonstrate the federal government's belief that a well-travelled or university-educated "Indian" was a contradiction in terms. Any First Nations person who exhibited any of the qualities considered "civilized" could no longer remain a First Nations person in the eyes of the government. The long-term objective of the federal government was succinctly stated by Superintendent General of Indian Affairs, Duncan Campbell Scott, in 1920:

> Our objective is to continue until there is not a single Indian in Canada that has not been absorbed into the body politic, and there is no Indian question and no Indian Department (cited in Jamieson 1978, 50).

Despite the hopes of Indian Department officials and missionaries, however, the involuntary enfranchisement provision was repealed after a few years, following considerable opposition from First Nations leadership. In 1933 involuntary enfranchisement was slipped into the *Indian Act* once more and while it remained in effect until 1951 it was made ineffectual and eventually abandoned because of First Nations protest (Canada, SC 1932-33, c.42, s.110(14)).

The state and the churches denounced the personal autonomy of Indian women as an outrage and a major threat to the Christian patriarchal order they intended to impose (LaFramboise 1990). Accordingly, traditional marriage patterns, the right to divorce (and remarry), and female sexual autonomy were undermined and/or outlawed. Customary marriage practices conducted outside the church were strenuously denounced by missionaries and the validity of such marriages concerned the Indian Department as early as 1860. At that time the Department objected strenuously to the continuation of customary marriage practices but could not outright prohibit them because a number of court cases had already established the validity of customary marriage in law (Saunders 1975). Despite the protests of churches, the Indian Department was forced to accept traditional First Nation marriages until 1951. One of the ways the Department got around the law, however, was to refuse to acknowledge polygamy. In an attempt to curb polygamy and impose monogamy, the Indian Department withheld treaty annuities and Band revenues from any persons engaged in polygamous unions. While this strategy appeared effective, it merely encouraged traditional families to conceal their polygamous arrangements (Saunders 1975).

In 1951, the federal Indian Department outright disregarded Canadian common law on customary marriages. The revised 1951 *Indian Act* amendments required all marriages to be legally solemnized according to provincial marriage legislation. The only exceptions to this rule applied to the Longhouse marriages of the Iroquois Confederacy (Six Nations) Bands. After numerous petitions and much lobbying by the Iroquois, the Department agreed to accept Longhouse customary marriages on two conditions: first, that the marriages be between members of the Six Nations Bands; second, that the marriages would be recognized only so long as no subsequent marriages occurred (Canada, SC 1951, c.29; Sanders 1975, 666). In effect, the government conditionally acknowledged customary marriages of the Confederacy Peoples. Other First Nations were denied this proviso despite the fact that marriages of other minorities in Canada — the Mennonites, Hutterites, Doukabours, Mormons — were accepted and recognized under law.

Women who had children out of wedlock also came under attack. The *Indian Act* stipulated that illegitimate children would be excluded from membership in their mothers' First Nation unless the Chief and Council accepted them and agreed to give them equal share in Band revenues. The acceptance of illegitimate children by Chiefs and Councils, however, had to be sanctioned by the Superintendent General of Indian Affairs (Canada, SC 1876, c.18, s.3(3)a) who had absolute power to refuse membership to illegitimate children. Clearly this provision demonstrates the government's assimilationist agenda as well as its intent to impose Victorian moral standards on First Nations women.

The sexual autonomy of Indigenous women and their right to divorce were also violated in the 1876 *Indian Act*. Again, annuity and revenue monies were withheld from any woman with "no children, who deserts her husband and lives immorally [common law] with another man" (Canada, SC 1876, c.18, s.72). This provision was a major blow to First Nations women who always had the right to divorce and remarry. It was an outright attack on their sexual, marital, and divorce mores, and furthered the imposition of Judeo-Christian European values and standards.

A final assault on women's rights to divorce occurred when the federal government imposed federal divorce laws on status Indians. In order to obtain a legal divorce, Indian women were bound by Canadian law which required more burdensome grounds of proof for women than for men (Montour 1987). These grounds for divorce were far more rigid than traditional ones that allowed women to end a marriage because of irreconcilable differences or if she believed her husband was a poor hunter or provider. Furthermore, since divorce through the courts was even less accessible to First Nations women than Euro-Canadian women, it was an additional restriction on First Nations women's autonomy (Jamieson 1978, 45).

Another "morality" provision concerned Indian prostitution — in connection to a First Nations woman charged with prostitution, a fine ($10 to $100) and/or imprisonment (up to six months) was imposed on anyone keeping a house in which a First Nations woman was prostituting (Canada, SC 1879, c.34, s.7 & s.8). This was in addition to the *Canadian Criminal Code* prostitution laws (Jamieson 1978, 45).

Provisions in the 1869 *Gradual Enfranchisement of Indians Act* were the first to officially exclude First Nations women from participating in local First Nation governance. The impact this had on First Nations women varied from Nation to Nation. In those First Nation societies where women did not publicly participate in local governance, the impact was not as severe as it was for women in those First Nations were they were actively involved. In its attempt to destroy traditional First Nations governments the state introduced an elected local government system based on the European municipal model. The new local government consisted of one Chief and one counsellor for each one hundred Band members. Women were totally excluded from voting or running for office. The *Act* required that the Chief and council be elected "by the male members of each Indian settlement of the full age of twenty-one years at such time and place, and in such manner, as the Superintendent General of Indian Affairs may direct" (Canada, SC 1869, c.6, s.10). The final selection had to be authorized by the Superintendent General who was also authorized to depose any elected Indian official for "dishonesty, intemperance, or immorality" (Canada, SC 1869, c.6, s.10).

The introduction of this male-dominated elective system not only undermined traditional self-government, it also barred women from participating in the local decision-making process. For the Six Nations Iroquois, for example, this provision effected the breakdown of the traditional Longhouse system because traditional hereditary leadership was traced through the female line, and it was women (Clan Mothers) who selected and deposed leadership (Brown 1975). However, the Iroquois did not accept the *Indian Act* system without a fight. Their refusal to adopt the Chief and Council resulted in the creation of a Royal Commission Investigation in 1923. The Chair of the Commission, Andrew F. Thompson, concluded that the problem with the traditional Longhouse system of the Iroquois was that "a comparatively small number of old women have the selection of those who are entrusted with the transactions of the business of the Six Nations Indians" (cited in Taylor 1983, 160). Thompson believed that the "hope of the future" (assimilation) lay among the small number of "better educated and more progressive Indians" and so he recommended that the federal government intervene (cited in Taylor 1983, 160). In September of 1924 the Privy Council of Canada passed an Order which authorized the forceful replacement of the traditional Longhouse government of the Six Nations with the *Indian Act* elected Chief and Council system. The following month the military forcefully imposed the Order by rounding up and jailing the traditional Chiefs, then held a Band election in their absence.[17] The Privy Council Order basically destroyed the authority of the traditional Iroquois government. The old system did not collapse and still remains relatively intact today but it has no legal authority within the Canadian political system. The only Iroquois authority Canada will recognize is the elected Chief and Council. Through this process the voice and authority of Iroquois Clan Mothers was silenced. Women were denied the right to vote, the right to run for office, and the right to depose any leader who was not looking out for the best interests of the community. Regardless of how resistant traditional leaders were to the elective system, women were not allowed to participate at any level of local government until 1951 revisions to the *Indian Act* (Canada, SC 1951, c.29).

The *Indian Act* also undermined female authority by denying them the right to participate in decisions concerning the disposition of reserve lands. The authority of Iroquois women as guardians and inheritors of the land, for example, was thwarted by the *Indian Act* which gave the authority to release and surrender reserve lands exclusively to men. The regulation stated that land surrenders were to be "assented to by a majority of the male members of the band of the full age of twenty-one" (Canada, SC 1876, c.18, s.26(1)).

The *Indian Act* contained wills and estates provisions that regulated the transfer of personal estates upon the death of an Indian, or more precisely, the death of a male head of a family. An estate included the location ticket for an individual parcel of reserve land together with all personal property and chattels. Upon the death of a location title holder, his land, goods, and chattels were transferred to his children, not his widow, on the condition that the children provide for their mothers' maintenance (Canada, SC 1869, c.6, s.9). First Nations women suddenly went from being autonomous individuals to wards of their children when their husbands died. It was a vicious affront to women, especially those in matrilineal societies where grandmothers were heads of the household and all their children and grandchildren were under their authority (Brown 1975).

The 1876 *Indian Act* improved the wills and estates provisions somewhat by allowing widows with children one-third of their husband's full estates and widows without children the entire estate (Canada, SC 1876, c.18, s.4(9)). However, the Superintendent of Indian Affairs maintained the statutory right to remove any widow from the administration and charge of her husband's estate and the right to distribute the estate of a deceased man among his family members as he saw fit (Canada, SC 1880, c.28, s.20). A widow only attained the right to administer her children's share of the estate "provided she be a woman of good moral character and that she was living with her husband at the date of his death" (Canada, SC 1884, c.27, s.20(3)). The moral character of widows was judged by the local minister and Indian agent. This regulation stayed in its present form until it was repealed in the 1951 revised *Indian Act*. To this day, however, the private and personal property of any First Nation person who dies intestate falls under the control of the Department of Indian Affairs to distribute as the Minister deems appropriate.

The wills and estates regulations went entirely against the traditions of many horticultural tribes where land and household property were held by women and transmitted to proceeding generations through the female line. By placing responsibility over land in the hands of the men, traditional female control over the land and control over the distribution of the products of the land were seriously undermined.

CONCLUSION

From the time of first contact foreign governments coveted Aboriginal lands, foreign missionaries coveted Aboriginal souls and both wanted Aboriginal Peoples to disappear as Aboriginal Peoples — to transform them into Euro-Canadian prototypes. When these two agencies combined their energies in a collaborative effort to reach their common goals, Aboriginal Peoples were struck by a hegemonic force unlike any they had previously known. However, church and state could only achieve their intended goals in collaboration — missionaries provided the moral and ideological rationale, the state provided legal authority.

From the first arrival of missionaries in our lands the status and autonomy of First Nations women was attacked. When colonial authorities, later the Federal Government of Canada, assumed authority over First Nations Peoples the attack on First Nations women was institutionalized. Through various *Indian Act*s and amendments, First Nations women's autonomy in the areas of membership, marriage, divorce, and sexuality were undermined, along with female relations to land and family property, and political decision-making. The overall intent of this legislation was to reduce First Nations women to a condition of dependency on their male relatives.

However, First Nations women did not readily bow down to the foreign patriarchy. They resisted their oppression and retained much of their traditional knowledge and roles. Over time, many of the discriminatory sections of the *Indian Act* were repealed, but not in time to stay the internalization of many European patriarchal notions and practices. The irony in this story is that, in direct contrast to the experiences of Euro-Canadian women, Aboriginal women's "emancipation" in fact intended their subjugation.

While colonialist transformation programs wreaked terrible damage on First Nations communities, they were not entirely successful. Traditional knowledge and skills were hidden by those Aboriginal men and women who resisted total cultural transformation. The healing and spiritual revitalization efforts in our communities today attest to the tenacity of traditional Indigenous lifeways.

ACKNOWLEDGEMENTS

Portions of this chapter derive from a presentation given at the Australian/Canadian Labour History Symposium at the University of Sydney, Australia, in December 1993. Special thanks to the organizer of the symposium, Dr. Greg Kealey, to the University of Saskatchewan for providing travel funds to attend the conference, Sandra Ahenakew for editorial assistance, and Tracey (Splicey) Lindberg for her comments and suggestions.

NOTES

1. The focus of this paper is exclusively on First Nations Peoples. "Indians" is the legal designation applied to First Nations Peoples as per the Royal Proclamation of 1763 and the *Indian Act* (1876 and amendments). The self-designation "First Nations" was adopted to remind the "Founding Nations" that we are the original peoples of this land. Throughout this chapter "First Nations" will be used except where "Indian" is used by other sources. The term "Aboriginal" is inclusive of First Nations (Indian), Inuit, and Metis Peoples as per s.35(1) of the *Constitution of Canada* (1982). While "First Nations *Peoples*," may be grammatically incorrect by English standards, it is used here and elsewhere to stress that there are many distinct and unique First Nations societies within the geopolitical boundaries of Canada, and that we cannot all be lumped into one all-encompassing category.

2. The cut-off date for this overview was selected because it somewhat marks the end of the classical colonial era and the beginning of the neo-colonial or internal colonial era we presently experience.

3. For the purposes at hand, this chapter is necessarily general in its approach and analyses. A broad (a.k.a. Canadian) overview of any subject in Native Studies requires considerable sensitivity and rigour to avoid falling prey to overgeneralization and misrepresentation. The reality is that no one general study can fairly represent the lives and experiences of all Aboriginal women in Canada because not all Aboriginal Peoples are alike. Within the geopolitical boundaries of Canada there are hundreds of distinct and autonomous Aboriginal Nations and societies and all have unique traditions and histories. Readers are strongly urged to consult the growing numbers of more regionally and First Nations-specific studies.

4. For discussions on the various forms and impacts of colonialism on Aboriginal Peoples see Robert Blauner, "Colonized and Immigrant Minorities," in *From Different Shores: Perspectives on Race and Ethnicity in America*, ed. Ronald Takaki (New York: Oxford University Press, 1987), 149-60; Jeremy Beckett, "Colonialism in a Welfare State: The Case of the Australian Aborigines," in *The Future of Former Foragers: Australia and Southern Africa*, eds. Carmel Schrire and Robert Gordon (Cambridge: Cultural Survival Inc., 1985), 7-24; Beverley Gartrell, "Colonialism and the Fourth World: Notes on Variations in Colonial Situations," *Culture*, vol. 6, no. 1 (1986): 3-17; John H. Bodley, *Victims of Progress* (Menlo Park, CA: Benjamin-Cummings Publishing Co., 1982); James S. Frideres, *Aboriginal Peoples in Canada: Contemporary Conflicts*, 5th ed. (Scarborough: Prentice Hall, 1988); J. Rick Ponting, *First Nations in Canada: Perspectives on Opportunity, Empowerment, and Self-Determination* (Toronto: McGraw-Hill Ryerson, 1998); Terry Wotherspoon and Vic Satzewich, *First Nations: Race, Class, and Gender Relations* (Scarborough: Neslon Canada, 1993); Royal Commission on Aboriginal Peoples, *Final Report: Restructuring the Relationship*, Vols. 1 & 2 (Ottawa: Minister of Supply and Services, Canada, 1996); Winona Stevenson, "'Ethnic' Assimilates 'Indigenous': A Study in Intellectual Neocolonialism," *Wicaso Sa Review*, vol. 13, no. 1 (1997): 33-53.

5. Indian-White relations is a sub-field of history that focuses on relations between Aboriginal and European Peoples. See Olive Patricia Dickason, *Canada's First Nations: A History of Founding Peoples from Earliest Times* (Norman: University of Oklahoma Press, 1992) and Olive Patricia Dickason, ed., *The Native Imprint: The Contribution of First Peoples to Canada's Character*, Volume 1, to 1815 (Edmonton: Athabasca University, 1995); J. R. Miller, ed., *Sweet Promises: A Reader on Indian-White Relations in Canada* (Toronto: University of Toronto Press, 1991).

6. Almost 1,000 years before Cabot arrived, Aboriginal Peoples on the northeastern seaboard were visited by Norse fishermen. All existing evidence suggests that the Norsemen set up a few village sites and that relations between them and local Aboriginal communities were cordial. For reasons not altogether understood, the Norsemen abandoned their North American villages and returned

home. For a brief discussion see Arthur Ray, *"I Have Lived Here Since the World Began:" An Illustrated History of Canada's Native People* (Toronto: Lester Publishing, 1996); Dickason, *Canada's First Nations.*

7.   The New England colonies were located south of the primary beaver habitats and while some fur trapping occurred it was inconsequential because of the poor quality of southern furs.

8.   An English "stone" is the equivalent of 14 pounds, which makes ten stone 140 pounds.

9.   Historically and contemporarily the term "squaw" is loaded with negative connotations. It originates from "esqwew" or "iskwew" which in most Algonquian languages signifies woman. However, it has been bastardized by non-Aboriginal peoples into a derogative term embodying a range of nasty stereotypes.

10.   There is a growing body of literature on the rise of Metis nationalism and the Metis Resistance movements of the nineteenth century in the Canadian Northwest, far too many to list here. For example see Peterson and Brown (1985); D. N. Sprague *Canada and the Metis, 1869-1885* (Waterloo: Wilfred Laurier University Press, 1985).

11.   Historical evidence demonstrates that the more marginal sectors of Aboriginal societies — the physically challenged, orphans, widows, for example — were the first converts received by missionaries because conversion offered hope of spiritual and/or mundane advancement and they had less to lose for trying (Grant 1984).

12.   Treaty Annuity Paysheets provide excellent demographic data on individual Band members in Western Canada (1870s to 1940s). The numbers of "widows" bearing children begins to decrease after the first few decades of the reserve transition period. National Archives of Canada, Record Group 10, Indian Affairs Black Series, vols. 9350-9364 (NAC RG10).

13.   Considerable research has been done on the impact of colonial impositions on the political and economic realms of First Nations, which are perceived by scholars as predominantly male realms. Little has been done, however, from a gender studies approach on how colonialism impacted the social roles of First Nations men.

14.   In 1850 legislation was passed in Lower Canada that determined who was entitled to live on Indian lands. It included the first definition of an "Indian" — all persons of Indian ancestry, and all such persons married to such persons, belonging to or recognized as belonging to an Indian Band and living with that Band (*Statutes of the Province of Canada*, chap. 42). The following year the definition was amended to exclude non-Aboriginal spouses of both sexes but the children of mixed marriages were not excluded (Jamieson 1986, 116). Patriarchal definition was imposed in 1869.

15.   In 1869 the federal government's stated purpose in imposing this regulation was to prevent the relatively large numbers of non-Indian men who were married to First Nations women from living on reserves and dividing First Nation revenues into smaller per capita portions, which, the government claimed, impoverished Indians. However, First Nation revenues seldom accounted for much of their incomes. In reality, declining economic opportunities due to settler encroachments into hunting, trapping, and fishing territories were the primary sources of First Nations poverty (Canada, House of Commons 1869, 83; Fenton 1988, 161).

16.   The sexual discrimination against Indian women through this section of the *Indian Act* remained in effect until 1985. That year the *Indian Act* was revised by Bill C-31 which repealed the discrimina-tory sections of the *Act* and allowed for the reinstatement of women and their children who lost status and Band membership by marrying-out. Bill C-31 also transferred the authority to determine Band membership over to First Nations governments. See Joyce Green, "Sexual Equality and Indian Government: An Analysis of Bill C-31 Amendments to the Indian Act," *Native Studies Review*, vol. 1 (1985): 81-95.

17.   After the *Indian Act* Chief and Council were elected, the traditional Chiefs were released. Soon after the coup, one of the traditional Cayuga Chiefs of the Younger Bear Clan of the Six Nations named Deskaheh travelled to London, England and Geneva, Switzerland to present the Iroquois case before the British government and the League of Nations, but to little avail. After returning home in March of 1925, he lambasted the Canadian government during a radio interview:

>   To punish us for trying to preserve our rights, the Canadian government has now pretended to abolish our government by Royal Proclamation and has pretended to set up a Canadian-made government over us, composed of the few traitors among us willing to accept pay from Ottawa to do its bidding (cited in Petrone 1983, 153).

To this day the Six Nations reserves are divided between supporters of the Longhouse and supporters of the elected Chief and Council (Taylor 1983).

REFERENCES

Acoose, Janice. 1995. *Iskwewak Kah'ki yaw ni Wahkomakanak: Neither Indian Princess Nor Easy Squaws*. Toronto: Women's Press.

Albers, Patricia. 1983. "Introduction: New Perspectives on Plains Indian Women." In *The Hidden Half: Studies of Plains Indian Women*, eds. Patricia Albers and Beatrice Medicine. Lanham: University Press of America.

Albers, Patricia, and William R. James. 1987. "Illusions and Illumination: Visual Images of American Indian Women in the West." In *The Women's West*, eds. Susan Armitage and Elizabeth Jameson. Norman: University of Oklahoma Press.

Anderson, Karen. 1992. "Commodity Exchange and Subordination: Montagnais-Naskapi and Huron Women, 1600-1650." In *The First Ones: Readings in Indian/Native Studies*, eds. David Miller, Carl Beal, James Demspey, and R. Wes Heber. Piapot: Saskatchewan Indian Federated College.

Axtell, James. 1988. "Some Thoughts on the Ethnohistory of Missions." In *After Columbus: Essays in the Ethnohistory of Colonial North America*. New York: Oxford University Press.

Berreman, Gerald D. 1962. *Behind Many Masks: Ethnography and Impression Management in a Himalayan Village*. New York: Society for Applied Anthropology.

Blauner, Robert. 1987. "Colonized and Immigrant Minorities." In *From Different Shores: Perspectives on Race and Ethnicity in America*, ed. Ronald Takaki. New York: Oxford University Press.

Bourgeault, Ron. 1991. "Race, Class, and Gender: Colonial Domination of Indian Women." In *Racism in Canada*, ed. Ormond McKague. Saskatoon. Fifth House Publishers.

Brown, Jennifer S. H. 1976. "Changing Views of Fur Trade Marriage and Domesticity: James Hargrave, His Colleagues, and 'The Sex.'" *The Western Canadian Journal of Anthropology*, vol. 6, no. 4: 92-105.

———. 1980. *Strangers in Blood: Fur Trade Company Families in Indian Country*. Vancouver: University of British Columbia Press.

———. 1987. "The Metis: Genesis and Rebirth." In *Native Peoples, Native Land*, ed. Bruce Alden Cox. Ottawa: Carleton University Press.

Brown, Judith. 1975. "Iroquois Women: An Ethnohistorical Note." In *Towards an Anthropology of Women*, ed. Payna Peiter. New York: Monthly Review Press.

Buffalohead, Priscilla K. 1983. "Farmers, Warrior, Traders: A Fresh Look at Ojibway Women." *Minnesota History*, vol. 48, no. 6: 236-44.

Canada. *Statutes of the Province of Canada*. 1850, chap. 41; 1857, chap. 29.

———. House of Commons. 27 April 1869.

———. *Statutes of Canada*. 1868, 31 Victoria, chap. 42; 1869, 32-33 Victoria, chap. 6; 1876, 39 Victoria, chap. 18; 1884, 47 Victoria, chap. 27; 1951, 15 Victoria, chap. 29.

———. 1981. *Indian Acts and Amendments, 1968-1950*. Ottawa: Department of Indian Affairs and Northern Development, Treaties and Historical Research Centre.

———. 1981. *Contemporary Indian Legislation: 1951-1978*. Ottawa: Indian Affairs and Northern Development.

———. 1996. Royal Commission on Aboriginal Peoples, *Final Report: Restructuring the Relationship*. Vols. 1 & 2. Ottawa: Minister of Supply and Services, Canada.

Carter, Sarah. 1984. "The Missionaries' Indian: The Publications of John McDougall, John McLean and Egerton Ryerson Young." *Prairie Forum*, vol. 9, no. l: 27-44.

———. 1996a. "First Nations Women of Prairie Canada in the Early Reserves, the 1870s to the l920s: A Preliminary Inquiry." In *Women of the First Nations: Power, Wisdom, and Strength*, eds. Christine Miller and Patricia Chuchryck. Winnipeg: University of Manitoba Press.

———. 1996b. "Categories and Terrains of Exclusion: Constructing the 'Indian Woman' in the Early Settlement Era in Western Canada." In *Out of the Background: Readings on Canadian Native History*, eds. Ken S. Coates and Robin Fisher. Toronto: Copp Clark Ltd.

———. 1997. *Capturing Women: The Manipulation of Cultural Imagery in Canada's Prairie West*. Montreal: McGill-Queens University Press.

Cole, Douglas, and Ira Chaikin. 1990. *An Iron Hand upon the People: The Law Against the Potlatch on the Northwest Coast*. Toronto: University of Toronto Press.

Cominos, Peter T. 1963. "Late-Victorian Sexual Respectability and the Social System." *International Review of Social History*, vol. 8: 18-48.

Devens, Carol. 1992. *Countering Colonization: Native American Women and Great Lakes Missions, 1630-1900*. Berkeley: University of California Press.

Dick, Noel. 1985. "Representation and the 'Fourth World': A Concluding Statement." In *Indigenous Peoples and the Nation-State: Fourth World Politics in Canada and Norway*. St. John's: Memorial University of Newfoundland.

Dickason, Olive Patricia. 1985. "From 'One Nation' in the Northeast to 'New Nation' in the Northwest: A Look at the Emergence of the Metis." In *The New Peoples: Being and Becoming Metis in North America*, eds. Jacqueline Peterson and Jennifer S. H. Brown. Winnipeg: University of Manitoba Press.

———. 1992. *Canada's First Nations: A History of Founding Peoples from Earliest Times*. Norman: University of Oklahoma Press.

Etienne, Mona, and Eleanor Leacock, eds. 1980. *Women and Colonization: Anthropological Perspectives*. New York: Praeger Publishers.

Fee, Elizabeth. 1973. "The Sexual Politics of Victorian Social Anthropology." *Feminist Studies* (Winter-Spring): 23-39.

Fenton, William N. 1988. "The Iroquois in History." In *North American Indians in Historical Perspective*, eds. Eleanor Burke Leacock and Nancy Oestreich Lurie. Prospect Heights: Waveland Press, Inc.

Fisher, Robin. 1983. *Contact and Conflict: Indian-European Relations in British Columbia, 1774-1890*. Vancouver: University of British Columbia Press.

Fiske, Jo-Anne. 1987. "Fishing is Women's Business: Changing Economic Roles of Carrier Women and Men." In *Native Peoples, Native Lands: Canadian Indians, Inuit and Metis*, ed. Bruce Alden Cox. Ottawa: Carleton University Press.

Frideres, James A. 1998. *Aboriginal Peoples in Canada: Contemporary Conflicts*. 5th ed. Scarborough: Prentice Hall, Allyn and Bacon Canada.

Grant, John Webster. 1984. *Moon of the Wintertime: Missionaries and the Indians of Canada in Encounter Since 1534*. Toronto: University of Toronto Press.

Green, Joyce. 1985. "Sexual Equality and the Indian Government: An Analysis of Bill C-31 Amendments to the Indian Act." *Native Studies Review*, vol. 1, no. 2: 81-95.

Green, Rayna. 1990. "The Pocahontas Perplex: The Image of Indian Women in American Culture." In *Unequal Sisters: A Multicultural Reader in U.S. Women's History*, eds. Ellen Carol Dubois and V. L. Ruiz. New York: Routledge.

Grumet, Robert Steven. 1980. "Sunksquaws, Shamans, and Tradeswomen: Middle Atlantic Algonkian Women During the 17th and 18th Centuries." In *Women and Colonization*, eds. Mona Etienne and Eleanor Leacock. New York: Praeger Publishers.

Howley, James P., ed. 1915. *The Beothucks of Red Indians* Cambridge. Reprinted, Coles Canadiana Collection. Toronto.

Jaimes, M. Annette, with Theresa Halsey. 1992. "American Indian Women at the Center of Indigenous Resistance in Contemporary North America." In *The State of Native America: Genocide, Colonization, and Resistance*, ed. Annette M. Jaimes. Boston: South End Press.

Jamieson, Kathleen. 1978. *Indian Women and the Law in Canada: Citizens Minus*. Ottawa: Minister of Supply and Services, Canada.

———. 1986. "Sex Discrimination and the Indian Act." In *Arduous Journey: Canadian Indians and Decolonization*, ed. J. Rick Ponting. Toronto: McClelland and Stewart.

Jaenen, Cornelius. 1991. "French Sovereignty and Native Nationhood During the French Regime." In *Sweet Promises: A Reader on Indian-White Relations in Canada*, ed. J. R. Miller. Toronto: University of Toronto Press.

Jones, Peter. 1970. *History of the Ojebway Indians: With Especial Reference to Their Conversion to Christianity*. 1861. Reprint, Freeport: Books for Libraries.

Klein, Laura F. 1976. "'She's One of Us, You Know': The Public Life of Tlingit Women: Traditional, Historical, and Contemporary Perspectives." *The Western Canadian Journal of Anthropology*, vol. 6, no. 3: 164-83.

LaFramboise, Teresa, Anneliese M. Heyle, and Emily J. Ozer. 1990. "Changing and Diverse Roles of Women in American Indian Cultures." *Sex Roles*, vol. 22, nos. 7-8: 455-76.

Leacock, Eleanor. 1980, "Montagnais Women and the Jesuit Program for Colonization." In *Women and Colonization: Anthropological Perspectives*, eds. Mona Etienne and Eleanor Leacock. New York: Praeger.

------, ed. 1981. *Myths of Male Dominance: Collected Articles on Women Cross-Culturally*. New York: Monthly Review Press.

Littlefield, Lorraine. 1987. "Women Traders in the Maritime Fur Trade." In *Native People, Native Land*, ed. Bruce Alden Cox. Ottawa: Carleton University Press.

Lurie, Nancy O. 1972. "Indian Women: A Legacy of Freedom." In *Look to the Mountaintop*, ed. B. L. Fontana. San Jose: Gousha Publishers.

Lyon, Noel. 1985. "Constitutional Issues in Native Law." In *Aboriginal Peoples and the Law: Indian, Metis, and Inuit Rights in Canada*, ed. Brad W. Morse. Ottawa: Carleton University Press.

McDougall, John. 1895. *Pathfinding on Plain and Prairie: Stirring Scenes of Life in the Canadian Northwest*. Toronto: William Briggs.

McLean, John. 1889. *The Indians of Canada: Their Manners and Customs*. Toronto: William Briggs.

Medicine, Beatrice. 1993. "North American Indigenous Women and Cultural Domination." American
    Indian Culture and Research Journal, vol. 17, no. 3: 121-30.
Milloy, John. 1991. "The Early Indian Acts: Developmental Strategy and Constitutional Change." In
    Sweet Promises: A Reader on Indian-White Relations in Canada, ed. J. R. Miller. Toronto:
    University of Toronto Press.
Montour, Martha. 1987. "Iroquois Women's Rights with Respect to Matrimonial Property on Indian
    Reserves." Canadian Native Law Reporter, vol. 4: 1-10.
Morris, Alexander. 1971. The Treaties of Canada with the Indians of Manitoba and the North-West
    Territories. 1880. Reprint, Toronto: Coles Publishing Co.
National Archives of Canada. Record Group 10, Indian Affairs, Vols. 9350-9364, 1875-1895 Treaty
    Annuity Paysheets, Norway House/Fisher River.
Nock, David C. 1988. A Victorian Missionary and Canadian Indian Policy: Cultural Synthesis vs.
    Cultural Replacement. Waterloo: Wilfred Laurier Press.
Peterson, Jacqueline. 1978. "Prelude to Red River: A Social Portrait of the Great Lakes Metis."
    Ethnohistory, vol. 25, no. 1.
Peterson, Jacqueline, and Jennifer S. H. Brown, eds. 1985. The New Peoples: Being and Becoming
    Metis in North America. Winnipeg: University of Manitoba Press.
Petrone, Penny, ed. 1983. First People, First Voices. Toronto: University of Toronto Press.
Pettipas, Katherine. 1994. Severing the Ties that Bind: Government Repression of Indigenous
    Religious Ceremonies on the Prairies. Winnipeg: University of Manitoba Press.
Ray, Arthur. 1974. Indians and the Fur Trade. Toronto: University of Toronto Press.
———. 1996. "I Have Lived Here Since the World Began": An Illustrated History of Canada's
    Native People. Toronto: Lester Publishing.
Riley, Glenda. 1986. Inventing the American Woman: A Perspective on Women's History. Arlinton
    Heights: Harlan Davidson, Inc.
Rothenberg, Diane. 1980. "The Mothers of the Nation: Seneca Resistance to Quaker Intervention." In
    Women and Colonization: Anthropological Perspectives, eds. Mona Etienne and Eleanor
    Leacock. New York: Praeger.
Saunders, Douglas E. 1974. "Indian Act — Status of Women on Marriage to Persons without Indian
    Status." Saskatchewan Law Review, vol. 38: 243-9.
———. 1975. "Indian Women: A Brief History of Their Roles and Rights." McGill Law Journal, vol.
    21: 656-72.
———. 1984. "Indian Status: A Women's Issue or an Indian Issue?" Canadian Native Law Review,
    vol. 3: 30-9.
Scott, James C. 1990. Domination and the Arts of Resistance: Hidden Transcripts. New Haven: Yale
    University Press.
Shoemaker, Nancy. 1995. "Introduction." In Negotiators of Change: Historical Perspectives on
    Native American Women, ed. Nancy Shoemaker. New York: Routledge.
Smandych, Russell, and Gloria Lee. 1995. "Women, Colonization and Resistance: Elements of an
    Amerindian Autohistorical Approach to the Study of Law and Colonialism." Native Studies
    Review, vol. 10, no. 1: 21-46.
Smith, Sherry L. 1987. "Beyond the Princess and Squaw: Army Officers' Perceptions of Indian
    Women." In The Women's West, eds. Susan Armitage and Elizabeth Jameson. Norman: University
    of Oklahoma Press.
Smits, David D. 1982. "The 'Squaw Drudge': A Prime Index of Savagism," Ethnohistory, vol. 29, no.
    4: 281-306.
Stevenson, Winona L. 1988. "The Church Missionary Society Red River Mission and the Emergence of
    a Native Ministry, 1820-1860, with a Case Study of Charles Pratt of Touchwood Hills." Master's
    Thesis: University of British Columbia.
———. 1995. "Post-Colonial Reflections on the Past and Future Paths of Canadian Aboriginal Women
    (Or, Out from Under the Skirts of Her Majesty)." The London Journal of Canadian Studies, vol.
    11: 1-27.
———. 1997. "'Ethnic' Assimilates 'Indigenous': A Study in Intellectual Neocolonialism." Wicazo Sa
    Review, vol. 13, no. 1: 33-53.
Taylor, John L. 1983. Canadian Indian Policy During the Inter-War Years, 1918-1939. Ottawa:
    Department of Indian Affairs and Northern Development.
Tobias, John. 1991. "Protection, Civilization, Assimilation: An Outline History of Canada's Indian
    Policy." In Sweet Promises: A Reader on Indian-White Relations in Canada, ed. J. R. Miller.
    Toronto: University of Toronto Press.
Upton, L. F. S. 1991. "The Extermination of the Beothucks of Newfoundland." In Sweet Promises: A
    Reader on Indian-White Relations in Canada, ed. J. R. Miller. Toronto: University of Toronto
    Press.
Van Kirk, Sylvia. 1980. "Many Tender Ties": Women in Fur Trade Society, 1670-1870. Winnipeg:
    Watson & Dwyer.

————. 1987a. "The Role of Native Women in the Creation of Fur Trade Society in Western Canada, 1670-1830." In *The Women's West*, eds. Susan Armitage and Elizabeth Jameson. Norman: University of Oklahoma Press.

————. 1987b. "Toward a Feminist Perspective in Native History." In *Papers of the Eighteenth Algonquian Conference*, ed. William Cowen. Ottawa: Carleton University Press.

————. 1996. ""Women in Between': Indian Women in Fur Trade Society in Western Canada." Reprint. In *Out of the Background: Readings on Canadian History*, eds. Robin Fisher and Kenneth Coates. Toronto: Copp Clark Pitman Ltd.

Weist, Katherine M. 1983. "Beast of Burden and Menial Slaves: Nineteenth Century Observations of Northern Plains Indian Women." In *The Hidden Half: Studies of Plains Indian Women*, eds. Patricia Albers and Beatrice Medicine. Lanham: University Press of America.

West, John. 1823. *The Substance of a Journal During a Residence at the Red Colony, British North American in the Years 1820-1823*. Reprinted ed. Vancouver: 1967, Alcuin Society.

Young, Egerton R. 1893. *By Canoe and Dog Team Among the Cree and Saulteaux Indians*. London: Charles H. Kelly.

Young, Mary E. 1980. "Women, Civilization, and the Indian Question." In *Clio was a Woman: Studies in the History of American Women*, eds. Mabel E. Deutrich and Virginia C. Purdy. Washington: Howard University Press.

PART II

THE POST-COLONIAL ECONOMY AND THE CONSOLIDATION OF RACIALIZED LABOUR MARKETS

CHAPTER THREE

Black Women and Work

*The Impact of Racially Constructed Gender Roles on the Sexual Division of Labour**

DIONNE BRAND

PART ONE

Feminist chroniclers of the "woman question" use the term "woman" generically to define all women by what happens to some. The feminist chronicler who uses the term "women" generically attempts to expose the importantly generalizable conditions of women but the effect, often, indeed almost always, excludes the specific conditions of a particular and large part of the population of women — the reality of Black, working-class women and the complexity of working-class women's struggles in general. The articulation of the themes of women's liberation has applied directly only to the conditions of white, middle-class women.

To take just one chronicler, Olive Banks in *Faces of Feminism* is an example of such white, middle-class feminism. "Certainly," she says, "working-class women have their own sources of discontent and by and large these have appeared to be less a result of their sex than of their class." And even though she admits that, to some extent, white, middle-class feminists' views of the needs of working-class women were coloured by their own class position, she goes to great pains to assure us that "much more than for working-class women, it was clear (to white middle-class women) that their discontent was linked to their position as women, rather than to their class" (Banks 1981, 12). This, I assume, she meant in reference to *white*, working-class women. Consider the grave implications which her reasoning must have for Black women.

This lack of analysis has privatized the "woman question" to white, middle-class women and appropriates the sex oppression of women as a white, middle-class phenomenon. For example, Banks says that working-class women suffer more from their class condition than from their sex, but does not express the same

---

*   This essay is reprinted with permission from Dionne Brand and *Fireweed*. Part One appeared in *Fireweed*, Issue 25 (Fall 1987): 28-37. Part Two appeared in *Fireweed*, Issue 26 (Winter/Spring 1988): 87-92. At the time of the *Fireweed* printing, this essay was an excerpt from an M.A. thesis in progress. Due to the lack of literature on the history of women of colour and work, this essay, though more than a decade old, remains vital to understanding the historical construction of racialized labour markets, and the impact on women of colour. Thank you to Pat Murphy.

reservation about middle-class women's experiences, as if their middle-classness is "natural" to their sex. There is always debate about whether working-class women are affected more by class or by sex and which might take precedence at which instance. An even stronger debate goes on, albeit underground, about whether Black women are affected more by their blackness or by their sex and which comes first. This question, posed as though life, experience, and under-standing are linear and therefore race and class must necessarily jockey for posi-tion, is a non-question. But it is not without its use. By posing the question in this way, working-class women, Black and white, are relieved of their challenge to oppression of any sort. White, middle-class definitions of oppression blank out the specificity of the challenge that Black or white working-class women might pose. White, middle-class gendered oppression becomes the "oppression of *women.*" Despite this, however, Black working-class women's lives are still lim-ited to toil both outside and inside the home, are marked by poverty, and require analysis, and struggle.

A feminist theory must root out the borrowed, unchallenged categories which have informed a mode of discourse used to repress the identity and claims of Black women. If not the knowledge of Black women, the world, as felt by them and stolen from them, is lost.

What is actually political knowledge about the devastating experience of an economic exploitation rooted in being a Black woman is often mistaken in Black women as: a) lack of concern for feminist issues, b) the assumption that Black women do not see their issues as separate from those of Black men, c) that there is a contradiction between Black nationalism and Black women's liberation. The latter is not only a problem for white feminists but also for Black male national-ists. The fact is that feminist themes, at least so far, and feminist practice have refused to be informed by Black women's lives. And feminist themes have lent themselves to capitalist, racist, and imperialist ideologies in so doing. To say that Black women are more concerned with issues of race than issues of sex is, in fact, to deny the social formations in this society, formations which have at their root the founding myths of American society (I mean all of the Americas, Canada most definitely). These formations reinforce and perpetuate the constituents of the work force; that is the gendered, racial, and racially gendered hierarchies necessary for the continued exploitation of labour. These hierarchies ascribe cer-tain kinds of work and certain conditions of living to certain kinds of people, and in the present case, to certain kinds of women:

> The colonists were the 'advanced civilisation.' Such societies proved their historical significance by the destruction or domination of 'savage' and 'backward' peoples....
>
> Founding myths were substituted for history, providing the appearance of historical narrative....Endlessly elaborated, these myths were produced by ideologies who identified with the dominant creed and depended upon those classes in the society which possessed power and the capacities to extend social privilege....

These myths were to be recognised in the official instruments of class hegemony: national creeds, social ideologies, philosophical tenets, constitutions and the like, their function was to legitimate the social orders which had come into being... (Robinson 1983, 267).

The myth of the Black inferiority coupled with the paradoxical myth of white femininity and feminine weakness has served to obscure what Black women *think* about all of this.[1]

I want to look both historically and through argument at the conditions of Black women's lives, how these have been structured by capitalist relations of production from the time of the colonizers and the slave trade to the present. Further, an analysis of these relations informs a feminism relevant to Black women, one that has a basis in their lived experience and one that acknowledges that oppression is rooted in their sex as much as it is rooted in their race and class. Unlike most white women, Black women experience their race, class, and sex consciously and simultaneously. That is, Black women live their sex, race, and class as existentially inseparable and live them differently from Black men, white men, and white women. A feminism relevant to Black women would, therefore, hold much for radicalizing what is called "the movement" and the body of work emanating from it, since such a feminism would confront race, class, and sex as these converge in the dominant ideology. A feminism arising from a confrontation with the dominant ideology is necessarily class conscious since the conditions under which we live and have lived ever since coming to the "New World" have been wrought by capitalist relations of production, and since the true emancipation of Black women would have to consider capitalist exploitation as anathema to the very lives of Black women and their struggle to liberate themselves.

Madeline MacDonald, in her work on the reproduction of class and gender relations, posits that the category of gender is socially constructed and that class and gender relations, though at times separate, conjoin in the development of capitalism. She further poses patriarchal relations of male dominance over women as buttressing the structure of class domination and argues that this is evident in a variety of sites, such as the work place, the law, and the educational system. This can also be seen in the changes in the ideological forms of masculinity and femininity and in which elements of the two gain ascendancy in parallel to the needs of capital. For example, when capital demands a cheap and numerous labour force, the definition of femininity which gains ascendancy is that of the capable woman — good at detailed or boring work. When the demands for labour are not as high, however, the definition of femininity which gains ascendancy is that of the ultra-feminine, helpless female. MacDonald then sees a correlation between the needs of capitalist production and the concepts of masculinity and femininity. Added to that, she argues that class and gender relations conjoin as the definition of masculinity reinforces the categories of manager and experts in the social relations of capitalist production. More fundamentally, MacDonald states that the coincidence of the two structures — patriarchy (masculinity/femininity) and capitalism — facilitates the reproduction of the work-force and the sexual divisions of labour which delegates to women the prime responsibility for childcare and early education. This facilitates the private/public split between the "production of commodities for exchange and the production of use values such as food, garments, etc. for consumption in the family" (MacDonald 1981, 161).

The usefulness for capital of the private/public division lies in the source of hidden and unpaid labour which women represent, when this split is thus reified by the appeal to "natural" propensities, the claims of women are not seen as claims against the social relations of capitalist production but as claims against the "private" sphere, the individual situation. The claims of women are not mediated within the construct of social relations but rather "belong" in some other sphere. These claims are seen neither as "political" nor even "economic," as in the case of working-class men, but are "personal" or "domestic," or even worse, are the claims of those who are not full participants in social activity (MacDonald 1981, 160).

MacDonald's analysis is useful to a point. What she self-admittedly does not address is race as it is socially constructed. She does not see that the ideological forms of masculinity and femininity are race-specific and have been so since the slave trade, when Black women first began to be seen by white men and women as brood mares and infinitely suited to physically demanding field labour:

> Slave holders had little use for sentimental platitudes about the delicacy of the female constitution when it came to grading their hands according to physical strength and endurance. Judged on the basis of a standard set by a healthy adult man, most women were probably ranked as three-quarter hands; yet there were enough women like Susan Mabry of Virginia, who could pick 400 or 500 pounds of cotton a day (150 to 200 pounds was considered respectable for an average worker) to remove from a (slave holder's) mind all doubts about the ability of a strong healthy woman field worker (Jones 1985, 15).

This is where the ideological forms of femininity struck different paths on the road of history for Black women and white women. In the seminal experience of Black slavery, "white femininity" and "Black femininity" were defined. Black women, this ideology said, lacked the "natural" refinement of white women and could not only be used in the fields but their offspring could be sold away from them without thought to the "nature" of woman as mother. This, from the very practical standpoint of the ownership of Black women and their issue by white men, served well the purposes of labour, sexual exploitation, and propagation of the slave population. The social relations of production and the social relations of reproduction, therefore, did not merely conjoin but were crudely the same. Two details would distinguish "Black femininity," Black women would *always* be good for hard physical labour and the "benefits" of "natural refinement" would never accrue to them within the moral codes of the day.

Certainly the lives of slave women were marked by hard labour which belied

the rhetoric of the time that claimed feminine weakness. Of course this rhetoric
and its contradiction in the fact of Black women's lives still operates. From the
sixteenth century to the late nineteenth century, Black women were captured in
Africa and enslaved in the Americas. Their enslavement, along with that of Black
men, was strictly for the purpose of extracting the fruits of their labour in the
cotton, cane, indigo, and tobacco fields, in gold and silver mines (and so on) for
the European colonizers of the so-called New World. Their sex brought them no
considerations; they were not seen to have physical limitations nor were they
looked upon as the "weaker sex" and thus protected them from the brutal conditions of manual labour:

> I had to do everythin' dey was to do on de outside. Work in de field, chop
> wood, hoe corn, till sometimes I feels my back surely break. I done
> everythin' 'cept split rails. I never did split no rails.
>
> I split rails like man. I used a iron wedge drove into the wood with a
> maul.
>
> I drive the gin, what was run by two mules (Sterling 1984, 13).

Nor were Black women who resisted excluded from the slaveowner's fatal whip
and other torture devices. While the first waged workers were being made in
Britain, Black women were being enslaved and shipped to the Americas. The
majority of Black women worked as field hands — planting, hoeing, weeding,
and harvesting the crops which would be the source of the European capital
fuelling the industrial revolution.

The advent of emancipation did not alter that relationship perceptibly:

> Only an infinitesimal number of Black women had managed to escape
> from the fields, from the kitchen or from the washroom. According to
> the 1980 census, there were 2.7 million Black girls and women over the
> age of ten. More than a million of them worked for wages; 38.7 percent
> in agriculture; 30.8 percent in household domestic service; 15.6 percent
> in laundry work; and a negligible 2.8 percent in manufacturing. The few
> who found jobs in industry usually performed the dirtiest and lowest-
> paid work. And they had not really made a significant breakthrough, for
> their slave mothers had also worked in the Southern cotton mills, in the
> sugar refineries and even in the mines (Davis 1981, 87).

Slavery as an economic system became cumbersome and expensive, even with the
use of women as breeders in replenishing the supply of free (enslaved) labour.
The discovery of beet sugar in Europe increased the cost of producing sugar in the
Caribbean.

> The planters found it harder and harder to compete for sales, not
> only in England, the planters' home country, but also to other countries
> after the sugar was refined in England. In time what was important
> to the planters began to be of less and less interest in the halls of

Westminster and the laws favouring the goods from the colonies began to stir up resentment. By the time the English Parliament moved to do away with slavery in 1833-1834, the decline of the colonies had become very sharp indeed (K.B. Smith and F.C. Smith 1986, 18-19).

Similarly in the U.S. the industrial development of the North, fed by the slave labour of the South, now challenged the South for capitalist leadership in the U.S. civil war.

Women in the post-emancipation period would still work as breeders and labourers and began to work in agriculture as sharecroppers and farmworkers, in what Angela Davis calls "an indefinite state of peonage." Those who could leave sharecropping or plantation life moved to town to work as washerwomen, cooks, hucksters, market venders, maids, and general domestic workers. Some left the Caribbean for Latin America, and the U.S. Similar experiences would reach over the Black diaspora from Truro, Nova Scotia to Chatham, Ontario to Atlanta, Georgia to Morant Bay, Jamaica to Bahia, Brazil.

The resistance of Black women has rarely been documented as the struggle for women's rights. It is hardly likely that Black women did not see themselves as exploited because of their sex. They were, after all, used for breeding by slaveholders and landowners, and worked at forced labour in the houses and kitchens and cane and cotton fields of the Americas beginning with slavery. History has witnessed their incredible leadership and militancy in the fight for their rights in individual as well as collective ways:

> [My mother] worked so long and so often that once she went to sleep at the loom. Her master's boy saw her and told his mother. His mother told him to take a whip and wear her out. He took a stick and went out to beat her awake. When she woke up, she took a pole out of the loom and beat him nearly to death. She said, "I'm going to kill you. These black titties sucked you and then you come out here to beat me." And when she left him he wasn't able to walk. And that was the last I seen of her until freedom. She went out and got an old cow that she used to milk — Dolly, she called it. She rode away from the plantation (Sterling 1984, 59-60).

> During the busy harvest season in the fall of 1862, for instance, female field hands on a Louisiana sugar plantation in Union occupied territory engaged in a slowdown and then refused to work at all until the white landowner met their demand for wages. The men on the plantation also struck within a week. The planter fearful that his entire crop would be lost...agreed to pay them. And in 1866, the 'coloured' washerwomen of Jackson, Mississippi, organised themselves and established a price code for their services. Though the strike in June of that year was unsuccessful...it marked the "first known collective action of free Black working women in American history, as well as the first labour organisation of Black workers in Mississippi" (Jones 1986, 58).

Similarly, domestic workers in 1881 in the United States joined union locals of the Knights of Labour:

> Dora Jones found and led the New York Domestic Workers Union during the 1930's. By 1939 — five years after the union was founded — only 350 out of 1,000,000 domestics in the state had been recruited. Given the enormous difficulties in organising domestics, however, this was hardly a small accomplishment (Davis 1981, 95-6).

The reason resistance to the racial and sexual division of labour was not and is not seen within the context of the struggle for women's rights has more to do with the observers than with the phenomenon. The dualities of capital and labour, male and female, Black and white constitute not only social dichotomies but also hierarchies upon which both material and symbolic power are based.

White, middle-class women, on the other hand, were not and are not unaware of themselves as a class. Their struggle has had to do with taking their place next to middle-class, white men. The denial of the right to work outside of the home was not rooted in their sex but rather in their class. The fact is, certain kinds of women worked outside the home and certain kinds did not. And the kinds of work that they did "befitted" their class and race.

Black women enslaved and shipped to the Americas are the foremothers of the Black women who today live and work in Canada, whether the latter arrived here fleeing slavery in the U.S. or are descendants of slavery in Canada or whether they arrived fleeing the crisis of dependent capitalism in the Caribbean.

In Canada, the majority of Black women wage earners were excluded from the white women's traditional occupations of clerical, secretarial, and sales work until the late sixties and seventies. In Nova Scotia, with its large indigenous Black population it is still rare to find Black women in these jobs. Perhaps eight out of ten Black people in Canada have in their family women who have made or make their living "In Service." Being "In Service," engaged in domestic work, categorized and characterized the nature and type of Black women's work then and now, despite their later entry into white women's traditional occupations. Within and complimenting "In Service" is the back-breaking physical labour which Black women workers are expected to endure as labourers in factories, food services, and other personal services like nursing assistants and attendants, hotel cleaners and maids, etc. The category is distinguishable from the images of the less arduous work of white women. I say "images" here because certainly white, working-class women endure the same type of exploitation of their labour, but the dominant *image* of white women's work and the racist construction of work itself operates on the one hand to "pass" white, working-class women into other types of work as, on the other hand, it constructs what we can call "Black women's work."

"Black women's work" used to look like this: fourteen hours a day plowing fields; dropping seed; hoeing, ditching, picking cotton; planting sugar-cane cuttings; ginning and moting cotton; cutting cane; cutting and digging coconut; planting, digging, drying arrowroot; picking, sorting nutmeg; tending livestock; planting peas, corn; milling flour; threshing rice; cutting and hauling logs; splitting rails; spinning thread; cooking in the big house; tending children in the big house, and producing — babies, at which point they were considered a half hand in the fields. We still do some of this work if we live in agriculturally based economies, either as subsistence farmers or for new and old plantation owners.

Migration to the cities, towns, and the metropole saw Black women occupy jobs which mirrored the jobs which we had once occupied, if not insofar as the payment of wages were concerned, at least insofar as the station or social class which those jobs obtained and the low level of the wages. Another layer was added to the old myth of inferiority and subservience in order to continue the economic exploitation of Black women — "Black women's work."

"Black women's work" today looks like this: cleaning white people's houses, bathrooms, and hotel rooms; serving white people breakfast, lunch, and dinner in private homes, in office cafeterias, hospitals; lifting, feeding, minding, sweeping, boxing, scouring, washing, cooking.

Though some of their work in and of itself looks like work that white women do, when Black women do domestic work or are "In Service," the status of the job is clearly in the arena of "work" and further categorized as low-value work. The class position of these jobs is revealed by and is apparent in the supervisory status which whites, women or men, hold over these positions as opposed to the value and status of the job when white women do this type of work for their children or husbands or relatives. These jobs gain "moral value" as being nurturing and caring when done by white women in their own households. But when done by Black women for wages the same tasks are not valued in the society on any level. Indeed as paid work, and badly paid at that, these jobs are assigned to those who are thought not capable or worthy of other work.

The nature of the work is that it takes place in individual homes where conditions are not uniform or public, nor are the details of the tasks, nor the technology used in accomplishing them. The nature of the boss is such that s/he is an unregistered sole proprietor who generally has a sole employee and is rarely subject to restrictions of minimum wage, set hours, overtime payments or other regulations which apply to other business. Added too, this type of "business" is not referred to or considered to be a "business" since what is produced does not appear in the gross national product. Work actions, strikes, etc., are a rarity as domestic work is conducted and contracted super-privately.

Then too, the nature of the work is that it has so far "defied" standards, time and motion studies or a value placed on it, restricting workers to case-by-case negotiation and constant justification of a wage. These elements chart the "adhocary" of "Black women's work" (not only in the case of domestic work but in general), the ideological terms under which we live, the ideological codes which operate to exploit our labour.

A related area of "Black women's work" is institutionalized domestic work. I hope to deal with that area in the next issue. It is not by chance that more than half of nursing attendant jobs are filled by Black and Asian women. (Perhaps for the first time in Canadian labour history, a labour union, CUPE (Canadian Union of Public Employees) Local 79, has analyzed the issue of sexual division of labour as racially structured in institutionalized domestic work and has waged a struggle against the employer, the Metropolitan Municipality of Toronto, on that basis.) Also, I intend in the next issue to return to the theme of the ideological forms of masculinity and femininity which do more than prepare men for roles as supervisors and managers. The racial specificity of masculinity and femininity prepares both white men and women for roles as superiors, employers, and supervisors. And, these forms create racially constructed gender roles. Also I will look more closely at the adhocary of "Black women's work" as a key to the ideological terms under which we live.

PART TWO

In Part One, I discussed the impact of racially constructed gender roles on the sexual division of labour, indicating generally the extent to which "Black women's work" is historically rooted in slavery in the Americas. As a consequence, it is hidden, devalued, and marked by gender. In this article, I want to focus more closely on the "domestic" aspect of Black women's work, and discuss the racial construction of gender roles within this particular framework.

Because of the nature of "Black women's work," on one hand, it is seen as productive work, but, on the other hand, it is positioned in what we can call the reproduction of labour power in the society. Because of this, it has an ad hoc quality. That is, no one in the society acknowledges that it is socially important work, yet it is acknowledged at some level as work that has to be done; as a group "Black women" are appointed to do it. So although it is necessary labour, it is seen as degraded labour. Hence the terms of the relationship between worker and employer are always fluid, the disadvantage of the flexibility falling to the worker. Further, the degradation of the labour, coupled with its role within the reproduction of labour power in the society, makes the actual work and its means opaque, leaving Black women in the position of plugging the holes of the services with their own unpaid energies and labour.

Institutionalised domestic work on a large scale is performed in nursing homes, hospitals, homes for the aged, and so on (privately as well as publicly run) where nursing attendants and aides carry out the tasks of caring. These involve lifting, feeding, washing, dressing, clothing, and caring for largely older people who generally are white. Where, in the case of domestic work in individual homes, tasks such as lifting people might be minimal, and feeding, washing, and caring be "limited" to four or five people, nursing aides and attendants (NAs) have case loads of anywhere from ten to thirty human beings to be fed, washed, lifted, carried, dressed (clothing as well as bed sores) and generally tended and watched. Attendants also double as cooks and dishwashers in preparing breakfasts and snacks, and, in the more grossly understaffed, privately run institutions called "homes," they may have to prepare all meals. The inadequate ratio of caregiver to recipient means that work is intensive, labourious, hazardous (most NAs have chronic back problems, as do housekeepers), and stressful. The quality of the physical plant and "primary" staff (registered nurses and doctors) are largely dictated by the profit margins of these privately and publicly owned establishments.

Who Cares? CUPE Local 79 Campaign

As I mentioned in my first article, it is not by chance that more than half of nursing attendant jobs are filled by Black and Asian women. In the CUPE Local 79 struggle in the Municipal Homes for the Aged run by Metro Toronto, Black women make up some 50 percent of full-time nursing attendants and Black and immigrant women make up 79 percent of part-time nursing attendants. What was at issue in the CUPE Local 79 struggle was the plan by the Metro body to convert new full-time jobs into part-time hours, further narrowing an important area of work for Black women. The true effect of converting new full-time jobs into part-time *hours* is that a steady income and the security of full-time work will not be a possibility for Black women who historically occupy this job area. This way a woman can conceivably work many more hours trying to make do. The women in this case had a union to support their struggle, unlike many of the women in privately run homes. In these, the conditions of work are far more oppressive and attempts at unionizing dangerous to women's livelihood. The campaign by CUPE Local 79 to stop the conversion of full-time jobs to part-time hours rallied support from community and women's groups and temporarily put the brakes on Metro. So vociferous was the outcry and so organized the campaign that CUPE 79 was able to retain thirty of the possible seventy-one new full-time jobs threatened.

Part of the Family

It is a well-known joke among Black women in domestic work and institutionalized domestic work and other areas of Black women's work that employers, when trying to exact more work from them or when Black women reject disrespectful treatment or assert themselves, make an appeal to family. "But we treat her like part of the family" or "You know that you're part of the family" or "We are a family here" are some of the statements made. The derision with which Black women view these statements is a recognition of the attempts to "work them to the bone" while extracting that "free" (read unpaid) labour which stands for kinship, blood relations, and familial duty. Black women often remind employers that they have their own families where enough "free" labour is given up. The appeals to family which they encounter in situations of waged work reveal these expectations as well as they reveal the flexibility and durability of the ideological construct of "family" under capitalism. Through this one ideological construct a whole range of disparate relationships can be legitimated. So it cannot escape us that Black women reproduce white labour power in white households (extended to nursing homes where the aged or infirm are kept) as well as reproducing Black labour power in Black households where they are also often the only income earner.

To return to the theme of the ideological forms of masculinity and femininity, these forms do more than prepare men for roles as supervisors and managers. The racial specificity of masculinity and femininity prepares both white men and white women for their roles as superiors, thus as employers and supervisors because these forms are racially constructed. They also prepare Black men for roles of relative dominance as they prepare Black women for roles of subordination.

In Black women's experience, race and gender conjoin in the development of capitalism. White supremacy (racism) buttresses the structure of class domination as racist ideology demarcates Black subordination. Racial inferiority is ascribed to Blacks in general, positioning them within the mode of production under capitalism. According to the white supremacist ideology, whites are supposedly more intelligent, more human, more evolved, more advanced and more competent. Blacks are supposedly less intelligent (stupid, dumb), sub-human, backward, primitive, and incompetent. These attributes are supposed to be innate. It follows, then, that white dominance and Black subordination are "natural" underpinnings and outcomes in organizing the society; the structure of class and class relations mimics this "natural" selection. Because these are supposedly "natural" propensities, the possibilities for their use are logical and endless. White superiority reinforces categories within capitalist social relations of owners and managers. The fact that whites could own Blacks at one time in the Americas places these categories more concretely within capitalist social relations and reinforces certain categories of work labourers, underlings, and menials.

On both the continents and the islands of the Americas gradations of colour have historically denoted hierarchies of class and superiority. An intricate lattice-work of colour and shading stratified social position/class/power as synonymous with whiteness. So imbedded is this ideology that a well-known children's rhyme goes: "If you're white you're right/if you're brown stick around/if you're black get back!" This racial ideology creates a sub-group whose expectations are low, who do not rival the dominant group (whites) and who cannot claim equal treatment but who are a source of plentiful and ill-paid labour.

Thus, where Black women work as registered nurses, as many do, they are often assigned the heavy wards, i.e., the chronic care wards or wards requiring a lot of lifting and tending. As one hospital worker said, "The light wards are white; the heavy wards are black."

Both the resistance against white supremacy, imperialism, and class oppression, and the ability of capitalism to crush and co-opt movements which threaten it, have worked to make these racial ideological codes, though not always strictly enforced (there is a Black bourgeoisie and petty bourgeoisie), certainly never outdated and an important underpinning to the existence of capitalism.

For Black women, the structures are still more intricate. Having accepted

Madeline MacDonald's argument that gender relations buttress the structure of class domination, and, having examined racism or white supremacy which demarcates class domination, we may proceed to examine which ideological forms of masculinity and femininity operate in Black women's experience.

The construction of Black femininity has its foundation in Black women's relation to capitalist production and to reproduction. A particular category of femininity which is both neuter and oversexed, both strong and incompetent, prepares Black women for work as domestic workers/mammies/babysitters/caregivers/service givers/prostitutes, as well as for work as labourers. They are viewed as being at the lowest level of the productive forces. The paradoxes within the category operate to lower the esteem of those whom the category encompasses; they are seen as not good enough to encourage the "respect" afforded those in the category of "real" women (I don't mean the group Real Women). "Real" women wouldn't have to work or be made to work, and "real" women, if they did, would occupy the pink collar jobs which white women supposedly occupy. "Real" women would be considered first and foremost mothers, not workers.

Race and gender oppression conjoin and reinforce each other's validity or logic in Black women's experience. As part of a sub-group which is also sub-human, they are further divided into superior and subordinate through gender. White male dominance has its opposite in Black female subordination.

The correlation between the needs of capitalist production and this ideological form of Black femininity is that Black women remain at all times a source of ready, constant, ill-paid, and degraded labour. The forms of femininity which white women navigate as capitalist needs fluctuate, as MacDonald addresses them, are different from the forms which Black women navigate. White women are either capable or weak or dependent. Black women are either strong or lazy. Contradictions do not daunt the underlying bases — exploitation and oppression — of these forms.

So imprinted was the ideograph of Black femininity as different from white femininity that after their exodus from the fields after emancipation:

> Employers made little effort to hide their contempt for freed women who "played the lady" and refused to join workers in field. To apply the term ladylike to a Black woman was apparently the height of sarcasm; by socially prescribed definition, Black women could never become "ladies", though they might display pretensions in that direction. The term itself had predictable race and class connotations. White ladies remained cloistered at home, fulfilling their marriage vows of motherhood and genteel domesticity. But Black housewives appeared "most lazy"; they stayed "out in the fields, doing nothing" demanding that their husbands "support them in idleness" (Jones 1985, 59).

In a present-day example, the media as well as the state in Canada and the U.S. decry Black mothers on mothers' allowance as being lazy while they suggest that (white) women do not need daycare, that they should stay home with their children and preserve family life. Despite a similar reality in white, working-class women's lives, racism repeatedly obscures class alliances. Canadian immigration policy, which demanded that domestic workers coming from the Caribbean on work permits have no encumbrances (children) or appendages, indicates the ideological form of Black femininity accepted and recognized by the Canadian state (Silvera 1983).

Again, if there is any fluctuation in this form it is from strong to lazy and, I might add, from gendered to without gender. By the latter I mean that the jobs that Black women traditionally occupy fit into the group of jobs which "women" occupy, yet they are not the ones suitable to "ladies," which also means white women. (My own grandmother, who was born at the turn of the century, often rebuked and punished us children for calling a woman "woman," saying that it was rude and disrespectful of us to do so, that we should say "lady" as that was more respectful. "Woman" for her meant someone unprotected and disrespected.) Skilled work is denied Black women but not work itself and work of a certain kind; work which mirrors Black femininity or vice versa. So the ideological forms of Black femininity *prescribe* Black women's place in the labour force, *denote* a category called "Black women's work" and *proscribe* considerations of "feminine weakness."

I have laid out for the most part in this essay only the construction of Black women's work and the ideological forms which reinforce this category. I have not concentrated in this section on resistance to these forms and constructs. Were we to investigate further we would find that these resistance are responsible for the shifts and changes that manifest themselves as Black, working-class women struggle against oppression. And I have undertaken to look only at how the racial construction of gender roles affects one group of women — Black women, and Black women's work.

But more than an exercise in deconstructing Black women's work, lest we validate those forms of oppression by only pointing them out, it is necessary to say to what use we may put this exercise. For one thing, the examination of how gender roles are racially constructed can only deepen our analysis of how gender oppression actually *works* and how gender oppression is firmly tied to racial oppression and class oppression. For another, such an examination may take us beyond the crisis in feminism around race issues to a point where Black women and white women can meaningfully struggle together against sexual oppression. For it is the historical racial specificity of our oppression on which the current crisis hinges and which does not disappear behind platitudes of unity. Black women and white women must examine and expose the historical specificity of the ideological forms of Black femininity and white femininity in order to build the global movement. It is only within a rigorous examination of these forms that we may find the weapons to struggle.

NOTE

1.   Interestingly enough, I took a Women's Studies course at OISE (Ontario Institute for Studies in Education), where the word "primitive" was flung around quite openly, candidly, and ingenuously

in discussions about women in "primitive tribes" and matriarchy in primitive tribes. Someone was always searching for a primitive tribe or a woman in a primitive tribe for basing their argument on a primitive tribe. These primitive tribes were almost always in Africa and some apparently still existed, and some apparently were Native — Navaho or Sioux women. We were all women in the class. Only once did someone lower her voice, casting me a sidelong glance, as she uttered the word. Suspecting of course that I was probably one of "them." But generally, no one noticed the implications of what they were saying; what they had bought wholesale of white capitalist conquest and exploitation of the "New World."

For once, and with amazing difficulty, I held my tongue; I did not wade in for the fight. I pondered: would these women consider Elizabethan or Victorian women as women in "primitive" tribes? The historical period was just about the same.

Needless to say I rarely went to class.

REFERENCES

Banks, Olive. *Faces of Feminism*. New York: Martin Robinson, 1981.

Davis, Angela. *Women, Race and Class*. New York: Random House, 1981.

Jones, Jacqueline. *Labour of Love, Labour of Sorrow: Black Women, Work and Family, From Slavery to the Present*. New York: Vintage, 1985.

MacDonald, Madeline. "Schooling and Reproduction of Class and Gender Relations." In *Schooling, Ideology and Curriculum*, eds. L. Barton, R. Merghan, and S. Walker. London: Barcombe, Falmer Press, 1981.

Robinson, Cedric. *Black Marxism*. London: Zed Press, 1983.

Silvera, Makeda. *Silenced*. Toronto: Williams-Wallace International, 1983.

Smith, Keithlyn B., and Fernando C. Smith. *To Shoot Hard Labour*. Toronto: Edan's Publishers, 1986.

Sterling, Dorothy. *We Are Your Sisters*. New York: W.W. Norton, 1983.

CHAPTER FOUR

Do You Call Me "Sister"?

Women of Colour
*and the Canadian Labour Movement**

RONNIE JOY LEAH

THE LONG ROAD TO EQUALITY

Women of colour have travelled a long road in Canada over the past century, from the virulently racist rhetoric of the Vancouver Trades and Labour Council, calling for the exclusion of all Asian workers in the early 1900s, to union policies and programs in the 1990s which challenge practices of sexism and racism and promote an inclusive labour movement. The Canadian Auto Workers' 1988 video *Call Me Sister, Call Me Brother* and the Ontario Federation of Labour's 1995 Conference on Community Unionism exemplify some of the strategies currently being used by the labour movement to address its long-standing history of racism and sexism, and labour policies and practices which have excluded women and people of colour. Yet the journey to equality is far from over, especially for women of colour.

In the twentieth century, the relationship between women of colour and the Canadian labour movement has been a contradictory one, more often framed by racism and sexism than by solidarity and inclusion (Carniol 1990; Sugiman 1994). Efforts by women and people of colour to secure respect and equality in the workplace have been impeded by prevailing racist and patriarchal ideologies, exclusionary and discriminatory state policies, exploitation by employers in a labour market segmented by race and sex (Anderson 1991; Creese 1992; Sugiman 1994) and by the very policies and practices of the labour movement itself which is supposed to protect all workers.

Undeniably, many Canadian unions have reflected and promoted racialist and anti-immigrant perspectives by excluding Indigenous workers, Asian workers, Black workers, and other racial minority workers from union protection and membership (Anderson 1991; Calliste 1988; Creese 1992; Roy 1989; White 1993). For women of colour, their roles as workers and as trade unionists have been

---

* This chapter was researched and written in 1995, then revised and updated in March 1997 and February 1999. Contemporary union campaigns and strategies described in this chapter reflect, for the most part, union policies and practices current in 1995, with selected references to labour developments from 1996 to 1998.

constrained by the prototype of the "white male worker" (Sugiman 1994; White 1993) which has marginalized all women workers as secondary wage earners and constructed both women and immigrants as cheap labour threats to unionized white male labour.

It was not until after the Second World War that the labour movement began to systematically address the exclusion and inequality experienced by women and people of colour (Hill and Schiff 1986), although some progressive unions demonstrated instances of solidarity across gender and racial/ethnic barriers prior to that time (Avery 1979; Creese 1987; Frager 1986). Workers of colour, themselves, played a key role in mobilizing collectively against the exploitation and discrimination they experienced in the workplace, at times resorting to separate formations because of their exclusion from "white" unions (Calliste 1988; Creese 1987). In the past two decades, determined organizing efforts by women and people of colour within mainstream unions have challenged sexism and racism in the workplace and within unions themselves (Leah 1991, 1993). In response to rank-and-file pressure, as well as changing demographics of the labour force, unions and labour federations have begun to develop more inclusive strategies. Despite this progress, there is still a long way to go before women of colour gain real equality and respect in the labour movement (Leah 1991, 185).

The changing relationship between women of colour and the Canadian labour movement is difficult to explore given the lack of integrated studies on women, race and work (Brand 1991, 29; Sangster 1995, 7; White 1993, 3). Lack of attention to the interconnections of gender, race, and class can be traced to the patriarchal assumptions in studies of racial minority workers which exclude women's experiences, as well as one-dimensional feminist analysis which generalizes from white women's experiences and excludes women of colour (Brand 1991, 28; Leah 1991, 171).

Structural factors also account for the lack of integrated studies. Historically, gender and racial/ethnic divisions constituted two separate streams of workplace segregation (Sugiman 1994, 216). Because of racial discrimination and patriarchal assumptions about women's work, Black women, Asian women, and other women of colour were excluded from many industrial workplaces that employed white women and/or men of colour; this pattern continued until after the Second World War (Brand 1991, 15; Sugiman 1994, 217). Chinese and South Asian women, in particular, were prohibited by state policy from emigrating to Canada for many years (Adilman 1984; Das Gupta 1994). The evidence suggests that when Chinese and Japanese women did enter the paid labour force, their actual labour force participation rate was under-reported (Adilman 1984, 71; Kobayashi 1994, 59). To document the racist and exclusionary policies of the early Canadian labour movement, I have turned to the literature on racial minority male workers; when possible this material has been supplemented by the few accounts regarding women from racial/ethnic minorities.

While there are now many excellent, contemporary studies of women and unions, there have been few assessments to date of organizing efforts by racial minority women in the labour movement (Leah 1991; White 1993, 3). The tendency to address gender inequality and racial discrimination as two separate areas for education and action has marginalized the specific experiences and concerns of women of colour (Leah 1991, 169; Sugiman 1994, 217).

By studying how women of colour have organized over the past two decades, we gain important insights into organizing strategies which build a more effective labour movement: one which is based on inclusion, equity, sharing of power, democratic participation, and community linkages. This chapter describes and analyses strategies which have been effective for mobilizing women of colour, working within organizational structures, challenging racist and sexist policies, building links with allies, and educating for change. These are important lessons for women of colour, for unions, and for all social movements in Canada.

UNIONS: COLLECTIVE ACTION FOR WORKING PEOPLE

I always fight for the underdog...and that's...why I was in the union.

— *Grace Fowler, Black union activist born 1919*
Interviewed in Carty 1991, 191

For women of colour, as for other working people, unions have provided a means of organizing collectively for workers' rights and human dignity. Historically, unions have provided a means for working people to organize collectively against their economic exploitation (Carniol 1990). As a social movement which arose in response to injustices in the workplace, the labour movement represents the collective, organized strength of working people in the fight for better pay, benefits, and working conditions. Unions also provide a base for organizing around human rights and social justice issues both in the workplace and in the wider community.

Unions were illegal in Canada prior to 1872; however, even after the passage of the *Trade Unions Act of 1872*, unionization was resisted by employers and the state, often through violent measures. It was not until the 1940s, in a period of "unprecedented...working class mobilization and politicization" that the Canadian state "began to recognize the principle of freedom of association for workers...favouring union recognition and free collective bargaining" (Panitch and Swartz 1988, 18-19).

Unions have evolved over the past century, from the early craft unions which excluded all but the (white, male) skilled workers, to the (male) industrial unions of the early 1900s which organized workers in entire industries, to the more inclusive radical unions such as the International Workers of the World and the One Big Union which emphasized class solidarity in the struggle against capitalist exploitation (Carniol 1990). Growing numbers of workers joined unions in the 1940s in the mass-production, resource, and transportation industries (Heron 1989); by 1948, 30 percent of the non-agricultural workforce was unionized

(Panitch and Swartz 1988, 20). However, it was not until the 1960s and 1970s that women became a significant sector of the labour movement with the organization of public-sector workers at the federal, provincial and municipal levels (White 1990, chap. 2).

The number of women in unions in Canada has grown rapidly since the 1960s, increasing 510 percent between 1962 and 1989, to 1.5 million union members, and rising further to 1.6 million union members by 1997. Women have been joining unions at a faster rate than men, and this has resulted in a growing concentration of women in unions. Women as a proportion of union members have grown from 16 percent in 1989 to 39 percent in 1989, swelling to 45 percent of overall union membership by 1997 (Bourette 1997; White 1993a, 57).

The overall rate of unionization for employed women has been approaching the rate for men over the past three decades: from 16 percent of women and 41 percent of men in 1967, to 34 percent of women and 41 percent of men in 1989, and standing at 30 percent of women and 32 percent of men in 1997 (Little 1997; White 1993a, 164). Membership in unions climbed from 2.1 million Canadians in 1967 to a peak of 3.8 million in 1990; the numbers of unionized Canadians have declined slowly since that time (Bourette 1997).

There has been a dramatic shift in the labour movement away from the manufacturing sector towards the service sector, and a shift away from international (American) unions towards national unions and unions of government employees (White 1993a, 57). Women's concentration in the national unions and government unions (46 percent and 48 percent of membership, respectively) has provided a solid base for women's organizing in the labour movement (White 1993a, 58). In 1997, public sector employees were almost three times as likely to be unionized as private sector employees. Current trends indicate that women stand to lose a disproportionate share of these unionized public sector jobs due to government cutbacks (Bourette 1997).

According to data on ethnicity collected for the first time by Statistics Canada in the 1989 Labour Market Activity Study, racial minority workers are less likely to be unionized than other workers. In 1989, 32 percent of Native and visible minority workers belonged to unions compared with 38 percent of non racial minority workers; racial minority workers constituted 5.8 percent of all union members at this time (White 1993a, 165).

According to the 1989 data, racial minority women have the same 34 percent rate of unionization as non-racial minority women; this is a somewhat higher rate than the 30 percent unionization rate for racial minority men. White notes that these patterns give rise to a situation whereby racial minority women in unions outnumber racial minority men, comprising 51 percent of racial minority union members; this contrasts with the overall situation of women who still constitute a minority in the labour movement (White 1993a, 166-7). These figures have implications for the organizing efforts of racial minority women in unions.

While sexism and racism have been endemic to the labour movement as a whole, "social unionism" has been more receptive to the demands being raised by women and people of colour. Unlike business unionism, which focusses exclusively on narrow workplace issues, social unionism extends workplace struggles into the community (Sangster 1995, 197). Robert White, Canadian Labour Congress President, has noted that workers' lives don't start and stop at the door of the workplace (1992, 13-14). Unions embracing this approach of linking workplace and community, have incorporated equity struggles and social justice issues into their programs, and formed coalitions with community-based groups around common concerns (see Action Canada *Dossier* 1992; Leah 1992).

There is no doubt that union campaigns have improved the day-to-day conditions for working people. Panitch and Swartz (1988) argue, however, that the very state policies which guarantee unions collective bargaining rights also provide a means of controlling unions. The complex laws and regulations governing labour-management relations have pushed unions towards a legalistic and bureaucratic role, away from the mass mobilization of workers, which was the historic basis of workers' collective action (Panitch and Swartz 1988, 25-7).

Activism by women, people of colour and other marginalized groups of workers provides a countervailing force to these conservative tendencies: providing new impetus to rank-and-file organizing, mass mobilization of workers, democratization of unions, and strategic linking of union and community struggles for social justice. These struggles have radicalized the Canadian labour movement and challenged established relations of power.

FROM EXCLUSION TO SOLIDARITY:
HISTORY OF UNIONS, 1900-1939

Prior to World War Two, exclusion of racial minority workers was the norm and labour solidarity was the exception in the Canadian labour movement. Patterns of racial exclusion mirrored prevailing racial ideologies, racist state policies, and economic conditions. Instances of solidarity reflected radical labour politics, workers' militancy, and working-class solidarity. Racial minority women experienced the racism and exclusion directed against racial minority men, combined with the gendered patterns of work and patriarchal relations embedded in civil society.

Exclusion of Asian workers

The exclusion of male Chinese workers and other Asian workers from the early twentieth century labour movement in British Columbia has been well documented by historical studies (see Anderson 1991; Creese 1987, 1992; Ireland 1960; Roy 1989). While the research is less well developed with regard to other workers of colour in Canada, studies indicate that unions practised exclusion and discrimination directed against Native workers in the west coast fisheries (Muszynski 1988) and male Black porters working on the railroads (Calliste 1987, 1988). Overall, there is conclusive evidence that the union movement "promoted exclusion of non-whites from the country, from employment, and from the unions" (White 1990, 25; Creese 1987, 38).

Prevailing European and North American racial ideologies, which defined Chinese and other Asian workers as "inferior races," and state policies which denied political rights to Asian immigrants and defined them as "foreigners," contributed to racial divisions within the working class. This "ideology of difference" was central to the racial definition of the white working class in BC at the turn of the century (Anderson 1991, 72; Creese 1992, 316). It was mirrored in groups such as the Anti-Chinese Union, which organized boycotts against the employment of Chinese labour (Roy 1989, 60), the Vancouver Trades and Labour Congress, which agitated for the exclusion of Asian workers (Ireland 1960, 218), and the BC Miners Union, which called for the exclusion of Chinese and later Japanese workers from underground mining (Phillips 1967; Roy 1989, chap. 4). Anti-Asian sentiment occasionally escalated into violent actions such as the 1907 Vancouver racist riot against Chinese and Japanese homes and businesses (White 1990, 27).

State policies confirmed the outsider status of Asian immigrants. The head tax levied on Asian immigrants and the 1923 *Chinese Immigration Act* which prohibited the entry of Chinese people until 1947 were aimed specifically at the exclusion of Chinese workers. The BC *Provincial Election Act of 1895*, which denied the franchise to Chinese and Japanese people, sealed their alien status. Along with Native peoples in BC, who had earlier been disenfranchised, these immigrant peoples were defined by the state as legally inferior, without political rights (Anderson 1991, 53, 63).

Social and political inequality of non-Europeans based on race was closely linked to the demands of capitalist economic development, particularly the use of Asian immigrants as cheap wage-labourers by employers. Creese notes that "women and Asian workers were socially defined as more exploitable than white male workers" (1992, 313-4). Muszynski has documented the exploitation of Native men, women, and children in the west coast fishing and canning industry: "Native labourers, male and female, were paid lower wages than European labourers, women (and children) were paid the lowest wages." She notes that Native women and children were themselves replaced on the job by even lower paid male Chinese immigrant workers (1988, 135, 132).

During this period, unions implemented policies which reproduced prevailing racial ideologies and reinforced the exclusion of racial minority workers. Unions agitated against low-paid Chinese, Japanese, and East Indian labour because of white workers' fears of economic competition; at the same time, unions negotiated agreements which entrenched lower minimum wages for Asian workers (White 1990, 27). Mainstream unions excluded Asian workers and Native workers from membership, and in the west coast fishing industry, white, Japanese and Native fishers organized separately (Phillips 1967).

Chinese workers in BC responded to union exclusion by forming their own separate organizations, starting in 1916 with the Chinese Canadian Labour Union (Creese 1989, 3). The Trades and Labour Congress used segregated locals to accommodate the unionization of Japanese workers; the first all-Japanese local was admitted in 1927 (Ireland 1960, 219). This strategy paralleled the methods used by the American labour movement to segregate Black workers into separate locals (Ireland 1960). Black railway workers in Canada who were hired almost exclusively as porters, responded to white union exclusion and segregation by organizing themselves into separate unions (Calliste 1988).

Employers used "race-conscious" employment practices "to drive down the price of labour and undermine union organization" (Creese 1992, 317). At the same time, white workers in BC focussed on non-white workers, rather than employers, as their main enemy (Anderson 1991, 37). In British Columbia's racially stratified society, "class relations were shaped by practices of white domination and Asian subordination" (Creese 1992, 314).

Racial Minority Women

Very little research has been done regarding relations between racial minority women and the early Canadian labour movement. The evidence suggests that their experiences were shaped not only by race and ethnicity, but also by the prevailing relations of male domination and female subordination which underlay a labour market segmented by race/ethnicity and gender. Brand notes, for example, that the history of Black women cannot be assumed to be identical to that of Black men, since both groups were exploited in different ways by slavery and capitalism (1991, 13).

State policies which excluded Chinese women and restricted their entry into Canada from the 1880s until 1950 were shaped by the dominant racial and patriarchal ideologies (Adilman 1984, 54). Adilman (1984) argues that these discriminatory policies against women were implemented in order to maintain the temporary status of Chinese male labourers and to prevent their permanent settlement or the reproduction of Chinese communities.

South Asian women were allowed to enter Canada following a 1919 agreement with the Indian government, "after years of facing contrived rules and policies fabricated to justify the[ir] exclusion" (Doman 1984, 102). However, a restricted quota system impeded South Asian immigration until 1967 (Das Gupta 1994). While Japanese male immigration was limited by government policy, no restrictions were placed on immediate family members (Kobayashi 1994). Patterns of immigration for visible minority women were shaped, in large part, by state assumptions regarding women's predominant reproductive role and their dependence on men.

Racial minority women who emigrated from China, India, and Japan developed family survival strategies which combined unpaid family work and, to a lesser extent, paid employment (Adilman 1984; Das Gupta 1994; Kobayashi 1994). Brand notes that Black women worked in Ontario from the early 1800s on — in their homes, on farms, and in domestic service — in order to ensure the survival of their families (1991, 15).

Discrimination defined the limited work opportunities for Chinese women. As paid labourers, women worked mainly as home sewers or domestic labourers; until the 1920s few women worked in the industrial sector (Adilman 1984, 57). Research by Creese indicates that Chinese workers in BC remained "overwhelmingly male" until the Second World War (1987, 36). According to Das Gupta (1994), South Asian women did not enter the paid labour force in large numbers until the 1960s. Kobayashi reports that "nearly all the wives of Japanese fishermen worked in the fish canneries" and that domestic service was "very common" in the 1920s (1994, 59).

It is likely that Japanese women had some contact with the early labour movement given their high rate of participation in paid labour. Creese provides one brief account of white and Japanese men and women, organized under the radical Workers Unity League, who struck a Fraser Valley hop farm in 1933 (1992, 325). However, given the prevailing patriarchal assumptions regarding women's domesticity and dependence, Asian women's paid work was underreported — if not altogether invisible — in the official records (Adilman 1984; Kobayashi 1994). Institutional and systemic racism were facts of life for Japanese and Chinese women in Canada; both racism and sexism shaped their daily work lives in the workplace and in the home (Kobayashi 1994; Yee 1987).

Brand (1991; 1994) reports that Black women's paid work in Ontario was structured by the racial and sexual division of labour. Prior to World War Two, 80 percent of employed Black women in Canadian cities worked in domestic service; although Black women worked out of economic necessity to support their families, prior to the 1940s they had little access to industrial work (Brand 1991, 15). At the same time, Black women were active in community organizing and education, as well as in union auxiliaries in support of Black porters' organizing (Brand 1991, 16).

Although working women overall constituted only a small and transient segment of the Canadian labour force prior to World War One, immigrant women from a variety of ethnic backgrounds were active in the paid labour force. According to the 1911 Census of Canada, immigrants comprised 24 percent of employed women (see Table C, Leslie 1974, 96). In that same year, 58 percent of domestic workers in Toronto were immigrant women; the garment industry, which employed large numbers of women, was fragmented into different ethnic groups (White 1990, 13). Frager (1992a,b) provides one of the few accounts of immigrant women's labour activism prior to World War Two in her research on Toronto's Jewish Labour Movement in the garment industry.

Examples of Labour Solidarity

Despite the prevailing racism and sexism of the early Canadian labour movement, there were notable instances of labour solidarity and militancy. Studies by Creese (1987, 1992) and Avery (1979) analyse the conditions which gave rise to the class solidarity exhibited by radical unions and the militancy of (male) immigrant workers in the period from 1917 to 1939. Frager's (1992) studies of the Jewish Labour Movement of 1900 to 1939 incorporate gender into the analysis of immigrant worker's labour militancy.

Three factors can be identified which contributed to the struggle against racial cleavages in the labour movement. The first "necessary condition" was a change in the status of Asians and other immigrants, and their redefinition as workers instead of "foreigners" (Creese 1992, 327). The second factor was the growth of radical unions influenced by socialist politics which challenged prevailing racist ideology and practices. Radical unions such as the Industrial Workers of the World, the One Big Union, and the Communist-affiliated Workers Unity League emphasized class solidarity among workers and welcomed immigrant workers into their ranks (Avery 1979; Creese 1987). Creese notes that "increased labour solidarity between white and Asian workers" was a key feature of labour radicalism in British Columbia. For example, unions belonging to the Workers Unity League actively sought Asian members in the 1930s (1987, 40).

The third factor was labour militancy among racial minority and immigrant workers themselves. Creese (1987) notes that Asian workers demonstrated significant labour activism during periods of general labour unrest — in spite of their marginal economic position, lack of political rights, and anti-Asian agitation. According to her documentation, Chinese workers were involved in more than two dozen strikes in the Vancouver area during two periods, the end of World War One and the depression that preceded World War Two. Chinese workers' actions addressed not only traditional trade union concerns, but also specific issues of racial inequality and racist labour practices (Creese 1987).

Increasing labour solidarity by radical unions encouraged Asian workers' militancy; at the same time, Asian labour activism demonstrated the common class interests of Asian and white workers and encouraged even greater solidarity by white workers (Creese 1992). Such activism played an important role in undermining racial/ethnic divisions in the labour movement. These early anti-racist actions by Chinese workers also helped to place equality on the political agenda of the Canadian labour movement (Creese 1987, 44; 1992, 327).

The militancy of immigrants from continental Europe has been well documented by Avery (1979). European workers, many of whom faced hostility by Anglo-Canadian trade unionists and nativist groups, resisted exploitation through their support of industrial unions and socialist/communist organizations (Avery 1979, 62, 91).

Impact of Jewish Labour Movement

Frager's analysis of Toronto's Jewish labour movement provides a valuable account of the interaction of class, gender, and ethnicity in the lives of Jewish immigrant working women. Toronto's Jewish unions were concentrated in the garment industry where women constituted half the labour force. The unions were radical — primarily socialist — and by 1931, they had a cohesive community base of over

45,000 Eastern European Jews who had emigrated to Toronto to escape poverty and anti-Semitism (Frager 1992b, 507-8). Frager's research indicates that women's issues were subordinated to both class issues and ethnic identity within the Jewish labour movement. She notes that the gender subordination of women was simply not an issue, even for women activists, whose radical politics were shaped by their struggle against workers' exploitation and the anti-Semitism directed against them as Jews (Frager 1992b, 515).

Frager notes that Jewish ethnic identity had a two-fold effect. On the one hand, it provided a culture of protest for women which strengthened the labour movement; on the other hand, it continued women's subordination to men and their separation from other women in Canada (1992b; see also Loewen 1995). Male workers' solidarity with female workers was based on the notion of class consciousness expressed as the "common oppression of all workers." However, the labour movement's definition of class was, itself, based on a male concept of labour which assumed female dependence on men as the primary breadwinners and failed to address the special conditions of women's work (Frager 1992b, 513).

In an industry where women earned from one-half to one-third of men's wages, union strategies of across-the-board percentage increases in wages actually "increased the differential between women's pay and men's pay." Far from addressing women's exploitation, these policies reinforced women's economic subordination (Frager 1992b, 511).

Women's labour activism was impeded by the dominant patriarchal assumptions prevalent in the Jewish unions. Women's household responsibilities left them with less time and energy for union activity, and the male union culture excluded women from social networks and from leadership positions (Frager 1992b, 512). Despite these obstacles, a number of socialist labour women organized actively in the 1920s and 1930s around issues of justice for working people and against anti-Semitism (see Frager 1992b).

The Eaton's strike of 1912 was, according to Frager, "a rare example of male solidarity in support of women workers." She notes that "male self-interest and female self-interest coincided" when Jewish tailors went on strike in defence of their sister garment workers (Frager 1986, 96). Such labour solidarity existed in the face of continuing anti-Semitism and hostility by non-Jewish workers. Despite strike support by the Toronto District Labour Council and the Jewish community, non-Jewish garment workers at Eaton's failed to join the strike because, as Frager notes, the company successfully appealed to their "race and creed prejudice" (1986, 97).

Actions such as the 1912 Eaton's strike and a second strike against Eaton's in 1934 (see Frager 1992c) helped to promote militancy among female and male immigrant workers and to build solidarity in the labour movement. Militancy by Jewish immigrant workers, Asian workers' struggles against racial discrimination, and the solidarity exhibited by radical unions all provided openings for change in the labour movement. These developments helped to set the stage for anti-racist labour organizing after the Second World War.

EQUALITY ISSUES AS UNION ISSUES:
HISTORY OF UNIONS, 1940-1969

In the post-war period, unions began to systematically address the exclusion and inequality faced by workers of colour and immigrant workers (Hill and Schiff 1986; White 1993). Impetus for change came from several related factors: structural social and political changes arising from the war, sustained labour militancy, and organizing efforts by minority workers and their communities against racial and social inequality.

The Second World War was marked by labour shortages which tended to lessen the racial segregation faced by women of colour. As increasing numbers of men were mobilized out of the workplace into military service, increasing numbers of women were mobilized into the expanding wartime economy (see Pierson 1977). Brand notes that "...the war effort released Black women from the racialised, segregated, female employment that for them was domestic work and marked their entry into industrial labour and clerical work." (Brand 1991, 20). As a result of the war, "things opened up" for Black women and they moved into jobs which had previously been closed to them because of their race and their sex (Brand 1991, 20-21).

Experiences on the wartime shop floor inspired militancy among Black women and led to growing union activism (Brand 1991, 25). Similarly, Calliste points to the "new phase of activism" among Black railway workers that began as a result of the economic and political changes during wartime (1987, 9).

Labour legislation which protected workers' rights to organize supported this growing activism among workers of colour. Panitch and Swartz note that the 1940s was a period of almost unprecedented growth and militancy of the labour movement, "increasing with intensity under national mobilization for war and the return of full employment in the early 1940s" (1988, 19). Peacetime legislation in 1948, ensuring "free collective bargaining," was passed "largely because of this sustained (labour) militancy" (Panitch and Swartz 1988, 20).

A new awareness of human rights arose from people's wartime experiences of racism, anti-Semitism, and genocide. Pressure for human rights legislation came from two different sectors: the Jewish Labour Committee (Hill and Schiff 1986) and organized Black workers (Calliste 1987; 1988; Carty 1994). These efforts for progressive change stand in sharp contrast to the official wartime racism practised by the Canadian government: most notably, internment and expulsion of persons of Japanese ancestry regardless of Canadian citizenship (Ujimoto 1988) and refusal to accept Jewish refugees from Hitler's Europe (Hill and Schiff 1986).

Hill and Schiff identify the Jewish Labour Committee as the initial organizing force for anti-discrimination legislation in Canada. Founded in 1935 by progressive Jewish unions and community organizations to counter growing anti-Semitism, the committee began working with Canadian labour and other groups to press for anti-discrimination legislation. Committees against racial discrimination — labour committees for human rights — were established as early as

1946 in major Canadian cities, to focus on both collective bargaining and legislative remedies. The Canadian Labour Congress (CLC) supported these goals through its National Committee on Human Rights (Hill and Schiff 1986, 26-7).

During the 1940s and 1950s, the members of predominantly Black railway unions led the struggle around human rights issues. Through the Brotherhood of Sleeping Car Porters (BSCP), a predominantly Black union in the United States and Canada, Black, male workers organized for racial equality in both countries. They became active members of the CLC's Committee on Human Rights and joined with African Canadian community organizations to press for anti-discrimination legislation and to challenge racist immigration policy toward West Indian applicants (Carty 1994, 215). Within the Canadian Brotherhood of Railway Transport and General Workers (CBRT), Black porters intensified their resistance to racist practices of both management and union leadership (Calliste 1988, 41-3).

Several groups came together around their common interests in promoting human rights legislation. Together with the Jewish Labour Committee and the CLC Committee on Human Rights, Black porters organized for implementation of the *Federal Fair Employment Practices Act*, passed in 1953, as well as similar provincial acts for fair employment and accommodation practices (Calliste 1988; Hill and Schiff 1986). These legislative changes provided leverage for further organizing by workers of colour against discrimination in employment and within trade unions (Calliste 1987).

By the 1960s, with the enactment of human rights legislation at the federal and provincial levels, unions began to shift their focus from racism to other human rights struggles, namely women's rights. Groups outside the labour movement led the struggle against racism for the next twenty years, since anti-racism continued to be a major concern for people of colour in the community (Das Gupta 1997).

FROM MARGIN TO CENTRE:
THE CONTEMPORARY LABOUR MOVEMENT

In the past two-and-a-half decades, women of colour have begun to move from the margins toward the centre of the labour movement. Women's rights have become firmly entrenched in the labour movement, and workers of colour have organized to place racism on the agenda as a legitimate union issue. Despite these changes, Black union activists remain impatient with the slow rate of change, since "there is still a long way to go" before women of colour are fully represented in the labour movement (Muriel Collins and Yvonne Bobb, quoted in Leah 1993, 158).

Women of colour have made progress in the labour movement because of several interrelated factors: growing activism around women's rights and the emergence of a trade union women's movement in the 1970s; growing militancy and anti-racist organizing by immigrant communities and workers of colour in the 1980s; and the labour movement's growing realization that its survival into the 1990s and beyond depends on reaching new groups of workers and building more inclusive unions (Das Gupta 1997; Leah 1991, 1993; Modibo 1995). Support for anti-racism work by white union leaders reflects years of advocacy work by activists of colour both within and outside the labour movement (Das Gupta 1997). Immigrant and visible minority workers have a solid history of labour militancy in Canada; they have played an active role in many strikes and workplace struggles (Leah 1991).

In one recent example of militancy, women and men of colour, many of them recent immigrants, took the lead in an illegal strike by Calgary hospital laundry workers in November 1995; they successfully defended their jobs against contracting out and, in the process, mobilized labour and community groups against the devastating health care cutbacks (McGrath and Neu 1996).

Union policies, structural changes, and education programs have begun to address systemic discrimination within unions; however, activists note that resistance to change is deeply rooted among union members (Das Gupta 1997; Leah 1993; Modibo 1995). Union and community activists have also developed strategies to protect the rights of the many workers of colour who remain outside the labour movement. These strategies include: campaigns for organizing the unorganized workers, lobbying campaigns for legislative change, and coalition building between labour and community groups — building a new model of "community unionism" (Aggarwal 1995; Das Gupta 1996; Fudge 1991; Ladd 1995; Leah 1991).

Struggle within a Struggle: Racism and Women's Organizing

A trade union women's movement emerged in the 1970s; by the early 1980s union women were consolidating their positions with the formation of women's committees and activism around key women's demands such as daycare, equal pay, and affirmative action. Women's conferences, women's departments, and support for women's equality are now firmly established in labour centrals, public sector unions, and some private sector unions (Leah 1991; White 1993a). However, these gains in women's status have not been shared equally by all women. Women of colour have seen their concerns about racism pushed aside by white women who argue, "first we make these gains for women, then we'll deal with racism — your turn will come." Black union activists contend, on the contrary, that "it isn't first one group and then the others — we move together" (June Veecock, quoted in Leah 1993, 180). Women of colour maintain that "racism is a women's struggle," part of the struggle for women's rights (Yvonne Bobb, quoted in Leah 1993, 168).

Black union women report that, despite instances of solidarity and support by white union women, there is a still a struggle within the women's movement around issues of racism; some women have yet to come to terms with their own racism (Veecock and Bobb, quoted in Leah 1993, 168-9). Judy Darcy, President of CUPE (Canadian Union of Public Employees) National, confirms that "for those of us who are white...the first challenge is to confront our own racism" (1993, xi).

As a result of the obstacles they face, women of colour have emphasized the importance of fighting their own battles. They conclude: "Nobody is going to do this for you. It's your struggle, you have to do it for yourself" (Bobb, quoted in Leah 1993, 163).

Organizing by women of colour gained impetus in the 1980s, as workers of colour and immigrant workers began mobilizing in autonomous formations such as the Ontario Coalition of Black Trade Unionists (OCBTU) and within union human rights committees to challenge workplace racism, lobby for stronger human rights legislation, and demand equal rights within the labour movement itself (Leah 1991). These union struggles reflected growing militancy by workers of colour as well as community-based, anti-racist organizing in this period (Das Gupta 1997). By the 1980s, women of colour were becoming politicized and empowered through their involvement in community groups and grassroots organizations of immigrant and visible minority women (Das Gupta 1986; Leah 1991).

While today's labour movement has, for the most part, moved away from the virulent racism and exclusionary policies of the early 1900s, evidence suggests that unions continue to reflect and reinforce the racism prevalent in Canadian society (Leah 1993; Modibo 1995). Continuing racist incidents within unions create an urgent need for anti-racist education and action (Das Gupta 1997). Examples of racism range from the personal to the structural, from stereotyping and harassment to lack of representation in elected positions and staff appointments. According to the Ontario Federation of Labour (OFL) Human Rights Director June Veecock, a person of colour is "always perceived as an outsider" in the labour movement, no matter how long you've been in Canada (quoted in Leah 1993, 165). "As long as you are visibly different, the perception is you do not have an understanding [of unions]" (Veecock, quoted in Modibo 1995, 90). A member of OCBTU argues that there is a need for "affirmative action within affirmative action" to promote the movement of visible minority women into leadership positions, in cases where affirmative action positions created for women are filled exclusively by white women (quoted in Modibo 1995, 91).

There are a number of other barriers to union participation by women of colour and immigrant women. These include: absence of women of colour as role models, lack of knowledge about union culture, economic constraints for women who work in low-paying jobs, women's family responsibilities, lack of access to childcare, and differences of language and accent (Leah 1993; Modibo 1995). Two Black union activists describe how their "non-Canadian accents" have marginalized them in the labour movement. Yvonne Bobb and Muriel Collins explain: "If you don't have a Canadianized accent, you're not acceptable" (quoted in Leah 1993, 166).

Strategies for Institutional Change

Trade unionists organizing against racism and discrimination have developed strategies for institutional change which include: formal policy statements, union conferences, affirmative action within union structures, employment equity measures in the workplace, union policies against harassment, and union education programs.

Union activists usually begin with formal policy statements and resolutions which lay the groundwork for action programs, give legitimacy to their campaigns, and provide access to union resources. Anti-racism work in the Ontario Federation of Labour was initiated in 1981 with adoption of a policy statement, "Racism Hurts Everyone," by delegates to the annual convention. The campaign identified racism as a priority issue for labour and committed OFL resources and staff to the action plan (Leah 1991, 181). Unions affiliated with the federation were urged to take action on racism within their own ranks by the OFL's 1986 document "Racism and Discrimination." At the national level, the Canadian Labour Congress stated its commitment to "make human rights a priority" with adoption of a Human Rights Policy Statement at the 1992 Constitutional Convention; affiliated unions, locals, federations of labour, and labour councils were urged to take action around racism and other human rights issues.

Union conferences have enabled workers of colour to mobilize more effectively within the labour movement. The OFL's April 1986 conference, "Building the Participation of Workers of Colour in our Unions," provided the impetus for formation of the Ontario Coalition of Black Trade Unionists; the OCBTU, in turn, encouraged activism by workers of colour and provided them with a base for further organizing in the labour movement (Leah 1991, 182). Within the Canadian Union of Public Employees, the Ontario Division sponsors human rights conferences on a regular basis (Leah 1993). The Canadian Auto Workers held its first conference for workers of colour in 1996, with 140 delegates from across the country (Das Gupta 1997).

The Canadian Labour Congress was mandated to hold human rights conferences on a regular basis by its 1992 policy statement on human rights. Efforts were made to address the specific concerns of women of colour at the CLC's 1994 human rights conference, Confronting Racism: Strengthening Solidarity, through a workshop on "multiple oppression." Sunera Thobani, President of the National Action Committee on the Status of Women, was guest speaker for the plenary session (CLC Interim Report 1994).

In September 1998, close to 400 trade unionists and social activists gathered at the first CLC sponsored conference for Aboriginal workers and workers of colour. CLC's *Out Front* magazine (Fall 1998) reports that anti-racist activists challenged the labour movement to implement equality policies "at the bargaining table and in labour's own structures."

Structural Changes in Unions

Union members have lobbied for structural changes in the labour movement in order to ensure that issues of racism are addressed and that the work is led by people of colour. Demands by workers of colour for union staff positions, standing committees, and special departments have tested the labour movement's commitment to anti-racism work. Within the Ontario Federation of Labour, workers of colour and women activists successfully lobbied for a human rights director on race relations — in addition to the existing director of women's issues — after the OFL failed to renew the contract of the coordinator for its 1981 anti-racism campaign. June Veecock, a Black union activist, was hired into this new permanent position as Director for Race Relations (Leah 1991, 182).

CUPE has established a model for anti-racism work with formation of its National Rainbow Committee and appointment of Harminder Magon to a new staff position as Anti-Racism Coordinator. These structural changes can be traced to the union's 1987 national convention. At that time, outspoken discussion of racism by workers of colour led to adoption of a resolution calling for a vigorous anti-racism campaign and formation of a Working Committee on Racism, Discrimination and Employment Equity — known as the "National Rainbow Committee" (Das Gupta 1997; Leah 1993, 159). The National Rainbow Committee includes twelve CUPE members plus the coordinator, and it aims for gender parity as well as regional and ethnic representation (Leah 1993).

Publication of a newsletter and formation of Division Human Rights Committees in the provinces have helped to further the committee's goals of reaching racial minority and Aboriginal members and building a network of activists (Anti-Racism Communication 1993). These initiatives have combined with continuing pressure from the grassroots to promote change in the union. As Muriel Collins, a Black woman active in CUPE for many years, noted, "We got up on the convention floor in 1986 to fight for the Rainbow Committee, and we made a difference.... People are more receptive now, they've seen the results of our work" (quoted in Leah 1993, 159).

In the Canadian Auto Workers union (CAW), standing committees on human rights are mandated at the local level by Article 42 of the union's constitution. Staff member Hassan Yussuf — a well-known human rights activist — was appointed by the CAW's 1992 Canadian Council to coordinate the union's fight against racism (MacLennan 1992, 16). Yussuf's work has focussed on mobilizing workers of colour to become more active in the union, while workers of colour caucuses in union locals have helped to maintain pressure at the grassroots (Das Gupta 1997). As a result of this process, demands have surfaced for a CAW human rights department with a full-time coordinator; Das Gupta (1997) notes that the CAW is currently in the process of establishing this department.

At the national level, the Human Rights Committee and the Women's and Human Rights Department of the CLC help to coordinate anti-racism work. David Onyalo, Chair of CUPE's Rainbow Committee, holds a staff position with the CLC as National Representative, Women's and Human Rights Department.

Measures for Affirmative Action and Employment Equity

Workers of colour have organized for affirmative action measures to address their lack of representation at leadership levels in the labour movement. The "CAW Affirmative Action Plan," adopted at the union's 1991 Constitutional Convention, calls for "mandatory affirmative action measures" for women and visible minority workers on the National Executive Board, as well as more representative local leadership and staff appointments. These demands have come forward from the growing numbers of women and people of colour in the auto workers' union.

Veecock reports that pressure for greater representation in the Ontario Federation of Labour came from caucuses of Black workers, organized since 1985 at annual conventions (Leah 1993, 164). Delegates to the 1993 convention approved allocation of two vice-presidents to visible minority women, in addition to allocation of seven vice-presidents to women, one to a First Nations person and one to a person with a disability (OFL Constitution 1993, Article V, Section 1.1). Black caucuses have also been active at the national level, and at the 1992 CLC Convention, Black women held their own workshop. Activists Yvonne Bobb and June Veecock report that organizing by the Black Workers Caucus and the OCBTU exerted pressure for restructuring of the CLC Executive Council in 1992; two new positions for visible minority vice-presidents were added at that time (quoted in Leah 1993, 164). The positions for visible minority representatives were established ten years after the CLC took its first steps in 1982 to ensure greater representation of women on the executive council (CLC Report, Nov. 1993, 13).

Internal affirmative action measures taken by CUPE have included the appointment of a Black woman, Muriel Collins, as chair of CUPE's National Women's Committee and the appointment of Collins and an Aboriginal women, Lois Hill, as co-chairs of the Ontario Division Women's Committee (Leah 1993). Pressure for more substantial changes have come forward from the National Rainbow Committee and from caucuses of Racial Minority and Aboriginal workers in Ontario, the province with the largest proportion of union members of colour (Das Gupta 1997). A recommendation was brought forward by the Rainbow Committee that the National Executive Board (NEB) designate two positions of colour by 1995, one visible minority and one Aboriginal; at that time the NEB had one person of colour, a Black women, among the 14 positions. Despite strong advocacy by workers of colour at CUPE's annual convention, the proposal was defeated; this marked a painful setback for union members of colour (see Das Gupta 1997).

The labour movement has been more consistent in its support for affirmative action in the workplace than within its own internal structures. Workers of colour have joined together with women in support of employment equity measures. The OFL's 1987 "Statement on Equal Action in Employment" was jointly developed by the Women's and Human Rights Committees which also co-sponsored an employment equity forum at the 1991 OFL Convention (Leah 1993, 160). Within CUPE, the integration of race and gender issues has been highlighted by conferences which jointly address women's and human rights issues. The 1991 Ontario Division Women's Conference raised the issues of equality, discrimination, harassment and racism, while the 1991 Ontario Division Human Rights Conference on Employment Equity linked sexism with other forms of discrimination (Leah

1993, 161). Organizing around employment equity — and educating their members about this issue — has been a major priority of the labour movement, particularly in Ontario (Das Gupta 1997).

Policies on Harassment

Union policies combatting harassment have also begun to integrate issues of race and gender. CAW's 1988 policy on "Harassment in the Workplace" targets both sexual and racial harassment, as does the union's 1988 video *Call Me Sister, Call Me Brother*. United Steelworkers, District 6, has adopted policy papers "to prohibit and prevent" both sexual and racial harassment in the workplace, and both issues are combined in its educational booklet "Racial and Sexual Harassment, and Violence Against Women" (n.d.). The OFL's policy paper "Challenging Harassment," adopted unanimously in 1991, confirmed the labour movement's policy of zero tolerance to sexual, racial, and personal harassment (Leah 1993, 159). The policy document identified racism, sexism, homophobia and violence as important issues to be addressed by the labour movement (OFL 1991).

Implementation of Union Policies

Women of colour have raised concerns about the effectiveness of formal union policies at the local level. June Veecock is critical of "rhetorical statements" and policies that "are not always translated into action on the shop floor" (Leah 1993, 162). In describing the struggle for a human rights committee in her own CUPE local, Muriel Collins concludes: while the issues are being addressed in CUPE National and in the Ontario Region, "the issues are not being addressed the way we want" at the local level (Leah 1993, 163).

In the CAW, similar concerns have been voiced that national human rights policies are not always reflected in the union locals (Leah 1993; MacLennan 1992). Adoption of national union policy at the local level can be complicated by the semi-autonomous structure of individual union locals (OCBTU member, quoted in Modibo 1995, 91).

Union Education Programs

Effective union education is an essential part of anti-racist organizing in unions. Education programs can provide new information about racism and other human rights issues, promote critical awareness and support for policy changes, and create a more positive climate for addressing problems of racism among the membership (Das Gupta 1997; Leah 1993). Current labour human rights/anti-racism courses range from short modules of one to three hours to weekend or week-long courses, and they vary a good deal in both content and format. Popular education approaches to union education promote critical thinking and empowerment, and they incorporate experiential learning activities where participants learn by doing (Bernard 1997; Leah 1998; Worker Education Round Table 1997).

Canadian Auto Workers' comprehensive 1988 course, "Human Rights, Workers Rights: The Same Struggle," was one of the first efforts. It focusses primarily on human rights legislation and combines study of all areas of discrimination. Other unions offer courses which focus more specifically on challenging racism and promoting cross-cultural awareness. These include the United Steelworkers two-day and week-long courses, Solidarity in Diversity: Building a Multicultural Union (1989); Metro Labour Education Centre's course for unionists, Challenging Racism (1995); CUPE's courses, Combatting Workplace Racism and Cross-Cultural Awareness, and the CLC's 1993 anti-racism program of union seminars and weekend schools.

The Canadian Auto Workers' union and United Steelworkers of America have both successfully negotiated with employers for workplace instruction; this marks a significant advance for on-the-job human rights education. The CAW-GM program, implemented in 1987, provides three hours of instruction in its Human Rights Training Program for all General Motors employees (Leah 1993; CAW 1987). USWA's one-, two-, and three-hour anti-racism courses developed in 1991 — focusing on racism and racial harassment in the workplace — reached 35,000 members in Ontario workplaces within a two-year period (Das Gupta 1997; USWA 1991).

While most human rights courses have been aimed at sensitizing the "dominant group of white males," CAW's Assistant to the President Peggy Nash reports that in 1992, Canadian Auto Workers established two new courses specifically designed for women and workers of colour to "build their own networks, formulate their own demands and develop their own strategies." Women of colour were successfully recruited for both courses (Nash, quoted in Leah, 1993, 162).

Activists and educators have raised a number of concerns about the effectiveness of human rights and anti-racism education. Some unions have taken special steps to train the trainers: CLC put 70 union members (including workers of colour) through an extensive anti-racism training course in February 1993 (CLC Report, Nov. 1993, 13). CUPE trained rank-and-file members from diverse backgrounds to lead its two new courses (Das Gupta 1997).

Das Gupta (1997) identifies two problem areas for people of colour who lead anti-racism courses. While sharing personal experiences of discrimination may be effective in raising the consciousness of white workers, Das Gupta notes that workers of colour may find this role objectionable. Moreover, racial minority instructors may themselves face resistance from white union members participating in the courses.

CAW's Peggy Nash questions the effectiveness of human rights courses where "people get lectured to...and don't get a chance to really talk through their feelings" (quoted in Leah 1993, 163). Similarly, Mexican labour educator Patricia Fernandez has called for a participatory approach to labour education which recognizes that "workers are also individuals with feelings." She urges that education "take into account the rational and the emotional" aspects of learning (quoted in Cavanagh 1997, 57).

Fernandez was speaking at the recent "Educ-Action" conference held in Toronto, April 1997, which brought together labour and popular educators with a commitment to participatory and critical education (see Cavanagh 1997). Unless union courses on racism promote experiential learning and opportunity for self-reflection, there is a danger that participants will learn to speak the rhetoric of anti-racism discourse, without going deeper to explore their own racist attitudes and develop a personal commitment to real-life change.

"Honouring our Stories" workshops on cultural identity and racism, developed by Ronnie Leah (1998), provide an experiential approach to anti-racism training which begins with the premise: "Before you can respect other cultures, you must first honour your own culture." Primarily developed to address the racism directed against Native people, these workshops are designed for non-native participants: to express their fears and emotions, to become more aware of their own cultural identity and values, to re-examine everyday assumptions about Native people and cultural differences, and to develop greater openness to other cultures (Leah 1998). Evaluations by participants indicate that the workshops promote a positive experiential learning experience which increases self-awareness, encourages reflection on difficult questions, opens minds, and helps people get past their own dominant views (Leah 1998, workshop evaluations).

Union courses such as the Steelworkers 1989 course, which are based on active learning with discussion, case studies, and experiential exercises, are likely to prove more effective in changing the attitudes of members than straight, lecture-style courses. Courses such as Metro Labour's 1995 course, which have an explicit focus on strategies for challenging racism, are more likely to lead to action by union members. Instructors report that providing union members with new perspectives and more accurate information can begin to change their attitudes about workers of colour (Das Gupta 1997).

On a less optimistic note, human rights trainer Sherene Razack warns that union members still have "very strong resistance" to real change. Razack concludes that the labour movement must address issues of unequal power if education programs are to effectively challenge racism (quoted in Leah 1993, 163).

TOWARDS A NEW VISION OF COMMUNITY UNIONISM

Efforts to build a more inclusive labour movement, with full participation by women, immigrant workers, and workers of colour, are fundamental to building a revitalized, community-based labour movement that defends the rights of all workers. Contemporary union campaigns against racism and sexism have emphasized the need to build union solidarity: to overcome divisions of race and gender which weaken unions in the short term, and to build a more inclusive labour movement in the long term. Along with these efforts for equality within the labour movement, labour and community activists are developing strategies for reaching outside the organized labour movement to the many working people without union protection.

The strategy of "community unionism" — unions organizing in coalition with grassroots community groups for workers rights and justice — is changing the way unions organize and it is redefining the labour movement itself (Banks n.d.; Ladd 1995; Rachleff 1994). This development is especially significant for women of colour.

Organizing for Workers' Rights

Efforts to protect the rights of the most exploited workers have reached beyond unions' traditional emphasis on collective bargaining for unionized workers. Labour and community activists have organized in support of stronger human rights protection at the federal and provincial levels to protect all working people. They have mobilized for more effective employment equity provisions as a means of addressing "historic patterns of exclusion and discrimination" (OPSEU 1992, "Racism and Employment Equity"). Along with support for pay equity legislation, activists have argued in favour of higher minimum wage rates to improve conditions for workers at the bottom, many of whom are immigrant and visible minority women.

Groups promoting "workers' rights," such as the Workers Information and Action Centre of Toronto (WIACT), have mobilized for improved employment standards for all workers since the *Employment Standards Act* "is often the only instrument non-unionized workers have to protect themselves from unjust situations" (WIACT 1993, "Working for Dignity"; see also Fudge 1991). Campaigns have been waged in support of domestic workers and farm workers — many of them recent immigrants and women of colour — to have them covered by provincial labour standards (Epstein 1983; Hernandez 1987; Tatroff 1994). The Canadian Farmers Union (CFU) has led efforts to include BC farm workers under the province's minimum wage laws and to win better safety regulations (Tatroff 1994). Improvements to conditions for part-time and casual workers were achieved under the *Labour Standards Act* in Saskatchewan (see Broad and Foster 1995).

Innovative Organizing Strategies

In the face of economic restructuring and public sector cutbacks, anti-labour laws and attacks on workers' rights, unions have begun to develop new strategies for organizing the unorganized. Labour analyst Julie White has called for a "fourth wave" of unionization, directed at the private, service-producing sectors with traditionally low rates of unionization (1993b, 203). Innovative approaches will be needed to reach women, immigrant workers, people of colour, young workers — many of them part-time, casual workers in small, private sector workplaces (Armstrong 1993; Bourette 1996; Cornish and Spink 1994; Fudge 1993; White 1993b). With these goals in mind, the Ontario Federation of Labour sponsored its first conference on new organizing strategies in April 1997. More than 200 union activists attended the conference which highlighted effective, innovative organizing campaigns in Canada and the United States (Schenk 1997, 30).

In the past few years, Canadian Auto Workers has made noticeable gains in organizing service sector workers in British Columbia. Current membership stands at over 4,000 members in more than 50 bargaining units including Kentucky Fried Chicken, Whitespot, and Starbucks, and efforts are now underway to organize the first McDonalds Restaurant (Briere 1999). CAW Local 3000 President Denise Kellahan estimates that the membership is 70 percent women and 40 percent visible minority workers (Kellahan and Eaton 1997, 25). Whereas there were few women in CAW two decades ago, women comprised 30 percent of CAW's membership in 1997, and the figures are rising (Bourette 1997).

There is no question that unionization provides dramatic improvements in pay and working conditions for private sector service workers. According to Statscan analysis of 1997 labour force data, hourly wages and weekly earnings of union members were about 31 percent higher than for non-union workers. The differences were even more striking for part-timers in unions, who earned more than twice the amount of non-union, part-time workers (reported in Little 1997).

Local CAW President Kellahan, a waitress for twenty years and now a member of CAW's National Executive Board, reports that union members organize around more than higher wages; organizing issues include health and safety, scheduling of work hours, and "simply...dignity on the job" (1997, 26).

In 1998, employees at Suzy Shier retail outlets in Toronto successfully organized with support from the Union of Needletrades, Industrial and Textile Employees (UNITE). Union members include young women such as Kerrie-Ann Gunn, a 23-year-old single mother who moved to Canada from Jamaica 11 years ago, and Deborah De Angelis, the OFL's first vice-president representing youth. This campaign was another breakthrough for the "women, youth and visible minority workers who make up a disproportionate share of retail staff" (De Angelis and Eaton 1998, 23). UNITE also runs workplace citizenship classes to meet the needs of immigrant workers and their families (Eaton 1998, 7).

United Food and Commercial Workers' Union has initiated a "Special Project Union Representative" (SPUR) organizing program directed towards youth. Under the SPUR program, young stewards and activists are paid by the union to join organizing campaigns in similar, non-union jobs. UFCW reports "the best results we've had in eight years," organizing record numbers of new members into the union — including 1,400 members in Ontario during 1997, despite new anti-union laws (Kilgour 1998, 25).

Community-Based Organizing Strategies

CUPE Local 79 led the way in organizing part-time workers in the 1980s, utilizing a strategy of community-based support. The union had organized casual part-time workers in Metro Toronto Homes for the Aged; 90 percent of whom were women, mostly Black and Asian workers. After winning seniority and pro-rated benefits, CUPE was forced to defend these gains in the face of cutbacks. The union enlisted the support of community groups, gaining widespread support from groups representing women of colour (Leah 1991, 190).

Such strategies of coalition building with community groups have been especially effective in organizing for the rights of women of colour. The strategies
employed by Canadian Farmers Union (CFU) to win better pay and working conditions for farm workers has also reflected their strong roots in the community,
particularly with Indo-Canadian workers, many of them recent immigrant women
and elderly men. Never a "traditional trade union," the CFU is both union and
social movement (former president Chouhan, quoted in Tatroff 1994, 26).

The 1991 International Ladies Garment Workers Union (ILGWU) campaign
to organize homeworkers in the garment industry exemplifies innovative union
strategies for reaching the most exploited workers: "immigrant women sewing
clothing pieces in their basements...working for less than minimum wage and
with absolutely no job protection" (ILGWU Conference on Homeworking 1992,
Intro.). Organizing efforts were initiated by the Ontario District of the ILGWU
with Chinese and Vietnamese garment homeworkers, and followed in the South
Asian and Spanish communities (Ladd 1995; Yalnizyan 1993). In a departure
from the usual union organizing practices, ILGWU started from the ground up,
building social links among the garment workers through members of their own
communities, and building links between the organized and the unorganized.
They established the Homeworkers Association in 1992, and set about organizing
garment homeworkers in their individual workplaces. This was a different kind
of union, a pre-union with associate membership, for workers who were not yet
covered by a collective agreement (Dagg 1992, 19; Yalnizyan 1993, 295).

The union office became a drop-in centre providing a range of activities. The
Homeworkers Association reached out to its members with regular social events,
legal clinics, and workshops; it provided a health benefit plan, ESL training,
daycare, translation and education on workers rights — services that met the
needs of the workers. This process enabled the union "to build relationships and
trust with unorganized workers — especially immigrant women workers and
workers of colour," notes ILGWU organizer Deena Ladd (1995, 5).

The union's decision to hire staff representative of the workers was crucial,
insofar as it enabled the union "to communicate with members and do outreach
and make the links necessary in various ethnic and racial communities (Ladd
1995, 7). Coalition-building was part of the union's organizing strategy from the
beginning. The Coalition for Fair Wages and Working Conditions for Homeworkers
brought together women's groups, church groups, workers' rights groups, and
advocacy groups for immigrant workers to engage in education, lobbying, demonstrations, and rallies on behalf of homeworkers (Ladd 1995).

Community Unionism

The ILGWU campaign exemplifies a new model of community unionism. This
approach to organizing requires a long term commitment of several years instead
of the usual time frame of several months, and it requires a large outlay of money
and staff by the union. The strategy focusses on reaching workers in their communities and building relationships of trust with immigrant women. It promotes

coalition-building with grassroots community groups, and relies on political and social activism. Community activism is, in fact, an approach that goes back to the roots
of social unionism, "back to the origin of organizing as a social movement, organizing that is grounded in a sense of community" (Yalnizyn 1993, 297).

Activists in Canada, the United States and countries such as Mexico, are promoting the strategy of community unionism. They are organizing union campaigns as
social movements: to link workplaces and communities; mobilize women, minority
and immigrant workers; promote rank-and-file activism, militancy, and direct action;
and foster alliances and solidarity (Banks n.d.; Ladd 1995; Rachleff 1994). Ontario
Federation of Labour's Conference on Community Unionism held in April 1995,
demonstrates labour's growing interest and commitment to this strategy.

Community unionism has a strong potential to address the needs of women
of colour and to challenge inequalities of power within the labour movement. By
building an inclusive labour movement with organic links to the wider community, the labour movement is beginning to reconceptualize itself as a community-
wide movement; this can strengthen labour's commitment to justice for all workers, especially the most marginalized and exploited workers (Banks n.d.; Ladd
1995).

Community unionism and other innovative organizing strategies are proving to be crucial for the survival of trade unions in the current anti-labour climate. In Ontario, for example, anti-labour laws introduced by the Harris government led to a 56 percent decline in the number of workers organized between
November 1995 and November 1996. OFL research director Chris Schenk observes that the Ontario labour movement needs to organize 30,000 workers per
year in order to maintain its unionization rate of 31.5 percent; however, fewer
than 14,000 new workers were organized in the 1995 to 1996 period (Schenk
1997, 30). These figures provide a strong impetus for change in the labour
movement.

Union organizer Deena Ladd concludes: "community unionism is critical in
our surviving as a labour movement — and not just surviving but being a strong
movement, a representative movement and one that can take on the challenges that
we are facing right now" (OFL Conference on Community Unionism 1995, 1).

LESSONS FOR SOCIAL MOVEMENTS

This comprehensive overview of women of colour and the Canadian labour movement provides some valuable lessons for unions, for anti-racist organizing, and
for social movements in general. As a first step, unions and other progressive
organizations need to examine the extent to which racism and sexism have been
and continue to be embedded in their structures and traditions. The capacity to be
self-critical is an essential starting point. As noted by Canadian-born Elaine
Bernard, Executive Director of the Harvard Trade Union Program: "Developing
a critical culture within the labour movement — one that is more open to free-

ranging debates and the discussion of controversial internal issues — is essential to the growth and strengthening of organized labour" (Bernard 1997, 11).

Bernard goes on to say that "education, especially popular education, has an important role to play in this resurgence" (1997, 11). Popular education — which promotes critical thinking, empowerment, and action against oppression — plays an important role in developing critical awareness of structural inequalities and the need for systemic changes. Popular education starts with people's own experiences and understandings, and encourages popular participation and democratic practice.

Labour and popular educator Denise Nadeau maintains that it's only through a popular education process that "we can get people to feel that they are part of a union, that they own the struggle, that they are naming the issues, that the union is their own union" (quoted in Cavanagh 1997, 57). Ownership of unions is a crucial issue for women of colour and other groups of workers who have historically been excluded from full participation in the labour movement.

The strategy of coalition-building, developing links between unions and community-based groups, is essential for building effective struggles against sexism, racism, and other forms of discrimination. Women of colour live in families and communities; union organizing strategies should build on these strengths of community support and solidarity. Genuine coalition work involves a sharing of power among organizations and constituencies. The labour movement has often been reluctant to share power with community-based groups, even when engaged in labour-community coalitions such as the Action Canada Network (see Leah 1992).

Issues of power and privilege must be addressed by the labour movement, the women's movement, and other movements for social change — since unequal power relations are at the root of racism and sexism. This means challenging "white privilege" which maintains the power of white men and women on a daily basis in unions and other organizations (Das Gupta 1997; McIntosh 1990). And it means committing our organizations to programs of education and action for personal and structural change. Despite labour's many policies supporting equality measures, some unions remain reluctant to open up established structures of power.

In challenging issues of power and privilege within the Canadian labour movement, women of colour are raising fundamental questions about the restructuring of social relations within organizations and throughout society. Women of colour are changing the face of labour through their ongoing struggles for justice and equality. Their activism is providing new impetus for grass-roots organizing and empowerment, democratization of union policies and structures, strategic alliance-building with community, and mobilization for social transformation.

REFERENCES

Books and Articles

Action Canada Network (ACN). "Inside Coalition Politics." *Action Canada Dossier*, no. 37 (May-June 1992).

Adilman, Tamara. "A Preliminary Sketch of Chinese Women and Work in British Columbia 1858-1950." In *Not Just Pin Money*. Barbara Latham and Roberta Pazdro, eds. Victoria, BC: Comusun College, 1984.

Aggerwal, Pramila. "Business as Usual in the Factory." *Resources for Feminist Research/Documentation sur la recherche feministe*, vol. 16, no. 3 (1987): 42-3.

Anderson, Kay J. *Vancouver's Chinatown: Racial Discourse in Canada, 1975-1980*. Montreal: McGill-Queen's University Press, 1991.

Avery, Donald. *Dangerous Foreigners*. Toronto: McClelland and Stewart, 1979.

Banks, Andy. "The Power and Promise of Community Unionism." *Labor Research Review*, no. 18 (n.d.): 17-31.

Bernard, Elaine. "Education vs. Propaganda." *Our Times*, vol. 16, no. 5 (September/October 1997): 11.

Bourette, Susan. "Women Make Strides in Union Movement." *Globe and Mail*, August 29, 1997: B1.

Bourette, Susan. "Labour Looks to Youth." *Globe and Mail*, May 13, 1996: B1.

Brand, Dionne. "'We weren't allowed to go into factory work until Hitler started the war': The 1920s to the 1940s." In *'We're Rooted Here and They Can't Pull Us Up'*. Peggy Bristow, coord. Toronto: University of Toronto Press, 1994.

Brand, Dionne. *No Burden To Carry: Narratives of Black Working Women in Ontario 1920s-1950s*. Toronto: Women's Press, 1991.

Briere, Elaine. "Labour Deserves a Break Today at McDonald's." *Briarpatch*, vol. 28, no. 1 (February 1999): 13-16.

Briskin, Linda, and Patricia McDermott, eds. *Women Challenging Unions*. Toronto: University of Toronto Press, 1993.

Bristow, Peggy. "Introduction." In *'We're Rooted Here and They Can't Pull Us Up': Essays in African Canadian Women's History*. Bristow, coord. Toronto: University of Toronto Press, 1994.

Broad, Dave, and Lori Foster. "Saskatchewan Standards Struggle." *Our Times* (March 1995): 30-3.

Calliste, Agnes. "Canada's Immigration Policy and Domestics from the Caribbean." In *Race, Class, Gender: Bonds and Barriers*. Jesse Vorst, et al., eds. Toronto: Garamond, 1991.

Calliste, Agnes. "Blacks on Canadian Railways." *Canadian Ethnic Studies*, vol. 20, no. 2 (1988): 36-52.

Calliste, Agnes. "Sleeping Car Porters in Canada: An Ethnically Submerged Split Labour Market." *Canadian Ethnic Studies*, vol. 19, no. 1 (1987): 1-20.

Calvert, John. "The Need for a New Conception of Union Work." In *Working People and Hard Times*. Robert Argue, Charlene Gannage, and David W. Livingstone, eds. Toronto: Garamond, 1987.

Carniol Ben. "Social Work and the Labour Movement." In *Social Work and Social Change in Canada*. Brian Wharf, ed. Toronto: McClelland & Stewart, 1990.

Carty, Linda. "African Canadian Women and the State: 'Labour only, please.'" In *'We're Rooted Here and They Can't Pull Us Up.'* Peggy Bristow, coord. Toronto: University of Toronto Press, 1994.

Cavanagh, Chris. "When Two Rivers Meet: Popular and Labour Education." *Our Times*, vol. 16, no. 5 (September/October 1997): 53-7.

Christie, Gordon. "Dirty Laundry." *Briarpatch*, vol. 25, no. 1 (1996): 15-16.

Cornish, Mary, and Lynn Spink. *Organizing Unions*. Toronto: Second Story Press, 1994.

Creese, Gillian. "Exclusion or Solidarity? Vancouver Workers Confront the 'Oriental Problem.'" In *Canadian Working Class History*. Laurel Sefton MacDowell and Ian Radforth, eds. Toronto: Canadian Scholars Press, 1992.

Creese, Gillian. "Organizing Against Racism in the Workplace: Chinese Workers in Vancouver Before the Second World War." *Canadian Ethnic Studies*, vol. 19, no. 3 (1987): 29-40.

Cumsille, Alejandra, Egan, Klestorny, and Larrain. "Triple Oppression: Immigrant Women in the Labour Force." In *Union Sisters*. Linda Briskin and Lynda Yanz, eds. Toronto: Women's Press, 1983.

Darcy, Judy. "Foreword." In Briskin and McDermott, eds., *Women Challenging Unions*. Toronto: UTP, 1993: vii-xi.

Das Gupta, Tania. "Anti-Racism and the Organized Labour Movement." In *The Racist Imagination*. Vic Satzewich, ed. Toronto: University of Toronto Press, 1997.

———. *Racism and Paid Work*. Toronto: Garamond, 1996.

———. "Political Economy of Gender, Race and Class: Looking at South Asian Immigrant Women in Canada." *Canadian Ethnic Studies*, vol. 26, no. 1 (1994): 59-73.

———. "Unravelling the Web of History." *Resources for Feminist Research/Documentation sur la recherche feministe*, vol. 16, no. 1 (1987): 13-14.

———. *Learning from Our History*. Toronto: Cross Cultural Communications Centre, 1986.

De Angelis, Debora, and Jonathan Eaton. "Wake Up Little Suzy: Women Retail Workers Organize." *Our Times*, vol. 17, no. 2 (March/April 1998): 23-9.

Doman, Mahinder. "A Note on Asian Indian Women in British Columbia 1900-1935. In *Not Just Pin Money*. Barbara Latham and Roberta Pazdro, eds. Victoria, BC: Comusun College, 1984.

Eaton, Jonathan. "Citizens at Work." *Our Times*, vol. 17, no. 6 (November/December 1998): 7.

Epstein, Rachel. "Domestic Workers: The Experience in BC." In *Union Sisters*. Linda Briskin and Lynda Yanz, eds. Toronto: Women's Press, 1983.

Frager, Ruth A. *Sweatshop Strife: Class, Ethnicity and Gender in the Jewish Labour Movement of*

Toronto 1900-1939. Toronto: University of Toronto Press. 1992a.

————. "Class and Ethnic Barriers to Feminist Perspectives in Toronto's Jewish Labour Movement, 1919-1939." In *Canadian Working Class History*. Laurel Sefton MacDowell and Ian Radforth, eds. Toronto: Canadian Scholars Press, 1992b.

————. "Class, Ethnicity and Gender in the Eaton Strikes of 1912 and 1934." In *Gender Conflicts: New Essays in Women's History*. Franca Iacovetta and Mariana Valverde, eds. Toronto: University of Toronto Press. 1992c.

————. "Sewing Solidarity: The Eaton's Strike of 1912." *Canadian Woman Studies*, vol. 7, no. 3 (1986): 96-8.

————. "No Proper Deal: Women Workers and the Canadian Labour Movement, 1970-1940." In *Union Sisters*. Linda Briskin and Lynda Yanz, eds. Toronto: Women's Press, 1983.

Fudge, Judy. "The Gendered Dimensions of Labour Law: Why Women Need Inclusive Unionism and Broader-based Bargaining." In *Women Challenging Unions*. Linda Briskin and Patricia McDermott, eds. Toronto: University of Toronto Press, 1993.

————. *Labour Law's Little Sister: The Employment Standards Act and the Feminization of Labour*. Ottawa: Canadian Centre for Policy Alternatives, 1991.

Fudge, Judy, and Patricia McDermott. "Conclusion: Pay Equity in a Declining Economy: The Challenge Ahead." In *Just Wages*. Fudge and McDermott, eds. Toronto: University of Toronto Press, 1991.

Gannage, Charlene. *Double Day, Double Bind: Women Garment Workers*. Toronto: Women's Press, 1986.

Giles, Wenona. "'It's the Foreigners Who Do the Laundry': The Work of Portuguese Chambermaids in London Hotels." In *Maid in the Market*. Wenona Giles and Sedef Arat-Koc, eds. Halifax: Fernwood, 1994.

Golz, Annalee, David Millar, and Barbara Roberts. *A Decent Living: Women Workers in the Winnipeg Garment Industry*. Toronto: New Hogtown Press, 1991.

Gray, Stan. "Hospitals and Human Rights." *Our Times*, vol. 13, no. 6 (1994): 17-20.

Henry, Frances, and Carol Tator. "The Ideology of Racism — 'Democratic Racism.'" *Canadian Ethnic Studies*, vol. 26, no. 2 (1994): 1-14.

Hernandez, Carmencita. "Organizing Domestic Workers." In *Working People and Hard Times*. Robert Argue, Charlene Gannage, and David W. Livingstone, eds. Toronto: Garamond, 1987.

Heron, Craig. *The Canadian Labour Movement*. Toronto: Lorimer, 1989.

Hill, Daniel, and Marvin Schiff. *Human Rights in Canada*, 2nd ed. Ottawa: Canadian Labour Congress, February 1986.

Iacovetta, Franca. "From Contadina to Worker: Southern Italian Immigrant Working Women in Toronto, 1947-1962." In *Canadian Working Class History*. Laurel Sefton MacDowell and Ian Radforth, eds. Toronto: Canadian Scholars Press, 1992.

————. "'Famiglia e Lavoro': The Experience of Southern Italian Immigrant Women in Post-War Toronto." In *Working People and Hard Times*. Argue, Gannage, and Livingstone, eds. Toronto: Garamond, 1987.

Immigrant and Visible Minority Women's Organization. "Brief to the Ontario Employment Equity Commissioner." *Canadian Woman Studies*, vol. 12, no. 3 (1992): 37-8.

Ireland, Ralph. "Some Effects of Oriental Immigration on Canadian Trade Union Ideology." *American Journal of Economics and Sociology*, vol. 19 (1960): 217-20.

Johnson, Laura C., with Robert E. Johnson. *The Seam Allowance: Industrial Home Sewing in Canada*. Toronto: Women's Press, 1982.

Kellahan, Denise, and Jonathan Eaton. "Coffee to Go, Unions to Stay." *Our Times*, vol. 16, no. 2 (March/April 1997): 24-30.

Kilgour, Art. "Talking Youth Talking Union." *Our Times*, vol. 17, no. 4 (July/August 1998): 25-31.

Kobayashi, Audrey. "For the Sake of the Children: Japanese/Canadian Workers/Mothers." In *Women, Work, and Place*. Audrey Kobayashi, ed. Montreal: McGill-Queen's University Press, 1994.

Leah, Ronnie. "Honouring our Stories: Participatory Workshop on Cultural Identity, Aboriginal Peoples and Racism." Circle of Learning: Lethbridge, Alberta. Unpublished Reports. 1998.

————. "Anti-Racism Studies: An Integrative Perspective." *Race, Gender & Class*, vol. 2, no. 3 (1995a): 105-22.

————. "Aboriginal Women and Everyday Racism in Alberta." *The Journal of Human Justice*, vol. 6, no. 2 (1995b): 10-29.

————. "Black Women Speak Out: Racism and Unions." In *Women Challenging Unions*. Linda Briskin and Patricia McDermott, eds. Toronto: University of Toronto Press, 1993.

------, ed. *Taking a Stand: Strategies and Tactics of Organizing the Popular Movement in Canada*. Ottawa: Canadian Centre for Policy Alternatives, 1992.

————. "Linking the Struggles: Racism, Sexism and the Union Movement." In *Race, Class, Gender: Bonds and Barriers*. Jesse Vorst, et al., eds. Toronto: Garamond, 1991.

————. "Organizing for Daycare." In *Working People and Hard Times*. Argue, Gannage, and

Livingstone, eds. Toronto: Garamond, 1987.

Lerner, Stephen. "Let's Get Moving! Organizing for the 90s." *Labor Research Review*, no. 18 (n.d.): 1-15.

Leslie, Genevieve. "Domestic Service in Canada, 1880-1920." In *Women at Work, 1850-1930*. Janice Acton, Penny Goldsmith, and Bonnie Shepard, eds. Toronto: Canadian Women's Educational Press, 1974.

Little, Bruce. "A New Slant on the Benefits of Unionism." *Globe and Mail*, December 29, 1997.

Loewen, Royden. "Jews Inventing Ethnicity? A Review Essay." *Labour/Le Travail*, vol. 35 (Spring 1995): 309-18.

Macklin, Audrey. "On the Outside Looking In: Foreign Domestic Workers in Canada." In *Maid in the Market*. Wenona Giles and Sedef Arat-Koc, eds. Halifax: Fernwood, 1994.

MacLennan, John. "CAW Fights Racism." *Canadian Dimension*, vol. 26, no. 7 (1992): 12-16.

McGrath, Anne, and Dean Neu. "Washing Our Blues Away: The Laundry Workers' Strike." *Our Times*, vol. 15, no. 1 (1996): 25-36.

McIntosh, Peggy. "White Privilege: Unpacking the Invisible Knapsack." *Independent School* (Winter 1990): 31-6.

Modibo, Najja N. "Immigrant Women's Participation in Toronto Union Locals." *Race, Gender & Class*, vol. 2, no. 3 (1995): 83-103.

Muszynski, Alicja. "The Creation and Organization of Cheap Wage Labour in the BC Fishing Industry." Ph.D. Thesis, University of British Columbia, 1988.

Neal, Rusty. "Public Homes: Subcontracting and the Experience of Cleaning." In *Maid in the Market*. Wenona Giles and Sedef Arat-Koc, eds. Halifax: Fernwood, 1994.

Ng, Roxana. "Sexism, Racism, and Canadian Nationalism." In *Race, Class, Gender: Bonds and Barriers*. Jesse Vorst, et al., eds. Toronto: Garamond, 1991.

Ng, Roxana, and Alma Estable. "Immigrant Women in the Labour Force." *Resources for Feminist Research*, vol. 16, no. 1 (1987): 29-33.

Ng, Winnie. "In the Margins: Challenging Racism in the Labour Movement." M.A. Thesis, University of Toronto, Graduate Department of Education, 1995.

———. "The Garment Workers Action Centre." In *Working People and Hard Times*. Argue, Gannage, and Livingstone, eds. Toronto: Garamond, 1987.

Ontario Coalition of Visible Minority Women, Brief to the Ontario Employment Equity Commissioner. *Canadian Woman Studies*, vol. 12, no. 3 (1992): 33-4.

Panitch, Leo, and Donald Swartz. *The Assault on Trade Union Freedoms*. Toronto: Garamond, 1988.

Phillips, Paul. *No Power Greater: A Century of Labour in BC*. Vancouver: BC Federation of Labour Boag Foundation, 1967.

Phillips, Paul, and Erin Phillips. *Women and Work*. Toronto: James Lorimer, 1993.

Pierson, Ruth. "Women's Emancipation and the Recruitment of Women into the Labour Force in World War II." In *The Neglected Majority*. A. Prentice and S. Trofimenkoff, eds. Toronto: McClelland & Stewart, 1977.

Ritche, Laurell. "Why Are So Many Women Unorganized?" In *Union Sisters*. Linda Briskin and Lynda Yanz, eds. Toronto: Women's Press, 1983.

Rachleff, Peter. "Peering into the Crystal Ball: The Future of U.S. Labour." *Canadian Dimension*, vol. 28, no. 4 (1994): 23-5.

Roy, Patricia E. *A White Man's Province*. Vancouver: University of British Columbia Press, 1989.

Sangster, Joan. *Earning Respect: The Lives of Working Women in Small-Town Ontario, 1920-1960*. Toronto: University of Toronto Press, 1995.

Schenk, Chris. "Wanted! New Organizing Everywhere." *Our Times*, vol. 16, no. 4 (July/August 1997).

Seeseequasis, Paul. "Home and Native Lands: Aboriginal Workers and Unions." *Our Times* (August-September 1994): 23-7.

Sugiman, Pamela. *Labour's Dilemma: The Gender Politics of Auto Workers in Canada, 1937-1979*. Toronto: University of Toronto Press, 1994.

Tatroff, Daniel. "Fields of Fear." *Our Times*, vol. 13, no. 6 (1994): 22-7.

Ujimoto, K. Victor, "Racism, Discrimination and Internment: Japanese in Canada." In *Racial Oppression in Canada*. Bolaria and Li, eds. Toronto: Garamond, 1988.

White, Julie. *Sisters and Solidarity: Women and Unions in Canada*. Toronto: Thompson Educational Publishing, 1993a.

———. "Patterns of Unionization." In *Women Challenging Unions*. Briskin and McDermott, eds. Toronto: University of Toronto Press, 1993b.

White, Robert. "Unions and Coalitions: Broadening the Base." *Action Canada Dossier*, no. 37 (1992): 13-14.

Women's Book Committee, Chinese Canadian National Council. *Jin Guo: Voices of Chinese Canadian Women*. Toronto: Women's Press, 1992.

Worker Education Round Table. "Learning by Doing." *Our Times*, vol. 16, no. 5 (September/October 1997): 43-51.

Yee, May. "Chinese Canadian Women: Our Common Struggle." *Canadian Ethnic Studies*, vol. 19, no. 3 (1987a): 174-84.

———. "Out of the Silence: 'Voices of Chinese Canadian Women.'" *Resources for Feminist Research*, vol. 16, no. 1 (1987b): 15-16.

Yalnizyan, Armine, "From the DEW Line: The Experience of Canadian Garment Workers." In *Women Challenging Unions*. Briskin and McDermott, eds. Toronto: University of Toronto Press, 1993.

Documents, Reports, Interviews:
Unions and Community Groups

Canadian Auto Workers (CAW)
205 Placer Court, North York, ON, M2H 3H9

CAW. Peggy Nash, Assistant to the President, CAW. Interview, November, 1992.

CAW. "Building our Union: Solidarity in Diversity: A CAW Affirmative Action Plan." CAW Statement, 3rd Constitutional Convention, Halifax, September 1991.

CAW. "GM-CAW Human Rights Training Program." Workbook for 3-hour course, June 1990.

CAW. *Call Me Sister, Call Me Brother*. Video. 1988.

Human Rights, Workers' Rights: The Same Struggle. CAW Human Rights Course Workbook, 1988.

CAW. "Harrassment in the Workplace." Policy Paper, June 1988.

Canadian Labour Congress (CLC)
Women's and Human Rights Department
2841 Riverside Drive, Ottawa, ON, K1V 8X7

CLC. David Onyalo, National Representative, Women's and Human Rights Department, CLC. Correspondence and communications.

CLC. "Women at Work Everywhere!" CLC Ninth Biennial National Women's Conference. Ottawa, June 1995.

CLC. Submission to the Standing Committee on Human Rights and Status of Disabled Persons (regarding Bill C-64, An Act Respecting Employment Equity, Government of Canada). February 2, 1995.

CLC. "Confronting the Mean Society." Policy Statement, 20th Constitutional Convention, May 1994.

CLC. "Confronting Racism: Strengthening Solidarity." Interim Report, 1994 CLC Human Rights Conference, Ottawa, February-March 1994.

CLC. "Aboriginal Rights and the Labour Movement." Report, November 1993.

CLC. "Organizing for Strength." Report from the 8th Biennial CLC Women's Conference, Saskatoon, June 1993.

CLC. "Building Union Solidarity: Anti-Racism and the Activist." Readings and Resource Materials, February 1993.

CLC. "We Can Do It — Make Human Rights a Priority." Human Rights Policy Statement, Constitutional Convention, June 1992.

CLC. *Out Front*, Fall 1998.

Canadian Union of Public Employees (CUPE)
21 Florence Street, Ottawa, ON, K2P 0W6

CUPE. Muriel Collins, CUPE Local 79 and Chair of CUPE National Women's Committee. Interviews: December 1991; November 1992.

CUPE. Harminder Magon, CUPE Anti-Racism Coordinator. Correspondence and communications.

CUPE. *Anti-Racism Communication* (ARC), published by CUPE's National Rainbow Committee, vol. 1, no. 1 (October 1993).

International Ladies Garment Workers Union (ILGWU)
25 Cecil Street, 2nd floor, Toronto, ON, M5T 1N1

ILGWU. Deena Ladd, Interview: June 1995.

ILGWU. Deena Ladd, "Working with Community in Organizing Drives," OFL Conference on Community Unionism, April 1995.

ILGWU, et al. Conference Handbook Committee, "From the Double Day to the Endless Day."
    Proceedings from the Conference on Homeworking, November 1992, Toronto. Published by
    Canadian Centre for Policy Alternatives, Ottawa, 1992.
ILGWU, et al. "Fair Wages and Working Conditions for Homemworkers": A Brief to the
    Government of Ontario, December, 1991.

Labour Council of Metro Toronto and York Region (LCMT)
Metro Labour Education Centre, Equality Program
1209 King Street West, Suite 201A, Toronto, ON, M6K 1G2

LCMT. Meerai Cho, Equality Program Representative. Interview: June 1995.
LCMT. Challenging Racism — A Course for Unionists, Course Workbook, 1995.
LCMT, et al. Task Force for Anti-Racism Action Centre, "Proposal to Establish Anti-Racism
    Action Centre," Toronto, Summer 1994.
LCMT. "Developing Solidarity with Immigrant Members: A Report on Immigrant Participation
    within Unions," 1986.

Ontario Federation of Labour (OFL)
15 Gervais Drive, Suite 700, Don Mills, ON, M3C 1Y8

OFL. June Veecock, Human Rights Director, OFL. Interviews: October 1988; October 1992.
OFL. *Women's Rights Bulletin*, published bi-monthly by OFL Women's Committee.
OFL. Conference on Community Unionism, 1995.
OFL. *Constitution*, 1993.
OFL. "Challenging Harassment," Policy Statement, 1991.
OFL. "Statement on Equal Action in Employment," Women's Committee and Human Rights
    Committee, 1987.
OFL. "Racism and Discrimination," Policy Statement, 1986.
OFL. "Racism Hurts Everyone," Policy Statement, 1981.
    Ontario Public Service Employees Union (OPSEU)
    Toronto, ON

Ontario Public Service Employees Union (OPSEU)
100 Lesmill Road, North York, ON, M3B 3P8

OPSEU. Yvonne Bobb, President, OPSEU Local 520. Interviews: May 1989; November 1992.
OPSEU. "Racism and Employment Equity." *The Moment*, vol. 6, no. 1 (1992). Published by
    Jesuit Centre, Toronto.

United Steelworkers of America (USWA), District 6
200 Ronson Drive, Suite 607, Etobicoke, ON, M9W 5Z9

USWA. "Let's Talk About Employment Equity: Facts and Myths," Workshop Guides. Conference,
    Summer 1994.
USWA. "Understanding and Fighting Racism in the Workplace," Education Program (one- to
    three-hour course), 1992.
USWA. Solidarity in Diversity: Building a Multicultural Union, Course Workbook (written by M.
    Siemiatycki and P. Idahosa, Ryerson), 1989.
USWA. "Policy to Prohibit and Prevent Sexual Harassment in the Workplace," 1989.
USWA. "Policy to Prohibit and Prevent Racial Harassment in the Workplace," Steelworkers
    National Policy Conference, n.d.
USWA. "Racial and Sexual Harassment and Violence Against Women: Policy and Prevention,"
    Publication, n.d.

Workers Information and Action Centre of Toronto (WIACT)
277 Victoria Street, Suite 102, Toronto, ON, M5B 1W2

WIACT. Pramila Aggerwal, Community Liaison. Interview: June 1995.
WIACT. "Discrimination and Harassment at Work," Pamphlet, n.d.
WIACT. "Working for Dignity: The Employment Standards Act." *The Moment*, vol. 7, no. 2
    (1993). Published by Jesuit Centre, Toronto.

CHAPTER FIVE

Restructuring at the Margins

Women of Colour and the Changing Economy

CHRISTINA GABRIEL

INTRODUCTION

As the 1990s draw to a close it is not uncommon to see news stories with headlines such as "Canadians got poorer in '90s," "The Shrinking Pay Cheque," on the front pages of our national newspapers.[1] These articles are but one small symptom of the profound and dramatic economic changes occurring in Canada. Our economy is rapidly restructuring in response to the mobility of transnational capital, the growth of global markets, the development of new production and distribution techniques, and rapid technological advances.

The processes of "economic restructuring,"[2] however, are not confined solely to the market and are decidedly not neutral. They result in differential outcomes for various groups in society. Feminists have drawn attention to the ways in which gender is deeply implicated in the restructuring process. Different groups of women have been and continue to be unequally incorporated into a labour market constituted by intersecting and multiple social relations, including those of gender, class, 'race,' sexuality, age, disability, among others.

This chapter provides a labour market profile of women of colour[3] in Canada, a profile which is framed within the ongoing and contradictory processes of economic restructuring, and makes two general points. Firstly, it is not possible to develop a profile without considering the position that women in general, and women of colour in particular, play in the new economic order. Secondly, the structural position that many women of colour occupy as a group in the Canadian labour market, makes them vulnerable to some of the more adverse effects of restructuring and adjustment. Given these realties, the outcomes of restructuring will likely lead to a deepening of disparities that already exist among women,[4] which will have significant implications for women's social solidarity in Canada.

SHIFTING CONTEXTS

Canada, in the late 1990s, is experiencing profound economic and political changes forced by what many call the process of globalization. Although ambiguous, this term is frequently invoked to describe "how international developments are influencing domestic economic structures"[5] and to analyze this transformation. It embraces economic, political, and cultural realms.[6] Concepts such as "globalization,"[7] however, frequently neglect to consider the ways in which the changes in the international economy result in differential outcomes for various groups. For some groups, the costs of structural adjustment policies in the South or economic restructuring in the North are social and economic displacement and exclusion. While this claim can be read as suggesting that processes of globalization are inexorable and/or produce overwhelmingly negative adjustment and restructuring effects, I would emphasize the importance of considering the complex and oft contradictory implications that these processes also give rise to.

Recognizing these contradictions forces not only an important re-examination of the terms and conditions of economic restructuring, but can contribute to the development of a viable oppositional politics. The feminist economist, Diane Elson, puts the point simply and clearly:

> Restructuring opens up new opportunities as well as closing old opportunities. Oppressed and disadvantaged groups find that change creates conditions for new forms of struggle. Trying to resist the tide of change and to preserve precrisis social relations rarely works. A more creative approach, that tries to influence the terms of restructuring, to restructure not just production but also social relations, and to create new institutions and organizations of and for oppressed and disadvantaged groups may have more chance of success.[8]

Without minimizing the potential negative outcomes restructuring poses for vulnerable groups, Elson emphasizes the dialectical nature of the process.

A New Economic Order: Reading Globalization

The post-war Canadian economy was characterized by a long period of economic stability, during which the Canadian state adopted a model of economic growth premised on the development of social welfare provisions, macroeconomic stabilization policies, and increased trade with the United States. The Canadian economy, stimulated by keynesian demand management, experienced steady growth rates. By the 1970s there were signs the economy was in trouble.[9] Changes in the international political economy marked the end of the relatively stable post-war economic environment.[10] In the face of these changes, keynesianism unravelled.

Canada was not alone in experiencing economic difficulties. Most governments in the North were forced to confront changes in the international economy. In the South, rises in oil prices were accompanied both by a sudden fall in commodity prices and the adoption of protectionist policies by countries in the North.[11] Most countries were receiving lower prices for their exports but paying higher prices for imports. Interest rates skyrocketed and private lenders disappeared. It became more difficult for countries in the South to borrow money.[12] Many governments turned to the only available lender, the International Monetary Fund. The IMF demanded economic restructuring in the form of structural adjustment packages (SAPs) which imposed strict conditions on borrowing countries aimed at reducing deficits through drastic cuts in government expenditure, public sector employment and in social spending. The stated rationale behind these conditions was the promotion of economic growth, particularly export-led, in the private sector, ensuring a country's economic viability in the form of making debt payments and maintaining good credit.[13]

This rationale informs similar economic policy directions undertaken in Canada in response to changes in the global economy. It reflects the broader transformation underwriting state practices in which "the neo-liberal state is fashioning itself as a market player rather than as the purveyor of public goods or as the instrument of democratic will."[14] Increasingly a "neo-liberal consensus" dominates public policy and governing practices, which, Isabella Bakker argues, has narrowed the range of policy options available to nation states.[15]

More importantly, though market-orientated policies are often presented as "natural," "neutral," "inevitable," or "logical" responses to globalization, feminists have interrogated the quasi-scientific basis of such claims and have found them wanting. Both Isabella Bakker and Marjorie Cohen suggest that these assumptions tend to depoliticize the economic realm describing it as governed by forces over which ordinary people have no control. Marjorie Cohen argues that:

> ....both globalization and restructuring are terms which imply a kind of inevitability to the policy changes which are occurring.... In this sense restructuring appears apolitical and outside the purview of social analysis dealing with gender, class and racial issues.[16]

Current labour market experiences of women, and women's collective organizing in response to economic restructuring, have proved a powerful counterpoint to the assumptions underwriting neo-liberal orthodoxies.

The concept of "labour market flexibility," at the centre of some of these orthodoxies, is frequently presented as a way to respond quickly and rapidly to changes in the global economy. One definition of labour market flexibility stresses "changes in the regulations, contracts, customs and practices that govern the labour market so as to make it easier to hire, and more especially fire, workers."[17] And, as discussed later, the introduction of particular patterns of flexible work has contributed to increasing rates of part-time work and other forms of "non-standard work" in Canada.

The concept of flexibility, as Susan Bullock points out, needs further consideration. On the one hand, the introduction of imposed flexible work patterns can signal an overall deterioration in the conditions of work, pay, and benefits. In this case, flexibility is associated with an employer's bid to reduce costs — based on a low wage strategy — to meet the "imperatives" of the global economy. But, negotiated flexible work patterns can be in the interest of workers:

> Women's groups in the 1960s and 1970s were already arguing that greater flexibility in working hours would benefit workers and their families... Trade unions in industrialized countries now routinely bargain for a range of leave and break arrangements, as well as for reductions in total working hours.[18]

The terms and conditions of labour market flexibility are open to contestation. Sheila Rowbotham and Swasti Mitter emphasize that economic regulation and flexibility have pros and cons for both employers *and* workers. For Rowbotham and Mitter "the key issue is the extent to which poor women are able to gain greater control over their working conditions and more democratic power over state policies." And with regard to flexibility, they point out that the crucial question is "who has the power to decide what kind of flexibility?"[19]

The prevailing view of labour market flexibility favours such measures as repeal of employment standards, lowering wages, weakening collective bargaining provisions, strengthening employer control. It is a definition predicated on neo-liberal orthodoxy which views labour market regulation as a market rigidity. And it is often presented as the only "viable" choice for Canadians to meet the imperatives of the market. Yet, as illustrated above, flexibility can also be defined in terms which do not necessarily increase labour market insecurity.

While responses to changing conditions of globalization, such as flexibilization, are presented as "common sense" and beyond the scope of intervention, feminists have reminded us of the specious nature of such reasoning. Janine Brodie, for example, states neo-liberal assumptions are in fact "impositional claims — assertions about reality which are self-interested, biased, historically-specific, and thus subject to political contestation."[20] This insight is important when considering how processes of globalization and restructuring affect different groups of women. It encourages us to think, not just about the uneven impacts of these processes, but also about the possibilities of developing alternative strategies to ensure equitable outcomes.

Gender and Globalization: "The Third World Woman Worker"

Structural adjustment and restructuring policies are frequently cast in gender-neutral and aggregate terms.[21] Yet, in both the North and South, women, as a group, are more vulnerable to the costs of restructuring. More often than not, women have unequal access to material and political resources, work for lower wages, and their work is often undervalued.[22] The failure of policies to take into account these unequal relations of power has led to a "silencing of women's experiences and strategies of resistance."[23] Feminist insights have demonstrated that we need to consider how gender works within the dynamics of globalization.

In her work on globalization and restructuring, Isabella Bakker emphasizes the need for an approach that uses gender as a category of analysis but contends that:

> Feminist interventions on globalization do not call for an exclusive or

even primary focus on women; rather the goal is to reveal networks of power that are formed by the web of social relations.[24]

This represents an important shift from the tendency to view women's experiences and interests as the same everywhere despite differing class, ethnic, sexual, and racial locations. The rejection of the unitary category "women" is premised on the understanding that subjects have multiple, intersecting, and shifting identifications that are negotiated and transformed in relation to specific historic contexts.[25] This said, M. Jacqui Alexander and Chandra Mohanty make an important point when they argue that while current changes "may suggest more complicated forms of racialized identities, the hierarchical relationship among racial groups and geographies have not disappeared."[26]

Increasingly, many feminists emphasize the need to develop practices and strategies that are structured by coalition, and affinity, rather than identity.[27] However, as Inderpal Grewal and Caren Kaplan assert, forging this type of response demands a re-articulation of how the histories of "people in different locations and circumstances are linked by the spread of and resistance to modern capitalist social formations even as their experiences of these phenomena are not all the same or equal."[28]

In this area both Swasti Mitter and Chandra Mohanty, who have examined the positioning of women of colour in the global economy, make important contributions.[29] Chandra Mohanty argues that "women of colour" or "third world women" may share a common context of struggle. "It is third world women's oppositional *political* relation to sexist, racist, and imperialist structures that constitutes our potential commonality."[30] One potential space for an oppositional cross-national politic is "third world women workers'" experiences of multinational capital. Mohanty argues, "Third-World women workers occupy a specific social location in the international division of labour which *illuminates* and *explains* crucial features of the capitalist processes of exploitation and domination."[31] The "Third World" woman worker[32] can be found in the economies of the both South and North.

Swasti Mitter's work details how women are positioned in the operations of global capital. From the 1960s on, many transnational corporations moved labour-intensive production from the North to the South seeking cheap labour. In the South, governments have encouraged both export-led free trade zones and international subcontracting. The former are areas where raw materials or semi-processed goods are imported, processed into finished products and re-exported. In addition to exemption from duties, governments have added other incentives, including:

> ...provision of an infrastructure, tax-exemption, free repatriation of profits and freedom from foreign exchange controls, provisions of loans at favourable rates of interest and in most cases official discouragement of trade unions.[33]

Swasti Mitter also points out that cheap, young, female labour has been integral to the development and expansion of the free trade zones. A set of gender-based and racially-ascribed characteristics come to the fore. For example, in countries such as Taiwan and Malaysia, women were excluded from many sectors of the labour market and as a result were marginalized from the trade union movement. This, combined with their gender socialization (constructed as "docile") and "ability to work neatly and well (nimble fingers)" rendered them the "ideal worker." Moreover, Taiwanese and Malaysian women were expected to leave the workforce upon marriage.[34]

It is important not to overemphasize the directional nature of the transnational flow of capital, as it is estimated that "three of the four major source nations of transnational investment are also the major hosts of foreign direct investment"[35] and the numbers of women employed by multinationals in the countries of the South account for only a small proportion of the total female labour forces in these countries.[36] Yet, as Susan Bullock points out, we need to recognize that the effect of this type of investment goes beyond numbers alone, to include:

- The numbers of people, especially women, who work indirectly for foreign and global companies far exceeds those counted in the workforce
- The concessions made by government...and the fragmentation of work-places and workforces, have also had a significant negative impact on the development of trade unionism and the application of labour standards throughout the formal sectors of a number of countries.[37]

Mitter emphasizes how new patterns of work organization that characterize the new global economy have led to an increasing casualization of women's labour, including decentralized patterns of work organization — like flexible specialization — in the South and North.[38] Flexible specialization means large corporate organizations subcontracting much of their work to smaller subcontractors. As Mitter points out, workers in small subcontracting units are often entitled to fewer benefits and do not enjoy the same standard of legal employment protection.[39]

The growth of international subcontracting has led to an increase in the numbers of women working in home-based work which was encouraged by governments in the South, in part as a "cost-effective way of creating additional employment."[40] Homeworkers produce a range of goods for both domestic and international markets. A 1989 International Labour Organization (ILO) study reported:

> International sub-contracting is an important feature of homework and characterized by a long chain of contractors. Each contractor in the chain receives a commission which in some countries is 20-30% of the unit price. This means that for a baby's dress, for example, which sells for $15 in a department store in North America or Western Europe, the local producer who made it may get less than 10 cents.[41]

Researchers have documented a variety of goods produced under these conditions, from rattan furniture makers in the Phillipines to Indian women homeworkers producing footwear and lace.[42] Homeworking is a significant part of women's employment in the South. It is also an increasing feature of women's employment in countries of the North. In Canada, too, the "Third World" woman worker plays a key role. As Swasti Mitter states, in the countries of the North "it is the immigrants from the developing countries that get readily recruited into this form of clandestine work."[43]

Both Chandra Mohanty and Swasti Mitter emphasize potential links between "third world" women workers in the North and South. Chandra Mohanty highlights the differently located and specific positions occupied by lacemakers in India, electronic workers in the Silicon Valley, California, and migrant workers in Britain, to move toward defining the "common interests of Third-World women workers based on theorizing the common social identity of Third-World women as women/workers."[44] She argues for a consideration of the "process of gender and race domination" as opposed to the "content of 'Third World'"[45] and in doing so rejects:

> ...ahistorical notions of the common experience, exploitation, or strength of Third-World women or between third- and first-world women, which serve to naturalize normative Western feminist categories of self and other. If Third-World women are to be seen as the subjects of theory and of struggle, we must pay attention to the specificities of their/our common and different histories.[46]

This analysis is predicated on understanding the social identity of women as workers as not only class-based but located in gendered and racialized hierarchies.[47] Mohanty and Mitter's work is important insofar as it highlights the varying position(s) women of colour occupy within a changing global economy. Their insights offer a useful starting point for considering the labour market position of women of colour in Canada.

THE NATIONAL ECONOMY:
FEDERAL-PROVINCIAL POLICY RESPONSES

There is a tendency in assessments of globalization to focus on the international system and obscure the economic dynamics of specific national contexts. However, as Isabella Bakker argues, the outlines of the new global order are not yet fixed.

> ...it is crucial to distinguish between, on the one hand, the neo-liberals deterministic sense of system convergence that envisages the decline of nation states' political agency, and, on the other hand, the reality of national political economies continuing to strive to re-regulate and attenuate the disruption caused by various forces of globalization.[48]

In Canada, policy responses to changes in the global economic environment have, by and large, been informed by neo-liberal rationales. These rationales have helped to foster a "competitive" environment which has both shifted the balance of labour market power to the employer and actively encouraged the rise of particular kinds of flexible labour practices. The latter patterns of work have tended to polarize the labour market. The rise of non-standard working practices, especially subcontracting, have had a greater impact on some groups in Canadian society than on others. As the labour force becomes increasingly casualized, "economic and social vulnerability" arising from gender, class and 'race' will be exacerbated.[49] The nature of some of these policy directions and their relation to the labour market is worth scrutiny.

Commentators have focused on the apparent shift of power from the nation-state to transnational corporations.

> To compete for transnational investment, nation states and governments (including Canada) have surrendered some of their key sovereign powers and strategic policy tools required to improve the economic, social and environmental living conditions of their own citizens.[50]

What is actively promoted by government policies is export-led growth through a set of initiatives including regional trade integration, and deregulation of foreign investment and national economies. Alongside these policies are initiatives designed to enhance Canada's business climate: reduction of debt through cuts in social spending and public sector retrenchment, as well as the cuts in public revenue through lower corporate taxes and high interest rates.[51]

These initiatives are predicated on the assumption that social security provisions distort market forces, increase labour costs and deter investment. This reasoning informs the policy prescriptions of the Organization for Economic Co-operation and Development (OECD). Its 1994 *Jobs Study*, for example, suggested that unemployed workers — numbering some 50 million people in twenty-four OECD countries — adapt to the changing economy by "pricing themselves into jobs." Essentially, the jobless should be willing to accept lower paying jobs with less benefits. The OECD advised its member countries to adopt market-based solutions by "giving more weight to the market clearing role of wages" by limiting the extension of collective agreements, modifying minimum wage laws and removing the "disincentives to hiring" that result from social programs.[52] In varying degrees the Federal government and its provincial counterparts have moved in these directions.

Federal Policies
Trade Liberalization

At the forefront of the federal government's economic strategy is trade liberalization. In theory, each country seeks to maximize its comparative advantage through international trade, producing goods in which they have a comparative advantage — goods they can produce more cheaply than other countries — and exporting them. In turn, they pay lower prices for goods from abroad, because the goods for sale are those which are cheaper to produce abroad.[53]

In rapid succession Canada has entered into a number of trade and investment agreements that have intensified processes of regionalization and globalization. In 1988, Canada entered the Free Trade Agreement (CUFTA) with the United States.[54] Four years later, Canada entered into the wider North American Free Trade Agreement (NAFTA) which incorporated Mexico.[55] And, more recently, the government has participated in trade and economic forums such as the Asia Pacific Economic Cooperation (APEC) and entered negotiations on the Multilateral Agreement on Investment (MAI).[56]

As Canada pursues trade liberalization and seeks to maximize its export markets, it is inevitable that some industries and sectors will decline. Industries and sectors in which Canada does not have a comparative advantage can expect to see significant job loss. The trade-led adjustment that took place in the wake of the free trade agreement saw many American firms, and some Canadian-owned ones, re-evaluate their commitment to manufacturing in Canada. Increasingly, many moved to take advantage of lower wages, lower taxes, weaker and non-enforced labour, and environmental laws in the United States, especially the southern states, and in Mexico[57] These types of decisions, combined with 1990-1992 recession, resulted in large-scale job losses in the manufacturing sector. Competition from low wage areas — as well as corporate threats to relocate — have been key elements, not only in job losses, but in the weakening of rights and benefits of those on the lower rungs of labour market in many industrialized countries.

Consequently, the CUFTA and NAFTA, while frequently presented as necessary agreements about such matters as tariffs and import quotas, go much beyond this.[58] Ricardo Grinspun and Robert Kreklewich have suggested that such agreements

> ...serve as a new form of conditionality that is being applied to restructure state-civil society relations in both industrialized and less developed economies. The main argument is that FTAs such as CUFTA and NAFTA serve as 'conditioning frameworks' to promote and consolidate neoliberal restructuring. Both the negotiation and the implementation of an FTA modify the conditions under which economic and social decision making is conducted domestically.[59]

Marjorie Cohen further points out that the institutionalization of the 'unfettered' market mechanism implies negative outcomes for women and disadvantaged groups because "economic and social policies designed precisely to counter market forces are being abandoned in favour of the marketization process."[60]

For example, federal and provincial social policies such as unemployment insurance, employment standards provisions, and social assistance insulated Canadians from the insecurities of the market. These protections are being eroded and stripped away. Marjorie Cohen emphasizes that the harmonization pressures of the FTA, NAFTA, and GATT have profound implications for Canadian economic and social programs.[61] Indeed, the demand for a "level playing field" was held by advocates of free trade as a necessity to ensure access to markets. The trajectory of Canada's Unemployment Insurance (UI) — now referred to as Employment Insurance — supports Marjorie Cohen's assessment.

In comparison to their counterparts in the U.S. and Mexico, Canadian workers enjoyed more generous unemployment insurance provisions. Mexican workers did not have a plan. The Ecumenical Council for Social Justice reports that when the FTA agreement took effect in 1989, 87 percent of unemployed Canadians qualified for benefits compared to only 52 percent of U.S. workers. As of October 1996 only 42 percent of Canadians qualified for UI.[62] Further new regulatory changes regarding eligibility — the "hours system" — were introduced. Since more women tend to work part-time than men, many of those affected were women. The outcome of cuts to programs such as Unemployment Insurance is to shift the balance of labour market power to employers.

The neo-liberal policy agenda embarked upon by the federal government has contributed towards an "employers' market characterized by low-wage labour and a flexible labour force."[63] In many ways, this agenda has also been followed by provincial administrations. The policies of the current government of Ontario provide a provincial example of this agenda in action.[64]

Provincial Policies

The influence of neo-liberalism in power is exemplified by Mike Harris' Tories who swept into power in Ontario in June 1995 on an electoral platform they called "The Common Sense Revolution." While the Tories campaigned on promises to "limit" and "downsize" the government along with personal income tax cuts, their agenda was much more sweeping than this. Once in power, Harris' Tories embarked on a series of legislative changes designed to "Open Ontario for Business."[65] It is beyond the scope of this section to outline all these changes and their implications.[66] However, a number had direct labour market consequences and it is useful to consider these briefly.

Public Sector Retrenchment

Public sector retrenchment is at the fore of efforts to "streamline" public expenditures. It signals cuts to health, welfare, education as well as the public service. The Ontario government enacted massive spending cuts, including $800 million in education, $1.3 billion in hospital spending, and $1.4 billion in transfers to municipalities.[67] By the government's own estimates, the public sector would be reduced by more than 10,000 jobs by 1997-1998.[68] It has been suggested that by the end of the Conservatives first term in office, 70,000 public sector jobs will have been cut.[69]

It has been argued that women are particularly hard hit by such measures. Firstly, there are direct implications for women's labour market status. Traditionally, the public sector — education, health, and social services — has been an important site of women's employment. Jobs in the public sector have been characterized by higher wages and benefits than those in the private sector.[70] Women in public sector unions broke new ground campaigning for such measures as strong maternity provisions, same-sex benefits and parental leave for lesbian employees, and the right to refuse work because of sexual or racial harassment.[71]

Moreover, job losses will be most acute for those recently- hired, working in temporary or short-term contract positions. This is more likely to affect some groups of people within the public sector than others. For example, the Ontario Government's *Employment Equity — Annual Report, 1991-1992*, offered a profile of the provincial civil service. It reported that designated groups — women, racial minorities, francophones, aboriginal peoples, and peoples with disabilities — were all overrepresented in the unclassified service of the government's workforce. Aboriginal workers experienced the highest rates of overrepresentation.[72] Unclassified service refers to temporary or seasonal work and therefore these groups were all more vulnerable than "classified" or full-time permanent workers to the subsequent and accelerated downsizing that took place under Harris.

Direct job losses are only part of the story of public sector retrenchment. Governments at both the federal and provincial levels are moving toward dismantling the collective institutions of social reproduction. Ontario has enacted widespread health care restructuring and closed several hospitals. In terms of child care, the Ontario Federation of Labour reported in 1996:

- 4,743 spaces lost in Metro Toronto,
- closed 19 municipal child care programs,
- frozen subsidized intake for 12 regions,
- 30,000 parents are on the waiting list for a subsidized space.[73]

It is assumed that the care deficit will be borne by families, as provisions of community care are dismantled. Some families will be able to afford privatized options. In some cases, women will purchase the services of other women as domestics. Many of the latter will be women of colour who have come to Canada under inequitable immigration programs (discussed elsewhere in the book). But, in other cases, the costs will be borne by individual women as they are chiefly responsible for family care. As a result women may "choose" to leave the labour market or interrupt their careers. One study "reported that one in three caregivers had either quit or adjusted their jobs to fit with their responsibilities for older family members."[74] In either case, there are long-term negative effects for women on pay, pensions, and career prospects.

Labour Market Regulation

The Ontario Conservatives attributed the province's high rates of unemployment to the overregulation of the labour market, rather than to free trade or related processes of economic restructuring. The previous NDP administration (1990-1995) had introduced measures such as anti-scab provisions that prohibited the hiring of replacement workers during strikes, the right to organize and picket on third party property such as shopping malls, and proposals to make it easier to organize labour unions.[75] The Harris administration moved quickly to repeal these measures.

The new Minister of Labour introduced Bill 7 (*Labour Relations and Employment Statute Law Amendment Act*) saying the Act was a way "to restore balance and stability to labour relations and to promote economic prosperity."[76] However, one unionized worker offered a more perceptive view:

> Bill 40 used to protect workers a little bit.... The company can turn around and bring in labourers, and that causes civil strife right here. And it causes a fight between two people who shouldn't be fighting each other. And who pits them against each other but the government itself which eliminated Bill 40, and the owners of big businesses, who want to turn around and use people against each other.[77]

The government's agenda also introduced workplace productivity goals, Workers Compensation Board reform, elimination of Employers Health Tax for small- to medium-sized establishments, and the removal of the Workplace Health and Safety Agency.[78] The minimum wage was frozen at $6.85 for five years.

The minimum wage has been identified as a measure that offers some degree of protection to low-wage earners. Women, young workers, and recent immigrants constitute the majority of workers who have relied on employment standards protections such as the minimum wage.[79] In terms of the incidence of low-paid employment, 1994 OECD figures, for example, indicate 34.3 percent for Canadian women are in low-paid employment — a figure second only to Japan.[80] In freezing minimum wage levels, the Ontario government has accepted the market rationale that minimum employment standards limit businesses ability to compete in the global economy. And, while not abolishing minimum wage outright, the government will effectively reduce employers' labour costs because the wage will be eroded through inflation. Freezing the minimum wage in Ontario will consequently result in wage deterioration for the most vulnerable of the province's workers, the working poor.

Equity Initiatives

The "Common Sense Revolution" also vigorously attacked the limited gains women had made, by reducing government interventions in the labour market. Through Bill 26, the *Omnibus Bill*, the Ontario government sought to limit the scope of pay equity by eliminating the proxy method of comparison. This method allowed the provisions of pay equity to be extended to female-dominated workplaces such as nursing homes, childcare centres, and social services organizations. Within such establishments it was difficult to claim pay equity adjustments, because there often was no appropriate "male comparator" necessary for pay equity comparisons. The proxy method offered a means of determining equitable pay for those women who most needed it. Through the government's actions, some 100,000 women stood to lose $81 million in pay equity payments. The government insisted that low wages are determined by the market and a direct comparison between men and women's jobs was not possible.[81] While the government attacked the provisions of pay equity and the scope of its coverage, it did not repeal the *Pay Equity Act* outright.

The same is not true of Ontario's *Employment Equity Act* 1993, which attempted to address processes of systemic discrimination that disadvantaged various groups — women, Aboriginal peoples, people with disabilities, and racial minorities — experience in the labour market, by ensuring that ability and qualifications were the only criteria for jobs, promotion, and benefits. While the legislation was weak, it did force employers to embark on a process of examining barriers to hiring and promoting for the four designated groups. The legislation called on employers to set their *own* numerical goals and required them to show *reasonable progress* toward the achievement of a representative workplace.[82] Once in power, the Harris government moved quickly to repeal Employment Equity through Bill 8, *The Job Quotas Repeal Act.*

Both pay equity and employment equity were designed to help various groups, including women, achieve economic equality. The repeal of the latter, in particular, "counters the spirit and intent of past legislation which recognized racism as a systematic rather than individualized component of Ontario society."[83] The retreat from workplace equity will have consequences for many women of colour as systemic discrimination will likely be deepened and entrenched. And this takes place in a context of rapid restructuring of the labour market and the growing increase in precarious, low-paid jobs.

Backlash

The neo-liberal agenda pursued by the Harris government has both opened the province for business and shifted the balance of labour market power to employers. The administration's policy directions and public rhetoric also generated a social climate of profound divisiveness, what Judy Rebick refered to as a "politics of polarization," used to distract people from the real issues at hand "by turning citizens' anger against poor people, the Harris government will attempt to sidetrack people from his real agenda — to increase benefits for the already rich people."[84] In a similar vein, Trickey points out that the neo-conservative agenda is premised on "domination" and "blaming." Economic insecurity has provided "a fertile terrain for ideologically constructing 'other' people as drains on the system, special interests groups, or as illegitimate or fraudulent immigrants."[85] These policy directions constitute a backlash against both progressive groups working for social equity and members of disadvantaged groups such as the poor, single mothers on social assistance, immigrants, and refugees.

In sum, state responses to the processes of globalization in the economic arena have by and large been an invocation of the market. The new buzz words of the 1980s have been competitiveness and flexibility. Countries in both the North and South are seeking to secure comparative advantage to compete in the global economy. Firms and sectors have sought to adapt to a changing world economic order by adopting flexible labour practices to improve their competitive position.

Competition, however, also takes place between groups and individuals within the labour market.[86] Indeed, the neo-liberal agenda, pursued in Ontario, for example, has added to the labour market insecurity of many workers. Some groups in Canada are better positioned to confront the outcomes of economic restructuring. But for those workers already positioned at the margins of the labour market, the new workplace reality may well be characterized by low-paid, non-standard work. For many women, especially women of colour, the costs of restructuring are high, as an analysis of the Canadian labour market will show.

THE DYNAMICS OF THE CANADIAN LABOUR MARKET[87]

Through statistical indicators a labour market profile of women can be developed, illustrating the specific ways in which, even in a gender-segregated market, many groups of women are positioned — albeit in shifting and varying ways — on its margins. This statistical overview largely draws on Statistics Canada terms. It is important to emphasize here that "Aboriginal," "immigrant" and "visible minority" women are not homogeneous blocs. Within each group are women of various social classes, different life histories and backgrounds. Further, membership in the category "immigrant" or "visible minority" is not necessarily a predicator of labour market disadvantage. And, while many recent immigrants are members of visible minorities, not all immigrant women are "visible minorities," nor are all "visible minorities" immigrants. This review of the ways in which women of colour are included in (and excluded from) the labour market need also consider some social representations of women of colour which structure their position in the labour market, and some of the structural factors contributing to labour market disadvantage.

Categorizations

In Canada, various categorizations function as devices to socially regulate women of colour, including, but are not limited to, "visible minority women" and "immigrant women." It is important to draw the distinction between the construction of a discursive category such as "immigrant women" and actual immigrant women themselves who are historical agents with diverse and complex backgrounds.[88] These social representations are nonetheless significant in their affect on the labour market experiences of women of colour.

Some feminists in Canada have attempted to highlight how racialized discourses interact with those of gender and class in varying social representations of women of colour. Himani Bannerji, in particular, dissects the apparently official category of "visible minority" and finds it wanting.

> This category "visibility" and the construction of one's self as a "minority" (a suffered member of society, even though a citizen and socially productive) are ways of rendering people powerless and vulnerable. They work as operative categories not because they possess any truth, but because they enforce the racist and imperialist relations which are already in place.[89]

Similarly, Dionne Brand's work dissects constructions of Black women which, she argues, occur in the way that patriarchy, class, and race intersect to produce an oppression particular to Black women.

> There is a historical characterization of Black women as fit for any kind of work — except for the jobs that white men want. We have always done manual work, i.e. "non-traditional" work. Our history knows no category called "women's work"; there is "white men's work," "white women's work," and "nigger work." "Nigger work" has its roots in slavery in the "new world," and in the ascriptions of less-than-human characteristics to Black peoples as a whole.[90]

Brand demonstrates that the types of work Black women actually do today and the types of work ascribed to them have not changed significantly from the time of enslaved labour. For example, the fact that many Black women are nurses or nursing aides in Toronto reflects, she argues, "a trajectory from maid/servant/ domestic help to helping, caring subordinates."[91]

Roxanna Ng specifically examines the ways that women of colour are con-structed as "immigrant women" through the activities of employment counsel-lors, and become a special type of labour market "commodity":

> In everyday life, when we think of an immigrant woman, we have an image of a woman who does not speak English properly, who is a member of a minority group, notably from the Third World, and who has a certain location in the labour market (i.e., as a sewing machine operator or a cleaning lady).[92]

The social representations of women of colour as exemplified by "visible mi-nority," "Black," or "immigrant women" are "common sense" notions that domi-nant culture "knows" about women of colour. As such, they also constitute im-portant sites of political struggle as women of colour seek to subvert such representations. They are also racialized and gendered categories that structure the labour market position of women of colour when the assumptions behind these categories operate directly and indirectly in the areas of education, training, and employment.

Economic Indicators[93]

Within the labour market, women of colour experience simultaneously racialized and gendered forms of class oppression. Women of colour do tend to share labour market characteristics very similar to those of other women, such as occupational segregation. However, labour market facts that focus on the category "woman" tend to underplay the extent to which differences among women may contribute to differences in labour market participation, work experience, earnings, and unemployment. Thus even within a gender-segregated labour market, women of colour may often be further disadvantaged than other women. A review of indica-tors such as participation, education, underemployment, earnings, and occupations reveals the degree to which some groups of women are marginalized in the labour market. What follows is a brief overview of the changing face of the Canadian labour market emphasizing the position of immigrants,[94] visible minority women and Aboriginal women.[95]

At the Margins of the Labour Force

The entry of women into the labour force — either working or looking for work — is among one of the most significant social changes of the post-war period. In Canada and other industrialized economies, female participation rates are on the rise, while male participation rates are declining. For example, the number of employed women in Canada, aged 15 and over, has been increasing from 42 percent in 1976 to 52 percent in 1994. In the same period, employment among men decreased from 73 percent in 1976 to 65 percent in 1994.

Statistics Canada reports that the participation rate for visible minority women and others was the same (59 percent). "Filipino women (72 percent) were most likely to be in the labour force, followed by Blacks (64 percent) and Pacific Islanders (62 percent). Participation rates were lowest among West Asian and Arab (50 percent) and South East Asian and Latin American (each 52 percent) women."[96] It has been suggested that their relatively recent arrival to Canada is one factor that may account for the lower participation rates for Latin Americans and South East Asians, as well as West Asians and Arabs.[97]

Employment and Unemployment

The importance of women in the labour market is reflected in their increasing weight in employment. In 1991, 52.8 percent of women age 15 or over were employed. Employment levels vary among different groups of women. For example, 54.7 percent of Canadian-born, 50.4 of immigrants, 55.6 percent of those in a visible minority, and 47 percent of Aboriginals were employed in 1991. Recent women immigrants are less likely to be employed than those women with longer Canadian residence.[98]

Since the mid-1960s, unemployment has continued to rise for men and women. Through the 1980s unemployment was high. Initially women (8.4 percent) experienced higher levels of unemployment than their male counterparts (6.9 percent). This situation has been reversed in the 1990s. In 1991, 9.7 percent of women were unemployed versus 10.9 percent of men. High unemployment rates for particular groups can also signal difficulty in integrating into the labour market. Data indicates some groups of women experience higher levels of unemployment than the female population as a whole. In 1991, the unemployment rate for those aged 15 and over was 10.7 percent for immigrant women, 13.4 percent for visible minority women, and 17.7 percent for Aboriginal women.

Education

Women's employment prospects — and by corollary women's ability to adjust to a changing economy — are markedly increased with educational attainment. "It has been estimated that 15.5 percent of all new jobs created between 1986 and the year 2,000 will require more than 12 years of education and training and an additional 48.8 percent will require 17 or more years of education and training."[99] In 1991, 10 percent of women aged 15 and over were university graduates compared with 13 percent of men. However, even with post-secondary training women are somewhat less likely than men to be employed.

The educational attainment of recent immigrants has been described as "polarized." A higher proportion of them are university graduates than among Canadian-born but the proportion of this group with relatively little education is also higher than Canadian born.[100]

Similarly, visible minorities are more likely to have a university degree than other adults. In 1991, 15 percent of visible minority women age 15 and over were university graduates, as were 21 percent of their male counterparts. Visible minority women were also more likely than other women and non-visible minority men to have degrees. As discussed below, despite their education levels, visible minority men and women are less likely than other people with degrees to be employed in higher paying professional or managerial occupations. In the case of Aboriginal women aged 15 and over only 6 percent had a university degree compared to 13 percent of non-Aboriginal women. Aboriginal women are also more likely than other women to have less than a high school diploma.

Women as a whole are also less likely to benefit from further education and training programs. Public training programs may often be designed to meet short-term needs, such as those of the recently unemployed. Barbara Cameron details the gendered impacts of the 1985 Canadian Jobs Strategy and 1990 Federal Labour Force Development Strategy (LFDS).[101] Changes under the LFDS effectively shifted funding responsibility for training from the Federal government to the Unemployment Insurance Fund. As a result, women who were previously eligible for training — those entering or re-entering the labour force — were now excluded. Barbara Cameron's data indicates that the shifts in funding resulted in a 30 percent reduction in spending on women's training programs between 1987/1988 and 1991/1992. This decline is part of a more general trend away from targeting spending to designated equity groups under the Canadian Jobs Strategy (CJS). She reports,

> ...women's share of total CJS spending dropped 53.8% in 1987/1988 to 33.9% in 1991/1992. The drop in expenditures for visible minorities between 1989/90 and 1991/92 was from 7% to 5%; for persons with disabilities, from 3% to 2.4%; and for aboriginal people from 9% to 8%.[102]

The design and criteria of other programs also prove problematic for women. For example, courses may be held at inconvenient times, require basic entry qualifications and/or not offer childcare facilities or subsidies for childcare. These same barriers are also characteristic of firm- or sector-specific training. In this case, women can also miss out, because they lack seniority. Women who are working part-time or on contract are often ineligible for these programs. Additionally, many women work in small establishments and these employers may lack resources and facilities to provide adequate job training.[103]

These problems are further compounded for different groups of women. In the area of formal education, feminists have waged numerous struggles to secure equal access, influence curriculum content, and change practices. However, as Ruth Roach Pierson acknowledges, "we have been slow to respond to the demands for change...to meet the educational needs of more marginalized girls and women."[104]

In other cases, women's immigrant status proves to be problematic. In 1992, 44.7 percent of female immigrants came to Canada under the provisions of the family class. Until very recently, immigration entry status affected the ability of an individual to access language training.[105] The National Action Committee on the Status of Women has pointed out that federal government cuts to English as a Second Language (ESL) programs have left many women unable to move out of the periphery of the labour market.[106] The employment opportunities of those women with little or no knowledge of either official language are limited. Further, as Monica Boyd has argued, language plays an important role in allocating workers to the formal and informal sectors of the Canadian labour market.

> The lower participation rate of women who do not know English or French may be an accurate portrayal of participation in the formal economy but it may not measure all income generating activity.[107]

Boyd suggests that these women may find work in the invisible economy as domestic workers and homeworkers. However, the nature of the invisible economy makes it difficult to ascertain the size and scope of this participation. Her findings lead her to conclude "that not knowing one of the official languages is associated with a high degree of occupational and industrial concentration for both men and women [however] it is women who bring home less and have higher unemployment rates.[108]

The issue of accreditation also contributes to the labour market disadvantage many recent immigrants — both men and women — experience.[109] The problem stems from the fact that many have professional or trades accreditation in their country of origin that may not be recognized in Canada. Lawyers, doctors, engineers, accountants, and many trades are among the regulated occupations affected. The Ontario Coalition of Agencies Serving Immigrants (OCASI) identified some of the barriers related to accreditation including:

> ...requirement for Canadian experience, levels of English language fluency which have little relationship to the language needs of a job, and the lack of appropriate mechanisms for ensuring fair and equitable assessment of prior learning, experience and qualifications.

OCASI also pointed out that these barriers, "impede an immigrant's ability to practice the profession or trade for which she or he had been trained."[110]

In sum, women are less likely to benefit from further education and training. And even when they do, they still have to compete in a labour market that recruits and allocates jobs on the basis of intersecting social relations, including those of gender and "race." For some groups of women, educational streaming, rigid admission requirements to training programs, accreditation, and inadequate language programs act as barriers that further contribute to their disadvantaged position in the labour market.

Unpaid Work

The sexual division of labour reinforces women's disadvantaged position in the labour market. As women entered the labour force, they have had to cope with the conflicting demands of employment and family responsibilities. Many women are being pressured to take on added responsibilities as the state withdraws from the provision of collective social care. Women have chosen to negotiate their conflicting roles in a number of ways. Some delay or don't have children. Others rely on family networks. Part-time work and job-sharing are often employment options. Those women with financial resources will hire other women to look after children, the elderly, and people with disabilities.

The demand for live-in domestic workers has risen dramatically. Increasingly, the women hired as live-in domestics, come from the Third World under the provisions of the Live-In Caregiver Program. This "privatized" state-supported solution is particularly problematic. Sedef Arat-Koc neatly encapsulates this when she argues that:

> Rather than solving the problem of gender inequality, it adds class and racial dimensions to it. Instead of housework and childcare being the responsibility of *all* women, it becomes the responsibility of *some* with subordinate class, racial and citizenship status, who are employed and supervised by those who are liberated from the direct physical burdens. By reinforcing divisions of mental and manual labour, this helps perpetuate low status and low pay for domestic service.[111]

The restructuring of the labour market means that more and more women will be drawn into both the formal and informal economy. This will happen in a context in which they will remain chiefly responsible for the domestic sphere and while the state is actively dismantling the collective institutions of social reproduction. Within this context, the increasing use of third world women's labour will allow some women to climb the professional ladder and secure high-paying, high-status jobs. In this case "one women is exercising class and citizenship privilege to buy her way out of sex oppression."[112]

The Reconstitution of the Labour Market: New Employment Patterns
From Goods-Producing to Service-Producing

At one time, Canada's industrial structure was dominated by goods-producing industries. Before World War Two, over 60 percent of the employed population worked in agriculture, fishing and hunting, forestry and logging, mining, manufacturing, utilities and constructions. This proportion has been gradually dropping and service industries expanding. Only 27 percent of employed people in 1993 were working in goods-producing industries.[113] Jobs in goods-producing industries have been particularly hard hit by changes in the global economy. "In 1992, there were 458,000 fewer people with full-time work than was the case in 1990. Ninety-six per cent of full-time job loss was in the goods-producing industries and three quarters of these jobs belonged to men."[114]

Women also lost jobs in goods-producing sectors.[115] Pat Armstrong reports that "two-thirds of women employed in the goods producing industries were employed in manufacturing and women in these industries saw their unemployment rate rise by three percentage points between 1990 and 1992."[116] Most of the women's jobs lost would be those held by immigrant women, as they account for more than two-fifths of the women working in product manufacturing.[117]

More specifically, women's employment in clothing manufacturing suffered under the impact of trade liberalization. Marjorie Cohen's work demonstrates that in the first three years of Free Trade, women's employment in manufacturing decreased by over 11 percent. The biggest job losses for women were in clothing (a 20 percent decline).[118] A high proportion of this workforce are women: three out of four workers as compared to one out of four in all other manufacturing industries. But in addition to this, a significant proportion have low levels of education and/or difficulties with English and French.[119]

The clothing industry has seen considerable job losses as a result of either plant closure or production shifts to low-wage areas in the U.S. or Mexico. In addition to job losses, there has also been a downward pressure on wages and working conditions. A substantial portion of what is now produced in Canada is produced by homeworkers working for wages below the minimum standards.[120]

As the goods-producing sector has contracted there has been significant expansion in the service sector. For every woman working in the goods sector, six work in the service sector.[121] The growth of service industries and the decline of others has produced an increase in women's employment in service industries. However, as Pat Armstrong points out, many of these new jobs are "what the Economic Council of Canada terms 'bad jobs', jobs that offer little security, little opportunity for promotion, little economic reward and require few recognized skills."[122] Female employment is characterized both by segregation in terms of the sectors in which women work and in terms of the jobs they do.

Occupational Segregation

Despite increases in women's education, labour force participation, and length of time in the workforce, women as a group remain segregated by gender. This remains a source of labour market inequality. Different value is attached to men and women's jobs. Female-dominated jobs are often characterized by low status, poor wages, and limited potential for acquisition of skills, training, or career advancement.

The majority of women work in either teaching, nursing and health-related occupations, clerical positions, or sales and service occupations. In 1994, 70 percent of all employed women worked in these occupations. A full 54 percent of employed women worked in clerical, sales, or service jobs. The broad occupational patterns of employed immigrant, visible minority, and Aboriginal women tended to mirror that of women as a whole. For example, in 1991, 53 percent of employed female immigrants worked in clerical, sales, or service jobs compared to 48 percent of employed visible minority women and 52 percent of employed Aboriginal women.

Clerical work is one of the largest single occupational categories in Canada. There is a restructuring of clerical employment as a consequence of the introduction of new technologies, the integration of managerial/professional positions with higher level clerical occupations and the growth of more routine computer-related jobs, such as data entry.[123] These trends, Marcy Cohen states, have led to a polarization in clerical employment.

> Given that there are a limited number of senior positions and given that employers are hiring college graduates to fill these positions, the professionalization of clerical work has pushed older, often less-educated women and women with family responsibilities further down the occupational ladder.... These women are increasingly ghettoized in data entry and what remained of routine manual work.[124]

The Canadian Labour Congress (CLC) reports that: "the number of full-time clerical jobs fell by 13% between 1990 and 1995."[125] A Toronto study of labour adjustment issues facing clerical workers offered this profile of Metro Toronto's 185,900 clerical workers:

> Most of them are women (over 80 percent); many are of different racial and ethnic origins; and almost two-thirds have high school or less educational background. Clerical workers are one of the five least well-paid occupations.[126]

Given the suggested correlation between education and higher status clerical jobs it is likely the adjustment process will be difficult for this group of workers.

Women have, however, increased representation in professional fields. Much has been made of the fact that more women have joined the ranks of the 25 highest paid professions between 1990 and 1995.[127] For example, in the period between 1986 and 1991 the number of women lawyers and notaries jumped by 71 percent.[128] Data indicates women now account for 42 percent of those employed in management and administrative positions. This is an increase from 29 percent in 1982. And there were more women employed in social sciences or religion, 56 percent of professionals compared to 43 percent in 1982.[129] Yet these figures can be deceptive.

Such gains are realized by some professional women, generally those with recognized experience and educational requirements. Moreover, of the professional jobs held by women, half were in traditional areas such as teaching and health care, and women were still seriously underrepresented in the fields of science, engineering, and mathematics.[130] As the National Action Committee on the Status of Women (NAC) wrote in its 1993 review:

> Although it may be true that very few high-profile, well educated, mostly white women are faring somewhat better in the workforce than twelve years ago...conditions for the vast majority of women who remain outside of professional work are worsening.[131]

Among the groups 'outside' are Aboriginal women, who are somewhat less likely than other women to be employed in professional and managerial positions.[132] And, while female immigrants, as a group, are about as likely as both Canadian-born women and immigrant men to be employed as managers and professions, the same is not true for recent female immigrants.

Visible minorities, even with education levels similar to others, are less likely to hold professional and managerial positions. Statistics Canada reports, "in 1991, 30% of visible minority women with a university degree worked in professional occupations compared with 48% of their non-visible minority counterparts."[133] Underemployment is also an issue for this group of women, with 18 percent of employed, visible minority women who hold university degrees working in clerical positions. This compared to just 10 percent of other educated women.[134] The gains made by some women in the labour market are all too often celebrated with headlines such as "working women gaining equality." Such assessments ignore how partial and uneven such gains are.

Part-time Work and the Casualization of Work

The emergence of new patterns of work and organization, such as flexible specialization and just-in-time, are closely linked to the growth in "non-standard" forms of employment. "Non-standard" forms of employment include part-time work, subcontracting, temporary and casual employment, homework, short-term employment, and self-employment. Women are found in all categories of non-standard employment. A vast majority of all part-time workers in Canada are women. Many women are employed in subcontracting relations.

Part-time work is an indicator of many of the consequences of flexible employment as it affects women. In 1991, approximately 1.5 million women, 25.4 percent of all those with jobs, worked part-time compared to 8.8 percent of their male counterparts. Immigrant women are less likely to work part-time than their Canadian-born counterparts: 23 percent compared to 28 percent. The same is true of visible minority women. In 1991, 23 percent of employed visible minority women were working part-time compared to 30 percent of other women. The rate of part-time employment for Aboriginal women — 30 percent — is very similar to non-Aboriginal women. In all cases, women were more likely than their male counterparts to work part-time. This is particularly problematic as one study of women working part-time indicated that for them, part-time work often meant "poor pay and benefits, irregular hours, insecurity, the difficulty in arranging part-time child care, being away from children, and 'being given dirt to do.'"[135]

As it becomes harder to find full-time work, more and more women have turned to part-time work out of necessity. "In 1994, a full-third of women part-time workers wanted to work full-time but could only find part-time employment according to the official count."[136]

Homework

The growth and spread of homework in Canada has been one outcome of economic restructuring. One estimate put homeworking in the clothing industry at three to four thousand in Toronto alone, and a minimum of 30,000 in Quebec.[137] Research also indicates that most of these workers earn less than the minimum wage, work long hours with no overtime pay, and receive few or no benefits. Many garment homeworkers in Toronto are women of colour.[138]

In September 1996, garment industry workers appeared before Ontario provincial government committee hearings on changes to Ontario's *Employment Standards Act*. They staged a "Sweatshop Fashion Show" and modelled clothes produced by women in homes and in sweatshop conditions. The workers highlighted how goods produced were retailed for many times over the cost of production. Giant tags attached to the clothes modelled indicated how little workers were making. One tag indicated the actual labour cost for clothes that sell for $77.90 at a retail store is $6.77. Hourly wage rates ranged from $4.50 to $6.50, below the legislated minimum wage for homeworkers of $7.37 and well below unionized rates.[139] Fanny Yuen, coordinator of the Toronto Homeworkers Association states, "Homeworkers know this is unfair but they are afraid to complain because they can't afford to lose the work."[140] In other cases workers are vulnerable because of their status. Avvy Go, a lawyer at the Metro Chinese and South-East Asian Legal Clinic reports:

> ...in Toronto we understand that some employers pay according to your immigration status: If you're a landed immigrant you get, say $4 an hour; if you're a refugee claimant with employment authorization, you get $3 an hour; if you don't have any status at all, you get $2. And it's not just happening in the garment industry.[141]

Increasingly, as Yuen and Go's comments underscore, the poorest and most vulnerable workers are drawn into this casualized workforce.

The Coalition for Fair Wages and Working Conditions for Homeworkers has sought to address the issue of homework. In the course of its campaign, it explicitly made the link between racism and homework:

> If homeworkers are often from certain immigrant or racial populations, it's because of racism in the labour market. In workplaces, employers will pit one ethnic or racial group against another by paying different wages and allocating different workloads.... Racism denies workers access to educational upgrading and language training, does not recognize skills

and experiences they gained in other places, and bars them from equal opportunity in the labour market.

In fighting for fair wages and working conditions for homeworkers we have to take into account the effect that racism has on workers.[142]

Part-time work and non-standard forms of employment, such as homework, are often presented as viable alternatives for various groups of women. They offer a job when none other is available. They appear to provide a solution to domestic labour issues. However, given that job security, conditions of work, and employment protections are usually inferior to full-time work, such options often serve to further marginalize women in the labour market.

Employment Earnings

The occupational segregation that exists between men and women is a major factor in the persistent disparity that exists between men and women's wages. Women employed full-time earn considerably less than their male counterparts, regardless of age or level of education. In 1993, earnings of women employed full-time throughout the year averaged $28,390, 72 percent of what men working full-time earned — $39,430. This proportion was up sharply from 66 percent in 1989 and 60 percent in 1975.[143]

The earnings of immigrant women working on a full-time, full-year basis is about the same as other women in Canada. In 1990, immigrant women aged 15 to 64 earned $26,600 versus $26,478 for Canadian-born. Like other groups of women, immigrant women earned less than immigrant men. In 1990, immigrant women employed on a full-time, full-year basis earned just 65 percent as much as immigrant men.

Both Aboriginal and visible minority women earned less than other women. In 1990, the average income for visible minority women was $24,700 or about $1,400 less than other women who earned an average of $26,000. In terms of the wage gap, visible minority women employed full-time, full-year earned much less than visible minority men.

Aboriginal women's average employment earnings are lower than other women in all age groups under 65. In 1990, Aboriginal women working full-time, full-year earned an average $23,800. This was over $2,000 less than the average earnings of non-Aboriginal women. As with other groups of women, employed Aboriginal women earn less than their male counterparts.

CONCLUSIONS
Flexible Labour Markets: Implications

The process of restructuring is increasing the socio-economic inequalities that already exist between many groups of women. The outcome of capital's drive toward a more "flexible" labour market and the nation state's invocation of a neo-liberal agenda may very well result in a labour market that is increasingly polarized along gender, "race," and class lines. This will likely find expression in a number of trends and outcomes.

One immediate outcome of the processes of trade-led restructuring and structural shifts in the economy is the decline of sectors or industries in which Canada is at a comparative disadvantage. Women in a range of manufacturing jobs are increasingly vulnerable to employment insecurity by virtue of the sector they work in — textiles, electrical products and clothing. It was estimated that in 1989 the workforce of the clothing industry, then the largest supplier of manufacturing jobs in Toronto, was 85 percent immigrant and 70 percent female. This group of workers shared a set of characteristics: they were older than the average worker, they had less than a high school diploma, and many had serious language difficulties.[144] These people constituted a cheap labour pool for their employers. What are their chances in the "new global economy"?

The competitive pressures generated by the economy pose particular dilemmas. How can women in areas such as clothing or clerical occupations be assisted to make the transition to new jobs? How can they obtain skills that are now needed in new industries? State measures such as income supports, childcare, training, and job search programs are all under threat as governments pursue neo-liberal options. Further, as the CLC points out, both the clerical and garment industry have seen little in the way of government-funded adjustment. The CLC speculates on what the government response would have been if job losses had been in sectors dominated by male workers. "Job losses and government responses have both a gendered and racialized effect. The powerlessness and vulnerability of these workers have made it so much easier for governments to walk away."[145] In the absence of government-supported programs targeted towards women of colour in vulnerable sectors, it is likely that many of these women will be further marginalized in the labour market, and vulnerable to both income and employment insecurity.

The labour market is becoming much more fragmented, as evidenced by the decline in full-time jobs and the rise in part-time work. This transformation is linked directly to the adoption of particular kinds of "flexible" labour strategies. It is likely that women will continue to enter the labour market in larger numbers, but it is highly likely that the kind of jobs that many will undertake will be characterized by low wages, insecurity, and little opportunity for advancement.

By corollary, one outcome to emerge may well be an acceleration of labour market polarization in terms of high- status occupations and well-paying jobs. The gap will widen between women in professional, managerial positions holding secure jobs, and those women in non-secure jobs who are poorly paid and over-exploited. To the extent that the changing structure of employment builds on existing social and economic vulnerability, a substantial portion of women in the lower tier will be women of colour. This latter group will not only be concentrated in low-paying routine service work but will be used for personal services such as childcare and domestic work provided in the homes of middle- and upper-class women.

The state itself, under the banner of a neo-liberal program, is withdrawing from active labour market intervention in two ways:

Explicit deregulation, whereby formal regulations have been eroded or abandoned by legislation means, and implicit deregulation whereby remaining regulations have been made less effective through inadequate implementation or systemic bypassing.[146]

Recent developments in Ontario, highlighted in the previous section, are indicative of this withdrawal.

In the context of a changing economy and rapid restructuring, women of colour have organized to contest both their position in the labour market and the outcomes of decisions made by governments and business. It is one thing to argue that women's experience of the labour market is mediated by gender, "race," and class and quite another to suggest that women of colour passively accept the terms and conditions of their work experience. Within the Canadian context there is sufficient evidence to demonstrate that women of colour have powerful insights about their own situation, and have struggled both individually, together, and in coalitions against the specific nature of their oppression.

This mobilization builds on many previous struggles.[147] It has been pointed out that domestic workers and homeworkers in the garment industry "represent the ultimate form of flexible labour"[148] in the new global economy. And, as highlighted above, many are women of colour, vulnerable to the outcomes of restructuring because of the precarious nature of their employment, their immigration status, or both. As Fely Vallisin, coordinator of the Toronto-based domestic workers organization INTERCEDE, states:

> Those who have very little to begin with end up having nil. The clawback on employment rights is really worse for those who have the least rights. In a time of global restructuring, there should be no exemption from minimum standards — be they babysitters, farm workers, domestic workers or any other workers with temporary status.[149]

Industrial garment workers and domestic workers have organized. Domestic workers' organizations, such as INTERCEDE and the West Coast Domestic Workers Association, have worked to secure fair and equal treatment of domestic workers. Domestic workers have mobilized to challenge the provisions of the Federal government's immigration programs as they effect domestics — the Foreign Domestic Movement Program (FDM) and more recently the Live-in Caregiver Program. They have also organized about workplace conditions and standards. INTERCEDE and a coalition of community groups lobbied the Ontario NDP government successfully for collective bargaining rights, only to see this legal victory rolled back by the Harris government.[150] The efforts of domestic workers organizations have not been confined to the national arena alone. INTERCEDE and NAC have organized a petition campaign in an attempt to lobby the federal government to sign the UN Convention on the Protection of the Rights of All Migrant Workers and Members of Their Families.[151]

Similarly, homeworkers working with the International Ladies Garment Workers Union (ILGWU) have formed an association.[152] The ILGWU played a very proactive role, by adopting a strategy to organize homeworkers into their own association. The strategy built upon experiences developed and pioneered by community and women's groups outside Canada. The aim was "to work with community and women's groups in a coalition to pressure for legislative change and accessible child care and to build a public campaign to resist the impact of economic restructuring on women's work."[153] By the end of its first year, the Homeworkers Association had fifty members. The efforts of garment homeworkers and domestic workers, in Ontario, have been supported by women's groups, labour organizations and other social justice groups.

More recently, NAC and the CLC worked together to organize Women's March Against Poverty, May 14-June 15, 1996.[154] This campaign mobilized thousands of women across Canada under the banner For Bread and Roses, For Jobs and Justice.[155] At the heart of the campaign was a call for social solidarity. This call embodies an alternative vision that recognizes "social and economic inequalities among people and then [works] for a system to set them right."[156] The Women's March culminated with a protest rally at Parliament Hill. The 40,000-strong rally was led by Aboriginal women and included women activists from various communities. As the CLC has observed, "from coast-to-coast, the women who are the most marginalized are also the ones who are standing firm."[157] The women's movement is attempting to build an alternative political vision to the neoliberal rationales adopted by the federal and provincial governments, that presents restructuring policies as "inevitable" and "common sense."[158]

While women's organizing is not the central focus of this discussion, it is important to highlight struggles which belie the claim that women of colour are docile or passive in the face of the economic changes affecting them. As stated, different groups of women are incorporated into the Canadian labour market that is constituted by intersecting and multiple social relations including those of "race" and gender. This labour market is becoming more competitive as a result of economic restructuring and the state's active withdrawal from labour market regulation, and within this context of market-driven development, some groups of women will be better positioned than others to "compete." A number of structural features combine in varying, shifting, and complex ways to position different groups of women at the margins of the Canadian labour market. Increasingly, the women's movement is recognizing that social solidarity begins with those most excluded.[159] In challenging the current neo-liberal agenda and its policy prescriptions, the women's movement is constructing an oppositional politics that not only attempts to expose the differential impacts of restructuring for various groups of women but actively espouses an alternative vision of change.

NOTES

I would like to thank Pat Armstrong, Isabella Bakker, Janine Brodie, Ena Dua, and William Walters for their helpful suggestions on earlier versions of this paper. Thanks also to Ann Decter for her careful editing and many comments.
1.   These stories appeared in the *Globe and Mail*, 13 May 1998.

2.   According to the Ontario Ministry of Labour, "Economic restructuring means many things: disinvesting by abandoning businesses, relocating to low wage zones such as Mexico, investing in new technology to improve product quality, subcontracting work or fashioning new relationships between employers and workers. Further, [in Canada] these events are occurring in the context of a long term shift from the goods producing to the service producing industries as the primary source of new job creation." Ontario, Ministry of Labour, *The Displaced Workers of Ontario: How Do they Fare* (Toronto: Ministry of Labour, 1993), 14.
      However, as Marjorie Griffin Cohen (1995) argues, the term economic restructuring has very specific implications that are anything but apolitical. Nor are they gender-, race-, and class-neutral. She cites Mackenzie: "Sometime in the late 1970s and early 1980s, discussion of 'recession' metamorphosed into discussion of 'economic restructuring.' This was not just a change of rhetoric. It was, rather, a shorthand for some enduring changes in our way of life in Canada. Recession had implied that we were living through a temporary hiccup in an otherwise sound economy. Restructuring implies something more fundamental: a change in people's relationship to wage work and the concomitant alteration of a pattern of life centred on full employment of men in permanent jobs sponsored by women's dual roles." Suzanne Mackenzie, "Neglected Spaces in Peripheral Places: Homeworkers and the Creation of a New Economic Centre," *Cahiers de Geographie du Quebec* 31.83 (1987), cited by Marjorie Griffin Cohen, "Feminism's Effect on Economic Policy," in *Canadian Women's Issues*, Vol. II, eds. Marjorie Cohen and Ruth Roach Pierson (Toronto: James Lorimer, 1995), 274.

3.   I use the term "women of colour" throughout this paper in an effort to suggest a political constituency as opposed to a racial category. This term references Chandra Talpade Mohanty who writes: "What seems to constitute women of colour or third world women as a viable oppositional alliance is a *common context of struggle* rather than colour or racial identifications." Chandra Talpade Mohanty, "Cartographies of Struggle," in *Third World Women and the Politics of Feminism*, eds. Chandra Mohanty, et al. (Bloomington: Indiana University Press, 1991), 7. In a similar vein Dionne Brand states that "women of colour" "is a term of coalition rather than a term of identification. When I say women who are Chinese, South Asian, of African ancestry, Phillipina, Malaysian, et cetera who share a commonality of how white power structures deal with us and a need to organize as women of colour against [those structures]." Dionne Brand, cited in Charmaine Perkins, et al., "Interview with Dionne Brand," *Kinesis* (October 1993).

4.   This trend was identitified as early as 1989. See Urban Dimensions Group, *Growth of the Contingent Workforce in Ontario: Structural Trends, Statistical Dimensions and Policy Implications* (Toronto: Ontario Women's Directorate, 1989). See also, Isabella Bakker, "Pay Equity and Economic Restructuring," in *Just Wages: A Feminist Assessment of Pay Equity*, eds. Judy Fudge and Patricia McDermott (Toronto: University of Toronto Press, 1991).

5.   Kenneth Woodside, "Trade and Industrial Policy: Hard Choices," in *Governing Canada: Institutions and Public Policy*, ed. Michael Atkinson (Toronto: Harcourt Brace, 1993), 259.

6.   Waters argues that globalizing processes are occurring in three arenas - the economy, the polity, and culture. "Economies trend toward liberalization, that is freedom from command, constraint and status and class monopolization; polities trend towards democratization, the deconcentration of power; and culture towards universalization, the abstraction of values and standards to a very high level of generality that will permit extreme levels of cultural differentiation." Malcolm Waters, *Globalization* (London: Routledge, 1995), 159.

7.   For more on the concept of globalization see: David Held, *Democracy and the Global Order* (Cambridge: Polity Press, 1995).

8.   Diane Elson, "From Survival Strategies to Transformation Strategies: Women's Needs and Structural Adjustment," in *Unequal Burden: Economic Crisis, Persistent Poverty and Women's Work*, eds. Shelley Feldman and Lourdes Beneria (Boulder: Westview Press, 1992), 29.

9.   For an overview of the crisis see for example: Jeanne Vickers, *Women and the World Economic Crisis* (London: Zed Books, 1991). For a discussion of the particular nature of Canada's post-war settlement and crisis see Jane Jenson, "'Different' But Not 'Exceptional': Canada's Permeable Fordism," *Canadian Review of Sociology and Anthropology*, vol. 26, no. 1 (1989).

10.   For a discussion of the demise of keynesianism in Canada see: chapters 6 and 7 of Janine Brodie, *The Political Economy of Canadian Regionalism* (Toronto: Harcourt Brace Jovanovich, 1991). Stephen McBride and John Shields, *Dismantling a Nation: Canada and the New World Order* (Halifax: Fernwood, 1993).

11.   "A World Bank study has concluded that the cost to developing countries of rich-country protectionism exceeds the value of international aid." *The Economist* (25-31, March 1989), cited by Jeanne Vickers, *Women and the World Economic Crisis* (London: Zed Books, 1991), 1.

12.   Jeanne Vickers, *Women and the World Economic Crisis* (London: Zed Books, 1991), 1.

13.   Jeanne Vickers, *Women and the World Economic Crisis* (London: Zed Books, 1991), 4-5.

14.   Janine Brodie, "Meso-Discourses, State Forms and the Gendering of Liberal-Democratic Citizenship," *Citizenship Studies*, vol. 1, no. 2 (1997): 234.

15. Isabella Bakker, "Introduction," in *Rethinking Restructuring: Gender and Change in Canada*, ed. Isabella Bakker (Toronto: University of Toronto Press, 1996), 4. The antecedents of neo-liberalism can be found in the work of early liberal political economists such as Adam Smith. "Smith's work formulated some of the principles which still constitute the foundation of contemporary neo-liberalism. The first of these principles is the assertion that free and unfettered commerce will benefit everyone in society. Smith postulated an 'invisible hand which leads the private interests and passions of men in the direction which is most agreeable to the interest of the whole society.'" The Ecumenical Coalition for Economic Justice, *Reweaving Canada's Social Programs: From Shredded Safety Net to Social Solidarity*, (Toronto: ECEJ, 1993), 31.

16. Marjorie Griffin Cohen, "From the Welfare State to Vampire Capitalism," in *Women and the Canadian Welfare State*, eds. Patricia M. Evans and Gerda R. Wekerle (Toronto: University of Toronto Press, 1997), 30.

17. Diane Elson, 1991, cited by Susan Bullock, *Women and Work* (London: Zed Books, 1994), 32.

18. Susan Bullock, *Women and Work* (London: Zed, 1994), 33.

19. Sheila Rowbotham and Swasti Mitter, "Conclusion," in *Dignity and Daily Bread*, eds. Swasti Mitter and Sheila Rowbotham (London: Routledge, 1994), 220.

20. Janine Brodie, *Politics on the Margins* (Halifax: Fernwood, 1995), 27.

21. Isabella Bakker, "Engendering Macro-economic Policy Reform in the Era of Global Restructuring and Adjustment," in *The Strategic Silence: Gender and Economic Policy*, ed. Isabella Bakker (London: Zed Books, 1994), 1. Some other contributions to the literature on gender and restructuring include: Lourdes Beneria and Shelley Feldman, eds., *Unequal Burden: Economic Crisis, Persistent Poverty and Women's Work* (Colorado: Westview Press, 1992); Centre for Research on Work and Society, *Gender and Economic Restructuring*, Working Paper No. 12 (North York: York University, 1995).

22. For a further discussion see: M. Patricia Connelly, "Gender Matters: Restructuring and Adjustment, South and North," *Gender and Economic Restructuring*, Working Paper No. 12, Centre for Research on Work and Society (North York: York University, 1995).

23. Isabella Bakker, "Introduction," in *The Strategic Silence: Gender and Economic Policy*, ed. Isabella Bakker (London: Zed Press, 1994), 1.

24. Isabella Bakker, "Introduction," in *Rethinking Restructuring*, ed. Isabella Bakker (Toronto: University of Toronto Press, 1996), 8.

25. Isabella Bakker, "Introduction," in *Rethinking Restructuring*, ed. Isabella Bakker (Toronto: University of Toronto Press, 1996), 9. For a further discussion see Linda Alcoff, "Cultural Feminism versus Poststructuralism: The Identity Crisis in Feminist Theory," *Signs*, vol. 13, no. 3: 433.

26. M. Jacqui Alexander and Chandra Mohanty, "Introduction: Genealogies, Legacies, Movements," in *Feminist Genealogies, Colonial Legacies, Democratic Futures*, eds. M. Jacqui Alexander and Chandra Mohanty (New York: Routledge, 1997), xvii.

27. Donna Haraway, "A Manifesto for Cyborgs: Science, Technology, and Socialist Feminism in the 1980s," in *Feminism/Postmodernism*, ed. Linda Nicholson (New York: Routledge, 1990), 197.

28. Inderpal Grewal and Caren Kaplan, "Introduction," in *Scattered Hegemonies*, eds. Inderpal Grewal and Caren Kaplan (Minneapolis: University of Minnesota Press, 1994), 5.

29. See for example: Chandra Talpade Mohanty, "Cartographies of Struggle: Third World Women and the Politics of Feminism," in *Third World Women and the Politics of Feminism*, eds. Chandra Talpade Mohanty, et al. (Bloomington: Indiana University Press, 1991); Chandra Talpade Mohanty, "Women Workers and Capitalist Scripts: Ideologies of Domination, Common Interests and the Politics of Solidarity," in *Feminist Genealogies, Colonial Legacies, Democratic Futures*, eds. M. Jacqui Alexander and Chandra Talpade Mohanty (New York: Routledge, 1997); Swasti Mitter, *Common Fate, Common Bond* (London: Zed Books, 1986); Swasti Mitter, "On Organizing Women in Casualized Work: A Global Overview," in *Dignity and Daily Bread*, eds. Sheila Rowbotham and Swasti Mitter (London: Routledge, 1994).

30. Chandra Mohanty, "Cartographies of Struggle: Third World Women and the Politics of Feminism," in *Third World Women and the Politics of Feminism*, eds. Chandra Mohanty, Ann Russo, and Lourdes Torres (Bloomington: Indiana University Press, 1991), 7.

31. Chandra Mohanty, "Women Workers and Capitalist Scripts," in *Feminist Genealogies, Colonial Legacies, Democratic Futures*, eds. Chandra Mohanty and Jacqui Alexander (London: Routledge, 1994), 7.

32. Chandra Mohanty is defining "Third World Women Workers" in "the development and operation of the 'new' world order" as "both women from geographical Third World and immigrant and indigenous women of color in the U.S. and Western Europe." Chandra Mohanty, "Women Workers and Capitalist Scripts," in *Feminist Genealogies, Colonial Legacies, Democratic Futures*, eds. M. Jacqui Alexander and Chandra Mohanty (New York: Routledge, 1997), 7.

33. Swasti Mitter, *Common Fate, Common Bond* (London: Pluto Press, 1986), 40.

34. Susan Bullock, *Women and Work* (London: Zed Books,1994), 73. See also: Diane Elson and Ruth Pierson, "Nimble Fingers Make Cheap Workers: An Analysis of Women's Employment in Third World Export Manufacturing," *Feminist Review*, vol. 7 (Spring 1981).

35. J. K. Gibson-Graham, *The End of Capitalism (As We Knew It)* (London: Basil Blackwell Publishers, 1996), 127.

36. Susan Bullock, *Women and Work* (London: Zed Books, 1994), 72.

37. Susan Bullock, *Women and Work* (London: Zed Books, 1994),

38. See: Swasti Mitter, *Common Fate, Common Bond* (London: Pluto 1986) and "Women Organizing in Casual Work," in *Dignity and Daily Bread*, eds. Swasti Mitter and Sheila Rowbotham (London: Routledge, 1994), 17.

39. Swasti Mitter, "Women Organizing in Casual Work," in *Dignity and Daily Bread*, eds. Sheila Rowbotham and Swasti Mitter (London: Routledge, 1994), 17.

40. Swasti Mitter, "Women Organizing in Casualized Work," in *Dignity and Daily Bread*, eds. Swasti Mitter and Sheila Rowbotham (London: Routledge, 1994), 21.

41. *Conditions of Work Digest*, "Homework," 8.2 (1989) (Geneva: International Labour Office), 9, cited by Sheila Rowbotham, *Homeworkers Worldwide* (London: Merlin, 1992), 33.

42. Sheila Rowbotham, *Homeworkers Worldwide* (London: Merlin Press, 1993), 33.

43. Swasti Mitter, "Women Organizing in Casualized Work," in *Dignity and Daily Bread*, eds. Swasti Mitter and Sheila Rowbotham (London: Routledge, 1994), 27.

44. Chandra Mohanty, "Women Workers and Capitalist Scripts," in *Feminist Genealogies, Colonial Legacies, Democratic Futures*, eds. M. Jacqui Alexander and Chandra Mohanty (New York: Routledge, 1997), 28-9.

45. Chandra Mohanty, "Women Workers and Capitalist Scripts," in *Feminist Genealogies, Colonial Legacies, Democratic Futures*, eds. M. Jacqui Alexander and Chandra Mohanty (New York: Routledge, 1997), 7.

46. Chandra Mohanty, "Women Workers and Capitalist Scripts," in *Feminist Genealogies, Colonial Legacies, Democratic Futures*, eds. Chandra Mohanty and M. Jacqui Alexander (London: Routledge, 1997), 28.

47. Chandra Mohanty, "Women Workers and Capitalist Scripts," in *Feminist Genealogies, Colonial Legacies, Democratic Futures*, eds. Chandra Mohanty and M. Jacqui Alexander (London: Routledge, 1997), 27.

48. Isabella Bakker, "Introduction: Engendering Macro-economic Policy Reform in the Era of Global Restructuring and Adjustment," in *The Strategic Silence*, ed. Isabella Bakker (London: Zed Books, 1993), 2-3.

49. Swasti Mitter and Sheila Rowbotham, "Conclusion" in *Dignity and Daily Bread*, eds. S. Rowbotham and Swasti Mitter (London: Routledge, 1993), 219.

50. Tony Clarke, "The Transnational Corporate Agenda Behind the Harris Regime," in *Open for Business. Closed to People*, eds. Diana Ralph, Andre Regimbald, and Nérée St-Amand (Halifax: Fernwood, 1997), 29.

51. Tony Clarke, "The Transnational Corporate Agenda Behind the Harris Regime," in *Open for Business. Closed to People*, eds. Diana Ralph, Andre Regimbald, and Nérée St-Amand (Halifax: Fernwood, 1997), 29. See also: Marjorie Cohen, "The Implications of Economic Restructuring for Women: The Canadian Situation," in *The Strategic Silence: Gender and Economic Policy*, ed. Isabella Bakker (London: Zed Books, 1994).

52. OECD, *Jobs Study* (Paris: OECD, 1994), 36, cited by Ecumenical Coalition for Economic Justice (ECEJ), "Jobs are the Key to Social Security," *Economic Justice Report*, vol. 5, no. 3 (Toronto: ECEJ, 1994): 4.

53. Kenneth Woodside, "Trade and Industrial Policy: Hard Choices," in *Governing Canada: Institutions and Public Policy*, ed. Michael Atkinson (Toronto: Harcourt Brace, 1993), 248.

54. The Federal government began negotiating a free trade agreement with the United States in 1985. The Canada-U.S. Free Trade Agreement was concluded in 1988 and went into effect January 1, 1989. Essentially the two countries agreed to remove all tariffs (within a specified period), permitted freer flows of certain categories of workers, and established a disputes settlement tribunal. Two other provisions are particularly significant. Firstly, the two countries agreed to extend national treatment to each other. And secondly, the agreement covers many services. See: Kenneth Woodside, "Trade and Industrial Policy: Hard Choices," in *Governing Canada: Institutions and Public Policy*, ed. Michael Atkinson (Toronto: Harcourt Brace, 1993); also Marjorie Cohen, "Feminism's Effect on Economic Policy," in *Canadian Women's Issues*, Vol. II, eds. Ruth Roach Pierson and Marjorie Cohen (Toronto: James Lorimer, 1995), 277-82.

55. The North American Free Trade deal supersedes the provisions of the Canada-U.S. Free Trade deal. The three countries involved, Canada, the U.S., and Mexico, agreed to eliminate tariffs among them. They have also agreed to phase out investment restrictions. This means that firms can locate anywhere in the three countries without fear of undue interference by government. For more about the implications of NAFTA see: "Which Way for the Americas? Analysis of NAFTA

Proposals and the Impact on Canada," (Ottawa: Canadian Centre for Policy Alternatives, Nov. 1992); Ian Robinson, "The NAFTA, Democracy and Continental Economic Integration: Trade Policy as if Democracy Matters," in *How Ottawa Spends: A More Democratic Canada...? (1993/1994)*, ed. Susan Phillips (Ottawa: Carleton University Press, 1994).

56. The future of the MAI is somewhat uncertain as MAI talks collapsed in the Paris negotiating sessions in February 1998.

57. Bruce Campbell, *Canada Under Siege: Three Years into the Free Trade Era* (Ottawa: Canadian Centre for Policy Alternatives, 1992), 19. Campbell has also documented job shifts from Canada to selected production areas in the U.S. predominantly but also Mexico.

58. Marjorie Cohen, "New International Trade Agreements: Their Reactionary Role in Creating Markets and Retarding Social Welfare," in *Rethinking Restructuring: Gender and Change in Canada*, ed. Isabella Bakker (Toronto: University of Toronto Press, 1996).

59. Ricardo Grinspun and Robert Krelewich, "Consolidating Neoliberal Reforms: Free Trade as a Conditioning Framework," *Studies in Political Economy* 43 (Spring 1994): 34, cited by Christina Gabriel and Laura Macdonald, "NAFTA, Women and Organizing in Canada and Mexico: Forging a 'Feminist Internationality,'" *Millennium*, vol. 23, no. 3 (Winter 1994).

60. Marjorie Cohen, "New International Trade Agreements: Their Reactionary Role in Creating Markets and Retarding Social Welfare," in *Rethinking Restructuring: Gender and Change in Canada*, ed. Isabella Bakker (Toronto: University of Toronto Press, 1996), 191.

61. Marjorie Cohen, "New International Trade Agreements: Their Reactionary Role in Creating Markets and Retarding Social Welfare," in *Rethinking Restructuring: Gender and Change in Canada*, ed. Isabella Bakker (Toronto: University of Toronto Press, 1996), 192-3.

62. Ecumenical Coalition for Economic Justice (ECEJ), "Confronting the Unemployment Crisis," *Economic Justice Report*, vol. 7, no. 4 (December 1996): 8.

63. Louise Noce and Anne O'Connell, *Take It or Leave It: The Ontario Government's Approach to Job Insecurity*, Speaking Out Project: Periodic Report No. 1 (Ottawa: Caledon Institute of Social Policy, 1998), 8.

64. For a brief overview of similar initiatives in other provinces see for example: ECEJ, "Provinces Play Follow the Leader," *Economic Justice Report*, vol. 7, no. 1 (May 1996).

65. Tony Clarke cites a government ad in the *Globe and Mail*: "Ontario is not just open for business; Ontario is Business." Tony Clarke, "The Transnational Corporate Agenda: Behind the Harris Regime," in *Open for Business. Closed to the People*, eds. Diana Ralph, Andre Regimbald, and Nérée St-Amand (Halifax: Fernwood, 1997), 36.

66. For an assessment and review of the Tories policy agenda see: Diana Ralph, Andre Regimbald, and Nérée St-Amand, eds., *Open for Business. Closed to the People* (Halifax: Fernwood, 1997); Luciana Ricciutelli, June Larkin, Eimear O'Neill, eds., *Confronting the Cuts* (North York: Inanna Publications, 1998).

67. Ontario Women's Declaration, "We Are Not Going Back!" excerpts in *Kinesis* (February 1996): 9.

68. Greg Albo and Robert MacDermid, "Divided Province, Growing Protests: Ontario Moves Right," in *The Provincial State: Politics in Canada's Provinces and Territories*, 2nd edition, eds. K. Brownsey and M. Howlett (Toronto: Irwin, 1998).

69. Ontario Federation of Labour, *The Common Sense Revolution: Two Years of Destruction* (Toronto: OFL, 1997), 23, cited by Louise Noce and Anne O'Connell, *Take It or Leave It: The Ontario Government's Approach to Job Insecurity* (Toronto: Caledon Institute of Social Policy, 1998), 9.

70. Morley Gunderson, Leon Muszynski, with Jennifer Keck, *Women and Labour Market Poverty* (Ottawa: Canadian Advisory Council on the Status of Women, 1990), 125.

71. Canadian Labour Congress, *Women's Work: A Report* (Ottawa: CLC, 1997), 71.

72. Ontario, Management Board Secretariat, *The OPS: Employment Equity Annual Report — June 1991 to May 1992* (Toronto: Management Board Secretariat, 1993), 37.

73. Ontario Federation of Labour, *Fight Back Facts: Harris Attacks Women*, 1996, cited by Ecumenical Coalition for Economic Justice, "Provinces Play Follow the Federal Leader," *Economic Justice Report*, vol. 7, no. 1 (May 1996): 5.

74. The Vanier Institute of the Family, *Profiling Canada's Families*, 118, cited by Canadian Labour Congress, *Women's Work: A Report* (Ottawa: CLC, 1997), 43.

75. Tony Clarke, "The Transnational Corporate Agenda Behind the Harris Regime," in *Open for Business. Closed to the People*, eds. Diana Ralph, Andre Regimbald, and Nérée St-Amand (Halifax: Fernwood, 1997), 35.

76. Government of Ontario Press Release, "Government Acts to Repeal Bill 40 to Spur Growth and Create Jobs," October 4, 1995, cited by Louise Noce and Anne O'Connell, *Take It or Leave It: The Ontario Government's Approach to Job Insecurity* (Ottawa: Caledon Institute of Social Policy, 1998), 12.

77. Rick, participant in "Speaking Out Project," cited by Louise Noce and Anne O'Connell, *Take It or Leave It: The Ontario Government's Approach to Job Insecurity* (Ottawa: Caledon Institute of Social Policy, 1998), 13.
78. Tony Clarke, "The Transnational Corporate Agenda Behind the Harris Regime," in *Open for Business. Closed to the People*, eds. Diana Ralph, Andre Regimbald, and Nérée St-Amand (Halifax: Fernwood, 1997), 35.
79. Judy Fudge, "Fragmentation and Feminization: The Challenge of Equity for Labour Relations Policy," in *Women and Canadian Public Policy*, ed. Janine Brodie (Toronto: Harcourt Brace, 1996), 70.
80. Canadian Labour Congress, *Women's Work: A Report* (Ottawa: CLC, 1997), 3.
81. Brigitte Kitchen, "'Common Sense' Assaults on Families," in *Open for Business. Closed to the People*, eds. Diana Ralph, Andre Regimbald, and Nérée St-Amand (Halifax: Fernwood, 1997), 105.
82. Judy Fudge, "Fragmentation and Feminization: The Challenge of Equity for Labour-Relations Policy," in *Women and Canadian Public Policy*, ed. Janine Brodie (Toronto: Harcourt Brace, 1996), 80.
83. Jean Trickey, "The Racist Face of 'Common Sense,'" in *Open for Business. Closed to the People*, eds. Diana Ralph, Andre Regimbald, and Nérée St-Amand (Halifax: Fernwood, 1997), 115.
84. Judy Rebick, "Right Turn Leads to Dead End," *Kinesis* (July/August 1995).
85. Jean Trickey, "The Racist Face of 'Common Sense,'" in *Open for Business. Closed to the People*, eds. Diana Ralph, Andre Regimbald, and Nérée St-Amand (Halifax: Fernwood, 1997), 114.
86. This point is made in reference to Europe by Phillip Brown and Rosemary Crompton, "Introduction," in *Economic Restructuring and Social Exclusion*, eds. Phillip Brown and Rosemary Crompton (London: UCL Press, 1994).
87. Unless otherwise noted all figures in cited in this section are from Statistics Canada, *Women in Canada: A Statistical Report*, 3rd edition, Target Groups Project, Cat. No. 89-503E (Ottawa: Statistics Canada, 1995).
88. These points are inspired in part by a framework developed by Avtar Brah, "South Asian Young Muslim Women and the Labour Market," in *The Dynamics of Gender and Race*, eds. Halef Afshar and Mary Maynard (London: Taylor and Francis, 1994).
89. Himani Bannerji, "Popular Images of South Asian Women," in *Returning the Gaze* (Toronto: Sistervision Press, 1993), 149.
90. Dionne Brand, "A Working Paper on Black Women in Toronto: Gender, Race and Class," in *Returning the Gaze*, ed. Himani Bannerji (Toronto: Sistervision Press, 1993), 224.
91. Dionne Brand, "A Working Paper on Black Women in Toronto: Gender, Race and Class," in *Returning the Gaze*, ed. Himani Bannerji (Toronto: Sistervision Press, 1993), 224.
92. Roxanna Ng, "Immigrant Women: The Construction of a Labour Market Category," *Canadian Journal of Women and the Law*, vol. 4 (1990): 97.
93. Portions of this section are revised from material in Appendix I in Christina Gabriel, "Recasting Citizenship: The Politics of Multicultural Policy in Canada," diss., York University, Ontario, 1998.
94. Where possible data in this section will focus on "recent immigrants," i.e. those who immigrated in the 1986 to 1991 period because the majority of this group have come from countries outside Europe. Statistics Canada reports there have been major shifts in the country of birth of female immigrants. For example in 1991, women born in Asia or the Middle East made up 52 percent of all immigrant women living in Canada who arrived between 1988 and 1991. Whereas just 4 percent were born in the United Kingdom and 19 percent in other parts of Europe. "In contrast, among immigrant women living in Canada in 1991 who immigrated in the 1961-1970 period, 12% were born in Asia and the Middle East, while 22% were born in the United Kingdom and 46% in other parts of Europe." From: *Women in Canada*, 118.
95. The use of Statistics Canada data necessitates the adoption of its definitions. It has very specific definitions for each of these groups.
     • *Immigrant* — population consists of people who are, or have been, landed immigrants. Landed immigrants have been granted the right to live in Canada permanently. Non-permanent residents — that is, refugee claimants and persons holding student or employment authorizations or Minister's permits - are not included in the immigrant population. See: Tina Chui and Mary Sue Devereaux, "Canada's Newest Workers," *Perspectives* (Ottawa: Statistics Canada, Cat. No. 75-001E, Spring 1995), 17.
     • *Visible Minority* — the visible minority subgroups derived from the 1986 and 1991 Census include Blacks, South Asians (referred to as Indo-Pakistanis in 1986), Chinese, Koreans, Japanese, South East Asians, Filipinos, West Asians and Arabs, Latin Americans and Other Pacific Islanders. *Women in Canada* (Ottawa: Statistics Canada, Cat. No. 89-503E), 138.

- *Aboriginal women* — "includes women who are registered Indians but who do not have Aboriginal origins, for example women with no Aboriginal origins who were granted registered Indian status when they married Aboriginal men," (153). "Almost half (47%) of Aboriginal women in Canada in 1991 had Aboriginal origins only, that is, they had either North American Indian, Metis, or Inuit origins only, or some combination of the three. That year, 36% of all Aboriginal women had North American Indian ancestry only, while 7% reported Metis origins only, 3% had Inuit ancestry only, and 1% had multiple Aboriginal origins. At the same time, 51% of Aboriginal women reported Aboriginal ancestry along with other ethnic origins, while 2% were registered Indian women without Aboriginal Origins." From: *Women in Canada: A Statistical Report*, 3rd edition, 147.

96. Karen Kelly, "Visible Minorities: A Diverse Group," *Canadian Social Trends*, Summer 1995 (Ottawa: Statistics Canada, Cat. No. 11-008E), 6.

97. Karen Kelly, "Visible Minorities: A Diverse Group," *Canadian Social Trends*, Summer 1995 (Ottawa: Statistics Canada, Cat. No. 11-008E), 7.

98. "In 1991, 49% of women who immigrated from 1986-1991 and 54% of those who arrived during the 1981-1985 period were employed, compared with over 60% of immigrant women who arrived between 1961 and 1980." From: *Women in Canada: A Statistical Report* (Ottawa: Statistics Canada, 1995), 121.

99. *Success in the Works: A Profile of Canada's Emerging Workforce* (Employment and Immigration Canada, 1989), cited by Ontario Council of Agencies Serving Immigrants (OCASI), "The Ontario Training and Adjustment Board," Brief submitted to Honourable Richard Allen, Minister of Skills Development, May 1992, 15.

100. In the group, ages 25 to 44, 24 percent of recent female immigrant workers compared with 17 percent of Canadian-born had a university degree. However, in 1991, 7 percent of recent female immigrants had less than Grade 9 versus 2 percent of Canadian born. From: Tina Chui and Mary Sue Devereaux, "Canada's Newest Workers," *Perspectives*, Spring 1995 (Ottawa: Statistics Canada, Cat. No. 75-001E), 19.

101. Barbara Cameron, "From Equal Opportunity to Symbolic Equity: Three Decades of Federal Training Policy for Women," in *Rethinking Restructuring: Gender and Change in Canada*, ed. Isabella Bakker (Toronto: University of Toronto Press, 1996).

102. Barbara Cameron, "From Equal Opportunity to Symbolic Equity: Three Decades of Federal Training Policy for Women," in *Rethinking Restructuring: Gender and Change in Canada*, ed. Isabella Bakker (Toronto: University of Toronto Press, 1996), 73-4.

103. Organization for Economic Co-operation and Development, *Women and Structural Change: New Perspectives* (Paris: OECD, 1994), 27.

104. Ruth Roach Pierson, "Education and Training," *Canadian Women's Issues*, Vol II, eds. Ruth Roach Pierson and Marjorie Cohen (Toronto: Lorimer, 1994), 163.

105. For a discussion see Monica Boyd, "Migration Policy, Female Dependency, Family Membership," in *Women and the Canadian Welfare State*, eds. Patricia Evans and Gerda Wekerle (Toronto: University of Toronto, 1997).

106. Punam Khosla, "Review of the Situation of Women in Canada" (Toronto: National Action Committee on the Status of Women, 1993), 21.

107. Monica Boyd, "Immigrant Women: Language Socioeconomic Inequalities and Policy Issues," in *Ethnic Demography*, eds. Shiva Halli, Frank Trovanto, and Leo Driedger (Ottawa: Carleton, 1990), 285.

108. Monica Boyd, "Immigrant Women: Language Socioeconomic Inequalities and Policy Issues," in *Ethnic Demography*, eds. Shiva Halli, Frank Trovanto, and Leo Driedger (Ottawa: Carleton, 1990), 288.

109. For more on the issue of accreditation see: "Access! Task Force on Access to Professions and Trades in Ontario" (October 1989); and *Currents*, vol. 5, no. 4 (March 1990).

110. OCASI, "Employment Equity for Ontario," Brief submitted to Honourable Elaine Ziemba, Ministry of Citizenship, Feb. 1992, 5.

111. Sedef Arat-Koc, "In the Privacy of Our Own Home: Foreign Domestic Workers as Solution to the Crisis in the Domestic Sphere in Canada," *Studies in Political Economy*, no. 28 (Spring 1989): 53.

112. Audrey Macklin, "On the Inside Looking In: Foreign Domestic Workers in Canada," in *Maid in the Market*, eds. Sedef Arat-Koc and Wenona Giles (Halifax: Fernwood, 1994), 34.

113. Pamela Best, "Women, Men and Work," *Canadian Social Trends* Spring 1995 (Ottawa: Statistics Canada, Cat. No. 11-008E), 33.

114. Armstrong, 1993, cited by M. Patricia Connelly, "Gender Matters: Restructuring and Adjustment, South and North," *Gender and Economic Restructuring*, Working Paper No. 12 (North York: Centre for Work and Society, York University), 8.

115. "The Economic Council of Canada identifies industries at which Canada is at a comparative disadvantage, and thus which are at risk due to international competition. Two principal conclusions arise from this study. First, the process of adjustment is very likely to disproportionately affect women because women are over-represented in industries that are at risk...[knitting mills, clothing, leather, textiles, printing and publishing]. The proportion of women employed in the five industry groups that are most 'at risk' is substantially higher than the proportion of women in the five industry groups in which Canada is at a comparative advantage [wood, paper and allied products, primary metals, petroleum and coal products, transportation equipment]." Cited by Urban Dimensions Group, "Growth of the Contingent Workforce in Ontario: Structural Trends, Statistical Dimensions and Policy Implications" (Toronto: Ontario Women's Directorate, 1989), 15.

116. Pat Armstrong, "The Feminization of the Labour Force," *Rethinking Restructuring*, ed. Isabella Bakker (Toronto: University of Toronto Press, 1996), 35.

117. Jane Badets and Nancy McLaughlin, "Immigrants in Product Manufacturing," *Perspectives on Labour and Income* 1 (3 Winter) 1989, 40, cited by Pat Armstrong, "The Feminization of the Labour Force," in *Rethinking Restructuring*, ed. Isabella Bakker (Toronto: University of Toronto Press, 1996), 35.

118. Marjorie Griffin Cohen, "The Implications of Economic Restructuring for Women: The Canadian Situation," in *The Strategic Silence: Gender and Economic Policy*, ed. Isabella Bakker (London: Zed Books, 1994), 109.

119. Katherine Marshall, Denise Guevremont and Stephane Pronovost, "Sizing Up Employment in Clothing Manufacturing," *Perspectives*, Spring 1997 (Ottawa: Statistics Canada, Catalogue No. 75-001-XPE), 34-5.

120. Marjorie Griffin Cohen. "Feminism's Effect on Economic Policy," in *Canadian Women's Issues*, Vol. II, eds. Ruth Roach Pierson and Marjorie Griffin Cohen (Toronto: Lorimer, 1995), 281.

121. Canadian Labour Market and Productivity Centre, *Women and Economic Restructuring* (Ottawa: CLMPC, 1994), 18.

122. Economic Council of Canada, *Good Jobs, Bad Jobs: Employment in the Service Economy* (Ottawa: Ministry of Industry, Science and Technology, 1993), cited by Pat Armstrong, "The Feminization of the Labour Force," in *Rethinking Restructuring*, ed. Isabella Bakker (Toronto: University of Toronto Press, 1996), 35.

123. Marcy Cohen, "The Feminization of the Labour Market, Prospects for the 1990s," in *Getting on Track*, ed. Daniel Drache (Kingston: McGill Queens, 1992), 106.

124. Marcy Cohen, "The Feminization of the Labour Market, Prospects for the 1990s," in *Getting on Track*, ed. Daniel Drache (Kingston: McGill Queens University Press, 1992), 107-8.

125. CLC, *Women's Work: A Report* (Ottawa: CLC, 1997), 14.

126. Alice de Wolff, "Job Loss and Entry Level Information Workers: Training and Adjustment Strategies for Clerical Workers in Metropolitan Toronto," Report of the Metro Toronto Clerical Workers Labour Adjustment Committee, 1995, cited by CLC, *Women's Work: A Report* (Ottawa: CLC, 1997), 14.

127. See: Margaret Philip, "Women Climbing Wage Ladder," *Globe and Mail*, 13 May 1998.

128. Alanna Mitchell, "Working Women Gaining Equality," *Globe and Mail*, 3 March 1993.

129. Pamela Best, "Women, Men and Work," *Canadian Social Trends* (Ottawa: Statistics Canada, Spring 1995), 33.

130. Canadian Labour Market and Productivity Centre, *Women and Economic Restructuring* (Ottawa: CLMPC, 1994), 20.

131. Punam Khosla, "Review of the Situation of Women in Canada" (Toronto: National Action Committee on the Status of Women, 1993), 13.

132. *Women in Canada: A Statistical Report* (Ottawa: Statistics Canada, 1995), 152.

133. *Women in Canada: A Statistical Report* (Ottawa: Statistics Canada, 1995), 137.

134. *Women in Canada: A Statistical Report* (Ottawa: Statistics Canada, 1995), 137.

135. Pat Armstrong and Hugh Armstrong, *Double Ghetto*, citing Duffy and Pupo (1992: 171).

136. CLC, *Women's Work: A Report* (Ottawa: CLC, 1997), 25.

137. Alex Dagg, "Trade Union Response to Global Restructuring," A Working Paper from the Centre for Work And Society, August 1993, 2.

138. Ontario District Council of International Ladies Garment Workers' Union and INTERCEDE, "Industrial Homeworkers and Domestic Workers: Proposals for Improved Employment Legislation and Its Enforcement and Proposals for Access to Collective Bargaining," Feb. 1993, 22.

139. Ecumenical Coalition for Economic Justice. "Sweatshop Fashions: A Thing of the Present," *Economic Justice Report*, vol. 7, no. 3 (September 1996).

140. Yuen, cited in Bob Jeffcott and Lynda Yanz, "Bridging the Gap: Exposing the Labour Behind the Label," *Our Times* (Feb. 1997): 28.

141. Bob Jeffcott and Lynda Yanz, "Bridging the Gap: Exposing the Labour Behind the Label," *Our Times* (Feb. 1997): 28.

142. "From the Double Day to the Endless Day," Proceeding from the Conference on Homeworking (Canadian Centre for Policy Alternatives, Nov. 1992), 38.
143. Pamela Best, "Women, Men and Work," *Canadian Social Trends*, Spring 1995 (Ottawa: Statistics Canada, Cat. No. 11-008E), 33.
144. Kathy Jones and Valerie Huff, "Plant Closure: Its Effect on Immigrant and Women Workers," *Our Times* (January 1989).
145. CLC, *Women's Work: A Report* (Ottawa: CLC, 1997), 15.
146. Guy Standing, "Global Feminization through Flexible Labour," *World Development*, vol. 17, no. 7: p. 1989.
147. See for example: Peggy Bristow, et al., *We're Rooted Here and They Can't Pull Us Up* (Toronto: University of Toronto Press, 1994); Dionne Brand, *No Burden to Carry* (Toronto, Women's Press, 1991); The Women's Book Committee, Chinese Canadian National Council, *Jin Guo* (Toronto: Women's Press, 1992); Tania Das Gupta, *Learning from Our History* (Toronto, CCCC, 1986).
148. Ontario District Council of International Ladies Garment Workers Union and INTERCEDE, "Industrial Homeworkers and Domestic Workers: Proposals for Improved Employment Legislation and Its Enforcement and Proposals for Access to Collective Bargaining," Feb. 1993, 5.
149. Fely Vallisin, quoted in Canadian Labour Congress, *Women's Work: A Report* (Ottawa: CLC, 1997), 18.
150. Judy Fudge, "Little Victories and Big Defeats," *Not One of the Family: Foreign Domestic Workers in Canada*, eds. Abigail Bakan and Daiva Stasiulis (Toronto: University of Toronto Press, 1997).
151. Canadian Labour Congress, *Women's Work: A Report* (Ottawa: CLC, 1997), 18.
152. For an account of this see: Alex Dagg. "Trade Union Response to Global Restructuring: The Case of the ILGWU," Working Paper No. 5 (North York: Centre for Research on Work and Society, 1993); and Jan Borowy, et al., "Are These Clothes Clean?" *And Still We Rise*, ed. Linda Carty (Toronto: Women's Press, 1993).
153. Jan Borowy, et al., "Are These Clothes Clean?" *And Still We Rise*, ed. Linda Carty (Toronto: Women's Press, 1993), 309.
154. For more about this March see: Fatima Jaffer and Anges Huang, "A NAC for Movement Building," *Kinesis* (June 1996): 10-11. CLC, *Women's Work: A Report*, 65-6. ECEJ, "Women Call for Social Solidarity," *Economic Justice Report*, vol. 7, no. 3 (September 1996).
155. Demands included, "raising the minimum wage to $7.85 an hour, a real job creation program for women, a national child care program, abolishing the racist and sexist head tax, the inclusion of sexual orientation as one of the prohibited grounds of discrimination under the Canadian Human Rights Act...." CLC, *Women's Work: A Report* (Ottawa: CLC, 1997), 65.
156. ECEJ, "Women Call for Social Solidarity," *Economic Justice Report*, vol. 7, no. 3 (September 1996): 5.
157. CLC, *Women's Work: A Report* (Ottawa: CLC, 1997), 67.
158 See interview with Sunera Thobani - Fatima Jaffer and Anges Huang, "A NAC for Movement Building," *Kinesis* (June 1996): 10-11. Marjorie Cohen also makes this point well in "From the Welfare State to Vampire Capitalism," in *Women and the Welfare State*, eds. Patricia Evans and Gerda Wekerle (Toronto: University of Toronto Press, 1997).
159. ECEJ, "Women Call For Social Solidarity," *Economic Justice Report*, vol. 7, no. 3 (September 1996): 5.

REFERENCES

Albo, Greg, and Robert MacDermid. "Divided Province, Growing Protests: Ontario Moves Right. In K. Brownsey and M. Howlett, eds., *The Provincial State: Politics in Canada's Provinces and Territories*, 2nd edition. Toronto: Irwin, Forthcoming.

Alcoff, Linda. "Cultural Feminism versus Poststructuralism," *Signs*, vol. 13, no. 3.

Alexander, M. Jacqui, and Chandra Talpade Mohanty. "Introduction." In M. Jacqui Alexander and Chandra Talpade Mohanty, eds., *Feminist Genealogies, Colonial Legacies, Democratic Futures*. New York: Routledge, 1997.

Arat-Koc, Sedef. "In the Privacy of Our Own Home: Foreign Domestic Workers as Solution to the Crisis in the Domestic Sphere in Canada," *Studies in Political Economy*, no. 28 (Spring 1989).

Armstrong, Pat. "The Feminization of the Labour Force." In Isabella Bakker, ed., *Rethinking Restructuring*. Toronto: University of Toronto Press, 1996.

Baachi, Carol Lee. *The Politics of Affirmative Action*. London: Sage, 1996.

Bakker, Isabella. "Pay Equity and Economic Restructuring." In Judy Fudge and Patricia McDermott, eds., *Just Wages: A Feminist Assessment of Pay Equity*. Toronto: University of Toronto Press, 1991.

————, ed. *Rethinking Restructuring: Gender and Change in Canada*. Toronto: University of Toronto Press, 1996.

————, ed. *The Strategic Silence: Gender and Economic Policy*. London: Zed Books, 1994.

Bannerji, Himani. "Popular Images of South Asian Women." In Himani Bannerji, ed., *Returning the Gaze*. Toronto: Sister Vision Press, 1993.

Beneria, Lourdes, and Shelley Feldman, eds. *Unequal Burden: Economic Crisis, Persistent Poverty and Women's Work*. Boulder, Colorado: Westview Press, 1992.

Best, Pamela. "Women, Men and Work." In *Canadian Social Trends*. Ottawa: Statistics Canada, Cat. No. 11-008E, Spring 1995.

Borowy, Jan, et al. "Are These Clothes Clean?" In Linda Carty, ed., *And Still We Rise*. Toronto: Women's Press, 1993.

Boyd, Monica. "Immigrant Women: Language Socioeconomic Inequalities and Policy Issues." In Shiva Halli, Frank Trovanto, and Leo Driedger, eds., *Ethnic Demography*. Ottawa: Carleton University Press, 1990.

————. "Migration Policy, Female Dependency, Family Membership." In Pat Evans and Gerda Wekerle, eds., *Women and the Canadian Welfare State*. Toronto: University of Toronto Press, 1997.

Brah, Avtar. "South Asian Young Muslim Women and the Labour Market." In Halef Afshar and Mary Maynard, eds., *The Dynamics of Gender and Race*. London: Taylor and Francis, 1994.

Brand, Dionne. "A Working Paper on Black Women in Toronto: Gender, Race and Class." In Himani Bannerji, ed., *Returning the Gaze*. Toronto: Sister Vision Press, 1993.

————. *No Burden to Carry*. Toronto: Women's Press, 1991.

Bristow, Peggy, et al., eds. *We're Rooted Here and They Can't Pull Us Up*. Toronto: University of Toronto Press, 1994.

Brodie, Janine. "Meso-Discourses, State Forms and the Gendering of Liberal-Democratic Citizenship." *Citizenship Studies*, vol. 1, no. 2 (1997).

————. *The Political Economy of Canadian Regionalism*. Toronto: Harcourt Brace Jovanovich, 1991.

————. *Politics on the Margins. Restructuring and the Canadian Women's Movement*. Halifax: Fernwood, 1995.

Brown, Phillip, and Rosemary Crompton, eds. *Economic Restructuring and Social Exclusion*. London: UCL, 1994.

Bullock, Susan. *Women and Work*. London: Zed Books, 1994.

Cameron, Barbara. "From Equal Opportunity to Symbolic Equity: Three Decades of Federal Training Policy for Women." In Isabella Bakker, ed., *Rethinking Restructuring. Gender and Change in Canada*. Toronto: University of Toronto, 1996.

Campbell, Bruce. *Canada Under Siege: Three Years into the Free Trade Era*. Ottawa: Canadian Centre for Policy Alternatives, 1992.

Canadian Centre For Policy Alternatives. "Which Way for the Americas: Analysis of NAFTA Proposals and Impact on Canada." Ottawa: CCPA, 1992.

Canadian Labour Congress. *Women's Work: A Report*. Ottawa: CLC, 1997.

Canadian Labour Market and Productivity Centre. *Women and Economic Restructuring*. Ottawa: CLMPC, 1994.

Clarke, Tony. "The Transnational Corporate Agenda Behind the Harris Regime." In Diana Ralph, Andre Regimbald, and Nérée St-Amand, eds., *Open for Business. Closed to People*. Halifax: Fernwood, 1997.

Centre for Research on Work and Society. *Gender and Economic Restructuring*. Working Paper No. 12. North York: York University, 1995.

Chinese Canadian National Council. *Jin Guo*. Toronto: Women's Press, 1992.

Chui, Tina, and Mary Sue Devereaux. "Canada's Newest Workers." In *Perspectives*. Ottawa: Statistics Canada, Cat. No. 75-001E, Spring 1995.

Cohen, Marcy. "The Feminization of the Labour Market: Prospects for the 1990s." In Daniel Drache, ed., *Getting on Track*. Kingston: McGill-Queens University Press, 1992.

Cohen, Marjorie Griffin. "Feminism's Effect on Economic Policy." In Marjorie Cohen and Ruth Roach Pierson, eds., *Canadian Women's Issues*, Vol. III. Toronto: James Lorimer, 1995.

————. "From the Welfare State to Vampire Capitalism." In Patricia M. Evans and Gerda R. Wekerle, eds., *Women and the Canadian Welfare State*. Toronto: University of Toronto Press, 1997.

————. "The Implications of Economic Restructuring for Women: The Canadian Situation." In Isabella Bakker, ed., *The Strategic Silence: Gender and Economic Policy*. London: Zed Books, 1994.

————. "New International Trade Agreements: Their Reactionary Role in Creating Markets and Retarding Social Welfare." In Isabella Bakker, ed., *Rethinking Restructuring: Gender and Change in Canada*. Toronto: University of Toronto Press, 1996.

Connelly, M. Patricia. "Gender Matters: Restructuring and Adjustment, South and North." In Centre for Research on Work and Society, *Gender and Economic Restructuring*. Working Paper No. 12. North York: York University, September 1995.

Dagg, Alex. *Trade Union Response to Global Restructuring*. North York: Centre for Research on Work and Society, York University, 1993.

Das Gupta, Tania. *Learning From Our History*. Toronto: Cross Cultural Communication Centre, 1986.

Ecumenical Coalition for Economic Justice. *Reweaving Canada's Social Programs: From Shredded Safety Net to Social Solidarity*. Toronto: ECEJ, 1993.

———. "Confronting the Unemployment Crisis." *Economic Justice Report*, vol. 7, no. 4 (December 1996).

———. "Jobs are the Key to Social Security." *Economic Justice Report,* vol. 7, no. 3 (October 1994).

———. "Provinces Play Follow the Federal Leader." *Economic Justice Report*, vol. 7, no. 1 (May 1996).

———. "Sweatshop Fashions: A Thing for the Present." *Economic Justice Report*, vol. 7, no. 3 (September 1996).

———. "Women Call for Social Solidarity." *Economic Justice Report*, vol. 7, no. 3 (September 1996).

Elson, Diane. "From Survival Strategies to Transformation Strategies: Women's Needs and Structural Adjustment." In Shelley Feldman and Lourdes Beneria, eds., *Unequal Burden: Economic Crisis, Persistent Poverty and Women's Work*. Boulder, Co: Westview Press, 1992.

Elson, Diane, and Ruth Pierson. "Nimble Fingers Make Cheap Workers: An Analysis of Women's Employment in Third World Export Manufacturing." *Feminist Review*, vol. 7 (Spring 1981).

"From the Double Day to the Endless Day." Proceeding from the Conference on Homeworking, November 1992. Ottawa: Centre for Policy Alternatives.

Fudge, Judy. "Fragmentation and Feminization: The Challenge of Equity for Labour Relations Policy." In Janine Brodie, ed., *Women and Canadian Public Policy*. Toronto: Harcourt Brace, 1996.

———. "Little Victories and Big Defeats: The Rise and Fall of Collective Bargaining Rights for Domestic Workers in Ontario." In Abigail Bakan and Daiva Stasiulis, eds., *Not One of the Family*. Toronto: University of Toronto Press, 1997.

Fudge, Judy, and Patricia McDermott. "Conclusion: Pay Equity in a Declining Economy: The Challenge Ahead." In Judy Fudge and Patricia McDermott, eds., *Just Wages: A Feminist Assessment of Pay Equity*. Toronto: University of Toronto Press, 1991.

Gabriel, Christina. "Recasting Citizenship: The Politics of Multiculturalism Policy in Canada." Diss. York University, 1997.

———. "Women and Economic Restructuring: Current Trends and Issues." In Centre for Research on Work and Society, *Gender and Economic Restructuring*. Working Paper No. 12. North York: York University, September 1995.

Gabriel, Christina, and Laura Macdonald. "NAFTA, Women and Organizing in Canada and Mexico: Forging A 'Feminist Internationality.'" *Millennium*, vol. 23, no. 3 (Winter 1994).

Gibson-Graham, J. K. *The End of Capitalism as We Knew It*. London: Basil Blackwell Publishers, 1996.

Grewal, Inderpal, and Caren Kaplan, eds. *Scattered Hegemonies: Postmodernity and Transnational Politics*. Minneapolis: University of Minnesota Press, 1994.

Grinspun, Ricardo, and Robert Krelewich. "Consolidating Neoliberal Reforms: Free Trade as a Conditioning Framework." *Studies in Political Economy*, vol. 43 (Spring 1994).

Gunderson, Morley, Leon Muszynski with Jennifer Keck. *Women and Labour Market Poverty*. Ottawa: Canadian Advisory Council on the Status of Women, 1990.

Haraway, Donna. "A Manifesto for Cyborgs: Science, Technology, and Socialist Feminism in the 1980s." In Linda Nicholson ed., *Feminism/Postmodernism*. New York: Routledge, 1990.

Held, David. *Democracy and the Global Order*. Cambridge: Polity Press, 1995.

Jaffer, Fatima, and Agnes Huang. "NAC President Sunera Thobani Leaves a Legacy: A NAC for Movement Building." *Kinesis* (June 1996).

Jeffcott, Bob, and Lynda Yanz. "Bridging the Gap: Exposing the Labour Behind the Label." *Our Times* (Feb. 1997).

Jenson, Jane. "'Different' But Not 'Exceptional.'" *Canadian Review of Sociology and Anthropology*, vol. 26, no. 1 (1989).

Jones, Kathy, and Valerie Huff. "Plant Closure: Its Effect on Immigrant and Women Workers." *Our Times* (January 1989).

Kelly, Karen. "Visible Minorities: A Diverse Group." In *Canadian Social Trends*. Ottawa: Statistics Canada, Cat. No. 11-008E, Summer 1995.

Khosla, Punam. "Review of the Situation of Women in Canada" Toronto: National Action Committee on the Status of Women, 1993.

Kitchen, Brigitte. "'Common Sense' Assaults on Families" in Diana Ralph, Andre Regimbald, and Nérée St-Amand, eds., *Open for Business. Closed to the People*. Halifax: Fernwood, 1997.

Laghi, Brian. "Minorities Don't Share in Canada's Boom." *Globe and Mail*, 13 May 1998.

Macklin, Audrey. "On the Inside Looking In: Foreign Domestic Workers in Canada." In Wenona Giles and Sedef Arat-Koc, eds., *Maid in the Market*. Halifax: Fernwood, 1994.

Marshall, Katherine, Denise Guevremont, and Stephen Pronovost. "Sizing Up Employment in Clothing Manufacturing." In *Perspectives*. Ottawa: Statistics Canada, Catalogue No. 75-001-XPE, Spring 1997.

McBride, Stephen, and John Sheilds. *Dismantling a Nation: Canada and the New World Order*. Halifax: Fernwood, 1993.

Mitchell, Alana. "Women Working to Gain Equality." *Globe and Mail*, 3 March 1993.

Mitter, Swasti. *Common Fate, Common Bond: Women in the Global Economy*. Pluto: Zed Press, 1986.

———. "On Organizing Women in Casualized Work: A Global Overview." In Sheila Rowbotham and Swasti Mitter, eds., *Dignity and Daily Bread*. London: Routledge, 1994.

Mohanty, Chandra Talpade. "Cartographies of Struggle." In Chandra Mohanty, Ann Russo, and Lourdes Torres, eds., *Third World Women and the Politics of Feminism*. Bloomington, Indiana: Indiana University Press, 1991.

———. "Women Workers and Capitalist Scripts: Ideologies of Domination, Common Interests and the Politics of Solidarity." In M. Jacqui Alexander and Chandra Talpade Mohanty, eds., *Feminist Genealogies, Colonial Legacies, Democratic Futures*. New York: Routledge, 1997.

Ng, Roxanna. "Immigrant Women: The Construction of a Labour Market Category." *Canadian Journal of Women and the Law*, vol. 4 (1990).

Noce, Louise, and Anne O'Connell. *Take It or Leave It: The Ontario Government's Approach to Job Insecurity*. Speaking Out Project: Periodic Report No. 1. Ottawa: Caledon Institute of Social Policy, 1998.

Ontario Council of Agencies Serving Immigrants (OCASI). "Employment Equity for Ontario." Brief submitted to Honourable Elaine Ziemba, Minister of Citizenship, Feb. 1992.

———. "The Ontario Training and Adjustment Board." Brief submitted to Honourable Richard Allen, Minister of Skills Development, May 1992.

Ontario District Council of International Ladies Garment Workers' Union and INTERCEDE. "Industrial Homeworkers and Domestic Workers: Proposals for Improved Employment Legislation and Its Enforcement and Proposals for Access to Collective Bargaining." Feb. 1993.

Ontario, Ministry of Labour. "The Displaced Workers of Ontario: How Do They Fare." Toronto: Ministry of Labour, 1993.

Ontario, Management Board Secretariat. "The OPS: Employment Equity Annual Report - June 1991 to May 1992." Toronto: Management Board Secretariat, 1993.

Organization for Economic Co-operation and Development. *Women and Structural Change. New Perspectives*. Paris: OECD, 1994.

Perkins, Charmaine, et al. "Interview with Dionne Brand." *Kinesis* (October 1993).

Philip, Margaret. "Women Climbing Wage Ladder." *Globe and Mail*, 13 May 1998.

Pierson, Ruth Roach. "Education and Training." In Ruth Roach Pierson and Marjorie Cohen, eds., *Canadian Women's Issues*, Vol. II. Toronto: Lorimer, 1994.

Ralph, Diana, Andre Regimbald, and Nérée St-Amand, eds. *Open for Business. Closed to the People*. Halifax: Fernwood, 1997.

Rebick, Judy. "Right Turn Leads to Dead End." *Kinesis* (July/August 1995).

Ricciutelli, Luciana, June Larkin, Eimear O'Neill, eds. *Confronting the Cuts*. North York: Inanna Publications, 1998.

Robinson, Ian. "The NAFTA, Democracy and Continental Economic Integration: Trade Policy as if Democracy Matters." In Susan Phillips, ed., *How Ottawa Spends: A More Democratic Canada...? (1993/1994)*. Ottawa: Carleton University Press, 1994.

Rowbotham, Sheila. *Homeworkers Worldwide*. London: Merlin, 1992.

Rowbotham, Sheila, and Swasti Mitter. *Dignity and Daily Bread*. London: Routledge, 1994.

"Sloganeering on Employment Equity." Editorial. *Toronto Star*, 14 May 1995.

Standing, Guy. "Global Feminization through Flexible Labor." *World Development*, vol. 17, no. 7: 1989.

Statistics Canada, Housing, Family and Social Statistics Division. *Women in Canada: A Statistical Report*, 3rd edition. Target Groups Project. Cat. No. 89-503E. Ottawa: Statistics Canada, 1995.

Urban Dimensions Group. "Growth of Contingent Workforce in Ontario: Structural Trends, Statistical Dimensions and Policy Implications." Toronto: Ontario Women's Directorate, 1989.

Trickey, Jean. "The Racist Face of 'Common Sense.'" In Diana Ralph, Andre Regimbald, and Nérée St-Amand, eds., *Open for Business. Closed to the People*. Halifax: Fernwood, 1997.

Vickers, Jeanne. *Women and the World Economic Crisis*. London: Zed Books, 1991.

Waters, Malcolm. *Globalization*. London: Routledge, 1995.

Woodside, Kenneth. "Trade and Industrial Policy: Hard Choices." In Michael Atkinson, ed., *Governing Canada: Institutions and Public Policy*. Toronto: Harcourt Brace, 1993.

PART III

THE CANADIAN STATE
AND THE INSTITUTIONALIZATION OF
RACE AND GENDER RELATIONS

CHAPTER SIX

Self-Government
and Aboriginal Women

SHARON DONNA MCIVOR

The eagles of war
whose wings lent you glory
they were nothing but
carrion crows;
push'd the wrens from
their nest
stole their eggs
chang'd their story[1]

Aboriginal peoples, collectively and individually, have the inherent right to self-government and the right to self-determination. In plain language, women and men have the collective and individual right to govern themselves, their land, people, and resources. This is a right that accrues to all human beings living a social existence among other human beings. The right to self-government is an individual right, exercised when individuals decide to live as a group and be governed by rules of social, moral, political, and cultural behaviour upon which they agree.

Collective and individual rights are inherent, protected in, but not created by, the Canadian *Constitution*. They are rights that have existed since people existed, and the right of self-government is one of them. It is foundational and fundamental, and cannot be taken away from individuals or groups in society. There has been a misunderstanding of the concept of self-government rights, as was seen in the Charlottetown process, where Aboriginal women were not allowed to be equal participants in defining their constitutional place in Canadian and Aboriginal society.

In the constitutional process leading to the development of the Charlottetown accord, there was a notion that Aboriginal women advocated individual rights to protect gender equality, and that the predominantly male Aboriginal leadership advocated collective rights. This is a false dichotomy. Collective and individual rights coexist in domestic and international law, as do the rights of self-government and self-determination.[2] Self-determination relates to the "self," to the individual, and collectively may refer to a group of individuals who share fundamental traits like race, language, culture, tradition and values.

In examining the meaning of the inherent right to self-government, it is important to remember that women and men had and retain traditional political, social, economic, and cultural roles, responsibilities, and rights, within Aboriginal societies. These roles, responsibilities, and rights are protected within the inherent right to self-government. The traditional roles of women are protected in section 35(1) of the *Constitution*, and their rights in section 35(4). Aboriginal women and men share the same desire for self-government, although their visions may differ.[3]

The scope and content of the inherent right to Aboriginal self-government have yet to be set out in the *Constitution* and Canadian legal framework. All governments and male Aboriginal leaders have been reluctant to commit principles to paper that will govern the implementation of the right to self-government. There has been an absence of trust by governments and Aboriginal peoples.[4]

GENDER EQUALITY AND SELF-GOVERNMENT

The inherent right brings forward the recognition and affirmation of the participatory right to self-government of Aboriginal women that they enjoyed under traditional matriarchies. The inherent right to self-government recognizes and affirms matriarchal governments. Women's right to participate politically, socially, culturally, and militarily is part of the custom and tradition recognized and affirmed within the existing right to Aboriginal self-government in section 35(1) of the *Constitution*.

This balance between women and men's participation in government-making is also inherent. Indian, Inuit, and Metis women have individual rights that abridge the collective rights.[5] This includes restoring the gender relations that existed between Aboriginal women and men since time immemorial. Restoring this gender balance requires throwing aside women's obedience and men's sexual powers over women, eradicating patriarchy, and returning harmony to human relations in the home and in communities.[6] The American Indian case law is clear that rights exist even if they are not practiced, or if they are suppressed.

To deny Aboriginal women their participatory rights because Canadian laws expelled women from the communities and denied them their traditional rights would run completely contrary to the willingness of all parties to recognize the inherent right to self-government. It would recognize only the patriarchal interpretation of the inherent right while blatantly denying the traditional, political roles of women. I reject the assumption that the recognition of women's gender rights abridging collective rights is a purely European idea. Much of the literature on individual rights shows clearly that the liberal tradition of individual rights emanates from North American Indian philosophies.

This modern-day quest by Aboriginal women to be involved in decision-making which affects their future, and that of their children, reflects their immediate past. Kathleen Jamieson described the situation of Indian women plainly: "one thing is clear — that to be born poor, an Indian and a female is to be a member of the most disadvantaged minority in Canada today, a citizen minus. It is to be victimised, and utterly powerless, and to be, by government decree, without legal recourse of any kind."[7]

Women's Rights as "Existing" Aboriginal Rights

As with other "existing" Aboriginal rights, Aboriginal women's civil and political rights are foundational and do not derive from documents or treaties.[8] The right of women to establish and maintain their civic and political role within the context of Aboriginal self-government has always existed. The regulation of women's political rights through successive Indian Acts did not extinguish their fundamental civil and political rights. Even if the suppression of women's rights was so oppressive it led to their banishment from Aboriginal communities, this, in itself, did not lead to extinguishment of their rights. There is no "extinguishment by regulation" in the Aboriginal field.[9] Even though it is regulated, an Aboriginal right continues to exist.[10]

Are Aboriginal women's civil and political rights part of the existing Aboriginal and treaty rights? These rights are part of the inherent right to self-government, of customary laws of Aboriginal people. As such, civil and political rights of Aboriginal women are now recognized as part of the common law. "Such practices or forms of social organisation do not require the imprimatur of state action to qualify as rights."[11] Self-government is central to Aboriginal nationhood, culture, and existence. The civil and political rights of women are central to traditional, matriarchal, and equalitarian forms of government. If Aboriginal self-government is central to the existence of Aboriginal nations, the ability to determine civil and political rights of members must also be central to exercising the right of Aboriginal self-government, which includes self-defining the roles of women.[12]

Fundamental human rights, like civil and political rights of Aboriginal women, can never be extinguished, and these rights existed in some form in 1982. The distinction between the *Indian Act* civil and political rights of Aboriginal women and their inherent rights lies in the regulation of women's rights. The questionable aspect of Aboriginal women's civil and political rights arose in the period from 1982 to 1985 when the *Indian Act* was amended to end sex discrimination against Indian women. After the passage of Bill C-31, *An Act to Amend the Indian Act*, the Government of Canada reinstated Indian women and their children to their communities and ended legislated sex discrimination. The legislation effectively restored the civil and political rights of Indian women who regained their Band membership and right to vote. The *Constitution Act, 1982* did not revive Aboriginal women's civil and political rights, but did confirm their existence.[13]

The *Sparrow* decision makes it clear that Aboriginal women's civil and political rights were not frozen in their regulated form. The Supreme Court ruled that "an existing aboriginal right cannot be read so as to incorporate the specific manner in which it was regulated before 1982. The notion of freezing existing rights would incorporate into the Constitution a crazy patchwork of regulations."[14] The Supreme Court agreed with Brian Slattery that "existing" means "unextinguished" instead of "exercisable at a certain time in history."[15] The Court held that the term "existing" must be interpreted flexibly to permit its evolution over time.[16] Using the Court's interpretation, the civil and political rights of Aboriginal women were affirmed in their contemporary form "rather than in their primeval simplicity and vigour."[17] Aboriginal women's rights were not frozen in time in their regulated form, but were affirmed as amended in 1985, with sex discrimination removed.[18]

In the *Sparrow* case, the government attempted to prove that the right of Musqueam Indians to fish in the Fraser River had been extinguished by regulation. The Court disagreed with this position.[19] Similarly, the civil and political rights of Aboriginal women have been regulated to the point where they have been denied participation in elections of *Indian Act* Chiefs and Councillors. When Indian women married non-Indians they were banished from their communities and their legal right to be an "Indian" was stripped from them. This directly affected 12,000 Indian women. In 1985, these women and approximately 40,000 descendants were restored to their previous Indian status and Band membership. It would be absurd to use the "patchwork" of regulation approach to examine the existence of Aboriginal women's civil and political rights. The Court's approach is correct; in *Sparrow*, it held "that the right is controlled in great detail by the regulations does not mean that the right is thereby extinguished."[20] Thus, if a right is not extinguished, it exists.

Prior to the 1985 amendments to the *Indian Act*, Parliament made it clear in law that Indian women who intermarried with non-Indian men lost their civil and political rights within their communities. In this context, the *Lavell* decision of the Supreme Court of Canada agreed that parliamentary supremacy gave parliamentarians the right to determine who had Indian status. The Court refused to use the Canadian *Bill of Rights* to strike down the offensive sections of the *Indian Act*, and refused to recognize that it discriminated on the basis of sex against Indian women. After the 1985 amendments to the *Indian Act*, it was equally clear that Parliament intended to restore status and Band membership to women who lost those rights. The legislation was retroactive. Even if an Indian woman had lost status forty years earlier than 1985, she could have that status restored. If she had since died, she could still have her status restored. In either case, her descendants could apply to have Indian status and Band membership. The legislation also restored control of Band membership and regulation of Indian lands to *Indian Act* governments.

The *Sparrow* decision held that there must be "clear and plain" intention on the part of the government where it intends to extinguish Aboriginal and treaty rights. The Court also held that in "the context of aboriginal rights, it could be argued that before 1982, an aboriginal right was automatically extinguished to the extent that it was inconsistent with a statute."[21] On this point, Aboriginal women would have had to overcome this argument, had Bill C-31 not reinstated them and attempted to end sex discrimination against Indian women. After the 1985 amendments to the *Indian Act*, Parliament's clear and plain intention was restorative of rights that had been regulated.[22] In *Sparrow*, the Court noted that Justice Hall in *Calder* held that, "the onus of proving that the Sovereign intended to extinguish the Indian title lies on the respondent and that intention must be 'clear and plain.'"[23]

The scope of modern-day Aboriginal women's civil and political rights will be determined in the context of the inherent right of self-government. Over the past few years, Aboriginal women's groups like the Native Women's Association of Canada have fought for participatory rights. They demand participation in the policy and legislative processes defining, developing, and interpreting their forms of Aboriginal government. This includes defining who is a member of the "group" or members of the "collective." What Bill C-31, *An Act to Amend the Indian Act*, restored women and their descendants to the "base group," Band, or Tribe that will exercise the right of self-government.

Some Aboriginal leaders and governments will look to the nature of Aboriginal women's civil and political rights and believe that the manner in which the rights were regulated will determine the scope of the rights. The Court in *Sparrow* rejected that approach. Aboriginal women, themselves, must be part of the process of delineating their civil and political rights. The Court also held that, "Government policy can, however, regulate the exercise of that right, but such regulation must be in keeping with section 35(1)."[24] Aboriginal women can use section 35(1) to negotiate the definition of their modern civil and political rights. If legislated forms of Aboriginal self-government will involve provincial governments as well as the federal government, the *Sparrow* decision makes it clear that Aboriginal rights are protected from provincial legislative power.[25]

At least since 1867, Parliament has relied on section 91(24) of the *Constitution Act, 1867* to pass laws governing Indians and lands reserved for Indians. Until 1985, when the *Charter of Rights and Freedoms* came into effect, Parliament was recognized as having the power to pass laws under section 91(24) whose effect was to discriminate against Indian women based on sex. The effect of section 35(1) upon section 91(24) powers has not yet been determined. I would argue, however, that section 35(1) has established new rules where courts can question sovereign claims made by the Crown.[26] It diminishes parliamentary supremacy. For Aboriginal women, it means they must be consulted by governments that intend to discriminate against them on the basis of sex. Such discrimination is no longer allowed under section 15 of the *Charter*. It means Parliament cannot establish new rules in the *Indian Act* in the future that discriminate on the basis of sex.

The Supreme Court of Canada held in *Sparrow* that section 35(1) was to be interpreted in a purposive way.[27] "When the purposes of the affirmation of aboriginal rights are considered, it is clear that a generous, liberal interpretation of the words in the constitutional provision is demanded."[28] Section 35(1) recognized and affirmed existing Aboriginal and treaty rights including civil and political rights of Aboriginal women. Evidently, women as well as men comprise members of First Nations and First Peoples of Canada. In 1983, Aboriginal women were successful in lobbying federal and provincial governments, and Aboriginal leaders, to have section 35(4) added to the *Constitution Act, 1982*. Section 35(4) affirmed that Aboriginal and treaty rights were guaranteed equally to men and women. This, to women, was a double confirmation of their rights. The section did not create new rights, but confirmed that women's rights are contained in section 35(1).[29]

The Supreme Court of Canada has also held that Aboriginal and treaty rights should be interpreted while taking into account Aboriginal history and tradition.[30] In interpreting Aboriginal women's civil and political rights as Aboriginal and treaty rights under section 35(1), the Court must consider the historic roles of women within their traditional as well as contemporary Aboriginal societies. Part of the history of Aboriginal women is one of an oppressive state government that has attempted to deny women their civil, political, and property rights within their communities. Rather than suppressing the civil, political, and property rights of Aboriginal women, it is argued that the federal government has an active responsibility to respect and protect the rights of Aboriginal women. The federal fiduciary trust responsibility may also require the Government of Canada to protect the civil and political roles of Aboriginal women within their societies. The Supreme Court of Canada reconfirmed the *Guerin* trust in *Sparrow* and decided the "government has the responsibility to act in a fiduciary capacity with respect to aboriginal peoples. The relationship between the government and aboriginals is trust-like, rather than adversarial, and contemporary recognition and affirmation of aboriginal rights must be defined in light of this historic relationship."[31]

The Court found that section 35(1) was not subject to section 1 of the *Charter of Rights and Freedoms*. Under section 52, federal and provincial laws which conflict with Aboriginal and treaty rights under section 35(1) would be of no force and effect. This view was rejected in *Sparrow*.[32] The Court held the legislation would be valid if it met the test for justifying an interference with a right recognized and affirmed under section 35(1).

Women's Fundamental Rights

The fundamental human rights of Aboriginal women — including civil and political rights — form part of the inherent right to Aboriginal self-government in section 35(1) of the *Constitution Act, 1982*.[33] The Supreme Court of Canada has determined in *Sparrow* that certain Aboriginal and treaty rights may be regulated.[34] Even if Aboriginal women's civil and political rights were regulated since 1867 by removal of women from Indian lands for intermarrying with non-Indians,[35] this was rectified by the 1985 amendments to the *Indian Act*.[36] One of the purposes of the legislation was to remove sex discrimination from the *Indian Act*[37] and bring the legislation in line with the *Charter of Rights and Freedoms*.[38] Civil and political rights are fundamental human rights that cannot be extinguished, even if the exercise of those rights is denied.

The civil and political rights of Aboriginal women differ according to culture and Tribal traditions, although most Aboriginal societies were matriarchal and matrilineal, including hunting and gathering societies. The rights of women were not written in the treaties, but they are rights which women have exercised since the formation of their Indigenous societies. They are rights women had upon contact with non-Aboriginal settlers and, in some cases, these rights were suppressed by non-Aboriginal laws. This is a form of regulation that has been removed with respect to political rights. Civil and property rights are the subject of sex discrimination in the current *Indian Act* and still need to be challenged under the *Charter*.

International law dictates the recognition of fundamental civil and political rights of Aboriginal women in the documents: *International Covenant on Civil and Political Rights*; *Elimination of All Forms of Discrimination Against Women*; and *Universal Declaration of Human Rights*. The *Charter of Rights and Freedoms* provides for governments to respect the civil and political rights of all women, including Aboriginal women. Human rights codes of the provinces and territories also call for the adherence to fundamental human rights without discrimination based on race or sex. The *Calder* decision recognized that Aboriginal persons can rely on Aboriginal and treaty rights as binding on the Government of Canada.

Thus, three events have occurred in constitutional history that lead to the conclusion that Aboriginal women's civil and political rights are "existing" Aboriginal and treaty rights. In 1982, the *Constitution Act* recognized gender equality in sections 15 and 28, and existing Aboriginal and treaty rights. In 1983, all First Ministers and Aboriginal representatives endorsed the inclusion of section 35(4) in the *Constitution Act, 1982* to recognize that men and women equally enjoy Aboriginal and treaty rights. In 1985, Parliament passed amendments to the *Indian Act* purportedly to eradicate sex discrimination against Indian women. The *Sparrow* decision ends the federal theory that Aboriginal rights have been extinguished by regulations. Just as the Aboriginal right to fish was not extinguished by specific fisheries' legislation, so, too, the *Indian Act* has not extinguished female civil and political rights. There can be no extinguishment by regulation of Aboriginal women's civil, political, and property rights.[39]

THE PRIMACY OF WOMEN'S RIGHTS

The struggle for equality for Native women is continuing today.... Our goal is to enjoy our place in society as did our mothers and grandmothers in their day.[40]

The Battle of Rights

It is useful to examine the primacy of Aboriginal women's rights as fundamental rights in the context of the Aboriginal community or collective.[41] Aboriginal women have struggled to have their "first generation" rights recognized. "First generation" rights include civil and political rights, which are fundamental to human beings.[42] Aboriginal men's organizations have always actively sought to suppress Indian women's struggle for sexual equality, claiming it interfered with their struggle for collective rights.[43] "Group rights" are described by Blaustein and Tenney as "fourth generation" rights that include "indigenous" rights. They include "the special rights of indigenous peoples — rights based on race, language and ethnicity, and rights that flow from membership in a particular tribe or caste. This is well illustrated by Article 27 of the *International Covenant on Civil and Political Rights*."[44] That battle has been described as women's rights versus Indian rights.[45]

Are Aboriginal and treaty rights collective or individual rights? Are these rights transportable with the individual? For example, do they move with the individual from the reserve to the city? The courts have attempted to answer this question in the context of linguistic rights guaranteed under the *Charter of Rights and Freedoms* to French-language speakers. In the case of language rights guaranteed under sections 16 to 23 of the *Charter*, the right invoked is collective, not individual. These rights require a critical mass of persons entitled to the right in order to invoke the right. However, where there is a French school that will not admit a child of a French-speaker, the right is individual.[46] Thus, the simple answer is that Aboriginal and treaty rights are both collective and individual rights, exercisable by both the collective and individuals.

Sub-Committee on Indian Women and the Indian Act

The battle lines between individual and group rights were drawn in 1982 before the Sub-Committee on Indian Women and the Indian Act.[47] The National Indian Brotherhood wanted immediate control of Band membership.48 It was prepared to act with no resolution over reinstatement of men and women who had lost their rights under the *Indian Act*. While the Assembly of First Nations advocated control of membership and indicated that men and women would then decide the form of self-government and membership criteria, only those then in the group would make such decisions. The 100,000 disenfranchised Indians who eventually registered under Bill C-31, *An Act to Amend the Indian Act*, were not intended to have any voice in determining membership criteria or the form self-government would take in their former communities. The Assembly of First Nations asked legislators to remember that collective rights, including the right to determine membership, was also protected in international human rights instruments. The organization stated that many of the international standards which Canada signed support First Nations' rights, and that the nationhood of First Nations is based on culture.[49] The Chiefs of the Assembly of First Nations supported equality for Indian women provided that the government paid for that equality; they claimed they did not want to harm the collective that was already living in poverty.[50]

Indian women were equally clear that they wanted reinstatement before the recognition of Indian self-government and a legislated end to sex discrimination in the *Indian Act*.[51] The Native Women's Association of Canada insisted that the women and their descendants be reinstated first, so that collectively with men and women on reserves, they would decide membership criteria and the form of self-government. The Native Women's Association of Canada claimed "discrimination on the basis of sex goes against international covenants which Canada has signed. It is therefore within the realm of human rights protection."[52] In a parliamentary submission, the Native Women's Association of Canada asked that legislators remember Indian women have paid psychologically, economically, socially, culturally, and politically because of state sex discrimination, and women have been denied millions of dollars in government programs, services, and lands.

The Commissioner of the Canadian Human Rights Commission noted to the legislators in 1982 that Canada had been found in violation of Article 27 of the *International Covenant on Civil and Political Rights*.[53] He also noted that Canada had acceded to the *United Nations Convention on the Elimination of All Forms of Discrimination Against Women*.[54] The Supreme Court of Canada has not anticipated the changing world of women's rights. The Court was, however, instrumental in inspiring women, including Aboriginal women, to take political action to achieve sexual equality.

At the time of the "Indian Women and the Indian Act" hearings, the *Charter of Rights and Freedoms* was not available to Indian women. The battle for the *Charter* was related to the defeat of women's struggle for equality in the Supreme Court of Canada. Canadian Indian women, like their female counterparts in the United States, had little or no domestic redress for gender bias in Band or Tribal rules. Neither group had the opportunity to bring their Nation to task for gender-based discrimination under the *Convention on the Elimination of All Forms of Discrimination Against Women*. While it is evident that Canadian Indian women can still pursue domestic remedies, it is not clear whether United States Tribal women have similar options as I point out later.

Individual Rights in the Context of Collective Rights

Where collective and individual rights conflict, group rights accede to individual rights. There ought to be a hierarchy of rights in which individual rights prevail. For example, first generation rights of women — civil and political rights — ought to predominate over fourth generation rights of Aboriginal collectivities.

In *Thomas* v. *Norris*, the British Columbia Supreme Court dealt with the civil rights of an Aboriginal man and gave his rights priority over group rights of his Aboriginal Nation.[55] This case questions whether group rights to traditional spiritual practices ought to yield to individual charter rights to security of the person. The facts of *Thomas* are that Mr. Thomas was seized against his will and forced to take part in an Indian spiritual dancing ceremony. During the ceremony he was assaulted, beaten, and forced to dance. The ceremony is a tradition and practice of a number of West Coast Indian Tribes. Part of the practice is to seize persons against their will and initiate them into the ceremony. The Court ruled against the Indian Tribe and held that Mr. Thomas had been assaulted, battered, and imprisoned.[56] That decision is not favoured by proponents of collective rights.[57] One author found the Court's decision to be "culturally vulgar."[58]

The British Columbia Supreme Court in *Thomas* considered the conflict between an Indian individual's common-law right not to be assaulted in the context of an Aboriginal community's practice to induct individuals into traditional spiritual practices.[59] The facts accepted by the judge included recognizing that the defendant had been assaulted, battered, and falsely imprisoned without consent. Section 25 of the *Constitution Act, 1982* was not invoked because the litigation was between private parties.[60] The judge also held that spirit dancing of the Coast Salish people was not proven to be an "existing" Aboriginal right protected by sections 35 and 52 of the *Constitution Act, 1982*.[61]

The defendants — those who grabbed the plaintiff — asked the Court to consider the question: "Are the individual rights of aboriginal persons subject to the collective rights of the aboriginal nation to which he belongs?"[62] The judge concluded that "the assumed aboriginal right...is not absolute and the Supreme Court of Canada affirmed this in *Sparrow*. Like most freedoms or rights it is, and must be, limited by laws, both civil and criminal, which protect those who may be injured by the exercise of that practice."63 Judge Hood found that Aboriginal rights are abridged by criminal and civil laws where they are in conflict.64 This interpretation, however, has yet to be decided by a higher court, whether there is an abridgement of an existing Aboriginal right without an explicit reference in legislation. There is no law against spirit dancing as practiced by the Coast Salish Indians since time immemorial. The author noted that certain Acts were extended to Indians prior to Confederation that may have impacted adversely upon Aboriginal jurisdiction over civil matters arising in this case.65 Judge Hood decided that the plaintiff's civil rights could not be subjected to the collective rights "of the aboriginal nation to which he belongs."66

Aboriginal Women's "Group" Rights

The other difficulty encountered by Aboriginal women is the severability of collective rights into group rights. It is rare for collective rights to be discussed in terms of rights based on class or gender.67 The exception may be gender rights of Aboriginal women that are guaranteed by section 35(4) of the *Constitution Act, 1982*. Under that section, Aboriginal and treaty rights are guaranteed equally to male and female persons. Section 35(4) is evidence that collective Aboriginal and treaty rights may be enjoyed by two groups within the Aboriginal community: men and women. This section has not been considered by the courts.

Two other sections of the *Constitution* make it evident that women, as a group, enjoy rights and freedoms: section 15 and 28. Section 15 provides that men and women, as individuals and groups, have the right to be equal under and before the law, and the right to enjoy the benefits of the law in Canadian society. Section 28 guarantees men and women, as individuals and groups, the right to equally enjoy *Charter* rights and freedoms. It would seem, then, that collective rights are severable into group rights, and that women are a prime beneficiary of this severability. The same applies to men — the group most likely to litigate under section 15.

In attempting to resolve the matter of concurrent group and individual rights, it may be important to consider the distinction made by the Royal Commission on Aboriginal Peoples between the right and the exercise of the right. A proper interpretation of the *Thomas* decision may be that the group had a collective right, but the manner in which it was exercised conflicted with Canadian law on assault, battery, and false imprisonment.[68] The *Thomas* decision may explain, in part, Aboriginal women's fears that their individual rights could be obliterated by collective rights.[69] Thomas Isaac suggested:

> The importance of the *Thomas* decision, is further evidence which supports the claims made by some Aboriginal women and their representative associations that any constitutional recognition of an inherent right of Aboriginal self-government must be subject to the *Charter* and its sexual equality provisions. Aboriginal women's organisations have stated that the constitutionalization of an inherent right of Aboriginal self-government may have the effect of curtailing their individual rights as women.

The author noted that the Quebec Native Women's Association wanted both collective and individual rights recognized, and for that reason they wanted the Canadian *Charter of Rights and Freedoms* to apply to Aboriginal governments. The Native Women's Association of Canada, as a national umbrella group, also asked that the *Charter* apply to Aboriginal governments. Not only must the individual have rights, but she must have the freedom to exercise those rights.[70]

Should "collective" rights take precedence over women's rights individually or as a group? One theory is that collective rights are protected by the *Charter*.[71] These collective rights are intended to protect minority groups from the majority.[72] Do individuals within the minority group have individual rights? What about women's rights within the collective? One court decided individual rights should not take a subservient role. Placing the collective above the individual is akin to living in a totalitarian state, the court found. Every individual has a right to enjoy his or her rights to the fullest without having such rights eroded by collective rights.[73]

The collective, the group and individuals in the group, all claim the right of self-definition. The Aboriginal group claims the right to define its own membership; women claim the right to define themselves as Indigenous first, women second.[74] Evidently some Indian Tribes and Metis groups will exclude certain members on the basis of sex. In the United States, Tribes may define their own membership, but programs and services will be offered only to those whom the government recognizes as quarter-blood Indians.[75] In Canada, membership is decided by Indian Bands and Metis associations, but the federal government will only recognize persons who meet the *Indian Act* criteria for status and Band membership. The group finds it repugnant to have an outside force, like legislation, determine who is a member of the group.[76]

The United States and Aboriginal Rights

Like the *Lavell* case in Canada, the *Santa Clara Pueblo* case in the United States froze the efforts of Tribal women to have their individual right to sexual equality endorsed by the courts. Mrs. Martinez, a member of the Santa Clara Pueblo before her marriage, married a non-Pueblo man and was struck from the membership list. Her children would not be entitled to membership because of her marriage. Pueblo men could marry non-Pueblo women and not suffer the same fate. Mrs. Martinez claimed sex discrimination in the Pueblo membership rules and went to court arguing that this discrimination was contrary to federal law, namely the *Indian Civil Rights Act of 1978*.[77] The statute was passed by the United States Congress to protect individuals like Mrs. Martinez from human rights abuses not available to them under the Articles of Confederation. The Articles do not apply because Tribes had existed long before the coming into being of the American *Constitution*. The court found in the Martinez case that it was without jurisdiction. This left Mrs. Martinez in a legal limbo with no recourse to regain her Tribal membership. In considering the right of individuals against the rights of the Tribe, the Supreme Court ruled that *habeas corpus* was the only mechanism for judicial review.[78] This decision has left Native women in the United States virtually paralyzed within a system that subordinates women's right to collective rights at the Tribal level. Carla Christofferson argued that there is a need to expand the *Indian Civil Rights Act of 1978* to protect women's Tribal rights in the United States.

One Native American woman has stated: "My only crime is being born a female. I want the same rights as men — the right to vote for a chief and the right to live on the reservation." Women who are discriminated against because of gender-biased Tribal membership codes suffer both financially and psychologically. They no longer receive federal Indian benefits, such as annuities from the Tribe, access to education and health programs, and housing. Moreover, they suffer the loss of their cultural identity, because they lose the right to live on the reservation with their family and friends.[79]

American Native women are in a different constitutional position than Aboriginal women in Canada, particularly "Indian women." In Canada, the state established the criteria for who is an "Indian" and the state is subject to the Canadian *Charter of Rights and Freedoms*, a constitutional document. Tribes in the United States are not subject to the *Constitution* and their Articles. Some members of Congress and the U.S. Senate believed that this could be overcome by passing the *Indian Civil Rights Act of 1978*. This legislation, while granting human and civil rights to American Indians, cannot be imposed upon United States Tribes without their concurrence. Gender-biased Tribal membership codes can, therefore, withstand constitutional challenges based on sex discrimination. Gender-biased Band membership codes in Canada are not likely to withstand a *Charter* challenge because of sections 15, 28, and 35(4), and the inherent rights of women contained in section 35(1). Because of this difference, at least one author argued there is a need for gender-specific protection in the United States to protect Tribal women from Tribal sex bias to ensure they have the same protection as other women.[80]

Canadian Aboriginal women have justiciable rights to sexual equality within the collective. It has been suggested that group rights are not justiciable because such rights are inherently political.[81] Language rights are group rights in Canada and they are justiciable and are exercised by individuals. Women also have group rights under sections 15, 28, and 35(4), and these rights are justiciable.

The adjudication of collective or group rights will require that the exercise of the right be considered in a cultural context. Because of the variety of Aboriginal cultures across the country, it may be that particularization is required in adjudication.[82] Which court ought to adjudicate cultural matters where a conflict arises between the Aboriginal community and its members? One author has proposed a national human rights panel composed of appointees from the Assembly of First Nations, the Congress of Aboriginal Peoples, and the Native Women's Association of Canada.[83] Such a suggestion is likely to meet with substantial resistance from Aboriginal communities that want the centre of power and jurisdiction to remain at the local level.

Aboriginal Collectives as "Legal Fictions"

Aboriginal collectivities, where they are created by Parliament, are "legal fictions" having little foundation in reality. The lands reserved for Indians were selected by non-Indian settlers and do not represent "Indian lands." The entire province of British Columbia is under claim by 27 Tribal groups living in 197 communities carved out of the territory in 1911. The people living in those communities are also a legal fiction having been defined by a non-Indian government in such a way as to diminish the actual number of persons entitled to live on Indian lands. Because *Indian Act* Indians and *Indian Act* governments are legal fictions created by federal law, since 1850, Parliament has arbitrarily decided who was an Indian in Canada for purposes of benefitting from programs and services and for determining who would live on Indian reserve lands. Until 1985, Parliament allowed non-Indian women who married Indian men to become Indians. The law also stated that Indian women who married non-Indians were no longer deemed Indians. The *Indian Act* and its regulations do not allow off-reserve Indians to vote for Chief and Band Councillors, thus disenfranchising over 300,000 Indians from democratically exercising their rights to determine their own political leadership. The *Indian Act* community is a fictitious body, "composed of the individual persons who are considered as constituting...its members."[84]

Conclusion

The flaw in the debate between collective and individual rights in the Aboriginal community is the creation of a legal fiction by government that the Aboriginal collective is an entity in itself. When parliamentary supremacy went unchecked by the *Charter*, it could declare Indians to be non-Indians, and vice-versa. It created an artificial group of "Indians" who qualified for programs and services under the *Indian Act.*

The individual has legal rights. The community has collective rights exercisable by individuals or by a collection of entitled individuals. For example, the determination of membership and control of land and assets are collective rights of the Aboriginal community. The distinction that needs to be made if Aboriginal women are to exercise their equality rights is that all community members share in these rights: they cannot be limited just to members of the artificially created "community" as set out in the *Indian Act.* Where collective rights are violated, the wrong accrues to the individual members of the collective. "In this sense, aboriginal rights are personal in that their violation affects the individual Band members' enjoyment of those rights."[85]

Today, Aboriginal Peoples embark upon a road less travelled in government-Aboriginal relations. There is a lot of brush on the road. There is our oppressive past and there is our murky present. In 1992, we heard governments — federal and provincial — state that they recognize the "inherent right" of self-government as contained in section 35(1) of the *Constitution Act, 1982.* They did not explain the meaning of these words. As Aboriginal leaders we accepted their words as if they had meaning.

We have heard the federal Minister of Indian Affairs and Northern Development state that he is dismantling the Department, and devolving its programs and services to the Indian Bands. This process has been going on for over twenty years. Political accords have been signed between ministers and Aboriginal leaders on Indian programs and services; on gaming; on land claims; and on a plethora of services. In this context, it is left to us, as men and women of Aboriginal Nations, to determine the government agenda. As women of Aboriginal Nations we have to be concerned about the impact of these activities upon women and future generations. National, provincial, and local women's groups must be involved in the day-to-day negotiations on implementing self-government rights. Historically, women have been excluded from the national, regional, Tribal, and Band government organizations. Thus a conscious effort must be made to include women and their organizations.[86]

As women of Aboriginal Nations, as Metis women, and as Inuit women, we have the freedom to exercise our right to self-government and self-determination within our Nations. In November 1994, plans were announced for governing bodies for the territory of Nunavut that will be carved out of the present Northwest Territories. The territory will be almost exclusively Inuit. The new government, it was announced, would have equal representation from Inuit women and Inuit men, but when put to a referendum, it was defeated.

As a group of Aboriginal women in the organized movement, since 1971, we had a vision. It is a simple vision where we see ourselves united with our own people, on our own lands, determining our forms of government, deciding rules for membership in our Nations, and deciding who will live on our lands. That is the vision. We see ourselves home, among our own people — that place from which our mother, our aunts, our sisters, and our grandmothers were banished by law. We see ourselves back there. When the road is lonely and dark, and we are cold from the reception we receive when we speak of our right to participate, of our right to be at negotiating tables, and of our right to vote in our communities, that is the vision that sustains us.

NOTES

1. Song by Aboriginal singer, Buffy Ste. Marie.
2. Lillianne Ernestine Krosenbrink-Gelissen, *Sexual Equality as an Aboriginal Right: The Native Women's Association of Canada and the Constitutional Process on Aboriginal Matters, 1982-1987* (Saarbrucken, Germany: Verlag Breitenback Publishers, 1991), 7:

    In statements to the United Nations, Canadian government representatives have explained that they refuse to recognize the Indigenous peoples as 'peoples' because under international law 'peoples' have a right to self-determination — a right they do not want to recognize for Indigenous peoples, because Canada claims that Indigenous peoples would use this right to seek independence. Canada claims that, at the level of international law, it will recognize Indigenous rights only as individual rights. This effort to deny the reality of the Indigenous peoples as 'peoples' in order to avoid the obvious consequence in international law, may well prove to be counterproductive to Canada's interests. And it reminds us of the 'Person's Case' *Edwards* v. *Attorney-General of Canada* (1929) P.C., Canada's infamous refusal to refer to its female citizens as 'persons' to avoid the effects of a law which gave 'persons' the right to be appointed to the Senate.
3. Canada, Department of Justice, *Federal Issues Document on Violence Against Women* (Ottawa: Department of Justice, May 1994), 7.
4. Christos Sirross, Minister of Natural Resources and Minister Responsible for Native Affairs, "Notes for a Speech to the Federal-Provincial-Territorial Meeting of Ministers Responsible for Native Affairs and Leaders of the National Aboriginal Organizations," Quebec City, 17 May 1994, 3: "When we adopt this approach, we often realize that the difficulties stem from the fear we have of each other, and that this fear is rooted in our mutual ignorance."
5. Ibid.
6. Krosenbrink-Gelissen, *supra*, 44. "Moreover, the missionaries made serious efforts to change Indian gender relations. Women's obedience and men's sexual rights over women were gradually imposed in the Indian systems."
7. Kathleen Jamieson, *Indian Women and the Law in Canada: Citizens Minus* (Ottawa: Department of Indian Affairs and Northern Development, 1978), 9.
8. *R.* v. *Sparrow* (1990), 70 D.L.R. (4th) 385 (S.C.C.), 390.
9. Ibid., 391.
10. Ibid.
11. Michael Asch and Patrick Macklem, "Aboriginal Rights and Canadian Sovereignty: An Essay on *R.* v. *Sparrow*," *Alberta Law Review*, vol. 29, no. 2 (1991): 506.
12. Ibid., 505.
13. *Sparrow*, *supra*, 395.
14. Ibid., 396.
15. Ibid. See Brian Slattery, "Understanding Aboriginal Rights," *Canadian Bar Review*, vol. 66 (1987): 781-2; Kent McNeil, "The Constitutional Rights of Aboriginal Peoples of Canada," *Supreme Court Law Review*, vol. 4 (1982): 258; William Pentney, "The Rights of the Aboriginal Peoples of Canada in the Constitution Act, 1982, Part II, Section 35: The Substantive Guarantee," *University of British Columbia Law Review*, vol. 22 (1987): 207.
16. Ibid., 397.
17. Ibid.
18. Ibid.
19. Ibid., 400.
20. Ibid.
21. Ibid., 401.
22. Ibid.
23. *Calder* v. *A-G. B.C.* (1973), 34 D.L.R. (3d) 145, at 216.
24. *Sparrow*, *supra*, 401.
25. Ibid., 406.
26. Ibid, citing Professor Noel Lyon, "An Essay on Constitutional Interpretation," *Osgoode Hall Law Journal*, vol. 26 (1988): 100, "the context of 1982 is surely enough to tell us that this is not just a codification of the case law on aboriginal rights that had accumulated by 1982. Section 35 calls for a just settlement for aboriginal peoples. It renounces the old rules of the game under which the

Crown established courts of law and denied those courts the authority to question sovereign claims made by the Crown."

27. Ibid., 407.
28. Ibid.
29. *Nowegijick* v. *The Queen* (1983), 144 D.L.R. (3d) 193, at 198.
30. *Sparrow, supra*, 408, citing *R.* v. *Agawa* (1988), 43 C.C.C. (3d) 266, 28 O.A.C. 201, 215-6: "The second principle...emphasized the importance of Indian History and traditions as well as the perceived effect of a treaty at the time of its execution. He also cautioned against determining Indian rights in a vacuum. The honour of the Crown is involved in the interpretation of Indian treaties, as a consequence, fairness to the Indians is a governing consideration.... This view is reflected in recent judicial decisions which have emphasized the responsibility of government to protect the rights of Indians arising from the special trust relationship created by history, treaties and legislation: see *Guerin* v. *The Queen* (1984), 13 D.L.R. (4th) 321."
31. Ibid.
32. Ibid., 409.
33. *Constitution Act, 1982*, 35(1): "The existing aboriginal and treaty rights of the aboriginal peoples of Canada are hereby recognized and affirmed."
34. *R.* v. *Sparrow* (1990), 70 D.L.R. (4th) 385 (S.C.C.).
35. John Leslie and Ron Macguire, *The Historical Development of the Indian Act* (Ottawa: Department of Indian and Northern Affairs Canada, 1979), 25. An Act of 1851, 14-15 Victoria, c. 59, was the first to exclude white men married to Indian women from being "legal Indians," but white women married to Indian men and their children would henceforth be "Indians." At page 55, the authors reported that the *Act* of 1869 "was the first Canadian statute governing status of native women after marriage to non-Indians, or to Indians of other bands." The 1876 *Act* disenfranchised illegitimate children, Indians who lived continuously outside Canada for five years, and half-breeds.
36. Bill C-31, *An Act to Amend the Indian Act*, R.S.C. 1985, c. 32 (1st Supp. 1985).
37. *Indian Act*, R.S.C. 1970, c. I-6, s. 12(1)(b).
38. Part I of the *Constitution Act, 1982*, being Schedule B to the *Canada Act, 1982* (U.K.), 1982, c. 11.
39. W. I. C. Binnie, "The Sparrow Doctrine: Beginning of the End or End of the Beginning?" *Queen's Law Journal*, vol. 15 (1992): 226. "In fact, extinguishment by regulation has for many years been a premise of the federal Indian claims policy. If the doctrine has 'no merit,' which is certainly the view for the time being of the Supreme Court of Canada, then a substantial chunk of the governmental defences against Aboriginal rights claims across Canada...may collapse."
40. Verna Kirkness, "Emerging Native Women," *Canadian Journal of Women and the Law*, vol. 2 (1987-88): 415.
41. I use the term "collective" to identify the Tribal group to which women belong; for example, an Interior Salish woman belongs to an Interior Salish Tribe, a Sioux woman belongs to the Sioux Nation. In Canada, the legislature created artificial groups known as Indian "Bands." A community or collective includes an Indian Band.
42. Albert P. Blaustein and Carol Tenney, "Understanding 'Rights' and Bills of Rights," *University of Richmond Law Review*, vol. 25, no. 3 (1991): 414. The authors coined civil and political rights as "first generation rights" and I adopt their terminology.
43. I refer to Aboriginal men's organizations mentioned in the case *Native Women's Association of Canada* v. *Canada* (1992), 95 D.L.R. (4th) 106 (F.C.A.).
44. Blaustein and Tenney, *supra*, 415.
45. Sally M. Weaver, "Indian Women, Marriage and Legal Status," in *Marriage and Divorce in Canada*, ed. K. Kishwaran (Toronto: McGraw-Hill Ryerson, 1978), 18.
46. Michael McDonald, "Should Communities Have Rights? Reflections on Liberal Individualism," *Canadian Journal of Law and Jurisprudence*, vol. 4, no. 2 (1991), 245 (hereinafter "Communities").
47. Canada, Parliament of Canada, Standing Committee on Indian Affairs and Northern Development, *Report of the Sub-Committee on Indian Women and the Indian Act*, Chair, Keith Penner (Ottawa: Queen's Printer, 1982) Issue 58 (hereinafter "Report on Indian Women").
48. The National Indian Brotherhood in 1994 is now called the Assembly of First Nations. I use the name "Assembly of First Nations."
49. *Report on Indian Women*.
50. Ibid., 17.
51. Ibid., 19.

The Assembly of First Nations said that by concentrating upon the discrimination in the *Indian Act* against individual women, there was a danger that remedies might be damaging to internationally recognized collective rights. 'Under international standards the collective rights under civil and political rights is recognized...all we are saying is that if you deal with the individual right in isolation of the collective right, part of the collective right for men and women to form their own government and to determine their own policy on citizenship questions, that is part of the civil and political rights issue that we are talking about under international standards. So you are taking away from it. By dealing with the one issue on a sex basis, you are discriminating against all Indians, never mind women, under those standards you are citing to me now.' The Assembly of First Nations felt that the problem of discrimination against Indian women in the *Indian Act* was a symptom of the non-recognition of the collective rights of the Indian community, which include the right of the men and women together to decide their own form of government.

52.   Ibid.
53.   Ibid., 18.
54.   *Declaration on Elimination of Discrimination Against Women*, Art. 5, 1967 U.N.Y.B. 518, U.N. Doc. A/6716/1967. The United Nations declared that "women shall have the same rights as men to acquire, change or retain their nationality" and that "marriage to an alien shall not automatically affect the nationality of the wife either by rendering her stateless or by forcing on her nationality of her husband." *Declaration on Human Rights*, 1948 3 Y.B. Int'l L. Comm'n 15, U.N. Doc. A/811/ 1948.
55.   *Thomas* v. *Norris*, 1992 2 C.N.L.R. 139 (B.C.S.C.).
56.   Thomas Isaac, "Individual Versus Collective Rights: Aboriginal People and the Significance of *Thomas* v. *Norris*," *Manitoba Law Journal*, vol. 3 (1992): 626 (hereinafter "Individual v. Collective"). "As outlined earlier, Hood J. decided in favour of the individual's right to security of the person over the group right to practice spirit dancing. This raises the issue of whether group rights should succumb to individual rights for Aboriginal peoples."
57.   Robert Matas, "Native Rite Ruled Subject to Law," *The Globe and Mail*, 8 February 1992, A6.
58.   Isaac, "Individual v. Collective," *supra*, 630.
59.   Ibid., 618. "The facts and reasons for judgment of the decision provide a superb opportunity to examine the issue of individual rights of Aboriginal people versus group Aboriginal rights."
60.   Ibid.
61.   Ibid., 621.
62.   Ibid., 622, quoting *Thomas, supra*, 159.
63.   *Thomas, supra*, 160.
64.   Isaac, "Individual v. Collective," *supra*, 623. "Thus, section 35 rights are to be exercised in accordance with the criminal law (which prohibits certain kinds of conduct) and the civil law which protects persons who may be injured by the exercise, in this instance, of Aboriginal rights."
65.   Ibid., 625. "An 1803 Act, and an 1821 Act, extended the jurisdiction of the colonial governments to include crimes and offenses within 'Indian territories.' Thus, the criminal law was clearly applicable to Aboriginal people long before Confederation. Bruce Clark notes that this restricts any Aboriginal claims of an inherent right to self-government to 'civil matters.'" The author's references included: *An Act for Extending the Jurisdiction of the Courts of Justice in the Provinces of Lower and Upper Canada, to the Trial and Punishment of Persons Guilty of Crimes and Offenses within Certain Parts of North America Adjoining to the Said Provinces* (U.K.) (1803), 43 Geo. 3, c. 138; *An Act for Regulating the Fur Trade, and Establishing a Criminal and Civil Jurisdiction within Certain Parts of North America* (U.K.) (1821), 1 and 2, Geo. 4, c. 66; Bruce Clark, *Native Liberty, Crown Sovereignty: The Existing Right of Aboriginal Self-Government in Canada* (Montreal: McGill-Queen's University Press, 1990), 125.
66.   *Thomas, supra*, 232. "He lives in a free society and his rights are inviolable. He is free to believe in, and to practise, any religion or tradition, if he chooses to do so. He cannot be coerced or forced to participate in one of any group purporting to exercise their collective rights in doing so. His freedoms and rights are not 'subject to the collective rights of the aboriginal nation to which he belongs.'"
67.   Michael Hartney, "Some Confusions Concerning Collective Rights," *Canadian Journal of Law and Jurisprudence*, vol. 4, no. 2 (1991): 239.
68.   Philip P. Frickey, "Marshalling Past and Present: Colonialism, Constitutionalism and Interpretation in Federal Indian Law," *Harvard Law Review*, vol. 107, no. 2 (1993): 395. The author found that the existence of congressional plenary power has been established by the courts, but the exercise of the power is open to scrutiny. Similarly, the exercise of powers under sections 91 and 92 are open to the *Charter* tests. In other words, parliamentary supremacy is not an issue. The question is whether legislatures under section 32 exercised their legislative powers in keeping with the *Charter of Rights and Freedoms*.
69.   Isaac, "Individual v. Collective," *supra*, 627.
70.   McDonald, "Communities," *supra*, 225. "In a liberal state, right-holders must be more than merely passive beneficiaries of rights; right-holders must be active exercisers of their rights."
71.   Ibid., 227.
72.   Ibid.

73. Ibid., 226-7. McDonald quotes Justice Deschenes in *Quebec Protestant School Board* v. *Quebec A.-G.*, 140 D.L.R. (3d) 33, 64-5:

    The court is amazed, to use a euphemism, to hear this argument from a government which prides itself in maintaining in America the flame of French civilization with its promotion of spiritual values and its traditional respect for liberty.

    In fact, Quebec's argument is based on a totalitarian conception of society to which this court does not subscribe. Human beings are, to us, of paramount importance and nothing should be allowed to diminish the respect due to them. Other societies place the collectivity above the individual. They use the Kolkhoze steamroller and see merit only in the collective result even if some individuals are left by the wayside in the process.

    This concept of society has never taken root here — even if certain political initiatives seem at times to come dangerously close to it — and this court will not honour it with its approval. Every individual in Canada should enjoy his rights to the full when in Quebec, whether alone or as a member of a group; and if the group numbers 100 persons, the one hundredth has as much right to benefit from all privileges of citizens as the other ninety-nine. The alleged restriction of a collective right which would deprive the one hundredth member of the group of the right guaranteed by the *Charter* constitutes, for this one hundredth member, a real denial of his rights. He cannot simply be counted as an accidental loss in a collective operation; our concept of human beings does not accommodate such a theory.

74. Wendy Moss, "Indigenous Self-Government in Canada and Sexual Equality Under the Indian Act: Resolving Conflicts Between Collective and Individual Rights," *Queen's Law Journal*, vol. 15 (1990): 279.

75. *Santa Clara Pueblo* v. *Martinez*, 436 U.S. 49 (1978).

76. Moss, *supra*, 289.

77. *Indian Civil Rights Act of 1978*, Public Law No. 90-284, 88 Stat. 77 cited in Carla Christofferson, "Tribal Courts' Failure to Protect Native American Women: A Reevaluation of the Indian Civil Rights Act of 1978," *The Yale Law Journal*, vol. 101 (1991): 170.

78. Carla Christofferson, "Tribal Courts' Failure to Protect Native American Women: A Reevaluation of the Indian Civil Rights Act," *The Yale Law Journal*, vol. 101 (1991): 170.

79. Ibid.

80. Ibid., 175.

81. McDonald, "Communities," *supra*, 228: "from a liberal perspective group rights, like individual rights, appear to be non-justiciable because they are inherently political. Thus, Dworkin assigns to the judiciary the task of adjudicating claims on the basis of rights. The role of judges is to postulate foundational rights, which Dworkin contends will centre on individual autonomy. This leaves the care of groups to the legislature, which has the task of advancing the general good in a totalitarian way."

82. Darlene Johnson, "Native Rights as Collective Rights: A Question of Group Self-Preservation," *Canadian Journal of Law and Jurisprudence*, vol. 2, no. 1 (1989): 28.

83. Moss, *supra*, 301.

84. McDonald, "Communities," *supra*, 219.

85. Storrow and Morellato, "Aboriginal Law," *supra*, 1.1.09 citing *Pasco* v. *C.N.R.* (1989), 34 B.C.L.R. (2d) 344; *Joe* v. *Findlay* (1981), 26 B.C.L.R. 376 (B.C.C.A.). In *Pasco*, the court noted: "It is a mistake...to ignore the historical fact that the rights Aboriginal are communal, and that they are possessed today by the descendants of persons who originally held them. They are not personal rights in the sense that they exist independently of the community, but are personal in the sense that a violation of the communal rights affects the individual members' enjoyment of those rights."

86. Jamieson, supra, 91-2: "At the time of the *Lavell* case there were no women on the National Indian Brotherhood NIB executive council and the Iroquois and Allied Indian group, who first enlisted the help of the Solicitor-General and turned the tide against Lavell, represented 20,000 Indian men. At present (February 1978) the Indian Brotherhood executive council has eleven members none of whom are women. At the September 1977 annual NIB conference, out of 68 delegates, only one was a woman (from B.C.)."

REFERENCES

Articles

Asch, Michael, and Patrick Macklem. "Aboriginal Rights and Canadian Sovereignty: An Essay on *R.* v. *Sparrow*." *Alberta Law Review*, vol. 29, no. 2 (1991).

Binnie, W. Ian C. "The Sparrow Doctrine: Beginning of the End or End of the Beginning?" *Queen's Law Journal*, vol. 15 (1992).

Blaustein, Albert P., and Carol Tenney. "Understanding 'Rights' and Bills of Rights." *University of Richmond Law Review*, vol. 25, no. 3 (1991).

Christofferson, Carla. "Tribal Courts' Failure to Protect Native American Women: A Reevaluation of the Indian Civil Rights Act." *The Yale Law Journal*, vol. 101 (1991).

Frickey, Philip P. "Marshalling Past and Present: Colonialism, Constitutionalism, and Interpretation in Federal Indian Law." *Harvard Law Review*, vol. 107, no. 2 (1993).

Hartney, Michael. "Some Confusions Concerning Collective Rights." *Canadian Journal of Law and Jurisprudence*, vol. 4, no. 2 (1991).

Isaac, Thomas. "Individual Versus Collective Rights: Aboriginal People and the Significance of *Thomas* v. *Norris*." *Manitoba Law Journal*, vol. 3 (1992).

Isaac, Thomas, and Mary Sue Maloughney. "Dually Disadvantaged and Historically Forgotten? Aboriginal Women and the Inherent Right to Self-Government." *Manitoba Law Journal* (1992).

Johnson, Darlene M. "Native Rights as Collective Rights: A Question of Group Self-Preservation." *Canadian Journal of Law and Jurisprudence*, vol. 2, no. 1 (1989).

Kirkness, Verna. "Emerging Native Women." *Canadian Journal of Women and the Law*, vol. 2 (1987-88).

Matas, Robert. "Native Rite Ruled Subject to Law." *The Globe and Mail*, 8 February 1992, A6.

McDonald, Michael. "Should Communities Have Rights? Reflections on Liberal Individualism." *Canadian Journal of Law and Jurisprudence*, vol. 4, no. 2 (1991).

Moss, Wendy. "Indigenous Self-Government in Canada and Sexual Equality Under the Indian Act: Resolving Conflicts Between Collective and Individual Rights." *Queen's Law Journal*, vol. 15 (1990).

Pentney, William. "The Rights of the Aboriginal Peoples of Canada in the Constitution Act, 1982, Part II, Section 35: The Substantive Guarantee." *University of British Columbia Law Review*, vol. 22 (1987).

Slattery, Brian. "Understanding Aboriginal Rights." *Canadian Bar Review*, vol. 66 (1987).

Weaver, Sally M. "Indian Women, Marriage and Legal Status." In *Marriage and Divorce in Canada*, ed. K. Kriswaren. Toronto: McGraw-Hill Ryerson, 1978.

Books

Canada. Department of Justice. *Federal Issues Document on Violence Against Women*. Ottawa: Department of Justice, May 1994.

Canada. Department of Justice. *Draft Report on the Role of Aboriginal Women in Justice Reform*. Ottawa: Department of Justice, May 24, 1994.

Canada. Parliament. House of Commons. *Report of the Sub-Committee on Indian Women and the Indian Act*. Ottawa: Queen's Printer, 1982.

Canada. *The Elimination of Sex Discrimination from the Indian Act*. Ottawa: Minister of Indian Affairs and Northern Development, 1982.

Hobsbawn, Eric, and Terence Banger. *The Invention of Tradition*. Cambridge: Cambridge University Press, 1983.

Jamieson, Kathleen. *Indian Women and the Law in Canada: Citizens Minus*. Ottawa: Department of Indian Affairs and Northern Development, 1978.

Krosenbrink-Gelissen, Lillianne Ernestine. *Sexual Equality as an Aboriginal Right: The Native Women's Association of Canada and the Constitutional Process on Aboriginal Matters, 1982-1987*. Saarbrucken, Germany: Verlag Breitenback Publishers, 1991.

Leslie, John, and Ron Macguire. *The Historical Development of the Indian Act*. Ottawa: Department of Indian and Northern Affairs Canada, 1979.

Lowes, Warren. *Indian Giver: A Legacy of North American Native People*. Toronto: Canadian Alliance in Solidarity with Native Peoples, 1985.

Storrow, R.V., and Maria A. Morellato. *Aboriginal Law: Fishing Rights and the Sparrow Case*. Vancouver: Continuing Legal Education, 1990.

Trigger, Bruce G. *Natives and Newcomers: Canada's "Heroic Age" Reconsidered*. Montreal: McGill-Queen's Press, 1986.

Unpublished Works

Christos Sirross, Minister of Natural Resources and Minister Responsible for Native Affairs. "Notes for a Speech to the Federal-Provincial-Territorial Meeting of Ministers Responsible for Native Affairs and Leaders of the National Aboriginal Organizations." Quebec City, 17 May 1994.

Cases

A.-G. B.C. v. *MacDonald* (1961), 131 C.C.C. 126.

A.-G. Canada v. *Lavell* (1973), 38 D.L.R. (3d) 481 (S.C.C.).

A.-G. Canada v. *Lavell, Isaac* v. *Bedard* (1973), 1974 S.C.R. 1349.
Calder v. *A.-G. B.C.* (1973), 34 D.L.R. (3d) 145 (S.C.C.).
Cunningham v. *Tomey Homma* 1903 A.C. 151.
Derrickson v. *Derrickson* (1986), 26 D.L.R. (4th) 175 (S.C.C.C.).
Edwards v. *A.-G. Canada* 1930 A.C. 124.
*In the Matter of a Reference as to the Meaning of the Word "Persons" in section 24 of the British
    North America Act, 1867* 1928 S.C.R. 276.
Joe v. *Findlay* (1981), 26 B.C.L.R. 376 (B.C.C.A.).
Lovelace v. *Canada* 1982 1 C.N.L.R. 1.
Native Women's Association of Canada v. *Canada* (1992), 95 D.L.R. (4th) 106 (F.C.A.).
Pasco v. *C.N.R.* (1989), 34 B.C.L.R. (2d) 344.
Paul v. *Paul* (1986), 26 D.L.R. (4th) 196 (S.C.C.).
Quebec Protestant School Boards v. *Quebec A.-G.*, 140 D.L.R. (3d) 33.
R. v. *Flett* (1989), 6 W.W.R. 166.
R. v. *Sparrow* (1990), 70 D.L.R. (4th) 385 (S.C.C.).
Re Lavell and A.-G. of Canada (1971), 22 D.L.R. (3d) 182 (Co. Ct.); rev'd (1971), 22 D.L.R. (3d)
    188 (F.C.A.).
Santa Clara Pueblo v. *Martinez*, 436 U.S. 49 (1978).
Simon v. *The Queen* (1985), 24 D.L.R. (4th) 390, 410-12 (S.C.C.)
Thomas v. *Norris* 1992 2 C.N.L.R. 139 (B.C.S.C.).
Union Colliery v. *Bryden* 1899 A.C. 580.

Statutes

An Act for the Better Protection of the Lands and Property of the Indians in Lower Canada, 1850.
An Act to Encourage the Gradual Civilization of the Indian Tribes, 1857.
*An Act for the Gradual Enfranchisement of Indians, the Better Management of Indian Affairs, and to
    Extend the Provisions of the Act 31st Victoria, Chapter 42*, S.C. 1869, c. 6.
Bill C-31, *An Act to Amend the Indian Act*. R.S.C. 1985, c. 32 (1st Supp. 1985).
Electoral Franchise Act. S.C. 1885, c. 40, s. 2.
Family Relations Act. R.S.B.C. 1979, c. 121, s. 77.
Fisheries Act. R.S.C. 1985, c. F-14.
Indian Act. R.S.C. 1970, s. 12(1)(b).

International Instruments

Declaration on Elimination of All Forms of Discrimination Against Women. Art. 5, 1967 U.N.Y.B.
    518, U.N. Doc. A/6716/1967.
Declaration on Human Rights. 1948 3 Y.B. Int'l Comm'n 15, U.N. Doc. AK/811/1948.
Indian Civil Rights Act of 1978. Public Law No. 90-284, 82 Stat. 77.

CHAPTER SEVEN

The Politics of Multiculturalism

"Immigrant Women" and the Canadian State[1]

TANIA DAS GUPTA

This chapter presents a critical, anti-racist, and feminist perspective on the policy, programs, and practices of multiculturalism in Canada, spe cifically from 1981 to 1986. During these years, I worked as a full-time community worker in Toronto in a community centre that dealt directly with immigrant women, multiculturalism, and racism. I argue that as multiculturalism has developed historically, it has become a state ideology.

Today, any discussion on multiculturalism raises a heated debate involving views from the range of the political spectrum. Some from the political left have called for the elimination of the policy saying it has been totally ineffective in fighting racism and has served as a means of controlling ethnic groups (Mazurek 1987; Brand and Bhaggiyadatta 1986, 19). Others (Gairdner 1990) from the political right, have called for its elimination saying it is a drain on government resources given the fiscal crisis of the last decade and that there are "more important" priorities for Canada as a nation. Both the left and the right end up as "bedfellows" advocating to throw multiculturalism out.

My own work is in the tradition of Ng (1991) and Stasiulis (1990) who see multiculturalism as a highly problematic and contradictory policy which has at times been beneficial to, and frequently regressive of, the interests of immigrants and people of colour. Multiculturalism policies and programs have limited anti-racist objectives by creating the conditions for co-opting anti-racism activism within state goals and discursively constructing particular notions of "immigrant women" and "Canadians" — gendered, raced, and classed — in line with dominant Canadian nationalism. Multiculturalism has also empowered some middle-class people of colour to appropriate anti-racist activism from their working-class counterparts, smoothing out its critical edge in the process.

On the positive side, multiculturalism has provided a context in which disempowered and marginalized groupings have been able to make progressive demands from the state. It has provided a political climate in which overt racism and discrimination has been made illegal. However, it has also produced a peculiar brand of "Canadian racism" described by many as "polite," "subtle," "systemic," and even "democratic."

187

KEY TERMS

The nature and role of "the state" has been a source of much debate in the litera-ture. Hall (1984) reminds us that "the state is a historical phenomenon: it is a product of human association." Thus, we must resist developing all-encompass-ing, global, and reified assertions with regard to states. However, Hall asserts that, in general, states imply a notion of "power," the power to "rule" including the capacity to enforce their will by coercion and/or consent. The coercive power of the state in Canada is illustrated by the varied occasions on which it has called on the armed forces to counteract any threats, real or otherwise, to itself, such as overseeing the internment of Japanese Canadians during World War Two, during the break up of militant strike activities and to strike back at First Nations Peo-ples when they resist the encroachment on their land. Power maintained through consensual means is seen in the elimination of employment equity legislation in Ontario following Premier Harris' election victory on an anti-equity platform, in which he denounced the legislation as a quota system. His strong electoral victory signalled that Harris' anti-equity bias had popular support and that knowledge allowed him to unilaterally dismantle almost all anti-racist initiatives undertaken by the previous government. The capacity to enforce by consent or by coercion is socially recognized as legitimate.

Neo-Marxist theorist, Ralph Miliband (1973), defines "the capitalist state" as a system of several institutions, including the government, the administration, the military and the police, the judicial branch, sub-central government and par-liamentary assemblies" (Miliband 1973, 50). He also defines a larger entity, namely a "political system," including parties and pressure groups, which must be taken into account in understanding "political power." In this conception, the network of community organizations for immigrants and ethno-racial minorities, many of which receive state funding, would be considered part of the political system. Miliband confirms Marx and Engels' view that "the holders of state power are, for many different reasons, the agents of private economic power...." Miliband argues that even though those with economic power do not actually govern, they are drawn from the same class backgrounds.

Nicos Poulantzas debated Miliband on the exact nature of state "structures" and their "relative autonomy" from different fractions of capitalist classes. Un-like Miliband, he did not believe that capitalists were a united class devoid of major divisions. Therefore, he theorized that states play the role of maintaining capitalist interests as a whole, managing intra-class contradictions and regulat-ing inter-class struggles. The manner in which the Canadian state has imple-mented progressive reforms such as pay equity, employment equity, or even multiculturalism policy illustrates the management of popular struggles led by women, people of colour, or minorities. In this process, it can be argued that some members of the state have been supportive of popular demands. For instance, the New Democratic Party government in Ontario revealed a marked interest in de-mands for employment equity while the Progressive Conservative government is opposed to it. However, the diluted nature of progressive reforms, such as human rights or equity legislations, and their inherent limitations in the final analysis, show they are more facade than genuine attempts to remove inequities.

Contemporary Marxists, such as Corrigan, Ramsey, and Sayer (1980), have argued that "the state" is a "formation" and that it is "no simple structure, but a changing pattern of relations, primarily between classes, which we can understand as an organization or orchestration of the relations of production." The state's role is that of a "regulator" so that the status quo — capitalist relations — seem the natural way of being. The specific state formation is shaped by inter- and intra-class struggles. Legitimacy of state forms and practices are maintained by the invalidation of any alternatives to the capitalist way of doing things. The process of legitimizing its rule demands that state formations relate not only to the political arena but also to other social, economic, and cultural formations. As mentioned, various levels of the Canadian state have had a direct relationship with non-profit community organizations through funding policies. Ng (1988) conducted a case study of an immigrant women's organization in Toronto and analysed how the state began to shape its activities through its regulative practices.

The problem of legitimizing the "rule" or "power" of states has preoccupied many theorists. Antonio Gramsci (1971, 206) said that this process involves an organic relationship between the "state" and "civil society." He referred to this alliance as "a mechanical block of social groups" (p. 54) consisting of the elements of force and consent. It is in the manufacture of the latter element that civil society or "subaltern groups" with autonomous status — including the church, schools, trade unions, media, etc. — have to be engaged. Here the important notions of "ideology" and "hegemony" emerge. Ideologies (Baldwin and Calder 1982; Wotherspoon 1987) are a body of connected and coherent beliefs which explain to us the world that we live in. A single ideology is usually accepted by most people, although it depicts reality from the perspective of the dominant class or group. Through this process of common acceptance, it becomes hegemonic or dominant. The dominant ideology acts as a "glue" to keep everyone together. It maintains social order and control and neutralizes resistance and conflict. Ideologies are neither true nor complete depictions of reality. They offer a simple, easy-to-understand picture of the world. Utilizing Antonio Gramsci's ideas, Wotherspoon has discussed the process of establishing and maintaining ideological hegemony. It is achieved by the active involvement and consensus of people in subordinate positions. Dominant ideologies have therefore to be made palatable to ordinary people by intertwining them with "national-popular" (Sarup 1986) aspirations and then declaring them as state ideology. According to Gramsci (1971, 59), a ruling social group "leads" its allies, but "dominates" its enemies. The latter may include anything from "absorption" of enemies to the use of force against them. Even when force is used, it must appear to be based on consent. Between force and consent stands corruption/fraud (p. 80), which could include demoralizing or paralysing the enemy by "buying" the leaders out.

In the context of Canada, Kas Mazurek (1987) has analyzed exactly how ideological hegemony was organized by the integration of popular demands of "minorities" for more power with the dominant ideology of meritocracy. Multiculturalism in practice has been a way of integrating minorities into the ideology of meritocracy and of perpetuating "equal opportunity," which remains a myth without "equality of condition." In the name of "equality," the inequality of mental and manual labour and assumptions about the innate inequalities in the talents and intelligence of people, as well as assumptions about individual's innate need to "have more," are all reproduced. These are not challenged by multicultural proponents. "Equal opportunity" for minorities is called for under multiculturalism, but not "equality" per se.

Before proceeding further, I will define the way in which I am using the phrase "immigrant women." In everyday discourse, the phrase is used interchangeably with the phrase "women of colour" by most Canadians, whether they are "of colour" or "white." This particular usage is underlaid with a notion of "who" a "Canadian" is or what a "Canadian looks like." The implication is that a Canadian is white, middle or upper class and Anglo or Francophone. Anybody who deviates from this stereotype — someone who is a person of colour, has a non-dominant accent, wears a "different" dress or headgear, coupled with a working-class occupation — would be referred to as "immigrant" or non-Canadian, even though they may be holding Canadian citizenship. Conversely, white, English-speaking immigrants from the U.K. or the U.S. are often immediately identified as "Canadians" even though they may not hold Canadian citizenship. In a nutshell, these categories are racially derived. To make matters more complex, community activists, specifically those who are first generation immigrants, have often reclaimed the phrase "immigrant women" as their own — recognizing that it refers to Southern European women and to women of colour — as a symbol of cultural resistence and a way of saying that they are proud to be "immigrant" and "different." I use the phrase "immigrant women" recognizing its problematic nature and acknowledging that it is offensive to many women of colour tired of being stereotyped as immigrant just because of the colour of their skin.

THE DEMOGRAPHIC COMPOSITION OF CANADA
— IMPLICATIONS FOR THE STATE

Based on 1996 Census data (Statistics Canada 1998), about 28 percent of the population reported origins other than Canadian, British, or French. About 1.1 million persons reported Aboriginal ancestry in 1996, an increase from 1 million in 1991. In 1996, 3.2 million persons or 11.2 percent of the total population of Canada identified themselves as visible minorities. The latter category includes Chinese, South Asians, Blacks, Arabs and West Asians, Filipinos, Southeast Asians, Latin Americans, Japanese, Koreans and Pacific Islanders. About three out of ten visible minorities were born in Canada. Three-quarters of the visible minority population of Canada reside in Ontario and British Columbia. Toronto was home to 42 percent of all visible minorities in Canada.

Canada, like most western European societies, had an explicitly racist and sexist immigration policy until 1967, when the Points System was introduced. A new Immigration Act of 1976 encouraged immigrants of colour to come to Canada as the "traditional" source countries were drying up. Of course, some, including me, would argue that immigration is still racist and sexist today but systemically so and couched in the language of "class" preference. Nevertheless, over half the immigrants who arrived in Canada since the 1970s and three-quarters of those who came in the 1990s are visible minority members.

These demographics show that Canada is composed of many ethnic and racial groups. The question remains, is multiculturalism a reality in Canada? Demographic heterogeneity does not automatically imply the success of a multicultural policy.

HISTORICAL DEVELOPMENT OF MULTICULTURALISM

"Multiculturalism" refers to the government policy launched in 1971 by then Prime Minister P. E. Trudeau. Its four central tenets (Mallea and Young 1990) were:

1. to assist all Canadians to develop culturally,
2. to assist all Canadians to overcome cultural barriers to full participation in Canadian society,
3. to arrange cultural encounters to promote unity,
4. to assist immigrants to learn one of the two official languages.

The interpretation of multiculturalism as a concept, its meaning in practice, and resources allocated to it, have changed in the interim twenty years, depending on pressures from various minority communities as well as on the fiscal health of the federal government.

Multiculturalism policy was initially launched in response to struggles in the non-British and non-French immigrant communities (sometimes referred to as the "other" ethnic groups), assertions by Canada's First Nations, and to resist the separatist movement in Quebec. It has been argued that the policy was a way to divert attention from the French-English question. The late 1960s in Canada brought to the public eye a strong and radical nationalist/separatist movement in Quebec, at times quite revolutionary in its approach. The government responded in a number of ways, including the establishment of a Royal Commission on Bilingualism and Biculturalism (the B & B Commission) in 1963. The B&B Commission was to"inquire into and report upon the existing state of bilingualism and biculturalism in Canada and to recommend what steps should be taken to develop the Canadian Confederation on the basis of equal partnership between the two *founding races*, taking into account the contributions made by the *other* ethnic groups to the cultural enrichment of Canada"(Fleras & Elliott 1992, 72, my emphases). The Report of the B & B Commission reconfirmed the special status of the British and French in Canada by defining them as "official minorities" (read separate and superior from "other" minorities) and by defining Canada fundamentally as a bilingual and bicultural country with a multicultural component. The First Nations are not mentioned in this discussion. They have always been seen as external to all the various ethnic and racial groups in Canada and indeed external to the Canadian nation itself. The silence on this question expresses the reality that the concerns of the First Nations have never been given any priority in discussions of Canadian nationhood, multiculturalism, or anti-racism. Serious consideration of the demand for self-government would fundamentally alter the conceptualization of multiculturalism policy.

Racism is also not acknowledged in the policy. Thus, we can see that there was already a hierarchy entrenched in the original terms of reference on the basis of ethnicity and racialization: British and French, "other" ethnic groups, First Nations in descending order. These power relations are historical and have continued to the present. A recent publication on multiculturalism states: "The multiculturalism policy aims to preserve and enhance and use of other languages while strengthening the status and use of official languages"(Mallea and Young 1990). This stated contradiction has been discussed in some detail by Stasiulis (1988) who points out the gross inequality in resource allocation to multilingualism ($3.83 million) as opposed to bilingualism ($218 million) in 1986-1987.

Various multicultural policies have circumvented the issue of power relations. In practice, cultural and linguistic principles (principles 1, 3, and 4) have been emphasized. These principles focus on the attitudinal part of discrimination rather than on structural barriers.

In its mission to maintain the status quo, multiculturalism has been institutionalized in a number of ways. In 1972, a multiculturalism directorate established at the federal level to assist in the implementation of multicultural policies, funded activities in the areas of human rights, citizenship involvement, and immigrant services, to name a few. A Ministry of Multiculturalism was formed in 1973 to monitor the multicultural initiatives within the government. Formal links with ethnic organizations were established via the Canadian Consultative Council on Multiculturalism in 1973 (later renamed Canadian Ethnocultural Council). In 1990, the government formed the Canadian Multiculturalism Advisory Committee to assist with the implementation of the *Multiculturalism Act* which was passed in July 1988 (Multiculturalism and Citizenship Canada 1990). The *Act* reiterated the original principles and reconfirmed governmental commitment to the *Official Languages Act* (1969), which is a cornerstone of biculturalism. On December 1, 1987, Bill C-93, *An Act for the Preservation and Enhancement of Multiculturalism in Canada*, was tabled in the House of Commons and on July 21, 1988, the *Act* became law. In 1991, a new department was created, the Department of Multiculturalism and Citizenship. There has been clear recognition by the government of a multicultural reality and, in theory, there is political and financial commitment to it.

Currently, multiculturalism discourse includes a discussion of "fighting racism" and national unity. There is also a greater inclusion of issues of the First Nations (Multiculturalism and Citizenship Canada 1990) and a greater acknowledgement of institutional racism. These developments illustrate the recognition that we are a multi-ethnic and multiracial society and racism is a problem that has to be addressed. A number of influential reports (Abella 1984; Henry and Ginzberg 1985) and community spokespersons have unambiguously pointed out that racism is a reality and that multiculturalism is a dream rather than a practice. However, a careful deconstruction of policy documents and formal practices reveal that even though there is a symbolic naming of "racism," the official government interpretation of words such as "race," "racism," and anti-racism" is very different from how they are interpreted by the ordinary person of colour. The lack of clarity on these concepts allow their popularity in discourse to coexist with their negligible existence in material practice.

Stated multicultural priorities are: cross cultural communications, race relations and multiculturalism in education. In fact, an internal discussion paper titled "Multiculturalism — Priorities" (Secretary of State 1982)[2] categorically recommends "a decreasing emphasis on purely ethnocentric activities" (p. 2).

The crucial question is whether multiculturalism programs and practices are changing the power imbalances and the inequalities that people of colour have historically experienced.

DISCOURSES ON IMMIGRANT WOMEN

The document (Secretary of State 1982) referred to above says the following: "Immigrant women are isolated both within their own and the larger society, often as a result of limiting cultural traditions and lack of basic life skills, particularly official language acquisition" (p. 4). A "blame the victim" scenario is painted here. The low socio-economic position and the isolation of immigrant women is seen as a result of "limitations of cultural traditions," "*their* lack of skills," "particularly lack of official language acquisition." The indigenous cultures of immigrant women are seen as inherently conservative, and pathological, not oriented to developing a high level of self-esteem or self-identity and, therefore, of success in participation in social life. This is reminiscent of the "culture of poverty theories" so prevalent in explaining the high rate of drop-out and failure of Black youth in advanced capitalist countries, such as England (Sarup 1986; Sivanandan 1990) and Canada (Martell 1974). No mention is made in this paragraph of the systemic racism and sexism experienced by immigrant women which lead to their exclusion from the larger society. The denial of training opportunities in official language programs through the imposition of criteria of priority, for example, being a non-citizen, a non-immigrant, "bread winners," an "independent immigrant," and so on, are not even hinted at even though report (Estable and Meyer 1989) after report — including those commissioned by the government — have confirmed these realities.

What is meant by isolation "within their own society" is a mystery. It remains inexplicable, specifically given that immigrant women are often very well integrated within their own community-based organizations and institutions. Isolation due to sexism within their own communities is not unique to immigrant women. It is a reality of all women in all societies. To say otherwise is to engage in the most gross ethnocentrism.

A popularly accepted reason for the isolation of immigrant women is given, namely "lack of information." This again is interesting because, in keeping with the approach of multiculturalism, it lays the blame for isolation and exclusion of immigrant women on the "ignorance" of the "victim," that is, not having the relevant facts and figures. The implication is that immigrant women's liberation from oppression will be achieved by becoming more educated, more knowledgeable. It removes the focus of analysis from power inequalities existing in society which deny women, in general, and immigrant women, in particular, equal opportunities in life. That lack of information is systematic and institutionalized, which contributes to the racism and sexism experienced by immigrant women, is not acknowledged.

Subsequently, the document lists projects and programs which will address problems mentioned above. The first types of examples given are to facilitate immigrant women to "develop personal skills," "gain better knowledge of their communities" and "their rights and obligations in Canada." This is a continuation of the themes of "remediation," developing themselves psychologically, gaining information — that is, overcoming their "disadvantaged family and ethnic cultures" to join the "mainstream," or white Anglo-Saxon, middle-class Canada.

The next two approaches are curious in that they seem to actually incorporate the aspirations of immigrant women who have been organizing collectively to oppose class, gender, and race issues through community development efforts (Das Gupta 1986), and include efforts to bring change for the community of immigrant women as a whole, not as individuals, through a process of empowerment. It advocates "permitting immigrant women, through *collective action* to gain better access to Canadian institutions and improve their status in society." This is expansive hegemony, using Gramscian terminology. The ruling class, in particular state institutions, can absorb some demands of the "grassroots" in order to neutralize popular resistance. It would rather go through some form of equity reform as far as its institutional structures are concerned than be made vulnerable in its core social relations. The latter would include questioning the core values and missions of capitalist institutions. Equity reform would instead focus on integrating immigrant women into the existing institutions without fundamental questioning of its basis. Sivanandan (1990) has discussed the phenomenon of affirmative action, or "positive action" as he refers to it, as a tool used by middle-class people of colour to gain a piece of the status quo. In Sivanandan's words, "none of these gives a fart for ordinary black people, but uses them and their struggles as cynically as any other bourgeois class or sub-class."

The federal document continues with a goal to promote "the participation of immigrant women within the established ethno-cultural community infrastructure," meaning their inclusion in the older, male-dominated, ethno-cultural organizations, which the government has supported so far. Disenfranchised citizens are a potential threat to the infrastructure if they are not involved in it themselves.

The last idea mentioned in the document is to "encourage research and educational materials directed at the specific problems of immigrant women." While this is the most neutral program mentioned in the paper, it is noteworthy that considerable research data exists testifying to the specific problems of immigrant women, most of which have been produced by community development organizations such as Women Working With Immigrant Women (WWIW) and Cross Cultural Communication Centre (CCCC) in Toronto. This thrust for "more research" is often a tactic for inaction as far as immigrant women are concerned. It is also another way of delegitimizing research conducted by the community of immigrant women through a process of non-recognition. Existing community research becomes invisible. This lays the stage for academic researchers and consultants to corner this sphere of knowledge production by, in effect, reinventing the wheels and renaming age-old realities.

Kirby and McKenna (1989) have talked about how "subordinate groups have been structurally blocked from the process of selecting, naming, disseminating, and evaluating knowledge. Knowledge production reflects both the distribution of power and the principles of social control." The non-recognition of community knowledge is a crystallization of who controls and owns the production and reproduction of social and economic resources.

ANTI-RACISM TRANSFORMED TO RACE RELATIONS

A paragraph is devoted to the other priority target group — separate from that of "immigrant women" — namely "visible minorities" (p. 4). First, the implication of the juxtaposition of these two categories is that they are mutually exclusive. By the time this government document was developed most immigrant women were women of colour. Immigrant women who are in the most adverse situations are women of colour and non-English-speaking women. I will come back to the significance of these varied categories in terms of state practices later.

The description of the basis on which "visible minorities" are deemed a target area for the Multiculturalism Directorate is an even more marked example of expansive hegemony. According to government analysts, their disadvantaged position is "a result of institutional discrimination, racial bias and the prevailing adverse socio-economic conditions," all of which sound anti-racist and Marxist in approach. It seems that there is a recognition here of the larger capitalist political economy and its impact on people of colour as well as on power inequalities which foster individual and systemic forms of racism.

Jean Burnet (Bujeau 1990) notes that it was in 1975 that government (with John Munro as the Minister Responsible for Multiculturalism) revised its interpretation and the focus of its multiculturalism policy to emphasize "group understanding and combatting discrimination," a trend which continued with the next minister, James Fleming. The latter took an even stronger stance in addressing racism by creating a race relations unit within the multiculturalism directorate. All this was happening obviously as a result of community pressure from the non-profit sector, particularly those representing cultural and racial minority communities, particularly women. Burnet adds that the ministers concerned had to deal with vehement resistance from established ethnic organizations, for example Ukrainian Canadians (Richmond 1991), who disapproved of using "multicultural" funds to deal with "racism and human rights issues." "Cultural retention" then became the holy cow of multiculturalism, one that seems to be untouchable.

Canada's demographic diversity is well recognized in internal documents on multiculturalism priorities (Secretary of State 1982). A new *Immigration Act* of 1976 encouraged people of colour from Third World Countries to come into Canada. At the same time, there was international pressure on Canada to bear some responsibility for the resettlement of the world's refugee populations. Unfortunately, these were also times of rising unemployment and recession and created the conditions for racist backlash against people of colour. The state, in trying to balance out its role in the accumulation cycle, on the one hand was directly responsible for the new push for immigrants of colour due to specific labour needs. On the other hand, it had to legitimize its policies at a time of racist strife. It did this by increasing the deportation powers of immigration officials, as well as setting up a commission on immigration which heard views from Canadians across the country on immigration, which turned out to be significantly racist and exclusionist. This was facilitated by the *Green Paper* (Richmond 1979), a report produced by government aimed at generating public discussion on immigration.

Concurrently, the state had to deal with popular resistance from organizations representing the demands of people of colour from across the country. Stasiulis (1990) has surveyed the Black and South Asian communities organizing in the mid-1970s, particularly around issues of police brutality, democratization of institutions, and education of minority children. The incidents of police shootings of Buddy Evans in December 1978 and Albert Johnson in August 1979 and a variety of police harassment cases in the South Asian community, brought the communities together to press for institutional changes. Groups such as National Black Coalition of Canada, Jamaica Canada Association, the Albert Johnson Support Committee and the Coalition of Concerned South Asians engaged in a series of marches, rallies, and fundraising events which attracted thousands of people, uniting such diverse groups as Arabs, Blacks, South Asians, Whites, women, gays, labour and left organizations. A number of academic studies further confirmed the rise of racism against people of colour, in particular, one authored by Henry (1977). At the same time incidence of "Paki bashing" and racial assaults in Toronto had increased dramatically.

In the federal document, the Directorate made an attempt to deal with these diverse pressures, as evident in the following quote: "While continuing to fully support cultural retention activities it is nevertheless imperative that the program also respond to the needs and pressures arising from increased social tension" (Secretary of State 1982, 1).

However, when we look at the policy recommendations to deal with this situation, we see references to "cross cultural communication," "race relations," and "multiculturalism in education," in which the analyses and actions prescribed for immigrant women reverberate in different forms. The other aspect of the pre-scribed strategy includes "the development of organizational and other necessary skills of visible minority communities to enable them to more effectively articu-late their needs and promote change" (p. 3).

Firstly, "encouraging and supporting" does not ensure institutional change, as experience has shown us. We only have to look at the voluntary affirmative action programs in both Canada (Allan 1988) and the U.S. to make that conclu-sion. Even incentive grants do not seem to be very effective. Such changes have to be made mandatory, be enforced, and monitored. Secondly, this statement implies that people of colour are in an adverse position socially because of their lack of "necessary" skills. This is a replay of "blaming the victim."

The first recommendation of skill development in the area of advocacy is useful, but it does not lead to transforming institutions per se or transforming power relations within them. It merely facilitates a strata of vocal and articulate minority members who invariably become the "spokespersons" of the community in question. Its underlying agenda is to obtain some level of personal power, but only for personal benefit. Sivanandan (1990) cynically comments that, "it was only when there was a white blockage in the system, preventing them from going up further, that the ethnics turned 'black'..." (p. 96).

Advocacy to "get a piece of the pie" is opportunism at its best. This serves to delegitimize the grassroots activists who have been pushing for institutional change of a more fundamental type to benefit the whole community. They are excluded from official discourses, giving way to the "professional advocates."

The final point in the document, re-establishes the need for research in race relations. As I argued before, this is a code for "paralysis of action" and also for reproducing the politics of knowledge production.

Similar themes are replicated once again under the sub-heading of "multiculturalism in education." Harmonizing therapy approaches are reiterated in order to "increase understanding and appreciation of the multicultural and multiracial diversity." Culture of poverty perspectives echo back when mention is made of "encoura(ging) in every student understanding and pride in his/her ethno-cultural identity..." (p. 3). The best cure for this apparent lack of identity and pride would be to increase equality of condition and opportunity, not therapeutic remedial classes or heritage programs (Davis 1989).

One of my contentions in the first part of this chapter was that the putting together of official policies, documents, programs, and funding criteria provides a terrain of class, race, and gender struggles. These struggles are integral ele-ments of the reproduction of ideological hegemony. Targeting "visible minori-ties" was the process the state used to integrate selective elements of popular community struggles against racism, in such a way that the critical edge was removed and the remnants were institutionalized.

CASE STUDY OF A CONSULTATION MEETING

In 1982, a number of multicultural and anti-racist organizations being funded by the federal government, as well as some individuals, were invited to meet with representatives from the Multiculturalism Directorate in Ottawa. In this highly selective consultation on changing multicultural priorities, the level of dissension among various so-called community groups was highly evident and discussions were far from smooth. This was a case of struggle between communities of colour and those who identify themselves as being part of "ethno-cultural communities." While those of us who represented the "anti-racism" stance (officially recognized as "race relations advocates") felt that we had presented a well-coordinated, well-planned, well-articulated, and vocal argument and had clearly won out the formal part of the discourse, in the end the "cultural retentionist" survived, as holy cows do. Clearly, manipulations and "networking" behind the scenes had had a significant impact on the end result. At the same time, the officials from the Directorate could also report that they had engaged in a "consultative" process where the "political types" had received full hearing but hadn't amounted to much. This maintains "passive" hegemony by neutralization. Nevertheless, following this consultation vocabulary shifted from phrases such as "cultural retention and preservation" and "ethnic studies" to "intergroup communication," "race relations," "barriers," "equality," "visible minority," "institutional change," "racial discrimination," and "racial prejudice." Particular emphasis was placed on the removal of barriers for "visible minorities" and immigrant women. So a symbolic, linguistic victory had been won by the latter constituencies, but not a material one.

At the same consultation meeting, several dynamics were aimed at co-opting representatives of the communities of colour. These dynamics, which I would describe as "state practices," are not new or unusual. One dynamic centred around who was represented. We were informed that we *only* represented "ourselves" as "individuals" rather than "organizations" or "communities." This amounted to depoliticizing our viewpoints, bringing them down to individual perceptions, rather than "collective" experiences and demands. A struggle ensued on this point and did not reach any meaningful settlement. We had been individually hand-picked and invited to participate in this consultation process. Observers were not allowed in. It was a closed, exclusionary process meant to keep out the "riff raff" and "troublemakers" in the community. The process had been subverted slightly; originally, the administrator of my organization had been invited, who in turn felt that I would be more appropriate as a representative since I had been involved in advocacy and lobbying work in various anti-racist and immigrant women's organizations. The Directorate was simply informed of this decision on our part. The exclusivity itself was a structural factor to co-opt those who were engaging in the consultative process.

Elsewhere (Das Gupta 1987), I have talked about how dominant institutions in society, including the government and academic institutions, are the gatekeepers and label-givers to legitimate versus illegitimate "knowledge-makers." Only people who are "acceptable" in the eyes of the dominant ideologues, those representing bourgeois, institutionalized white, male perspectives, have the kind of knowledge which is recognizable. They are recognized officially as "experts" and "knowers." Hence, people from the external sphere, such as people of colour, women, people with a lower socio-economic background and lacking in formal education, are not seen as possessing any ideas of value to these institutions. "Value" is subjectively endowed depending on whether the perspective is "adopting" or "resisting" the status quo. Hence, in engaging in these consultation processes, which are seen as legitimizing exercises, people being consulted are very carefully hand-picked. Vocal, dramatic, but conservative spokespersons are ideal candidates for these charades.

COMMUNITY DEVELOPMENT BY IMMIGRANT WOMEN, WOMEN OF COLOUR, AND NON-ENGLISH-SPEAKING WOMEN

I turn now to the community development efforts of the above-mentioned communities of women in Ontario, and to a certain extent in Canada, to illustrate the apparent contradictions and discuss how the state responded in light of these contradictions.

Immigrant women (Das Gupta 1986) had started organizing in a significant way from the mid-1970s onward. In Toronto, an informal group of women began to meet to support each other and share information with regard to their work with immigrant women. This group became known as Women Working With Immigrant Women (WWIW) and was to be the major voice of immigrant women in the community in the future. Other organizations such as Women's Community Employment Centre and the Immigrant Women's Centre emerged, organizing front-line services around employment and health issues respectively. Innovative English as a Second Language (ESL) programs had also been developed by Freirean (Freire 1970) teachers for Southern European immigrant women, together with such groups as Cleaners' Action, a resource group for Portuguese immigrant women who worked as cleaners. These groups were heavily based on voluntary labour, as the government had no formal commitment at that time to supporting them. However, this was to change due to the international pressure from the UN-declared International Year of Women, as well as pressure from such groups as WWIW. In 1978, the Multiculturalism Directorate commissioned a study on the needs of immigrant women, on the basis of which funding immigrant women's programs was finally adopted as a priority.

By this time, immigrant women in other cities had begun to organize collectively. In Thunder Bay, the Thunder Bay Multicultural Women's Committee was founded around providing information, referral services and employment orientation. Similarly, in Windsor, a conference on immigrant women in the workplace was organized in 1982 by a group of immigrant women calling themselves Windsor WWIW. A major concern of theirs was the plight of domestic workers. Immigrant women and women of colour were making an impact on other "mainstream" institutions and movements as well such as the women's movement and the labour movement (Leah 1989).

The Multiculturalism Directorate's growing interest in the demands of immigrant women's organizations was symbolized by a national conference it

organized in 1981, to which WWIW (Toronto) was invited to organize the plenary session. While the community organization saw it as an opportunity to dialogue directly with policy makers, the government may have seen it as a process
of legitimizing itself in "consultation" with the most outspoken community organization of immigrant women at the time.

In subsequent years, the relationship between the federal government and
community development groups was ambiguous. The ambiguity and tension
persisted because many of the community organizations were directly critical of
certain government policies and practices as antithetical to the principle of community development and contrary to the philosophy of the right to self-determination of immigrant women. The issue of "representation" has been a bone of
contention in almost every major consultation process, conference, and in coalition building. The underlying theme of such contestation has been the issue of
state control over immigrant women's movements in Canada. It started in 1976,
when government officials who had been part of WWIW (Toronto) had been
asked to leave the organization. It resurfaced again after the national conference
of 1981 when the idea of developing a national network of immigrant women
arose. At the end of that conference, a group of volunteers constituted themselves
as the National Follow-up Committee on recommendations that had emerged.
Their only task was to monitor the implementation of those recommendations.
Over time, however, these committee members became the official spokespersons
of "all" immigrant women in Canada with the blessing of some key government
officials. A struggle ensued on this, involving a concerted effort by community
organizations of immigrant women, chiefly from Ontario, loudly denouncing the
process that had been followed and replacing it with a democratic, decentralized,
grassroots approach to forming a national organization of immigrant women with
elected executive members and with full input from each of the provinces. This
contest was neither short nor straightforward. Issues of class difference among
immigrant women became apparent as middle-class participants, driven by am-
bition and need for recognition, were easily co-opted by the workings of the state.

The national organization, called National Organization of Immigrant and
Visible Minority Women (NOIVMW), was formed in 1986 in Winnipeg. Before
NOIVMW was formed, the Minister of Multiculturalism held another "consultation" meeting in 1985 with thirty-seven women, ostensibly from national immigrant and visible minority women's groups and ethnocultural organizations, basically hand-picked for this purpose. Most notably, some of the activist immigrant
and anti-racist community workers were not invited to this event. Here, we see
another example of the state organizing, naming, and limiting the "representatives" of immigrant and women of colour communities. The underlying processes were the same as before: recognizing individual women as spokespersons,
integrating them into state discourse and structures, thereby legitimizing state
policies and practices and marginalizing entire communities of immigrants and
women of colour. These hand-picked consultants developed a brief, refining recommendations made at the 1981 conference on immigrant women — another

exercise in recycling knowledge. However, the contradiction was that some activist women did get selected for the consultation and were able to challenge the
process and shape the discourse to a certain extent. A ten-member "Action Committee" was formed to continue "dialogue" with the Federal Government. By this
move, the government was able to bypass the existing provincial and local networks of immigrant women and women of colour. In hindsight, I understand the
construction of this Action Committee as a compromise response by the state to
appear to consider the delegitimization of the National Follow-up Committee by
the powerful critique of groups like WWIW, while at the same time retaining
control over the movement through another hand-picked committee.

Such struggles within the community of immigrant women show the perva-
siveness of ideological hegemony. We, ourselves, take an active role in reproducing our subordination, not because of our psychological or moral degeneration,
but because of our location within hierarchies of class and race. The latter limits
our perspective and our experience. As Wotherspoon (1987) says, "In a society
which is socially divided by class, gender and race, our experience is always
partial" (p. 9). In the early 1980's, the movement of immigrant women and that
of women of colour were divided. Women of colour insisted that racism had to be
explicitly named, prioritized, and addressed in terms of community and government programs and policy. Immigrant women (including white women) felt that
their movement implicitly included race issues and that the two sub-movements
should be linked. Moreover, immigrant women's concerns around class, immigration, and/or cultural discrimination were the underlying animators of many of
their experiences. Such disagreements often became bitter and unpleasant and
resulted in alienation of individuals and weakening of the movements. Other
than a few community activists who recognized the importance of maintaining
linkages, classism, sexism, and racism were not connected in practice. The government, at all levels, took turns in back-patting exercises in order to "cool off"
community anger wherever it was originating — immigrant women or women of
colour groups. In this context, government-defined, mutually-exclusive categories of "immigrant women" and "visible minority women" served to keep the
community divided. In the final analysis, reliance on government funding further
accentuated feelings of competition and resentment among different groupings of
women (Ng, Kwan, and Miedema 1991). Since then, government departments
seem to see the following as their major reference groups: labour, visible minorities, women, people with disabilities, and Native peoples. We can see that "immigrants and refugees" are not in this list, much to the dismay of groups like Ontario Council of Agencies serving Immigrants (OCASI) (Conway 1992).

CONCLUSION

Despite the progressive rhetoric on racism in multiculturalism policy in the 1990s,
the compatibility of the policy with capitalist goals is reconfirmed. Herein lies the
crucial link with the theme of "national unity." As Royal Bank chairman Allan
Taylor said pointing out that the "break up of Canada would be an economic

disaster" (Gerard 1992): "This isn't just an altruistic view. When we see a threat
to the economy of Canada we believe our 8 million customers are going to feel
some economic pressures. When they have difficulty, *we* have difficulty" (emphasis mine). The agenda of finance capitalists is passed off as the consumers', and
thus the national, agenda. This is the power of hegemonic ideologies. Taylor's
speech was distributed among employees by General Motors and McCain Foods,
as well as by some boards of education.

In answer to one of its rhetorical questions in *Multiculturalism: What Is It
Really About?* (Multiculturalism and Citizenship Canada 1991), the state aims
for the same result when it says that multiculturalism "makes *us* stronger and
more competitive." Like Taylor, the state is referring to "national" interest as
equally beneficial to employers and employees alike, denoted by the pronoun
"us." This obfuscates the polarities of class so fundamental in capitalist societies.
The business connection in this document continues in a discussion on how the
removal of discrimination gives owners "more access to the skilled employees as
our population grows older," meaning more access to exploit. Other benefits include the knowledge of cross-cultural communication and different languages
which gives companies, for example banks, "a competitive edge" internationally.
It is stated that more than 50 percent of our small businesses are owned or operated by minority entrepreneurs. No doubt this is a reflection of present immigration policies, which project a preference for entrepreneurial immigrants (National
Film Board 1989).

A class and gender bias is apparent here by omission. By not acknowledging
the fact that Canada has been built at least 50 percent by so-called unskilled
labourers, many of whom have been women, the state betrays its bias in describing the "economic" advantages of multiculturalism. Such an approach reached
a public zenith under Minister Otto Jelinek in 1986, with his rallying cry
"Multiculturalism Means Business." This blatant intertwining of
multiculturalism with capitalist interests was quickly stopped by outcries from
immigrant organizations across the country (Coalition Concerned About
Multiculturalism Policy 1986).

The policy of multiculturalism has evolved as state ideology and its hegemony
has been precarious, given resistance within government as well as in the community. In its various forms, it has successfully reproduced gender, race, and
class relations and ideologies. These have been socially organized by a complex
mesh of state practices, facilitated by divisions in the community. The definition
of such concepts as "community representation," "legitimate knowledge," and
the use of language in state documents, show how certain meanings and
epistemologies are highlighted and hegemony is maintained. Multiculturalism
advocates within government have produced rhetoric in policy formulations and
in their stated function of advocating within other levels and departments of government. Recent events show clearly that class, gender, and racial inequalities are
being perpetuated systemically even though government has repeatedly professed
the opposite.

As far as immigration policies are concerned, restrictions on family reunification are in place, while investor immigrants are being given official concession in order to make Canada more competitive in the "immigrant market." On the other hand, domestic workers from Third World Countries face new restrictions of inflated requirements of education and training.

The latest recommendation of the government (Minister of Public Works and Government Services 1998) is that family members should be encouraged to acquire official language skills before coming to Canada. Those who don't and who are over six years of age have to pay an additional fee to cover the cost of language instruction in Canada.

Hegemony is maintained while community organizations resist and agitate for an alternative viewpoint. To deal with this opposition, the state has practiced co-optation and neutralization of community leaders and their ideas. Despite these agendas, some community organizations still endeavour to advance alternative goals and visions.

A document titled *Strategic Evaluation of Multiculturalism Programs* (1996) reveals that an evaluation of multiculturalism programs was requested by the Corporate Review Branch of the Department of Canadian Heritage, formerly known as Secretary of State, on behalf of the Director General, Citizens' Participation and Multiculturalism. According to the evaluators, the primary objectives of multiculturalism policy should be "protecting the civil and political rights of individuals," to "ensure that all who call Canada home are able to take a full and active part in the affairs of their community and their country," and "to ensure that the benefits that Canadians derive from their participation are not constrained by their ascribed characteristics" (p. 71). It is notable that the language of "Canadians" has replaced other identity labels, such as immigrant women or visible minorities. The latter are referred to as "subgroupings" or "special interest groupings" of Canadians. Moreover, it is categorically recommended that funding of ethno-specific organizations should *not* continue and that multiculturalism activities should be carried out by public agencies and organizations rather than by agencies representing subgroups. While *mainstreaming multiculturalism* appears to be a laudatory goal, one that has been consistently advocated by anti-racist and immigrant women's organizations, the corollary of de-funding community groups that have been working with immigrant women and women of colour at the grassroots for the last two decades is deplorable. The document further adds that the de-funding of these subgroups does not preclude them working in partnership with mainstream organizations. How these community groups survive within this environment is another chapter in the history of multiculturalism in Canada.

REFERENCES

Abella, Rosalie. *Equality in Employment, A Commission Report.* Ottawa: November, 1984.

Allan, Jane. *Employment Equity: How Can We Use It To Fight Workplace Racism.* Toronto: Cross Cultural Communication Centre, 1988.

Baldwin, Douglas, and William Calder. *Ideologies.* Canada: McGraw-Hill Ryerson Ltd., 1982.

Brand, Dionne, and Krisantha Sri Bhaggiyadatta. *Rivers Have Sources Trees Have Roots.* Toronto:

Cross Cultural Communication Centre, 1986.

Bujeau, Carol. "Ethnic Pluralism in Canada: Can It Work?" *International Council for Canadian Studies*, vol. 9, no.2 (Autumn 1990).

Canadian Heritage. *Strategic Evaluation of Multiculturalism Programs, Final Report*. Corporate Review Branch, March 1996.

Coalition Concerned About Multiculturalism Policy. Letter to the Honourable Otto Jelinek. Toronto, May 26, 1986.

Conway, Brian. Interview, Toronto, Ontario Council of Agencies Serving Immigrants (OCASI), May 5, 1992.

Corrigan, Philip, Harvie Ramsay, and Derek Sayer. "The State As A Relation of Production." In *Capitalism, State Formation and Marxist Theory: Historical Investigations*. Philip Corrigan, ed. London: Quartet Books, 1980.

Das Gupta, Tania. *Learning From Our History: Community Development By Immigrant Women in Ontario, 1958-1986*. Toronto: Cross Cultural Communication Centre, 1986.

_____. "Unravelling the Web." *Resources For Feminist Research*, vol. 16, no. 1 (March 1987).

Davis, Bob. "Teaching the General Level Student." *Our Schools, Our Selves*, (Jan. 1989).

Estable, Alma, and Mechthild Meyer. *A Discussion Paper on Settlement Needs of Immigrant Women in Ontario*. Canada: Immigrant Settlement and Adaptation Program, March 1989.

Fleras, Augie, and Jean Leonard Elliott. *Multiculturalism in Canada: The Challenge of Diversity*. Ontario: Nelson Canada, 1992.

Freire, Paulo. *Pedagogy of the Oppressed*. New York: Seabury Press, 1970.

Gairdner, Bill. *The Trouble With Canada*. Toronto: Stoddart Publishing Co., 1990.

Gerard, Warren. "Unity Speech Stirs Emotions." *Toronto Star*, April 10, 1992, A27.

Gramsci, Antonio. *Selections From the Prison Notebooks*. New York: International Publishers, 1971.

Hall, Stuart. "The State in Question." In *The Idea of the Modern State*. Gregor McLennon, David Held, and Stuart Hall, eds. England: Open University Press, 1984.

Henry, Frances. "The Dynamics of Racism in Toronto." Mimeographed paper, York University, 1977.

Henry, Frances, and Effie Ginzberg. *Who Gets the Work: A Test of Racial Discrimination in Employment*. Toronto: Social Planning Council and Urban Alliance on Race Relations, 1985.

Kirby, Sandra, and Kate McKenna. *Experience, Research, Social Change: Methods From the Margins*. Toronto: Garamond Press, 1989.

Leah, Ronnie. "Linking the Struggles: Racism, Feminism and the Union Movement." In *Race, Class Gender: Bonds and Barriers*. Jesse Vorst, Tania Das Gupta, et al, eds. Toronto: Between the Lines, 1989.

Mallea, John, and Jonathan Young, eds. *Cultural Diversity and Canadian Education*. Ottawa: Carleton University Press, 1990.

Martell, George, ed. *The Politics of the Canadian Public School*. Toronto: James Lewis and Samuel Publishers, 1974.

Mazurek, Kas. "Multiculturalism, Education and the Ideology of Meritocracy." In *The Political Economy of Education*. Terry Wotherspoon, ed. Toronto: Methuen, 1987.

Miliband, Ralph. *The State in Capitalist Society*. London: Open University Press, 1973.

Minister of Public Works and Government Services. *Not Just Numbers: A Canadian Framework For Future Immigration*. Legislative Review Ministerial Consultations, Catalogue # C:63-21/1998E.

Multiculturalism and Citizenship Canada. *Operation of the Canadian Multiculturalism Act: Annual Report 1989/90*. Canada: Minister of Supply & Services, 1991.

_____. *The Multiculturalism Act: A Guide For Canadians*. Canada: Minister of Supply & Services, 1990.

_____. *Multiculturalism: What Is It Really About?* Canada: Ministry of Supply & Services, 1991.

National Film Board. *Who Gets In?* Canada, 1989.

Ng, Roxana. *The Politics of Community Services*. Toronto: Garamond Press, 1988.

Ng, Roxana, Elizabeth Kwan, and Bukje Niedema. "State Funding and Immigrant Services: the Experience of An Immigrant Women's Group in the Maritimes." *The Canadian Review of Social Policy*, vol. 27 (1991).

Richmond, Anthony. "Immigration and Multiculturalism in Canada and Australia: The Contradictions and Crisis of the 1980's." *International Journal of Canadian Studies*, vol. 3 (Spring 1991).

Richmond, Anthony. "Canadian Immigration: Recent Developments and Future Prospects." In *The Canadian Ethnic Mosaic*. Leo Driedger, ed. Toronto: McLelland & Stewart, 1979.

Sarup, Madan. *The Politics of Multiracial Education*. London: Routledge & Kegan Paul, 1986.

Secretary of State. "Multiculturalism — Priorities." Discussion paper, December 21, 1982.

Sivanandan, A. *Communities of Resistance: Writings on Black Struggles For Socialism*. London: Verso, 1990.

Stasiulis, Daiva. "The Politics of Minority Resistance Against Racism in the Local State." In *Commu-*

nity Organization and the Canadian State. Roxana Ng, Gillian Walker, and Jacob Muller, eds. Toronto: Garamond Press, 1990.

_____. "The Symbolic Mosaic Reaffirmed: Multiculturalism Policy." In *How Ottawa Spends*. Canada: Carleton University Press, 1988.

Statistics Canada. *The Daily Statistics Canada*. Tuesday, February 17, 1998.

Wotherspoon, Terry, ed. *The Political Economy of Education*. Toronto: Methuen, 1987.

NOTES

1. A much shorter version of this chapter was published by *Canadian Woman Studies*, vol. 14, no. 2 (Spring 1994): 72-5.
2. This internal discussion paper was not released as a policy document, however I refer to it here as an indication of how the policy of multiculturalism was being reformulated at that time and some of the theoretical and philosophical approaches implicit in it.

CHAPTER EIGHT

Gender and Race in "Non-discriminatory" Immigration Policies in Canada

1960s to the Present

SEDEF ARAT-KOC

Despite the emergence of a new "non-discriminatory" — in terms of race and gender — logic in immigration in the 1960s, race and gender remain very relevant to the development of immigration and settlement policy in Canada, as well as to the effects seemingly "neutral" policies have on people. This paper will analyze how certain groups of women, especially groups of women from "non-traditional" source countries (read: non-British and non-French) are affected by immigration and settlement policies in Canada since the 1960s. The first section analyzes how and why two groups of women — sponsored immigrant women and foreign domestic workers — have been affected by immigration and settlement policies since the 1960s. The second section focuses on changes taking place in immigration policy in the 1990s, a period when neo-liberalism is gaining dominance in state policies and discourses. The third and final section looks into the nature and possible implications on the shape of immigration and citizenship of new proposals under consideration at present. While issues of gender and race are also very relevant to policy and procedures affecting refugees, this paper does not focus on refugee women. The factors affecting refugee policies and refugee determination processes are very complex, highly contingent to historical context and they deserve special attention in a separate discussion.

Until the 1960s Canadian immigration policy was based on explicitly racist principles. While concerns, such as meeting labour market needs and populating the country were important factors in immigration policy, there was an integral relation between immigration and a nation-building project which aimed to develop Canada as a settler colony in the image of Britain.

Immigration has also been clearly gendered. In immigration, women were treated *as women*, whose natures and capacities were perceived very differently from men. As significantly, women were also treated differently on the basis of their racial categorization and ethnic membership, for they represented a different form of participation in the nation-building process (Anthias and Yuval-Davis 1989). In addition to their capacity as biological reproducers, women are per-

207

ceived as cultural reproducers, through their parenting and community participation, as transmitters of culture from one generation to another. Depending on their race and ethnicity, therefore, in Canadian history, different groups of women were seen as desirable immigrants, or as threats to "the nation."

Very few women came to Canada as independent immigrants in their own right. Women mostly came as wives and mothers of those who were seen as the real members of the nation being built. When single women came from Britain, as many did at the turn of the century, they came as domestic workers to meet the needs of middle-class women and with the expectation that they would eventually get married and be the "mothers of the nation" (Roberts 1979; Valverde 1991). Immigration of women of colour was often very contentious, as women of colour were seen as threats to the racial and cultural purity of the nation. When their immigration was tolerated, it was partly in the hope that their presence would alleviate the possibility for men of their own race entering into sexual, emotional, and social relations with white women (Dua, forthcoming). When women of colour immigrated as single women, they were allowed to do so not as full persons and potential citizens of the country, or even in a gendered status as future mothers of a nation, but for their "labour only," as mere commodities, to solve labour shortage in domestic work not otherwise filled by British or other European women (Carty 1994).

Against this background, the developments in Canadian immigration policy in the 1960s seem to constitute a radical turning point, ending a history of discrimination. At a time when post-war, European economic growth was reducing European emigration, Canada was pressured, by a booming economy and an increased need for skilled, technical, and professional labour in the economy, to consider a radically new approach to immigration (Li 1992; Whitaker 1991). Whatever motivated the shift in immigration policy in the 1960s, the elimination of the explicitly racist criteria and the introduction of the "points system" seems to have made certain ascribed characteristics, such as race and sex, irrelevant to immigration. The points system is supposed be based on "objective" criteria in order to effectively respond to needs of the labour market. It focuses on such criteria as formal education and training, occupational skills, occupational demand, occupational experience, knowledge of Canada's official languages, and the age of the applicant. In addition, there has been a growing emphasis in the 1980s on the amount of capital an immigrant would be willing to invest in Canada, leading to a growth of "business" immigrants (Wong and Netting 1992).

GENDER AND RACE IN IMMIGRATION
AND SETTLEMENT POLICIES IN A PERIOD OF "NON-DISCRIMINATION"

Race and gender have continued to play an important part in the structure and consequences of immigration and settlement policies since the 1960s, though policies are supposed to be based on "objective" criteria. The gendered and racialized effects of immigration operate in complex, subtle, and sometimes seemingly contradictory ways in this period. There is no question, for example, that immigration from "non-traditional" source countries has multiplied since the 1960s, affecting not just the composition of immigrants, but also the general composition of Canadian population. In the 1950s and 1960s, most immigrants to Canada were still from the United Kingdom, the United States, and Europe. By 1987, however, the percentage of immigrants coming from these more "traditional" sources was down to 30 percent, while the percentage of immigrants from "non-traditional" source regions of Africa, Asia, Caribbean, and South America was up to 70 percent (Boyd and Taylor 1989). In addition to the sheer numbers of immigrants, some indicators of immigrants' performance, such as occupational distribution in recent periods, may paint an overly optimistic picture of Canada as having transformed to an egalitarian society with endless opportunities for immigrants. When one looks at occupational distribution of women in the labour force, one finds that immigrant women are highly represented in the higher end of the occupational scale (Seward and McDade 1988). This is due to the nature of the points system in immigration, which emphasizes the recruitment of "creme de la creme" from around the world. When one looks at occupational distribution, however, one finds that immigrant women are also overrepresented in the lower end of the occupational scale (Seward and McDade 1988). Altogether, when earnings are adjusted for occupational qualifications, being an immigrant, and a member of a visible minority group or female, is associated with lower earnings (Boyd 1992). To make sense of these complex and seemingly contradictory facts about immigration, race, and gender, we need to look more closely into what role the points system plays in immigration.

The points system is supposed to be based on a "rationalization of immigration." It was introduced at a time when the nation-building as a specific racial/cultural project seemed to weaken. I would propose, however, that the points system can also be interpreted as increasing commodification of immigrants. While the history of immigration to Canada always involved concerns about the needs of the labour market, immigrants from "desirable" sources were also seen as contributors to a nation-building project. As future mothers and transmitters of culture, women also had a special place in this project. Despite emergence of multiculturalism as state policy and as an ideal to shape society, in post-1960s Canada, there does not seem to be an intimate link between immigration and a political, cultural project of nation-building. In this environment, I would suggest, immigrants are more likely to be seen only as commodities.

One of the implications of this commodification is that it leads to an evaluation of people's potential contribution to and value for Canada solely on the basis of their expected place in the labour market. Those people whose skills are considered useless, less useful, or irrelevant to the labour market are either totally excluded from or get differential treatment in immigration. This process may have a particular gendered dimension, as some of the skills women have, like the specifically "women's work" they do has, either no or very low value in the marketplace. Focus on two specific groups of immigrant women shows how the existing immigration system negatively affects their status and conditions in Canada.

Sponsored Immigrant Women

Not all immigrants who come to Canada are subject to the points system. In addition to the criteria used under the points system to evaluate independent immigrants on the basis of their potential contribution (and lack of "burden") to the Canadian economy, there are supposedly "humanitarian" considerations used to decide the entry of refugees and "family class" immigrants. What is significant about these different categories of immigration is that they are not only based on different considerations and criteria used for entry of immigrants, but also are the basis of differential status and differential treatment. For example, family class immigrants lack the relative stability of status that independent class immigrants have. They are not entitled to and lack some of the rights and benefits that independent class immigrants are eligible for.

Family class immigrants are close family members, such as spouses, unmarried children under 18 years of age, and parents of qualified Canadian citizens or permanent residents. They are admitted into Canada on the basis of a ten-year sponsorship agreement their sponsor enters into with the Canadian government in which the sponsor agrees to undertake the provision of accommodation, care, and maintenance for this family member. For these sponsored immigrants, "family" is defined in a rather narrow way. The definition of family used for immigration purposes is an ethnocentric and heterosexist one, focussing on members of the nuclear family and not considering how family and significant others may be defined in other cultures, sub-cultures, or by individuals themselves.

Family class immigration is a highly gendered category. Females are highly overrepresented in this category: 59 percent as sponsored to 41 percent male (Ng 1993, 283). When children and parents are accounted for in the male category, it becomes clear that adult, married women are even more highly represented than 59 percent. There are several reasons for such overrepresentation. Until 1974, regardless of their qualifications, women who were married were not allowed to enter Canada as the principal immigration applicant. Their husbands were automatically considered the applicant, and the women their dependents (Boyd 1975). Since 1974, in terms of formal policy, women have equal chance with men to be considered an independent immigrant. However, several factors make it likely that most women will qualify for immigration as family members rather than as independent immigrants. First, gender inequalities worldwide mean that women have less access to opportunities for education and employment. Second, women, whose labour force participation are often interrupted with family responsibilities, lack the opportunities to develop an employment record and job experience comparable to men. As a result of these inequalities, less women than men are able to qualify under the points system.

We cannot, however, explain away overrepresentation of women in "family class" immigration solely on the basis of inequalities that exist prior to and outside of immigration policy and criteria. There are factors in immigration policies and procedures themselves which play an important part in marginalization of women. In fact, as Roxana Ng argues, "immigration process systematically structures sexual inequality within the family by rendering one spouse (usually the wife) legally dependent on the other" (Ng 1993, 284).

One of the ways in which immigration disadvantages women has to do with the definitions of "education," "skill," and "work" used in the points system. Education is interpreted to refer exclusively to formal education. Work refers only to paid work in the formal labour market. Skill is a term which, despite its objective pretensions, is politically defined. Rather than being a "thing," an objective, "fixed attribute of a job or worker which will explain higher wages or unemployment" (Gaskell 1986), skill involves perceptions of a job and the worker doing it. Rather than being intrinsic to a job, skill is constructed and negotiated through ideological and political processes. One of the dimensions of the way skill is defined in modern capitalist societies is that it tends to either exclude or undervalue skills and personal qualities women tend to develop during gender socialization and in learning to perform domestic work (Fincher et al. 1994). The result is that many forms of knowledge, skill, experience, as well as personal attributes women tend to have which might be directly relevant to needs and requirements of the labour market, go unnoticed or are considered irrelevant to evaluations of one's potential contribution to economy and society. The gender biases in definitions of education, work, and skill are not unique to the points system. These biases are commonly found in a capitalist society. The immigration process, one the one hand, reproduces and relegitimates these notions, and on the other, uses them as the basis for designating people to different classes of unequal citizenship.

In addition to the structural forces and common biases that affect gender inequality, sexism of individual immigration officers also plays an important part in determining who becomes an independent class and who is a family class immigrant. Despite the legal and administrative possibility of doing otherwise, it has been quite a common practice in immigration to designate only one member of a family as the independent immigrant, and the others as family class. In most cases, it is the husband who is so designated, since some immigration officers automatically assume him to be the head of the household and the main breadwinner. Making such judgements, immigration officers fail to pay adequate attention to the qualifications of the female applicant. Or, they focus on a woman's previous lack of labour market experience, and automatically assume that she would not work outside the home in Canada and would be "dependent" on her husband (Ng 1993). In most cases, this judgement invalid. Labour force participation rates for immigrant women are higher than for Canadian-born women (Seward and McDade 1988).

While there is no problem with having different "considerations" guiding immigration, there are problems with attaching differential status and differential rights to people arriving under different "classes." The immigrant status of family class immigrants in Canada is conditional on the continuity, for up to ten years, of their sponsorship relationship to the family member who has sponsored them. In addition, sponsored, family class immigrants are ineligible to make claims for federally-sponsored language training programs, subsidized housing, and social assistance. This system of differential status and differential rights can be critiqued in two ways: on the logic of such a differentiation by questioning the assumptions behind it, and through some of the consequences of unequal treatment for the immigrants concerned. Different "classes" of immigration are based on a distinction made between "deserving" and "non-deserving" immigrants. Differential status and differential rights are based on the idea that one group of immigrants, namely independent class, is expected to make a contribution to Canadian society and the economy, whereas family class immigrants would not, and therefore would not deserve a status and rights.

To evaluate the legitimacy of differential status and differential rights for family class immigrants, we need to interrogate how "contribution" to Canada is being defined in the immigration system. A definition of contribution based on labour market participation totally disregards the value of contributions in the home and family. Even those family class immigrants most likely seen as non-contributors to Canadian society, such as elderly parents, not only ease the adjustment of their relatives to Canada, but also directly contribute their labour in care of children in the home or in family businesses. Another problem with the category of "family class" is that it is based on a dichotomous distinction between independent class immigrants as labour market participants and "family class" immigrants as non-participants in the labour market. Such a distinction is very simplistic and highly questionable. As stated, immigrant women are active participants in the labour force. Their participation rates exceed those of Canadian-born women (Seward and McDade 1988). Labour force participation, especially for women, is also something that cannot be anticipated at any arbitrary cross-section of their lives, but rather changes over the life cycle.

In addition to sexist, ageist, and other biases involved in the evaluation of how contribution to society and the economy are measured, the differential status and rights accorded to sponsored immigrants create consequences for the people affected. Two implications of family class status have the most serious negative consequences for women: differential access to language training and its consequences, and the implications of dependency on sponsorship and in the event of a breakdown of sponsorship.

Though the consequences of sponsored status are universal, they do not affect all immigrants equally or similarly. Studies have pointed that one of the groups most seriously affected are immigrant women who do not have a knowledge of English or French. Lack of language proficiency in either of Canada's official languages is most common among immigrants from Asia and southern European countries of Greece, Italy, and Portugal. Among these groups, women are more than twice as likely as their male counterparts to be lacking proficiency in English or French (Boyd 1992b, 143, 145).

As part of settlement services, several types of language training programs have been available. Many of these programs have been offered on a part-time basis by community centres, local schools, and churches. Even though all the programs have been free for immigrants, one program, the National Language Training Program (NLTP) offered by Employment and Immigration Canada, which prevailed until 1992, was particularly sought after. The reasons for NLTP's popularity had, first of all, to do with the several types of financial support the program offered. NLTP was the only language training program which offered a living allowance (called a basic training allowance). In addition, it provided an allowance for dependent care (used mostly for daycare), commuting, living away from home, and long-distance transportation, where applicable (Boyd 1992b). Since it is very difficult to combine income-earning activities with intensive language training, the living allowance, though small, was a deciding factor in whether an immigrant would or would not be able to successfully complete language education. Except for the few who were independently wealthy, costs of language training were prohibitive without an allowance scheme. In addition to the allowances it made available, NLTP's popularity had to do with the quality of language training offered on a full-time basis.

Despite its advantages and popularity, however, access to NLTP was very restricted. Shortage of seats and resulting long waiting lists presented one of the problems for access. Even though immigration levels went up by 82 percent between 1984 and 1988, and even though a significant percentage of new immigrants did not have prior knowledge of the official languages, the number of training seats in NLTP went up by only 2.5 percent in this period (Doherty 1992, 68). In addition to the general inaccessibility of NLTP, immigrant women in particular had problems of access due to the eligibility criteria used by this language training program.

Women have faced problems with the NLTP eligibility criteria for several reasons. Prior to 1974, the rules were blatantly gender biased, making NLTP available only to the "head of the household," a term which is seldom interpreted to mean the adult female in families where there is an adult male present (Giles 1988, 129). After 1974, the wording of the eligibility criteria changed to emphasize that the program is, first, for those "destined for the labour market," and second, for those for whom English or French was necessary to find "suitable employment." Both these criteria have been decided by employment councillors who could exercise significant levels of discretion to interpret and judge. For reasons discussed above, many immigrant women, especially women with small children, including those who work outside the home, have been judged by employment councillors as "housewives," not "destined for the labour market" and therefore ineligible for NTLP.

The criterion of need of a language for suitable employment is also wide open to interpretation and discretionary judgement. The historical existence of immigrant job ghettoes, for example, in the garment sector, hotel and office cleaning, and domestic work, has led to the automatic expectation among employment councillors that some immigrant women, especially those from certain racial/ethnic backgrounds, will take employment there. When certain forms of manufacturing and service sector work have been considered potential, suitable employment for working-class immigrant women, employment councillors have also concluded that immigrant women would not need to use the official languages of the country to perform their job.

A third factor which has excluded many women from access to NLTP is linked directly to immigrant class. Financial support for family class immigrants is, by definition, the responsibility of the sponsor. Family class immigrants are not eligible to receive a living allowance, even if they did otherwise attend courses organized by the NLTP (Doherty 1992; Paredes 1987). As women are overrepresented among sponsored immigrants, there have been a significant percentage of women who lacked access to the full benefits of NLTP even if they could prove that they were destined for the labour market and needed language training for "suitable employment."

Other than the biases involved in the decisions regarding whether one is destined for the labour market and needs a language to find suitable employment, what also needs to be questioned with regard to the eligibility criteria for NLTP is the emphasis on labour market needs as the only legitimate determinant of whether or not one could qualify for a living allowance. The notion that one does not need to learn English or French, nor be supported while doing so if one is a "housewife," suggests that housewives are less than full persons in their contribution to and participation in society.

In addition to general gender biases shaping access, there have possibly been racial and ethnic biases determining who had access to which programs. Doherty has observed that there was a predominance of immigrants of colour in programs offered in community centres and local schools, and an overrepresentation of Northern Europeans taking NTLP at community colleges (Doherty 1992, 69). Although this observation has not been based on a systematic analysis of racial/ethnic distribution of immigrants in different language training programs, it is possible that the discretion employment and immigration officers used to determine who was destined for the labour market and whose future employment would require fluency in English or French, worked in racially biased ways to favour some immigrants and disadvantage others.

Lack of language proficiency in the official languages plays a determining role in an immigrant's future status in Canada. Lack of access to a language training program with a living allowance has sometimes meant that some immigrants, especially working-class, immigrant women, never get a chance to develop proficiency in English or French. As Paredes argues, "the organization of the language program produces an unequal distribution of linguistic resources" (Paredes 1987, 23). This clearly has negative consequences for their mobility in the labour market. It has meant that some immigrants are stuck in certain job ghettoes forever, unable to improve their employment and earning potentials. Outside the labour market, it leads to difficulties in successfully integrating to Canadian society, as this group of immigrants would be unable to communicate with and relate to other individuals and central institutions such as the school system or medical institutions. The results have been marginalization, isolation, and extreme dependency on family members even to carry out basic daily activities and relationships.

Lack of language proficiency is not the only factor which leaves some immigrants overly dependent on family members. As mentioned earlier, the very legal status of the entry of family class immigrants to Canada is conditional upon the continuation of support from their sponsors. The awareness of the conditionality of one's status upon the support of a sponsor creates a strong sense of dependency among family class immigrants. In many cases, this increases the likelihood that a sponsored immigrant would stay in an abusive and/or unsatisfactory family relationship. If a family class immigrant has already secured landed immigrant status in Canada, the breakdown of sponsorship does not provide grounds for their deportation from Canada. Despite the legal security of their status; however, many people — including elderly relatives as well as women — continue to see their status in Canada as directly conditional upon sponsorship, and feel intimidated and frightened to end negative relationships.

There are also sponsored immigrants, whose legal status in Canada is in fact in jeopardy with the breakdown of sponsorship. These are fiances or family members who are already in Canada, whose applications for immigrant status are still being processed. In these cases, sponsorship is often withdrawn and the fiancé or family member is deported unless she can prove that she can independently establish herself in Canada (Pratt 1995).

Foreign Domestic Workers

Family class immigrants are not the only group for whom gender, and in some ways race, continue to be of relevance in immigration policies since the 1960s. Domestic workers constitute the other category of immigrants whose immigration status and conditions are highly gendered and racialized. Women are highly overrepresented in this category — 98 percent. Unlike family class immigrants, domestic workers are admitted to Canada on the basis of their response to a demand in the labour market. One would expect, therefore, that domestic workers would enter Canada as independent immigrants on the basis of points earned under the points system. What makes the case of domestic workers arriving in Canada since the early 1970s particularly interesting, however, is that despite the need in the labour market they clearly fill, domestic workers have been unable since the early 1970s to come to Canada as independent immigrants, but come under less-favourable conditions in different programs.

Because the pay, conditions, and general restrictions on one's life make live-in domestic work undesirable, working-class Canadian women, with any level of choice over their occupations, have historically tried to stay away from this type of employment. As a result of the shortage of domestic workers, Canada has, since the nineteenth century, imported domestic workers from abroad. While the British domestic workers who came in the late nineteenth and early twentieth century suffered class subordination and middle-class paternalism, they were also welcome to Canada as central participants in nation-building and were treated as future "mothers of the nation" (Arat-Koc 1997; Roberts 1979).

As the supply of British domestic workers fell behind Canadian demand, Scandinavian, Central and Eastern European women moved in during the early twentieth century. In the post-war period, as the efforts to import domestics from the preferred sources of Britain and Western Europe failed, Canada first resorted to women refugees from "displaced persons" (DP) camps in Eastern Europe and then entered into short-lived recruitment schemes with Italy, Greece, and Spain (Arat-Koc 1997). It was only after exhausting attempts to secure stable sources of domestic workers in Europe, that, as a last resort, immigration of women of colour was allowed. In 1955, Canada entered into domestic labour schemes with some Caribbean governments. Since then, the Third World has replaced Europe as the major source of foreign domestic workers. With this change of source countries, however, came a backward shift in the treatment of domestic workers in immigration policy.

What is most ironic about foreign domestic workers arriving in Canada since the 1960s is that, under a supposedly more "rationalized" system of immigration, which was expected to operate in non-discriminatory ways, their status and conditions, rather than improving, have worsened. This is ironic for several reasons. First, in a period characterized by "liberalization" of immigration policies, and development of ideas of "multiculturalism," one would expect that conditions of all, and especially Third World, immigrants should have improved. Second, the late 1960s and early 1970s was also a period when second wave feminism was growing in Canada. One could hope, therefore, that there would be strong and effective pressures from the women's movement to improve status and conditions of all immigrant women, and particularly those who were in a clearly female occupation. Contrary to what might have been expected of such a historical period, however, the status of domestic workers changed from being "permanent residents" (as immigrants are called in Canada) to temporary workers, with severe implications, not only in terms of their long-term status in the country, but also in terms of their working and living conditions.

The treatment of domestic workers under the points system reveals the biases against "women's work" in a most explicit way. It also demonstrates how, in a seemingly "objective" system of immigrant recruitment, measures can be developed to deliberately devalue domestic work in general, and domestic workers from certain parts of the world in particular. After the introduction of the points system in 1967, this devaluation was done through manipulation of points assigned for several evaluation criteria. Under the points system, occupations are rated on a scale of demand value. Accordingly, domestic work should have received high points; with few Canadians interested in entering this occupation, demand for this type of work has historically exceeded supply. In fact, in the late 1960s and early 1970s, with large numbers of middle-class women moving into the labour force, and effective and adequate alternatives for their childcare needs and domestic responsibilities not keeping pace, the demand for domestic workers was increasing rapidly. Despite this, in 1968, and several times subsequently, without any explanation or supporting evidence for decreasing demand, the occupational demand rating for some categories of domestic work were lowered (Daenzer 1993, 75, 96, 113; The Task Force on Immigration Practices and Procedures 1981). Nursemaids and nannies, who were predominantly from Britain, continued to receive high points; while the points for all other categories of domestic workers were lowered. Most of the other domestic workers in this period were from the Caribbean. As there were no formal training programs for nursemaids and nannies in Caribbean countries, Caribbean domestics could only apply in other categories (Daenzer 1993, 76).

Reflecting the general biases in modern capitalist society against informal education and training, and against gendered domestic work, the points system also assigned domestic workers very low points for occupational skill, occupational training and experience, even if they had years of training and experience in the field (Daenzer 1993, 116). The result was that most domestic workers, but especially those from Third World countries, were unable to get enough points to enter Canada as independent immigrants. Instead, more and more started coming in as non-immigrants on temporary work permits. By 1978, five out of six domestic workers who came to Canada came as temporary workers (Daenzer 1993, 92). The 1967 *Immigration Act* had effected neither equity nor racially neutral policy outcomes. European domestics continued to enter Canada predominantly as landed immigrants with full rights of citizenship, unlike non-immigrant, Caribbean domestics. (Daenzer 1993, 95)

The downward manipulation of points assigned to domestic workers for different criteria appears "arbitrary" according to the formal logic of the points system, as the system is intended to respond to labour demand as well as to recruit immigrants on the basis of their skills and other qualifications. When one considers the different considerations in and influences on immigration policy, however, one could conclude that rather than being "arbitrary," the assignment of low points were based on deliberate calculations to deny permanent status and associated rights of citizenship to domestic workers.

One of the factors working against domestic workers in immigration policy had to do with racist concerns about Caribbean immigration. Archival research on internal memos in the Ministry of Immigration and Citizenship reveals that throughout the 1960s — supposedly a period of opening in immigration — there was a great deal of ambiguity and anxiety about immigrants from the Caribbean. The anxiety was based largely on the possibility that a large number of sponsored immigrants could potentially follow every independent immigrant. In the 1960s, immigration authorities still thought of Black Caribbeans as social problems and did not believe that it was worth opening the door for future immigration from this region just for the "dubious skills" that some independent immigrants might provide (Daenzer 1993; MacKenzie 1988; Satzewich 1989).

The second consideration in immigration policy which led to what we can interpret as a deliberate lowering of points for domestic workers, had to do with pressures from existing and potential employers of domestic workers. It was feared that permanent immigrant status gave too much freedom and mobility to foreign domestic workers. When they had secure legal status in Canada, domestic workers felt free to change employers or to move on to other jobs if or when they had better opportunities. With high numbers of middle-class women moving into the labour force, and the government doing very little to provide socialized care arrangements, there was concern on the part of employers and government that people who worked in domestic service stay in the occupation and with the same employers. Without improving wages and working conditions, this would be achieved through creation of indentured status for domestic workers which would force them to stay in the occupation and with the same employer (Arat-Koc 1989).

The introduction of measures to eliminate the possibility of permanent immigrant status and the widespread use of temporary visas for domestic workers created a captive labour force whose condition could best be characterized as indentureship. Unlike other groups of workers and immigrants (those independent immigrants with permanent status), who enjoy mobility rights with respect to their place of residence, work, and employer, several forms of restrictions are placed on temporary workers. One major condition associated with temporary work permits has been the requirement that the domestic worker live with her employer. Temporary work permits not only dictated that the migrant women who came to do domestic work could only do this type of work, but they also specified the employer. Unable to leave domestic service without losing their right to stay in Canada, domestic workers also found it difficult to change employers. If she left or lost her job, the domestic worker theoretically had two weeks to find a new employer. The decision to issue a new visa, however, was at the discretion of immigration officers who judged whether the working conditions with the previous employer had, in fact, been intolerable. In addition to the hassle they often received from immigration officers, domestic workers had to abide by a regulation, which remained in effect until 1986, which required them to obtain a "release letter" from their former employers! (Arat-Koc 1989, 48).

The combination of the live-in requirement with the imposed attachment to one specific occupation and specific employer often created vulnerable workers and working conditions wide open to abuse. The restrictions imposed by the conditions of work permits, as well as the general tentativeness of the workers' legal status in Canada often prevented domestic workers from exercising their, albeit limited, rights. According to a survey answered by approximately 600 foreign domestic workers in Toronto in 1990, very long working hours, overtime work with no proper compensation, lack of privacy, poor quality room and board, restrictions placed on social and sexual life by employers, and vulnerability to sexual abuse were among typical conditions for many domestic workers on temporary status (Arat-Koc and Villasin 1990; Arat-Koc 1992).

While temporary work permits imposed these restrictions on the individual freedoms and working conditions of domestic workers, all they provided was a temporary status in Canada. The system of temporary work permits worked like a revolving door, expecting those who worked in Canada for a few years to leave and new workers to replace them. The workers who came under temporary status were treated as "guest workers" who had no rights to stay in Canada or make social security benefits. They paid generously for income tax, unemployment insurance, and Canada Pension Plan, but could claim no benefits, because of their status, which has, by definition, been temporary (Arat-Koc 1989, 49).

Since the early 1970s there have been two changes in the specific immigration programs applying to domestic workers. What have *not* changed, however, are two of the most negative characteristics of the temporary worker system. First, in all three programs which have prevailed since the 1970s, domestic workers have been treated as temporary workers, as opposed to independent immigrants with guaranteed, permanent status. Second, living with employers has not been eliminated as a requirement.

According to the system of temporary work permits applied through the 1970s, and until 1981, domestic workers had no chance to stay in Canada over the long term. In this policy, the message given to and about domestic workers was that they were "good enough to work, but not good enough to stay" as citizens of Canadian polity and members of Canadian society. This policy turned domestic workers into disposable commodities whose services could be consumed, but whose persons could not have rights.

In 1981, following the report of a federal task force (Task Force on Immigration Practices and Procedures 1981), a new immigration program was introduced to regulate entry and conditions of domestic workers in Canada. Called the Foreign Domestic Movement (FDM), the new program involved a compromise between the demands of employers to have a stable supply of domestic workers and the demands of domestic workers. According to regulations introduced under the FDM — which prevailed between 1981 and 1992 — domestic workers were no longer required to leave the country after a few years of temporary service. They were given an opportunity to apply for landed immigrant status after completing two years of domestic service in Canada on temporary status. Even though the provision of this possibility under the FDM seemed like a slight improvement from the previous policy, it failed to solve the problems of domestic workers. First, indentured status and restrictive conditions (including the live-in requirement) continued for at least two years (and often longer, as the processing of application for permanent status often took approximately another year). Second, there was no guarantee that permanent status would be granted. Domestic workers had to fulfill a number of extra requirements and criteria over and above those for other immigrants to qualify for independent immigrant status. Applicants needed to demonstrate abilities to "successfully establish themselves" and be "self-sufficient" in Canada. Given the low wages for domestic work, in practice, these criteria were interpreted to imply that domestic workers had to take upgrading courses and demonstrate that an ability to manage their finances (by proving savings with bankbooks). As a third requirement, they had to demonstrate "social adaptation" through involvement and volunteer work in community organizations. In addition to the incompatibility of these requirements with the reality of domestic workers, these extra requirements were problematic in another way. Ironically, they implied that domestic work (in terms of both its low status and the lack of financial security associated with the level of wages) was still not grounds to give independent immigrant status, that one had to move out of domestic work to obtain secure legal status in Canada. Although the new immigration program provided opportunities for individual upward mobility *out of* the profession, it confirmed and perpetuated notions of domestic work as low value, and domestic workers as undeserving immigrants (Arat-Koc 1989).

The criteria used in the evaluation of applicants for permanent immigrant status often led to discrimination against older domestic workers as well as women who had dependents and were seen as interested in sponsoring them from the country of origin (Macklin 1994, 18-19; Silvera 1983, 21). So, not only were domestic workers separated from their families during the two or more years of temporary status, but they were also looked upon unfavourably because of the possibility that they could reunite after receiving permanent status.

In 1992, immigration policy and procedures pertaining to domestic workers were changed once again. The new program, still in effect, is called the Live-in Caregiver Program (LCP). The only improvements for the domestic workers the LCP provided involved elimination of the "release letter" previously required to change employers, and relaxing of the criteria for permanent status. According to regulations under the LCP, the only requirement for permanent status became proof on the part of the domestic worker that she completed two years of full-time employment in domestic work. Upgrading and the other extra requirements for landing that the former FDM program had imposed were eliminated (Macklin 1994).

While providing limited improvements on freedom of movement, and relaxing criteria for immigrant status, however, the LCP continues several aspects of deplorable policies on domestic workers. By definition, living-in is still mandatory in this program. As well, the LCP continues the two-year indenture instituted under FDM. In addition, the LCP has introduced more demanding qualifications for initial entry of domestic workers. According to the new policy, women intending to do domestic work in Canada are admitted on the basis of their education and training in a specific area of care: of children, seniors, or disabled. Originally, the regulations of the program defined the required qualifications as the successful completion of Canadian Grade 12 education and six-months full-time formal training in the specific area of care one is applying for (CEIC 1992). The introduction of these new criteria met with immediate criticism from domestic workers' advocacy organizations who argued that the new program would exclude many applicants from Third World countries. Requirement for Grade 12 equivalent is either an arbitrary or deliberately racist criterion. In many countries, basic schooling only goes to Grade 10 or 11. As well, formal training in areas such as early childhood education, geriatric or pediatric nursing care is typically available only in Western European countries (DeMara 1992; Domestics Cross Cultural News 1992).

In 1993, responding more to concerns from employers about the decreasing number of domestic workers arriving under he program, than to pressures from domestic workers' organizations, the Minister of Employment and Immigration introduced an amendment to the requirements of the program. According to the amendment, the six months of formal training can be replaced by one year's experience in the area of caregiving one specializes in (Macklin 1994, 29). Despite this "compromise" in the qualification criteria, LCP fails to bring any radical improvement to the status and conditions of foreign domestic workers in Canada. Altogether, it can be characterized as a program which requires more from domestic workers, without offering them much more, a program which has been designed to "enable Canadian employers to obtain higher qualified labour for less pay" (Domestics Cross Cultural News 1992).

The status and conditions applying to both sponsored immigrant women and foreign domestic workers represent gender subordination in immigration and settlement policies. There are significant differences as well as parallels between the treatment of each group. Whereas sponsored "family class" immigrants are defined by their relationship to their family, the role of domestic workers as mothers to their own children is often unrecognized, ignored, or discouraged. The live-in requirement, as well as the nature of the temporary work permit which assigns domestic workers to a specific employer, however, forcefully makes domestics a part of the employer's family. What is common to the status of both sponsored immigrant women and foreign domestic workers is that neither group is seen and treated as persons and citizens in their own right, contributing, and being entitled, to benefit from the welfare state. Rather, their status as non-citizens implies that their conditions and welfare are not the responsibility of the welfare state, but the private responsibility of sponsoring relatives or employers. Such a status clearly makes both groups of women dependent and vulnerable on their families and employers respectively.

In the cases of both sponsored immigrant women and domestic workers, gender subordination does not exist in isolation. Rather, gender is found in intersection with race and class. Even though immigration policies affecting both groups are universal, they have differential effects on women from different parts of the world. Some of the negative aspects of family class status affects immigrant women from non-traditional source countries disproportionately. Among domestic workers, compared to women from the Caribbean and the Philippines, British and Northern European women are likely to be perceived and defined as "nannies" as opposed to general domestic workers. As a result, they are likely to benefit from a more favourable evaluation of their qualifications by immigration authorities, getting independent immigrant, as opposed to temporary worker, status. As well, Western and Northern European women are likely to enjoy higher social status and receive more respectable treatment by their employers (Macklin 1994).

CHANGES IN CANADIAN IMMIGRATION AND SETTLEMENT POLICIES
IN THE 1990s AND THEIR GENDER IMPLICATIONS

As we have seen, the supposedly race and gender "neutral" structure of the points system which shaped immigration decisions since 1967 entailed several race/ethnic and gender-specific effects which particularly disadvantaged groups of visible minority women. In the 1990s, as part of general attempts to restructure the state and weaken the welfare state in Canada, several changes have been introduced in immigration policy. These changes will once again disadvantage women of colour in immigration and settlement, either eliminating their possibilities of immigration altogether or strengthening unhealthy relations of dependency during settlement.

Changes in Language Training Policy and Programs

As mentioned in the previous section, although there have been a variety of language training programs available for immigrants, the National Language Training Program (NLTP) was the one most sought after by immigrants needing to acquire knowledge of the official languages. Funded by the federal government, NLTP not only offered full-time intensive training, but also provided a living allowance to immigrants during the six-month training period. The problem with NLTP, however, was that eligibility requirements of NLTP disadvantaged women, resulting in a significant gender gap in access to the program.

In response to the discriminatory nature of the eligibility criteria used for NLTP, a court challenge was launched by two immigrant women. The challenge was supported by the Centre for Spanish Speaking Peoples and the Women's Legal Education and Action Fund (LEAF), an organization which fights for women's equality by pursuing legal cases involving the equality provisions of the Canadian Charter of Rights and Freedoms (Doherty 1992).

In 1992, the Federal Government of Canada introduced a new language training policy. Instead of improving the NLTP by making the training allowance available to all immigrants, the new policy eliminated the living allowance completely. In introducing the new policy, the government claimed that it would rechannel the money saved from training allowances into development of more language courses.

The new policy introduced two types of language training programs. Language Instruction for Newcomers to Canada (LINC) is aimed at providing basic communication skills. Labour Market Language Training (LMLT), on the other hand, provides specialized or advanced language training targeting those individuals whose labour market skills are in demand (EIC 1992).

Immigrant groups have been immediately able to identify two major problems with the new language training policy. One problem is that both LINC and LMLT are restricted new immigrants who have been in Canada for less than a year. Given the fact that many women were excluded from the previous language training program and that, as a result, women are twice as likely as their male counterparts to be unable to speak one of the official languages, a significantly large group of immigrants will permanently lose their chance of acquiring language skills (Fincher et al. 1994, 180-3).

A second major problem with the new language training policy is that the two tiers of language programs are likely to reproduce the gender differences in access. LMLT, the program which provides advanced and specialized language training, assumes a basic knowledge of the languages. Given existing inequalities worldwide in access to formal education in general, and language education specifically, it is likely that this program is going to serve more men than women.

Even if the new language training policy affects men and women equally, the new policy makes it more difficult (and less likely) for immigrants who do not initially possess proficiency in Canada's official languages to develop it. The elimination of the living allowance means that the immigrants attending courses need independent financial means to survive a period of intensive training without employment income. Or, it would mean that they acquire language skills on a part-time basis, which compares unfavourably with full-time, intensive learning. For many immigrants, who do not have the independent wealth or large enough savings to support themselves for long periods without income, the training allowance was perhaps a small and symbolic, yet significant, form of support which enabled them to attend and successfully complete language training. The elimination of the training allowance represents an elimination of a privilege which mostly benefited male immigrants. It may therefore appear to create equality for women. Equality for the least common denominator, however, is not the kind of equality that women desire. In the words of the feminist lawyer Mary Eberts, it is only "equality with a vengeance."

Changes in Immigration Criteria
Regarding Knowledge of Official Languages

The elimination in 1992 of the living allowance attached to federally funded language training represented a backward step in state responsibility over settlement services. Later in the 1990s, there were other steps taken in immigration policy which would further decrease such responsibility. In November 1995, the federal government announced that it was looking for "immigrants who [could] hit the ground running." Part of this search was an increased emphasis in the proficiency of independent class (specifically, the skilled, as opposed to business-class) immigrants in Canada's official languages (Thompson 1995).

This new emphasis in immigration selection criteria is likely to have race and gender implications. As opposed to the older selection criteria, which seemed to emphasize occupational skills and resulted in a significant increase in immigration from Third World countries, the emphasis on knowledge of English or French is more likely to disadvantage immigrants from countries where these are not the spoken languages. Even though the history of colonialism and existing imperialism imposes a "necessity" on many peoples of the world to learn the imperial languages, access to such knowledge is still largely governed by class and gender. As women are less likely than men to learn foreign languages, the new immigration criteria are likely to make it even more difficult for women to achieve status as independent immigrants. Women are more likely than men to be excluded from immigration. If they are included, they are more likely to be included in family class immigration as dependents.

Measures Against Family Class Immigration

In 1994, the federal government carried out a "public consultation" process on immigration. There were two interesting things about the timing of this "public consultation." One, it took place in the middle of a serious economic recession. Two, it took place in a period of hysteria initiated and fuelled by the Reform Party and the media regarding crime committed by immigrants and refugee applicants (Greenspon 1994; Noorani and Wright 1995). Not surprisingly, the "consultation" process revealed a generally cynical and negative attitude towards immigrants (Campbell 1994; Citizenship and Immigration Canada 1994b).

In 1994, following the public consultation on immigration policy, the federal government announced two major changes affecting family class immigrants. The first change was in the composition of new immigrants. While the overall numbers of immigrants were being reduced, the change in the composition of immigration would involve a decrease in the percentage of family class immigrants and an increase in the percentage of independent immigrants. The government argued that the policy change was based on arguments that the average earnings of family class immigrants were below those of other immigrants and Canadian-born people, and that a significant percentage of family class immigrants received social assistance (Citizenship and Immigration Canada 1994a, 1994c; Sarick 1994b).

The other policy concerning family class immigrants involved the introduction of strict enforcement measures to guarantee the fulfilment of sponsorship obligations. Claiming that a sizeable 14 percent of sponsors failed to fulfill their sponsorship obligations, leading to the creation of a burden on the welfare system, the government proposed the creation of a "sponsorship bond." The bond would be savings or property put aside by sponsors to be forfeited by the federal government in case the sponsor was not able to honour one's responsibilities (Gratton 1994; Harper 1994; Sarick 1994c; Wilson-Smith 1994). The bond immediately became an effective means of intimidation against sponsorship. In an economic climate of growing job insecurity, many potential sponsors are unable to assume the risks associated with a "sponsorship bond." In combination with the later-introduced "head tax" (mentioned below), the sponsorship bond seems to have worked as intended to limit family class immigration. The measures discouraging family class immigration were so "successful" they probably played an important part in the government "exceeding" its immigration plans. The government plans in 1994 were to reduce family class immigration from 51 percent to 44 percent of overall immigration while increasing "economic" immigrants from 43 percent to 52 percent by the 1997-1999 period (Citizenship

and Immigration Canada 1994a, 13). The actual percentage of family class immigrants, however, went down to 30 percent by 1996 (*Globe and Mail*, March
18, 1997).

Introduction of the Modern "Head Tax"

In March 1995, the federal government introduced a "right of landing fee" to
each and every immigrant, including refugees, landing in Canada. The fee has so
far been equal to the substantial sum of $975 for adults. Resonating too closely
with the infamous taxes imposed on Chinese immigrants earlier in the century,
the "right of landing fee" was immediately dubbed the "head tax." The head tax
clearly involves considerable costs for any immigrant, but especially immigrants
from Third World countries, whose currencies might be suffering particularly
unfavourable exchange rates in relation to western currencies. In addition to its
effect on immigrants in general, the sponsorship bond seems to have created
particular hardship on refugees and family class immigrants (Thompson 1995).

In introducing the head tax the government claimed that it would be using
the revenues from the tax towards the costs of settlement services for new immigrants. The irony has been that the government has introduced the tax at a time
when it had already started to substantially cut settlement services. The announce-
ment in November 1995 of the change in immigration policy against immigrants
who do not have proficiency in the official languages, just months after the introduction of the head tax, raises further doubts as to what the right of landing fee is
intended to achieve.

The Meaning and Implications
of Policy Changes Introduced in the 1990s

Many of the changes introduced in immigration and settlement policies in the
1990s, namely the new language training programs, the introduction of new sponsorship requirements, and the head tax, were intended to privatize the costs of
settlement by downloading them on to individual immigrants and their sponsors.
In introducing some of these changes, government officials have argued that their
overriding concern has been deficit reduction and that all they have done is "shift
the cost burden for specific activities from the general taxpayer to the beneficiaries" (Thompson 1995). Specific assumptions are made in the assertion that it is
not the general "Canadian taxpayer" but the individual immigrant and/or their
sponsor who are the beneficiaries of immigration.

NEW PROPOSALS FOR CHANGE IN IMMIGRATION POLICY:
THE IMMIGRATION LEGISLATIVE REVIEW REPORT

At the time of writing, the federal government is in the process of reviewing the
Immigration Act. In January, 1998, a three-person panel commissioned by the
Liberal government unveiled its report entitled "Not Just Numbers: A Canadian
Framework for Future of Immigration." The report produced a detailed review of
all aspects of immigration and extensive recommendations (172 in total!) to shape

a new immigration act. Since the unveiling of the report, the federal government has engaged in a very short and limited process of public hearings. While at this point, it is not clear what aspects of the report will be adopted by the government in the formation of new legislation and policy, what is significant is that the report has set the agenda for a public debate on immigration.

The following is an analysis of parts of the report "Not Just Numbers," provided for several reasons. First, whether important parts of it are adopted or not, the report needs to be taken seriously, as it is the document that segments of the public have to respond to in order to participate in the present debate on immigration. Second, the document is culmination of a neo-liberal approach to immigration prevailing in aspects of immigration policy in the 1990s. In addition, despite the fact that its arguments are presented in a framework of economic rationality, the cynical tone of the report gives voice to some of the anti-immigration sentiments developing in Canada in the 1990s.

The title of the report "Not Just Numbers" is critical of some characteristics attributed to immigration policies of the last few decades. The title seems to target family class immigrants and refugees, who are thought to have benefited from recent immigration policies. "Just Numbers" implies that immigration of people in these categories has not only failed to benefit Canada, but has created of a burden on Canadian society. The title is in some ways reminiscent of a clearly racist debate over immigration that took place in Canada at the turn of the century. Early in the twentieth century, when the government of Canada decided in favour of eastern European immigration to populate western Canada and to open the land to agriculture, and debated whether the priority of immigration should be the quantity of immigrants or their "quality" — referring to their racial/cultural background.

Implying that many recent immigrants have not successfully integrated into Canadian society, "Not Just Numbers" argues that integration is one of the central issues guiding its recommendations. The report argues for selection of immigrants on the basis of their skills and means to integrate to Canadian society. Although the report is written in supposedly race- and gender-neutral terms, the ideal immigrant who would successfully "integrate" to Canada is depicted as someone with the characteristics and qualifications of an educated, white male from traditional source countries. In what has become the most controversial change recommended in immigration policies since the 1960s, the report recommends introduction of new criteria for the selection of independent class immigrants (called "self-supporting immigrants" in the report) over and above the already demanding criteria used under the point system. This is the requirement that each and every independent, including business class immigrants, have proficiency in at least one of Canada's official languages (Recommendations 53, 58, 59).

Moreover, the report takes a neo-liberal approach to integration, treating it almost solely as the responsibility of immigrants — which they are supposed to accomplish through the education, language, labour market skills, and money they are expected to bring with them — but not equally a responsibility of Canadian society and the state. The report recommends that every independent immigrant be financially capable of personally meeting the full costs of establishing themselves in Canada during their first six months after immigrating (Recommendation 52). Along the lines of a neo-liberal approach to "integration," the report recommends a downloading of settlement costs to immigrant families, making sponsorship a financially onerous and intimidating responsibility which would, in practice, be undertaken and carried out by only a privileged few. For example, the report suggests that family class immigrants who do not have prior knowledge or high proficiency of Canada's official languages may be admitted to the country, but only on the condition that their sponsor pay the whole costs of their language training (Recommendations 35, 41, 64). In addition, the report recommends the entrenchment of harsh enforcement measures for sponsorship in law (Recommendation 36).

This approach overlooks the significance of racism and sexism in setting obstacles to "successful integration" of immigrants. It also overlooks the ways in which immigration and settlement policies, as discussed earlier, contribute to difficulties of integration. Rather than finding the Canadian state partially responsible for integration problems, this approach eliminates many responsibilities the state has historically assumed in the settlement process. The implication of this approach becomes a "blame the victim" attitude. If there are problems in "successful integration" among immigrants already in Canada, they are attributed to the immigrants' own shortcomings, rather than obstacles set by discrimination, disfavour policies, or unfavourable labour market conditions. In immigration policy, the objective becomes one of recruiting those immigrants who are least likely to become "burdens" on Canadian society and the state. The judgements as to who would become a "burden" versus who would be "self-supporting" are based on gender- and class-biased notions as to who "contributes" to society and the economy.

The neo-liberal perspective of "Not Just Numbers" overshadows and undermines the potentially positive implications of what could otherwise be interpreted as its better recommendations. One significant aspect of the document, for example, is the liberalization it proposes to the definitions of "spouse" and "family" used in discussions of family class immigration. Responding to criticisms made over the years regarding the homophobic as well as ethnocentric biases prevailing in the existing definitions of spouse and family, the report recommends that family class immigration be expanded to include partners in same-sex relationships as well as notions of family that may be culturally different (Recommendations 32, 34). While these specific recommendations seem to represent an improvement over existing regulations, other recommendations contradict and limit their positive implications. They suggest that the document may be doing little more than paying lip-service to a liberalized approach to family class. For example, Recommendation 40 suggests that a three-tier structure be created for family class immigrants composed of: 1) spouses and dependent children; 2) fiancé(e)s, parents and (if the sponsor's parents have deceased) grandparents; 3) relatives or close personal acquaintances of the sponsor's choice. This three-tier system introduces a hierarchy in the definition of "family." once again repeating ethnocentric biases as to who would be considered significant family members. Coupled with this hierarchy in the definition of family are different and demanding requirements and conditions for immigration and settlement, especially for Tier 3 - not very different from those of self-supporting immigrants ("Not Just Numbers" Table 5.1, p. 51). The tier system demands that Tier 3, and sometimes Tier 2, applicants meet very high requirements for education, language skills, and medical screening over and above those required in Tier 1. In addition, the report argues for a reduction in the sponsorship period for spouses and dependent children (Tier 1) - shortening their dependency on the sponsor (Recommendation 37) - but explicitly recommends a ten-year period of sponsorship for those in Tiers 2 and 3.

These extra conditions and requirements for immigration and settlement of people in Tiers 2 and 3 of family class immigration, along with the excessive costs involved in paying for immigration application, right of landing, and language fees, suggest that, under the proposed regulations, very few relatives, if any, would realistically be sponsored to come to Canada. Despite the seeming liberalization in the definition of the family, therefore, the report is arguing, in effect, for a closing of family class immigration.

Foreign Domestic Workers

"Not Just Numbers" automatically categorizes domestic workers as "foreign workers" as opposed to immigrants, assigning them temporary status. This categorization represents a further step back from the existing policy which guarantees domestic workers ("live-in caregivers" since 1992) permanent status after completion of two years of service under temporary status. Recommendation 75 suggests that domestic workers would come to Canada as temporary workers, but could apply for landed immigrant status if they could obtain a valid, permanent job offer. Permanent status, therefore, is not guaranteed, but conditional. The condition is a very difficult one to achieve, as it is not clear what would constitute a "permanent" job offer for a caregiver in a private home. Furthermore, the condition for the achievement of permanent status is highly questionable, as it creates a strong relationship of dependency for the worker who needs the employer to accomplish a status.

The report seems to suggest an improvement of the existing policy when it recommends the elimination of the compulsory live-in status as a government requirement. As with some other recommendations, however, the report takes back with one hand what it has given with the other. On the issue of living-in, it once again endorses the dependency of domestic workers when it leaves the issue to "the arrangement they make with their employer." In tune with the neo-liberal spirit of the document, the terms of the contract, as well as the status of the worker, therefore, are decided privately by the employer. Another example of this spirit is demonstrated in Recommendation 71. This recommendation assigns responsibility of health coverage for all temporary workers (including domestic workers) to their employer. It does not, however, suggest any measures to enforce this.

The document seems to recommend a relaxation of direct state regulation over foreign domestic workers which prevailed in its most visible forms since the early 1970s. It also, however, allows the state to rid itself of responsibility over working conditions.

Altogether, "Not Just Numbers" epitomizes some of the shifts that have occurred in Canadian approaches to immigration and settlement in the 1990s. Whereas recommendations such as the one encouraging a more liberal definition of family are welcome as correctives to the heterosexism and ethnocentrism in immigration processes, most of the recommendations in the report represent a culmination of a neo-liberal logic. This logic prevails in both the narrowly "economic" approach to the selection of immigrants, and the downloading of the complete costs of settlement on to the immigrants. The document contributes ideologically to the generally hostile sentiments surrounding immigration to Canada in the 1990s. In addition to the general ideological tone, the specific recommendations also have direct material implications for the lives of most female immigrants, except for the privileged few.

CONCLUSION

Even though changes in Canadian immigration policy in the 1960s have been heralded as "liberalization" by some observers, a gender/race/class analysis of developments in immigration and settlement since the 1960s reveals that women immigrants, and especially working-class women of colour, have been disadvantaged in their chances of their entry into Canada as well as in the status and conditions they have experienced once they have entered Canada. The reality of systemic inequalities in the conditions of women immigrants of colour is particularly ironic in the context of a growing women's movement in Canada since the 1960s, and the emergence in the 1980s of a Canadian *Charter of Rights and Freedoms* with seemingly strong equality clauses.

I have argued that the subordination of women of colour has continued, while gaining new meanings and dimensions under a "liberalized" immigration system, because this "liberalization" has largely consisted of "rationalization" of immigration criteria based on labour market principles. So, while "rationalization" has, on the one hand, meant *formal* equality in the treatment of immigrants on the basis of gender, race, and nationality, it has, on the other hand, meant increased commodification of immigrants. Increased commodification of immigrants has caused several disadvantages for women of colour. First, it has meant that in modern times, women immigrants have lost their status as perceived contributors to nation-building. Compared to British immigrant women of the past, whose racial and cultural background privileged and often made them valued immigrants for their potentials as the future "mothers of the nation" and transmitters of (British) culture, women immigrants of colour are not seen, either biologically or culturally, to be contributing towards the building of a nation. Second, even when women immigrants promise to make much-needed contributions in the labour market, a "rationalized" immigration system does not necessarily guarantee equality. When definitions of such labour market criteria as education and skill are gendered, formal equality may be vacuous for women immigrants.

As demonstrated, the economic logic in Canadian immigration and settlement policies has gained further force and new dimensions in the 1990s. Restructuring of the Canadian state in the 1990s has led to changes in immigration policy emphasizing selection of immigrants to maximize their economic contributions to Canada, while minimizing any costs in their settlement and welfare. These new developments, while clearly making immigration to Canada difficult for all potential immigrants, are likely to have particularly negative effects on women immigrants of colour. On the one hand, they further disadvantage women and Third World immigrants in the immigration selection process. On the other hand, they weaken membership and rights of immigrants in the Canadian state, and deepen relations of dependence in immigrant families which tend to have negative consequences especially for women and elderly people.

This overview of the difficulties immigrant women in Canada have faced since the 1960s — despite the alleged elimination of explicit racism and sexism in immigration and settlement policies — has several implications for anti-sexist and anti-racist theorizing and strategies. One major implication is that there are radical differences between *non*-racism and *non*-sexism in policies and *anti*-racism and *anti*-sexism. The former set of principles are often limited to elimination of formal and explicit discrimination, but may be perfectly compatible and co-existent with unequal and exploitative treatment of differently situated immigrants (Simmons 1998). Political strategies aiming to challenge problems facing immigrant women in Canada have to involve, but cannot simply be content with, elimination of such discrimination, and must continue developing an *anti*-racist and *anti*-sexist agenda. Such an agenda would necessarily involve an examination and challenge of differential impacts of immigration and settlement policy on the basis of gender and race, as well as ethnicity, language, class, sexuality and able-bodiedness. In addition, however, an *anti*-racist and *anti*-sexist agenda needs to interrogate and challenge some of the central premises involved in Canadian nation-building and immigration, as well as in recent neo-liberal policies: notions of who "builds" a nation (and who doesn't), who is a "contributing" (as opposed to "dependent") member of society and nation, and what are the values of housework, care-giving work, and different types of labour market work.

REFERENCES

Agnew, Vijay. 1996. *Resisting Discrimination: Women from Asia, Africa and the Caribbean and the Women's Movement in Canada*. Toronto: University of Toronto Press.

Anthias, Floya, and Nira Yuval-Davis. 1989. "Introduction" in *Woman-Nation-State*. Houndsmills, Basingstoke: Macmillan.

Arat-Koc, Sedef. 1989. "In the Privacy of Our Own Home: Foreign Domestic Workers as Solution to the Crisis of the Domestic Sphere in Canada." *Studies in Political Economy*, no. 28 (Spring 1989).

———. 1992. "Immigration Policies, Foreign Domestic Workers and the Definition of Citizenship in Canada." In Vic Satzewich, ed., *Deconstructing a Nation: Immigration, Multiculturalism and Racism in 1990s Canada*. Halifax: Fernwood.

———. 1997. "From 'Mothers of the Nation' to Migrant Workers." In Abigail B. Bakan and Daiva Stasiulis, eds., *Not One of the Family: Foreign Domestic Workers in Canada*. Toronto: University of Toronto Press.

———. 1998. *National Action Committee on the Status of Women (NAC) Response to the Immigration Legislative Review Report: "Not Just Numbers: A Canadian Framework for Future Immigration."*

Arat-Koc, Sedef, and Felicita Villasin. 1990. *Report and Recommendations on the Foreign Domestic Movement Program*. Report prepared for INTERCEDE to be submitted to the Ministry of Employment and Immigration.

Arnopoulos, Sheila MacLeod. 1979. *Problems of Immigrant Women in the Canadian Labour Force*. Ottawa: Canadian Advisory Council on the Status of Women.

Bakan, Abigail, and Daiva Stasiulis. 1995. "Making the Match: Domestic Placement Agencies and the Racialization of Women's Household Work." *Signs*, vol. 20, no. 2 (Winter 1995).

Bakan, Abigail, and Daiva Stasiulis. 1997. "Foreign Domestic Worker Policy and the Social Boundaries of Modern Citizenship." In Abigail B. Bakan and Daiva Stasiulis, eds., *Not One of the Family: Foreign Domestic Workers in Canada*. Toronto: University of Toronto Press.

Boyd, Monica. 1975. "The Status of Immigrant Women in Canada" *Canadian Review of Sociology and Anthropology*, no. 12, part II (November 1975).

———. 1992a. "Gender, Visible Minority and Immigrant Earnings Inequality: Assessing an Employment Equity Premise." In Vic Satzewich, ed., *Deconstructing a Nation: Immigration, Multiculturalism and Racism in 1990s Canada*. Halifax: Fernwood.

———. 1992b. "Immigrant Women: Language, Socio-Economic Inequalities and Policy Issues." In Barbara Burnaby and Alister Cumming, eds., *Socio-Political Aspects of ESL*. Toronto: OISE.

Boyd, Monica, and Chris Taylor. 1989. "Canada: International Migration Policies, Trends and Issues." In Charles Nam, William Serow, David Sly, and Robert Wellner, eds., *International Handbook on International Migration*. Westport, Connecticut: Greenwood Press.

Brodie, Janine. 1997. "Meso-Discourses, State Forms and the Gendering of Liberal Democratic Citizenship." *Citizenship Studies*, vol. 1, no. 2.

Campbell, Murray. 1994. "Too Many Immigrants, Many Say: Federal Survey Shows Relatively Less Compassion, Less Tolerance," *Globe and Mail*, March 10, 1994, A1, A6.

Carty, Linda. 1994. "African Canadian Women and the State: 'Labour Only, Please.'" In Peggy Bristow et al. *'We're Rooted Here and They Can't Pull Us Up: Essays In African Canadian Women's History*. Toronto: University of Toronto Press.

Canada Employment and Immigration Commission. 1992. *Immigrant Regulations*, 1978 as amended by SOR/92-214, P.C. 1992-685 (April 1992).

Citizenship and Immigration Canada. 1994a. *A Broader Vision: Immigration and Citizenship Plan 1995-2000 Annual Report to Parliament*. Ottawa.

———. 1994b. *Immigration Consultations Report*. Ottawa.

———. 1994c. *Into the 21st Century: A Strategy for Immigration and Citizenship*. Ottawa.

Daenzer, Patricia. 1993. *Regulating Class Privilege: Immigrant Servants in Canada, 1940s-1990s*. Toronto: Canadian Scholars' Press.

———. 1997. "An Affair Between Nations: International Relations and the Movement of Household Domestic Workers." In Abigail B. Bakan and Daiva Stasiulis, eds., *Not One of the Family: Foreign Domestic Workers in Canada*. Toronto: University of Toronto Press.

Das Gupta, Tania. 1995. "Families of Native Peoples, Immigrants and People of Colour." In Nancy Mandell and Ann Duffy, eds., *Canadian Families: Diversity, Conflict and Change*. Harcourt, Brace and Co.

DeMara, Bruce. 1992. "New Immigration Rules Racist Domestic Workers Rally Told," *Toronto Star*, February 3, 1992.

Doherty, Nuala. 1992 "Challenging Systemic Sexism in the language Training Program." In Barbara Burnaby and Alister Cumming, eds., *Socio-Political Aspects of ESL*. Toronto: OISE.

Domestics Cross Cultural News. 1992. INTERCEDE monthly newsletter, June 1992.

Dua, Ena. Forthcoming. "'The Hindu Woman's Question': Canadian Nation-Building and the Social

Construction of Gender for South-Asian Canadian Women." In Agnes Calliste and George Dei, eds., *Anti-Racism and Critical Race, Gender and Class Studies: A Canadian Reader*. Toronto: University of Toronto Press.

Fincher, Ruth, Lois Foster, Wenona Giles, and Valerie Preston. 1994. "Gender and Migration Policy." In Howard Adelman, Allan Borowski, Meyer Burstein, and Lois Foster, eds., *Immigration and Refugee Policy: Australia and Canada Compared*, Vol. I. Toronto: University of Toronto Press.

Gaskell, Jane. 1986. "Conceptions of Skill and the Work of Women: Some Historical and Political Issues." In Roberta Hamilton and Michele Barrett, eds., *The Politics of Diversity*. London: Verso.

Giles, Wenona. 1988. "Language Rights are Women's Rights: Discrimination Against Immigrant Women in Canadian Language Training Policies." *Resources for Feminist Research*, vol 17, no. 3.

Globe and Mail. 1997. "Immigration Goals Exceeded," March 18, 1997, A2.

Gratton, Michael. 1994. "A Policy Worthy of Reform," *Ottawa Sun*, November 6, 1994.

Greenspon, Edward. 1994. "Reform Releases Refugee Crime Data," *Globe and Mail*, November 5, A1, A10.

Harper, Tim, and David Vieneau. 1994. "Clampdown on Immigration: Families to Risk Houses or Cars to Bring in Kin," *Toronto Star*, October 29, 1994, A1, A22.

Inglis, Christine, Anthony Birch, Geoffrey Sherington. 1994. "An Overview of Australian and Canadian Migration Patterns and Policies." In Howard Adelman, Allan Borowski, Meyer Burstein, and Lois Foster, eds., *Immigration and Refugee Policy: Australia and Canada Compared*, Vol. I. Toronto: University of Toronto Press.

Lanphier, Michael. 1997. "Overview: Devolution in post-Multicultural Society." *Refuge*, vol. 15, no. 6. Law Union of Canada.

Law Union of Ontario. 1981. "History of Immigration Laws and Policy." In *The Immigrant's Handbook*. Montreal: Black Rose Books.

Li, Peter. 1992. "The Economics of Brain Drain: Recruitment of Skilled Labour to Canada: 1954-1986." In Vic Satzewich, ed., *Deconstructing a Nation: Immigration, Multiculturalism and Racism in 1990's Canada*. Halifax: Fernwood.

Macklin, Audrey. 1994. "On the Inside Looking In: Foreign Domestic Workers in Canada." In Wenona Giles and Sedef Arat-Koc, eds., *Maid in the Market: Women's Paid Domestic Labour*. Halifax: Fernwood.

MacKenzie, Ian. 1988. "Early Movements of Domestics from the Caribbean and Canadian Immigration Policy: A Research Note." *Alternate Routes*, no. 8.

Morris, John. 1997, "Neo-Liberal Strategies to Cut Costs in Settlement Services: Cost Recovery and Devolution." *Refuge*, vol. 15, no. 6.

Ng, Roxana. 1993. "Racism, Sexism and Immigrant Women." In Sandra Burt, Lorraine Code, and Lindsay Dorney, eds., *Changing Patterns: Women in Canada*. Toronto: McClelland and Stewart.

Noorani Arif, and Cynthia Wright. 1995. "They Believed the Hype" *This Magazine*, no. 28 (December/January 1995).

"Not Just Numbers: A Canadian Framework for the Future of Immigration" (Immigration Legislative Review). Ottawa, 1997.

Opoku-Dapaah, and Michael Lanphier. 1997. "Family-Class Immigration: Implications for Post-Multiculturalism." *Refuge*, vol. 15, no. 6.

Paredes, Milagros. 1987."Immigrant Women and Second-Language Education: A Study of Access to Linguistic Resources." *Resources for Feminist Research*, vol. 16, no. 1 (March 1987).

Pratt, Anna. 1995. "New Immigrant and Refugee Battered Women: The Intersection of Immigration and Criminal Justice Policy." In Mariana Valverde, L. MacLeod, and K. Johnsten, eds., *Wife Assault and the Canadian Criminal Justice System: Issues and Policies*. Toronto: Centre of Criminology, University of Toronto.

Roberts, Barbara. 1979. "'A Work of Empire': Canadian Reformers and British Female Immigration." In Linda Kealey, ed., *A Not Unreasonable Claim: Women and Reform in Canada: 1880s-1920s*. Toronto: The Women's Press.

Sarick, Lila. 1994a. "Immigration from Europe, a Priority, Marchi Says," *Globe and Mail*, Sept. 13, A4.

———. 1994b. "Family Immigration Faces Change" *Globe and Mail*, October 24, 1994 A1, A2.

———. 1994c. "Less Help for Immigrants Planned: Policy Dashes Man's Hope of Sponsoring His Mother," *Globe and Mail*, November 2, 1994, A1, A6.

Satzewich, Vic. 1989. "Racism and Caribbean Immigration Policy: The Government's View of Caribbean Immigration, 1962-1966." *Canadian Ethnic Studies*, vol. 21, no. 1.

Seward, Shirley, and Kathryn McDade. 1988. "Immigrant Women in Canada: A Policy Perspective." A Background Paper Prepared for the Canadian Advisory Council on the Status of Women.

Silvera, Makeda. 1983. *Silenced: Talks with Working Class Caribbean Women about Their Lives and Struggles as Domestic Workers in Canada*. Toronto: Sister Vision.

Simmons, Alan. 1998. "Racism and Immigration Policy." In Vic Satzewich, ed., *Racism and Social Inequality in Canada*. Toronto: Thompson.

Stasiulis, Daiva, and Radha Jhappan. 1995. "The Fractious Politics of a Settler Society." In Daiva Stasiulis and Nira Yuval-Davis, eds., *Unsettling Settler Societies: Articulations of Gender, Race, Ethnicity and Class*. London and Thousand Oaks, California: Sage Publications.

Task Force on Immigration Practices and Procedures. 1981. *Domestic Workers on Employment Authorizations*. Ottawa: Canada Employment and Immigration Commission.

Thanh Ha, Tu. 1994. "Less Help for Immigrants Planned," *Globe and Mail*, November 2, 1994, A1, A6.

Thompson, Allan. 1995a. "Immigration Tax: How It Really Hurts Refugees," *Toronto Star*, March 5, A2.

————. 1995b. "Immigration Changes Attacked: Stressing French and English is Unfair, Critics Say," *Toronto Star*, November 18, 1995, A16.

Valverde, Mariana. 1991. "Racial Purity, Sexual Purity and Immigration Policy." In *The Age of Light, Soap and Water*. Toronto: McClelland and Stewart.

Whitaker, Reg. 1991. *Canadian Immigration Policy Since Confederation*. Ottawa: Canadian Historical Association.

Wilson-Smith, Anthony. 1994. "Debating the Numbers: Ottawa Acts to Dampen Public Concern over Immigration," *Maclean's*, November 7, 1994.

Wong, Lloyd, and Nancy Netting. 1992. "Business Immigration to Canada: Social Impact and Racism." In Vic Satzewich, ed., *Deconstructing a Nation: Immigration, Multiculturalism and Racism in 1990s Canada*. Halifax: Fernwood.

PART IV

THE RACIALIZED
CONSTRUCTION OF GENDER

CHAPTER NINE

Beyond Diversity

Exploring the Ways in Which the Discourse of Race has Shaped the Institution of the Nuclear Family

ENAKSHI DUA

For more than a decade, feminists have been debating the relative importance of the nuclear family in shaping the ways in which women of colour experience gender oppression. For many mainstream feminists, the nuclear family has been the starting point for exploring the roots of gender oppression in society. Mainstream feminists have argued that the institution of the nuclear family is the primary site in which gender oppression is produced and experienced by women. They point out that it is through the nuclear family that gender socialization, the appropriation of women's unpaid labour, and the unequal power relationships between men and women are organized in society (Barrett and McCintosh 1982). However, in *Ain't I a Woman* (1981), bell hooks shattered the hegemony of mainstream feminist analyses, when she argued that these theories failed to address the ways in which racism shape the social construction of gender. hooks and others went on to argue that due to the racism in western societies, women of colour's experiences with the family deviate considerably from the model put forward in mainstream feminist analyses (see for example Parmar and Amos 1984).

Based on this critique, many feminist scholars have called for theorizing that is inclusive of how women of colour experience the family and that take into account the diversity of women's experiences with the family. For example, Mandell argues that "previous historical accounts...have uncritically superimposed a European framework onto a Canadian past" and calls for research "that stress[es] the diversity and multiplicity of family histories" (1995, 17). The starting point for such research has been the task of integrating the historical dimensions of racism into investigations of gender and class.

Not all feminists agree that integrating racism into analyses of gender would alter feminist theorizing on the family. Recently, Okin dismissed the significance of such diversity in experiences with the family, cautioning scholars "not to overreact to differences by losing sight of their broadly relevant insights about families, their gendered division of labour, and its effect on sex inequality in all spheres

237

of life" (1997, 19). Okin calls for a re-evaluation of feminist theories of the family, arguing that "there are obvious benefits to such reevaluations of earlier second-wave feminist theories about families that a decade or more of scholarship had been inclined to jettison as racist, classist, ethnocentric or heterosexist. Indeed when such theories are given a fair second chance rather than rejected as essentialist, they can sometimes be found to apply or to have considerable relevance to those persons they had thought to neglect and thereby discriminate against" (1997, 20).

Despite such disagreements over the relevance of mainstream feminist theories on the nuclear family for women of colour, feminist analyses of the family have failed to investigate the ways in which racism has shaped the institution of the nuclear family. While mainstream feminist analyses have been preoccupied with investigating the forces that led to the historical emergence of the nuclear family, they have assumed that the discourse of race has had little to do with the nuclear family. As a result this body of work has concentrated on discerning the ways in which male power interacted with the historical development of capitalism to produce the nuclear family as a sexist institution. For writers such as Okin, racism as a discourse and as a form of systemic discrimination[1] seems to have little to do with the way in which gender has come to be socially organized or with the historical development of the family.

In contrast, writers who attempt to integrate race and gender have challenged the universalizing tendencies in mainstream feminist analyses, pointing out that the family is experienced differently according to a woman's social class, race, and sexual orientation. Surprisingly, though, these writers do not tell us why such diversity exists. In particular, they do not explain why racism alters a woman of colour's experience with the family, nor how the dynamics of racism have shaped the way in which the institution of the nuclear family has historically come to be organized. As a result, racism is seen as only relevant in explaining how women of colour experience the family, not in how white women experience the family, nor in explaining the social organization of sexism.

This chapter explores the role of the discourse of race in the emergence of the nuclear family as a sexist institution. First, through a review of mainstream feminist approaches to the family, I examine the ways in which the historical development of patriarchy and capitalism led to the emergence of the nuclear family in Canada. Next, through a review of integrative feminist approaches, I show that the nuclear family operated very differently in Canadian communities of colour. The last section outlines the ways in which the discourse of racism led to the emergence of the nuclear family. Drawing on an emerging body of literature which explores the social construction of race and gender in both metropolitan and white settler societies, I will demonstrate that the familial, gender, and sexual relationships characteristic of the nuclear family emerge out of the imperatives of racialized projects of nineteenth century nation-building. In addition to organizing gender relations, the institution of the nuclear family also organizes race relations in society. It is these politics of race and nation that explain why white women and women of colour[2] have different experiences with the nuclear family.

MAINSTREAM FEMINIST APPROACHES TO THE NUCLEAR FAMILY: PATRIARCHY OR CAPITALISM?

The question of how the nuclear family emerged as a sexist institution has been a central concern in mainstream feminist theory. In the 1960s and 1970s, feminists began challenging the hegemonic idea that the institution of the family was a complementary unit which provides for the needs of all of its members. Starting with Betty Friedan's *The Feminine Mystique* (1963), mainstream feminists have argued that the gender division of labour within the family, which delegated to women unpaid motherwork and domestic work, created power differences as unpaid domestic work made women dependent on a male wage. These writers linked the division of labour within the family to the subordination of women in society. As the private sphere (domestic and mother work) was associated with women, the public sphere (paid work) became associated with men; the private sphere also became devalued.[3]

Given that the family was identified as one of the main institutions that organized gender inequality, it is not surprising that mainstream feminists invested considerable energy in exploring which historical and social forces shaped its sexist character. The initial investigation into the social origins of the nuclear family was characterized by an intense debate between marxist and radical feminists, a debate that not only resulted in initially polarizing feminist analyses of the family but, as importantly, in limiting future discussion to an investigation of the respective roles of patriarchy or capitalism in the emergence of the nuclear family. Unfortunately, as the attention of writers became focused on exploring either patriarchy or capitalism, the possibility that racism may also have played a role in the emergence of the nuclear family was not considered.[4]

Marxist feminists argued that the origins of the nuclear family were located in the social relations of capitalism. These writers began their analysis by extending conventional marxist categories of production and class exploitation, illustrating that domestic work was indeed a form of labour and that social reproduction was a form of production. Benston (1969), Dalla Costa (1972) argued that the nuclear family served the interests of capitalism, which required the reproduction of cheap labour. Subsequently, others argued that not only did the nuclear family serve the needs of capitalism but its origins are located in the transition from feudal to capitalist society (Fox 1980; Secombe 1980). In contrast, radical feminists argued that the origins of the sex-gender system predated capitalism, and were located in earlier cleavages between men and women. Firestone (1970) argued that these cleavages arose out of a male imperative to control women's reproduction — where such control was socially organized through the institutions of marriage and the family.

Rather than asserting the primacy of one over the other, one resolution of this debate was to integrate the two approaches. The attention of theorists shifted to how the historical development of capitalist relations of production combined with the historical development of social relations of reproduction to create gender oppression (see for example Coontz and Henderson 1986; Lerner 1986; Fox 1988; Eisenstein 1979; Armstrong and Armstrong 1984; Ursel 1992). As a result, feminist scholars began to undertake detailed historical studies of the nuclear family. However, given the intellectual context of theorizing on the nuclear family, the role of racism continued to be treated as irrelevant to the historical development of capitalism, the organization of social reproduction in a capitalist society and the institution of the nuclear family.

Despite their narrow focus, these historical studies offer important insights into the possible ways in which racism has shaped the nuclear family. In particular, these studies suggest that the development of the nuclear family cannot simply be seen as the inevitable consequence of any structural force, capitalism or patriarchy (Faladrin 1979; Secombe 1986; Stone 1977; Davis 1977). Instead, this body of work suggests that in most western countries the emergence of the nuclear family as a dominant pattern organizing gender and sexual relations was the consequence of complex interaction between male power, the tensions inherent in a capitalist society, state intervention, and bourgeois morality.

In Canada, the nuclear family, as an institution, begins to emerge for the bourgeoisie during the late eighteenth century, typified by a strong sense of separation of parents and children from the extended family, marked by a norm of complementarity between husband and wife, and the special role of the mother in shaping the character of her children (Bradbury 1981). Several writers have demonstrated that the institutionalization of the nuclear family among working class and settler households, in part, was a response to the changes brought about by industrialization, particularly to the extension of wage labour to a larger proportion of the population.[5] After 1850, what constitutes the character of household life begins to change for working-class and settler households, as relations of production give way to relations of sexuality, intimacy, and consumption.

As Armstrong and Armstrong (1984) and Ursel (1992) have shown, the shift to industrialization meant that men, women, and children became dependent on the wages earned by family members for survival. In the initial period of industrialization, all members of a household worked in the wage labour force, and wages were pooled. As Ursel (1992) has shown, the entry of all members of the household into the paid labour force was accompanied by a breakdown in the power of the patriarch. In addition, declining birth rates in this period led to a societal concern for social reproduction. The crisis in social reproduction gave legitimacy to the notion of the family wage, which in turn allowed the nuclear family to be institutionalized and women's labour to once again be tied to the household (1992, 61-122). The family was transformed into a set of relations that specialized in procreation, child rearing, consumption, and affection. Notably, the nuclear family widened the division between many men's and women's tasks: husbands became responsible for breadwinning and wives became responsible for homemaking and child-rearing.

Several agents participated in the process of institutionalizing the nuclear family. The most noted role is that of state managers. The Canadian state, through a variety of social welfare and family protection legislation, preserved the concept of the household as a distinct unit. As Ursel (1992) and Pupo (1988) show, child labour legislation, protective labour legislation for women, the creation of Mother's Pensions, reform of property and divorce legislation, and the notion of the family wage were measures designed to preserve both familial and patriarchal relations. Such interventions allowed women's labour to once again become tied to the household. By transforming men into breadwinners, male authority was both maintained and transformed.

However, the state was not the only agent working to preserve patriarchal authority. In Canada, as well as elsewhere, the entrenchment of the nuclear family was located in a politics of bourgeois morality. As noted earlier, the nuclear family first became entrenched in middle-class homes, leading the middle class to glorify motherhood and the ideology of domesticity, and to work towards institutionalizing these gender and familial relations in society. As several researchers have shown, in the late nineteenth and early twentieth century, the nuclear family was the focus of social reform movements in most western societies (Pupo 1988; Ursel 1992). Social reformers worked to entrench the bourgeois ideal of the nuclear family among the working class, as well as immigrants and First Nations people (see also Dubinisky 1992; Iacovetta 1992; Marks 1992). Private charities spearheaded attempts to make poor and immigrant European families conform to the new ideal of domesticity. These organizations advocated legislation that would keep families intact, where husbands were engaged in paid work, wives laboured in domestic work and childcare, children went to school, and no one other than parents and children lived within the home.[6] Notably, middle-class women dominated the social reform movement, playing a major role in shaping state policies as activists, lobbyists, and clients.

This literature suggests the importance of a more contingent, historically-sensitive approach that locates the development of the nuclear family in several forces — such as patriarchy, capitalism, wage labour, the social organization of reproduction, state authority, and bourgeois morality. However, these studies treat the development of the nuclear family as isolated from the social organization of racism. This work is missing an analysis of how these forces operate in the lives of women of colour. While there is a recognition of the complexities of class and gender, these writers assume that these forces have organized familial relations in the same way for women of colour. Moreover, how racism has shaped the social organization of white male power, "Black" male power, wage labour, reproduction, and bourgeois morality are unexplored.

INTEGRATIVE PERSPECTIVES ON THE FAMILY

It was not until women of colour began to challenge mainstream feminist thought that the issue of racism was raised. Perhaps reflecting the importance of the family not only in feminist theorizing but also in all women's lives, women of colour began deconstructing mainstream feminist theories by pointing to the absence of an analysis of how racism alters women's experiences with the family.

In a series of articles, Amos and Parmar (1985), Bhavani and Coulson (1986), and hooks (1981) argue that in the context of a racist society, the family becomes not only a site of gender oppression but, as importantly, a refuge against racism. As Bhavani and Coulson state:

> Whatever inequalities exist in such households, they are clearly also sites of support for their members. In saying this we are recognising that black women may have significant issues to face within black households.... But at the same time the black family is a source of support in the context of harassment and attacks from white people (1986, 88).

These writers point out that, for women of colour, the struggle has not been to escape the constraints of the nuclear family, but to be able to participate in a nuclear family. Collins (1991) and Das Gupta (1995) have pointed out, in the context of the historical inadequacy of the Black male wage and of high rates of Black female labour force participation rates, the ability to do unpaid domestic work becomes a form of resistance against racism. As Collins states,

> by emphasising Black women's contributions to Black family well-being, such as keeping families together and teaching children survival skills...such work suggests that Black women see their unpaid domestic work more as a form of resistance to oppression than as a form of exploitation by men (1991, 44).

As a result, many writers rejected the idea that the family is the main institution that structures inequality for women of colour (see also Parmar 1982; Trivedi 1984; Bhavani and Coulson 1986; Ramazanoglu 1986; Kazi 1986; Lees 1986). Others, such as Collins (1991), Dua (1994), and Das Gupta (1995), argue that while the family does operate differently in the lives of women of colour, it would be premature to deny that it does not also organize gender and sexual relations for women of colour.[7] One way to resolve this debate is to distinguish between how women of colour experience the family, and how the family is socially organized in communities of colour (see Collins 1991; Dua 1992). Dua (1994) and Das Gupta (1995) have called for work which identifies the historically specific characteristics of the institution of the family in communities of colour.

While very few studies have specifically focused on this question, there is a large body of historical research from which we can begin to discern how the family has been organized in Canadian communities of colour. This literature suggests that there are several important differences in how the institution of the family is organized in communities of colour. Das Gupta summarizes these differences, arguing that people of colour and immigrants have often been denied the right to live in a family context, or the right to have the "family" form of their choice, a denial that has been historically constructed by the Canadian state (1995, 142-4).

Indeed, the following examination of state policies towards familial relations in First Nations, Asian-Canadian, and Caribbean-Canadian communities supports this argument. In all of these cases, Canadian state managers have acted to destroy, prevent, or disrupt the ability of people of colour to participate in family relations. This body of research suggests that women of colour do experience the family in very different ways than women of European descent. Through this research we can begin to see the ways in which racism operates to (dis)organize familial and gender relations.

Both French and British colonizers undertook a series of campaigns to reconstruct familial relations in First Nations communities (Anderson 1988; Bourgelaut 1988; Stevenson 1998).[8] The attack on family forms in First Nations communities began in the seventeenth century when French colonial authorities through the missions identified the familial practices in First Nations communities as problematic. As Anderson (1988) shows, French colonizers were threatened by the social organization of social, gender, and sexual relations in First Nations communities: the economic, social, and political equality men and women possessed; the absence of hierarchal relationships; the personal freedom enjoyed by men and women; the existence of consensual conjugal relations, spousal autonomy, sexual freedom inside and outside marriage; the ease with which spousal relations could be ended; the indulgence of children, and absence of physical punishment (also see McIvor and Stevenson in this collection).

In contrast, the world of the colonizers was hierarchial and patriarchal. Authority was vested in a few senior officers; soldiers and traders were subject to harsh discipline. French ideas of familial relations were bound by relations of authority, discipline, and dependency. As a result, the French colonizers, through the missions, undertook an active campaign to not only destroy gender, sexual and familial relations in First Nations communities, but moreover to replace them with an alternate set of relationships organized around monogamy, patriarchy, and bounded by discipline and dependency (Andersen 1988). As Andersen (1988) suggests, the transformation of gender and familial relations was part of a larger project to bring First Nation people into the nexus of authoritarian and hierarchial relations of the colonial regime.

British colonizers also focused on familial relationships in First Nations communities. However, the focus shifted from an attempt to transform familial relations, to an attempt to disrupt the ability of First Nations people to participate in either European or First Nations patterns of families. As Ponting (1986) and Jamieson (1986) show, after 1806, customary marriages were outlawed by the North West Company. Several factors account for this change. First, as the fur trade declined in importance, and the Canadian economy shifted to agriculture production for the world market, the importance of the labour of First Nations people to the fur trade declined (Laxer 1973, 1989; Naylor 1975). Second, as Jamieson (1986) notes, there was a shift in British colonial policy after the Hudson Bay Company merged with the North West Company. During this period, trading companies were further tied to British imperial interests. These political and economic changes were accompanied by an increasing emphasis on British moral codes, especially class and racial classification codes. These changes meant that company officials, government representatives and missionaries began to denounce interracial marriages in an effort to promote racial segregation. As Bourgelaut suggests, the shift to a politics of racial purity needs to be located in the project of creating a white settler colony with political power in the hands of white settlers (Bourgelaut 1988).

With Confederation, the politics of racial purity would not only encourage state officials to regulate intermarriages but also to regulate the ability of First Nations men and women to participate in familial relations. Under the policy of assimilation, government policies set out to destroy languages, familial relations, and community structures in these communities (Ponting 1986). A series of acts, culminating in the *Indian Act* of 1876, legislated the system of reservations and policies which regulated all aspects of social life in First Nations communities. State regulation focused on family forms. Residential schools and later child welfare policies were mechanisms used to destroy the fabric of social, familial, gender, and sexual relations. Through residential schools and child welfare agencies, children were forcibly separated from biological parents and First Nations communities. Notably, child welfare officers were most likely to remove these children from parents who did not conform to the norms of a patriarchal nuclear family (Locust 1990; Brant 1988). Monture (1995) has argued that the purpose behind such polices was not simply to alter family practices but to destroy the fabric of First Nations communities (Monture 1995; McIvor and Stevenson in this collection). Thus, an examination of the institution of the family in First Nations communities demonstrates that colonial and Canadian state policies have often denied First Nations people the right to live in a family context and the right to have the "family" form of their choice.

The experience of Asian migrants to Canada has been similar to that of First Nations peoples. Asian migration to Canada began in the mid-1850s. British colonial settlement policies in Canada and, later, Canadian immigration policies were based on creating a white, settler nation. However, in the late nineteenth century as the Canadian economy made an uneven transition to a peripheral capitalist economy, it experienced a demand for low-wage labour. The Canadian government experienced difficulty in attracting British and European migrants, forcing it to allow limited migration from Asia: China, India and Japan. However, in the context of a white, settler policy and the politics of racial purity, Asian migrants were defined as temporary workers rather than potential citizens of Canada. During the next 100 years, successive governments regulated the entry of Chinese, South Asian, and Japanese men according to labour market needs, as well as enforced a differential residency and citizenship status (Bolaria and Li 1988). Asian men were unable to vote, denied naturalization, legally prohibited from owning certain kinds of property, and entering into certain occupations.

The status of Asian migrants as temporary workers had profound implications for these men being able to participate in familial relations. Unlike British and European male migrants who were encouraged to sponsor their wives and children, until 1947, the Canadian state imposed a series of regulations designed to prevent Asian men from sponsoring spouses and children. These restrictions varied, as different methods were used in different periods and for different nationalities (see Bolaria and Li 1988; Das Gupta 1995; Dua forthcoming). The result was that the majority of migrants from these countries were men — many of whom were forced to leave their wives and children. In addition, the politics of racial purity made it difficult for these men to enter into familial relations with women of European descent.[9] As Das Gupta notes, these conditions led to bachelor societies, households where groups of Asian men would live together, often sharing domestic work and pooling resources (1995, 162). Given such oppressive state practices, the demand for a "family" became a central issue in communities of colour (Dua forthcoming). By the turn of the century, Chinese, Japanese, and South Asian men began to challenge the restrictions on the entry of their spouses.

After the Second World War, such overt restrictions were removed, but as critics of Canadian immigration policies have pointed out, the Canadian state continued to employ immigration polices to disrupt the ability of Asian and other migrants to participate in family life (Law Union of Canada 1981: Das Gupta 1995, 153-9). Recent reports have suggested that on average it takes over ten years to sponsor a spouse and children from India (NAC 1998). In addition, immigration policies require that immigrants undergo interviews in which they are required to reveal intimate aspects of their lives to "prove" that they are married (NAC 1989). A recent newspaper article reported that migrants from Asia are more likely to be subjected to interviews and delays in sponsorship than those from Europe or the United States (*Toronto Star*, May 12, 1996).

Not only has the Canadian state acted to restrict or prevent people of colour from living in families, it has also acted to transform their relations into nuclear (and heterosexual) forms. Immigration policies require that immigrants can only sponsor one wife, and only their biological children under the age of 18. Immigrants are unable to sponsor members of an extended household as well as children older than 18. As Das Gupta (1995) notes, this regulation disregards that households in China, Japan and India often consisted of parents, adult children and their spouses and children, as well as other relatives. The aim of these policies is clear — they are designed to impose monogamous relationships and to stop the practice of extended families. An examination of the experiences of Asians with the family also suggests that Asian people have often been denied the right to live in a family context, or the right to have the "family" form of their choice.

The experience of Black women from the Caribbean demonstrates an even more complex relationship between people of colour and the institution of the nuclear family. Their experiences suggest that not only are women of colour prevented from participating in familial relationships — when they do it is often as paid domestic workers. As several researchers have pointed out, the social organization of domestic work has not only been gendered, but as importantly has been racialized (hooks 1983; Calliste 1991; Silvera 1983; Arat-Koc 1992; Bakan and Stasiulis 1997). As these writers have pointed out, the reproduction of the labour force does not only take place through women's unpaid labour, but also through paid labour. In the past as well as today, women of colour have been concentrated in paid domestic work — often at subsistence wages for affluent families. It is through the role of women of colour as paid domestic workers that we can begin to see the ways in which women of colour have a different relationship to the institution of the family.[10]

As discussed earlier, until the point system was adopted in the late 1960s, immigration policies had restricted the entry of people of colour into Canada. Given such restrictions, it is significant that one of the few ways in which women of colour have been able to gain immigration status has been through the various domestic worker recruitment schemes (see Bolaria and Li 1988; Arat-Koc 1992; Bakan and Stasiulis 1997). Canada has had a series of immigration policies aimed at recruiting domestic workers to Canada — women from Europe as well as from the Third World. However, as Calliste (1991), Arat-Koc (1992), Bakan and Stasiulis (1997) have demonstrated, since their inception in the nineteenth century, domestic worker recruitment schemes have been racialized. While domestic worker recruitment schemes have preferred women from the British Isles and northern Europe, these programs have been forced to allow women of colour to enter into Canada as the number of European women applying for such work declined. Importantly, the two groups of women have been treated very differently. In the nineteenth and early twentieth century, when the majority of women who entered Canada under these schemes were from Europe, these women were encouraged to marry with white, male settlers and reproduce a white population.[11] In contrast, women of colour entering as domestic workers have been expected to enter domestic work as a life-long occupation — and to return to their country of origin when they are no longer able to carry out such work. The expectation that women of colour would return to their country of origin has been entrenched in immigration policies, as foreign domestic workers have been entitled to only temporary work visas.[12] Through such policies, the Canadian state has effectively ensured that the position women of colour occupy in the Canadian political economy is tied to paid domestic work.

This body of research points to the importance of paid domestic work in the social organization of reproduction. The social reproduction of the labour force has not been completely privatized. Through cooking, cleaning, washing, and the care of white children, paid domestic workers have made substantial contributions to the process of social reproduction in Canada. Women of colour's work as inexpensive paid domestic workers has allowed the Canadian state to avoid the costs of a national childcare program as well as enabled middle-class women to participate in the labour force (Arat-Koc 1992; Bakan and Stasiulis 1997).

The concentration of women of colour in paid domestic work and white women in unpaid domestic work points to the ways in which the private/public split in the social organization of reproduction is racialized. In this split, state policies have encouraged white women into the private realm, while positioning women of colour in the public realm. Moreover, as women of colour have been channelled into paid domestic work, domestic requirement schemes have restricted their ability to participate in private familial relations.

In addition to imposing a differential legal status, until recently immigration policies have required that foreign domestic workers be single — unmarried without children.[13] Foreign domestic workers are often required to live with employers as a condition of their contracts. These regulations ensured that foreign paid domestic workers raise other people's children at the expense of their own families and children, suggesting that the "mothering" of children of colour is an unimportant social concern. As Leah and Morgan (1979), Arat-Koc (1992), and Das Gupta (1995) have noted, these regulations point to the complex ways in which racism has structured familial relations in Canada. It suggests that while emphasizing domesticity and motherhood as ideal roles for white women, dominant ideologies and institutions in Canada see women of colour simply in terms of their labour power (Brand 1988; Arat-Koc 1992).

Canadian state policies regarding familial relations in First Nations, Asian-Canadian, and Caribbean communities have had remarkable similarities. In all of these cases we can see a pattern in which the state has acted to destroy, prevent, or disrupt the ability of people of colour to participate in family relations. In the cases of First Nations and Asian-Canadian communities, the state has spent considerable effort to target existing familial practices in these communities as problematic and developed strategies to eliminate such practices. In the case of First Nations communities this involved replacing egalitarian or matrilineal familial relationships with patriarchal ones. In the case of Asian-Canadian communities this has taken the form of imposing new forms of patriarchal relations — those associated with a nuclear family structure. This body of research suggests that women of colour do experience the family in very different ways than women of European descent. This difference can be summed up quite simply: while the Canadian state has acted in ways to ensure the participation of white women in nuclear familial relations, the state has acted to restrict women of colour's ability to participate in familial relations.

While this body of work has been important for suggesting that race matters — that white women and women of colour have significantly different relationships to the institution of the family — it does not explain why race matters. In other words, what remains unexplained is why women of colour experience the family differently than white women. Why have Canadian state managers instituted policies which encourage white women to participate in nuclear family relations, yet been reluctant to ensure that women of colour do so? Ironically, by not asking why race matters, such an examination does not tell us much about how racism has shaped the social organization of familial and gender relations in Canada. Without such an analysis, the restrictions that people of colour have faced appear as deviations from the way in which the nuclear family operates in Canadian society.

TOWARDS A TRINITY — INTEGRATING RACE, PATRIARCHY AND CAPITALISM: THEORIZING THE IMPACT OF RACISM ON THE FAMILY

In order to understand the ways in which racism has shaped the development of the nuclear family, we need to place it in the context of late nineteenth century projects of nation-building. An emerging literature in sociology, history, political science, post-colonial, and feminist studies explores the connections between nationalism and the social construction of race and gender in metropolitan and colonial settings. Importantly for our purposes, this literature points to the ways in which nineteenth century discourses of race influenced the social organization of capitalism, nations, bourgeois morality, and the nuclear family. During this period, as nations became constituted through a discourse of race, the nuclear family emerged as one of the main institutions for constructing a racialized and gendered nation-state. This link between the discourse of race, the nation, and the nuclear family explains why white women and women of colour experience the family differently.

Several important economic and political changes were taking place in the nineteenth century. In Europe, and many settler societies, this period was not only characterized by the consolidation of the capitalist mode of production, but also by the development of the nation-state. The emergence of the nation-state played an important role in ensuring capitalist relations of production. The spatial division of the world, and the formation of a centralized political authority claiming sovereignty within each space allowed for the organization of wage labour and the consolidation of markets (see Corrigan and Sayer 1986; Hobsbawm 1990; Miles 1989). As importantly, this spatial division of the world into nations allowed for the consolidation of a bourgeois project (Stoler 1995; Hobsbawm 1990).

However, as nations are far from "natural," the consolidation of nation-states required reconstituting social identities. The emergence of many, though not all, nineteenth century nations was accompanied by projects of nation-building.[14] As Anderson (1983) points out, these projects focused on creating an "imagined community," where members of a nation-state acquired a sense of fraternity with an extended community based on an emotional sense of shared distinctiveness. As Gellner (1983), Anderson (1983), and Hobsbawm (1990) show, despite the allegory of a historical continuum, national identities are a product of nation-states, rather than vice versa. Balibar suggests that in order to promote such a sense of distinctiveness, nineteenth century nationalists promoted a sense of a "fictive ethnicity," the notion that members of nation-states share a pre-existing unity with others who are part of the nation-state.

Historically, the discourse of race has played a significant role in the construction of a fictive ethnicity or national identity.[15] As several writers have illustrated, in both metropolis and colonial settings, nineteenth century nationalists often employed notions of race to imagine the nation (Miles 1989; Balibar 1991; Huttenback 1976; McClintock 1995; Stoler 1995). Miles describes this process:

during the nineteenth century, when the process of capitalist development and a conscious strategy of nation-state formation was at its most vigorous, many (but certainly not all) advocates of nationalism drew upon scientific racism in order to identify the supposedly distinct, natural collectivities.... Racism was specially appropriate for this task because it suggested natural differences between 'nations' were grounded in biology and this constituted perhaps the most solid defence of the idea of historical inevitability that is central to the nationalist doctrine (1989, 113).

The discourse of race allowed nationalists to put forward four interconnected representations of the nation. First, that a nation was composed of naturally occurring distinct populations. Second, the discourse of race allowed the distinct character of each nation to be located in biology — an inborn national spirit — so that each nation came to be seen as composed of races — of people who were biologically distinct from those in other nations. Third, as citizens of a nation-state came to be defined as belonging to a common race — nations came to be represented as natural and inevitable. Fourth, the discursive construction of the nation as composed of a common race linked such nationalist projects into a politics of racial purity, as nationalists argued that the biological stock of a nation needed to be protected, otherwise the nation would decline. In the language of the period, nationalists argued that nations need to be guarded against "race deterioration" or "race degeneration" (see Klug 1989; Davin 1978; Valverde 1991; McLaren 1990).

By the end of the nineteenth century, in Canada and elsewhere, the discourse of racial difference between nations was articulated in the pseudo-scientific rhetoric of eugenics. According to Lochhead, a Canadian eugenicist, the purpose of this new science was "the improvement of the race" (cited in McLaren 1990, 13). This was especially vital in the context of nineteenth century imperial expansion, as the importance of improving the racial stock of a nation was seen as the basis for national vitality, strength and the position of nations (and races) within empires (Davin 1978; Klug 1988).

Importantly, in both metropolitan and settler settings, this discourse shaped how national identities were constituted, for it tied those who resided within a nation-state together through the metaphors of blood, inborn essences, and biology. It is this racialized process of constituting national identities that underpins the institutionalization of the nuclear family in metropolitan and settler settings. For, a nation that imagines itself on the basis of race, in its imagining redefines the family, and gender relations within the family. As Balibar points out, a nation which is constituted through the imagery of a racial community has a tendency to present itself through the common envelope of family relations, or as one big family.[16] Indeed, in nineteenth century nationalist discourses, the icon of family became a powerful symbol through which the national identities were constructed and where individuals were tied to the nation through a national genealogy.

As importantly, as national identities were constituted through the meta-phors of blood, inborn essences, and biology, the nuclear family and its associated set of gender and sexual relations would become the anchoring point for a racialized nation. Balibar suggests that in a racialized nation, the importance of the family does not derive solely from the role it plays in the reproduction of labour, but from its role in physically reproducing the nation. Nations that are based on the notion of racially distinct groups require that such distinct groups be physically reproduced. By the end of the nineteenth century, in most metropolitan and white settler colonies, the importance of "race instinct for reproduction" (cited in McLaren 1990, 21), was an accepted notion (also see Valverde 1992).

In addition, in the context of fear of racial deterioration, nationalists argued that the physical reproduction of the nation could not be taken for granted, as it was subject to many kinds of dangers (see Klug 1989; Davin 1978; Valverde 1992; McLaren 1990; Stoler 1995). These included the danger posed by those who resided in the nation-state, especially the working class, poor, the disabled, and those considered to be sexually deviant. Eugenicists characterized these groups as having "inferior racial stock," and argued that they posed a threat of racial degeneration. In both metropolitan and colonial settings, the nation also needed to be protected from the dangerous racial stock of colonized peoples.

It is in this context that the nuclear family became entrenched. As the racialized and classed (re)production of the nation was not something nationalists could take for granted, nationalists focused considerable attention reorganizing familial relations, particularly in ensuring that the nuclear family and its concomitant racial, gender, sexual relations were adopted by those women deemed important for the reproduction of the nation. Eugenicists such as Lochhead systematically advocated that improving the race called for "more stringent marriage laws" (cited in McLaren 1990, 13). Eugenicists were not alone in advocating the institution-alization of the nuclear family. In the context of the moral panic over racial degeneration, several agents, ranging from social reformers to state managers, argued that the nuclear family was central to national strength and vitality (see Davin 1978; McLaren 1990; Ursel 1992; Valverde 1992).[17]

The institutionalization of the nuclear family allowed nationalists to organize race, class, gender, and sexuality according to the racialized nationalist project. Foremost, the institutionalization of the family allowed nationalists to entrench the class character of the nation-state. As Ursel (1992), Valverde (1992), and Stoler (1995) show, the fear of race deterioration allowed social reformers and state managers to link the nuclear family and its associated gender relations to bourgeois morality. As the racial stock of working-class women was suspect (see also Davin 1978; Klug 1989; McLaren 1990), nationalists, eugenicists and social reformers argued that no matter what the costs, middle-class women needed to focus their energies on reproducing a racialized and classed citizenry. For example, in a public lecture in 1885, Pearson, an eugenicist, advocated that "if child-bearing women must be intellectually handicapped then the penalty to be paid for race predominance is the subjugation of women" (cited in Klug 1989, 21).

This bourgeois project was not simply based on the notion of racial purity. It was also based on notions of colonized people. As Stoler has suggested, both the construction of bourgeois civility and the racial inferiority of the working class were juxtaposed against the inferiority of colonized peoples and the threat that they posed to the racial vitality of a nation (Stoler 1995; Huttenback 1976; Miles 1989). The danger posed by colonized people depended on the setting. In the metropolis, as Davin (1978), Ware (1991), and Stoler (1997) have shown, the dangers of racial deterioration were placed in the context of imperialism. As population was linked to power, the ability of white, middle-class women to re-produce a virile race was widely perceived as paramount to the imperial strength and success. Childbearing and improving the racial stock became not just a na-tional but also an imperial duty. As a British nationalist proclaimed in 1909, "the history of nations is determined not on the battlefields but in the nursery, and the battalions which give lasting victory are the battalion of babies. The politics of the future will be domestics" (cited in Davin 1978, 29).

Increasing European imperial rivalries combined with declining birth rates in the late nineteenth century led to a school of eugenics (in Britain and British settler colonies) which recommended that programs to encourage population growth not be restricted to middle and upper classes (see Davin 1978; Klug 1989; Valverde 1991; McLaren 1990). By the late nineteenth century, eugenicists began to advocate that the population as a whole needed to be improved — both in quality and quantity. As a result, eugenicists and social reformers began to advo-cate programs to "uplift" the working class. Programs of upliftment centred around extending the bourgeois nuclear family to working-class women and men. White middle-class women were assigned the task of ensuring that working-class women adhered to the gender, sexual, and familial practices of the nuclear family. In Canada, as elsewhere, white, bourgeois women, through the social reform move-ment, worked to encourage working-class and immigrant (European) women to participate in nuclear family relations (Dubinsky 1992; Valverde 1991). The in-stitutionalization of the nuclear family in complex and, at times, obscure ways secured the link between the nation, the politics of race, bourgeois morality, and class.

To reproduce the class and racial character of the nation, nationalists needed to transform gender and sexual practices. Most importantly, gender practices within bourgeois households needed to be reorganized so that white, bourgeois women's labour was tied to the re(production) of the nation. Several writers have demon-strated how in this period white bourgeois women came to be seen as exalted breeders of a virile race of nation- and empire-builders, as "mothers of the na-tion" (see Burton 1994; Yuval-Davis 1989). New emerging ideologies of mother-hood allowed this to take place. These ideologies of motherhood, domesticity, and childbearing stressed the importance of white bourgeois women's work in pre-serving the race and nation. According to a writer of a manual on motherhood published in 1911, "If every woman who takes upon herself the sacred relation-ship of motherhood could be led to realize how she is responsible for the future of the baby-life, and the true greatness of the individual constitutes the true grandeur of nations, we should have healthier babies and happier homes, and the disintegration of family life would be a menace no more" (cited in Davin, 24).

In the emerging rhetoric, white, bourgeois women were not only responsible for physically reproducing the nation but also for socially reproducing a generation of empire-builders. Davin (1978) illustrates that as theories of eugenics were used to bolster ideas of innate superiority of the white race in the late nineteenth century, the ideology of motherhood was redefined so that it was the duty and destiny of women not only to breed but also to raise healthy members of the race. As she states, "a responsible mother would study expert opinion so that the eugenically conceived baby would be reared to its best advantage" (1978, 21). The emerging ideology of femininity tied bourgeois women to raising citizens for the nation. A nineteenth century child welfare manual warned, "the child of today will be the citizen of the coming years and must take up duties of statesmanship, defence from foes, the conduct of labour, the direction of progress...and all other necessities for the perpetuation of an imperial race" (cited in Davin 1978, 43).

In addition to reorganizing gender relations, the reproduction of a racialized nation involved reorganizing sexuality. Eugenicists argued that it was the responsibility of each citizen to channel their sexual energies towards "race betterment" (see McLaren 1990, 68-88). In this context, eugenicists argued that masturbation, venereal disease, prostitution, sexuality outside of marriage, and homosexuality were dangerous as these practices would lead to the deterioration of the race. Eugenicists and social reformers sought to control and direct sexuality by bringing it under public scrutiny. In addition, eugenicists argued that a strong and healthy nation required that white, middle-class women ensure that men and children adhered to the sexual norms of the nuclear family (McLaren 1990; Valverde 1991). As Valverde and Stoler have argued, by making the nuclear family one of the sites of the regulation of sexuality, the tie between respectable bourgeois morality, the nuclear family, and the nation was secured (Valverde 1991; Stoler 1995).

In British, white settler colonies (Canada, South Africa, Australia, New Zealand, and United States), nationalist projects had a more complex racial politics. While white, working-class people were suspect, the racial inferiority of people of colour was immutable. Nationalists and eugenicists pointed out that the inclusion of colonized people made race deterioration an immediate threat. In these cases, nationalist projects were based on the creation of a white settler society. Foremost, this involved the marginalization of indigenous peoples from the emerging body politic, which involved legal, residential, and social separation. This included legal regulations of interracial sexuality.[18] They also were characterized by settlement and immigration policies that recruited suitable "white" settlers and excluded people of colour. Eugenicists preached the danger of waves of "defective immigrants" for racial deterioration (in Canada, see Mclaren 1990; Valverde 1991). However, while white, working-class immigrants were suspect, people of colour were defined as truly dangerous foreigners. In Canada, as well as other settler colonies, racial purity was premised on the Asian peril — the danger of

Anglo-Saxons being overrun by more fertile races (see Roy 1989; Valverde 1991; Dua forthcoming). As a result, a series of immigration and naturalization regulations prevented Asians from entering Canada.

In white settler colonies, the nuclear family organized more complex race and class relations. Only white women could produce a white race. With the threats posed by indigenous populations, the immigration of defective immigrants as well as Asian immigration, it was even more crucial that white, middle-class women channel their energies into the reproduction of the nation. As settlement policies recruited working-class and non-British migrants, the role of middle-class women in the upliftment of the race took on a particularly charged character. In Canada, women's groups such as The Independent Order of the Daughters of the Empire and the National Council of Women organized classes to teach newcomers Anglo-Saxon norms — particularly familial, gender, and sexual norms (see Roberts 1979).

Most significantly, the presence of people of colour within white settler colonies made interracial sexuality a possibility. As eugenicists linked miscegenation to the deterioration of the race and nation, sexual purity became a controlling metaphor for racial, economic and political power in settler colonies (Klug 1989; Valverde 1991; Stoler 1995). For white, middle-class women in settler colonies, controlling men's sexuality, exalting maternity and breeding a virile race of empire-builders took a more charged character as it was juxtaposed against the presence of colonized peoples (Stoler 1995; McClintock 1995). In this context, institutionalizing the nuclear family among white settlers (and workers) ensured that the nation would be protected from the dangerous racial stock of people of colour. Concomitantly, by charging white women with the responsibility of regulating male sexuality, socializing children, and upholding British moral values, these women became responsible for regulating interracial relations. George Hardy reflected these notions when he stated "a man remains a man as long as he remains under the watchful gaze of a woman of his race" (quoted in Stoler 1995, 129). In settler societies, the nuclear family is a site in which not only a racialized nation is produced, but as importantly, a site in which a racist imperial order was formed.

Not only would the discourse of race shape the organization of the nuclear family and its associated gender and sexual relations, moreover, nation-building projects would racialize the institution of the family itself. By the end of the nineteenth century, the family would become a symbolic signifier of national difference. McClintock (1995) shows that the institution of the nuclear family was employed to construct notions of modernity and progress. In colonialist narratives, the nuclear family was employed to construct a discourse of racial superiority as it was tied to civilization, superiority, and whiteness.[19] In contrast, symbols of alternative familial and gender relationship were employed to represent colonized people as backwards, arrested, natural, and in an unreasonable state of savagery. Projecting the emergence of the nuclear family into a discourse of national and imperial progress enabled colonial administrators to legitimate colonialism as modernizing, progressive, and as unfolding of natural decree. McClintock points out that after 1850, the image of the natural patriarchal family in alliance with social Darwinism came to constitute the organizing trope for marshalling an array of societies into a single global narrative, ordered and managed by Europeans (1995, 21-51).

As the nuclear family was employed to manage colonial relationships, departures from the nuclear family were seen not just as a danger to the nation, but, as importantly, the Empire. In this context, the danger of people of colour within white settler colonies was not simply linked to miscegenation, but to the possibility that white settlers would degenerate into "native" or primitive patterns of social and family practices. Stoler (1995,143-64) suggests that the entrenchment of the nuclear family in colonies was premised on fear of degeneracy. Notions of degeneracy characterized those who deviated from the familial, cultural, gender, or sexual norms of the nation as dangerous. By practising alternative familial and gender practices, people of colour posed a threat to the moral order that underlaid the racialized imperialist nation. Alternative familial patterns were seen as particularly dangerous for permitting unregulated sexuality. In Canada, as elsewhere, indigenous people, people of African descent, and Asians were linked to dangerous sexual behaviours and their presence was seen as opening up the possibility that white settlers would follow their paths. In 1910, a staff inspector of Toronto police accused Chinese men of enticing white girls into vice: "Immorality among young girls is increasing.... The lure of the Chinaman is also developing among this class of girls, to their utter demoralization in many instances" (cited in Valverde 1991, 111).

In this context, women of colour threatened the racialized project of nation-building in several ways. As the social organization of reproduction in the racialized nation was premised on the politics of racial purity, women of colour's reproductive activities posed a threat to the nation. In contrast to the exalted fertility of white, middle-class women, women of colour were depicted in the iconography of degeneration. In Canada, First Nations and Chinese women were linked to primitive sexuality (Roy 1989; Valverde 1991), while the submissiveness of Hindu women was linked to a decline into pre-modern conditions (Dua 1998). While white bourgeois women were racially gendered as mothers of the nation, colonized women were racially gendered as dangerous to the nation-state.

In the racialized narrative of the family, women became symbolic boundary markers of nations and empires (Yuval Davis and Anthias 1989; McClintock 1995). As colonial women and colonial patterns of gender relations became associated with power and progress, colonized women and colonized patterns of gender relations became associated with degeneracy and inferiority. Departures from bourgeois patterns of family life by colonized women were used to define these women simultaneously as racially inferior, in need of colonial relationships, and a danger to the nation-state and empire.

CONCLUSION

It is only by integrating the interconnections between the discourse of race and the forces of capitalism, imperialism, nation-building, and bourgeois morality that we can understand the emergence of the nuclear family and its concomitant gender and sexual relations. In important ways, the racialized projects of nation-building and imperialism both underpin the emergence of the nuclear family and shapes its associated gender and sexual relations. As Balibar (1991) points out, nationalism has a secret affinity with sexism: the inequality of sexual roles in conjugal love and childbearing constitute the anchoring point for the nation. The nuclear family was crucial to constituting the nation-state; projects of nationalism have been central in institutionalizing the nuclear family.

Through an exploration of the interconnections between nation-building, the politics of racial purity, and the nuclear family we can explain why white women and women of colour experience the family differently. As projects of nation-building were constituted on a discourse of race, the nuclear family organized gender and sexual relations to ensure a racialized nation. The nuclear family not only regulated gender relations in society, it also regulated race relations. In this process white women and women of colour were racially gendered in starkly different ways. White women were racially gendered as mothers of the nation whose participation in the nuclear family was crucial for the (re)production of the nation. In contrast, women of colour were racially gendered as posing a triple threat to the racialized nation as they could not reproduce a white population, allowed for the possibility of interracial sexuality, and challenged, by their presence within the nation-state, the very racialized moral order that the nuclear family was to protect. Given this, it is not surprising that the Canadian state has both disrupted the ability of women of colour to participate in families, and systematically attacked alternative ways of organizing familial relations.

NOTES

1. In this paper, following Miles (1989), I will define the discourse of race as the idea that human beings can be categorized into biologically distinct populations; racism as a representational form which by designating discrete human collectivities, necessarily functions as an ideology of inclusion and exclusion; and systemic discrimination as the exclusionary practices that arise from a racist discourse.
2. Despite their limitations, I will use the terms white women and women of colour. As we shall see, whiteness and colour were two of the crucial signifiers for racializing women. This process of racialization led white women and women of colour to be treated in radically different ways. As we shall see, this is not to deny that both categories hide other forms of racial distinctions.
3. Despite its lack of attention to diversity and racism, it is important to note that these writings had a strong resonance for many women of colour. See for example Rosemary Brown, *Being Brown* (1989).
4. Interestingly, several of these theorists had noted that there was a connection between racism and sexism — yet they failed to elaborate on the interconnections, assuming instead that the two forms of inequality operated independently of each other. For example, see Leacock (1981) and Rich (1980).
5. The focus on industrialization has led theorists to underemphasize the importance of other social changes that were taking place in this period, particularly the importance of the world market for wheat production which would lead to demand for petty-commodity producers. Notably, the demand for petty-commodity producers was tied to an aggressive white settlement policy for the western territories. In addition, the emergence of a nation-state also supported white settlement policies.

6. Nicholson (1997) has recently pointed out that it was not until the post-war era that the nuclear family became a mass phenomenon. It would be the boom of the 1950s that was accompanied by an increase in real wages that would allow white, working-class Americans to live in separate households.
7. For a more detailed critical evaluation of how women of colour experience sexism in communities of colour see Dua (1994) and Bannerji (in this collection).
8. While my discussion will focus on the role of the colonial authorities and the church, notably, male traders and First Nations people also participated in this process. As Bourgleault and Stevenson have shown, white, male traders and officers through the practice of "country wives" transformed First Nations women from independent members of First Nation communities to a dependent and gendered role as "wives."
9. For a discussion of the fear of miscegenation in this period see Valverde (1991).
10. While my discussion focuses mainly on women of colour who have been recruited to carry out paid domestic work, it is important to note that men of colour also were recruited to carry out domestic work. In the late nineteenth and early twentieth century male migrants from China were often employed as paid domestic workers.
11. It is important to note that while immigration policies favoured European women over people of colour, these polices differentiated between Europeans on the basis of nationality and class. See Roberts (1979), Boloria and Li (1988), Valverde (1991) for a discussion of how immigration policies discriminated on the basis of class and nationality.
12. As the majority of women who applied to the domestic recruitment programs were from Third World countries, these programs began to impose temporary residential status for domestic workers. Between 1973 and 1981, these schemes tied paid domestic work to temporary employment visas, prevented workers from changing employers, required that applicants be single and childless. See Arat-Koc (1992), Stasilus and Bakan (1995) for a more detailed description of these policies.
13. The determination of immigration officials to maintain the singleness of these workers was dramatized in 1976 when seven Jamaican workers applied to sponsor their children who had been unreported in their original visa applications. Upon receiving their applications, these workers were ordered to be deported for failing to disclose that they had children on their original applications (see Leah and Morgan 1978).
14. It is important to note that a number of nations have been constituted in the absence of projects of nation-building. These nations have been constituted through negotiation, legal procedure, or physical force. However, such processes were more common in earlier periods in European history, and in colonized countries. See Hobsbawm (1983) and Seton-Watson (1977) for a more detailed discussion.
15. Anderson (1983, 41-9) has suggested that the emergence of print language allowed for differences in language to legitimate the idea of distinct nations. However, as Miles (1989, 113) has argued, such legitimation took place by combining notions of linguistic differences with the idea of racial differences. Thus, in many ways the rhetoric of language was synonymous with the rhetoric of race.
16. It is interesting to note that Balibar (1991) has pointed out that imaginary kinship of the nation drew on earlier European discourses of the race and blood in the kinship structures of extended families.
17. It is important to note that it is precisely because the nuclear family is a place where the nation is reproduced that allows the state to penetrate and organize family relations. As Ursel demonstrates, it is at the moment in which the family becomes privatized (in that it becomes isolated from the public sphere of household production) that it also becomes subject to state regulation. As Balibar (1991) and Stoler (1995) note, it is because childbearing and rearing become a national duty that the state is allowed to intervene in family life. It is when the family becomes charged with the task of raising the next generation of citizens that the state becomes justified in regulating procreation, gender, and sexual relations. Thus, the new forms of state intervention in this period need to be seen as not only designed to ensure that social reproduction takes place, but moreover to ensure that it takes place according to the politics of a racialized nation.
18. In South Africa the nationalist project was accompanied by a series of laws that regulated marriages between white settlers and indigenous peoples (Ware 1991; Stoler 1995). In the United States, a series of laws prohibited sexual relations between white settlers and those of African descent (Ware 1991; Haney-Lopez 1997). While laws that overtly prohibited interracial sexuality were not implemented in Canada, they were often proposed. In Canada the regulation of interracial sexuality took place through other legal mechanisms. For example, the 1876 *Indian Act* was employed to govern marriage and sexual relations between white settlers and First Nations people (see Jamieson 1986).
19. What makes the family particularly suitable to this is that the family and domesticity was considered to be natural and universal in the first place.

REFERENCES

Amos, Valerie, and Pratibha Parmar. "Challenging Imperial Feminism." *Feminist Review*, vol. 17 (1984): 3-19.

Anderson, Bennidict. *Imagined Communities: Reflections on the Origins and Spread of Nationalism.* London: Verso, 1983.

Anderson, Karen. *Chain by Her Foot: The Subjection of Native Women in Seventeenth Century New France.* New York: Routledge, 1991.

Armstrong, Pat, and Hugh Armstrong. *The Double Ghetto: Canadian Women and Their Segregated Work.* Toronto: McClelland and Stewart, 1984.

Balibar, Etienne. "The Nation Form: History and Ideology." In *Race, Nation, Class*, eds. Etienne Balibar and Immanuel Wallerstein. London: Verso, 1991.

Barrett, Michele, and Mary McIntosh. *The Anti-Social Family.* London: Verso, 1982.

Benston, Margaret. "The Political Economy of Women's Liberation." *Monthly Review*, vol. 21 (Sept. 1969): 13-27.

Bhavnani, Kum-Kum, and Margaret Coulson. "Transforming Socialist-Feminism: The Challenge of Racism." *Feminist Review*, vol. 23 (1986): 81-92.

Bolaria, Singh, and Peter Li, eds. *Racial Oppression in Canada.* 2nd ed. Toronto: Garamond Press, 1988.

Bourgeault, Ron. "Race and Class Under Mercantilism: Indigenous People in Nineteenth-Century Canada." In *Racial Oppression in Canada*, eds. Singh Bolaria and Peter Li. Toronto: Garamond Press, 1988.

Bradbury, Bettina. "The Fragmented Family: Family Strategies in the Face of Death, Illness, and Poverty, Montreal, 1860-1885." In *Childhood and Family in Canadian History*, ed. Joy Parr. Toronto: McClelland and Stewart, 1982.

Brand, Dionne. "Black Women in Toronto: Gender, Race, and Class." *Fireweed* (Summer/Fall 1984): 26-43.

_____. *A Conceptual Analysis of How Gender Roles Are Racially Constructed: Black Women.* M.A. Thesis, University of Toronto, 1988.

Brant, Beth. "A Long Story." In *A Gathering of Spirit*, ed. Beth Brant. Toronto: Women's Press, 1988.

Burton, Antoinette. *Burden's of History: British Feminists, Indian Women, and Imperial Culture, 1865-1915.* Chapel Hill: University of North Carolina Press, 1994.

Calliste, Agnes. "Canada's Immigration Policy and Domestics from the Caribbean." In *Race, Class, and Gender: Bonds and Barriers*, eds. J. Vorst, et al. Toronto: Between The Lines Press, 1989.

Collins, Patricia. *Black Feminist Thought.* Boston: Unwin Hyman, 1990.

Coontz, Stephanie, and Peta Henderson. *Women's Work: The Origins of Gender and Class.* London: Verso, 1986.

Corrigan, P., and D. Sayer. *The Great Arch: English State Formation as Cultural Revolution.* Oxford: Basil Blackwell, 1986.

Dalla Costa, Mariarosa. *Women and the Subversion of the Community.* Bristol: Falling Wall Press, 1972.

Das Gupta, Tania. "Families of Native Peoples, Immigrants, and People of Colour." In *Canadian Families: Diversity, Conflict and Change*, eds. Nancy Mandell and Ann Duffy. Toronto: Harcourt Brace, 1995.

Davin, Anna. "Motherhood and Imperialism." *History Workshop* 5 (1978): 9-57.

Dickason, Olive. *Canada's First Nations.* Toronto: McClelland and Stewart, 1992.

Dickenson, Harley, and Terry Wotherspoon. "From Assimilation to Self-Government: Towards a Political Economy of Canada's Aboriginal Policies." In *Deconstructing a Nation: Immigration, Multiculturalism and Racism in '90s Canada*, ed. Vic Satzewich. Halifax, Nova Scotia: Fernwood Publishing House, 1992.

Dua, Enakshi. "Racism or Gender: Understanding Gender Oppression of South-Asian Canadian Women." *Canadian Woman Studies*, vol. 13, no. 1 (1992): 6-10.

_____. "The Hindu Woman's Question: Canadian Nation-Building and the Social Construction of Gender for South Asian-Canadian Women." In *Canadian Reader on Anti-Racism*, eds. George Dei and Agnes Calliste. Toronto: University of Toronto Press, forthcoming.

Dubinsky, Karen. "'Maidenly Girls' or 'Designing Women'? The Crime of Seduction in Turn-of-the-Century Toronto." In *Gender Conflicts: New Essays in Women's History*, eds. Franca Iacovetta and Mariana Valverde. Toronto: University of Toronto Press, 1992.

Eisenstein, Zillah. *Capitalist Patriarchy and the Case for Socialist Feminism.* New York: Monthly Review Press, 1979.

Firestone, Shulamith. *The Dialectic of Sex: The Case for Feminist Revolution.* New York: William Morrow, 1970.

Friedan, Betty. *The Feminist Mystique.* New York: Penguin, 1979.

Fox, Bonnie. *Hidden in the Household: Women's Domestic Labour Under Capitalism.* Toronto:

Women's Press, 1980.

____. "Conceptualizing 'Patriarchy.'" *Canadian Review of Sociology and Anthropology*, vol. 25, no. 2 (1988): 273-84.

Gellner, Ernest. *Nations and Nationalism*. Oxford: Basil and Blackwell, 1983.

Hobsbawm, Eric. *Nations and Nationalism Since 1780*. Cambridge: Cambridge University Press, 1990.

Hoodfar, Homa. "The Veil in Their Minds and on Our Heads: The Persistence of Colonial Images of Muslim Women." *Resources for Feminist Research*, vol. 22, nos. 3/4: 5-19.

Hooks, Bell. *Ain't I a Woman: Black Women and Feminism*. Boston: South End Press, 1981.

Huttenback, Robert. *Racism and Empire*. Ithaca: Cornell University Press, 1976.

Jamieson, Kathleen. "Sex Discrimination and the Indian Act." In *Arduous Journey: Canadian Indians and Decolonization*, ed. J. R. Ponting. Toronto: McClelland and Stewart, 1986.

Kazi, Hamida. "The Beginning of a Debate Long Due: Some Observations on Ethnocentrism and Socialist Feminist Theory." *Feminist Review*, vol. 17 (1986).

Laxer, Gordon. *Open for Business: The Routes of Foreign Ownership in Canada*. Don Mills, Ontario: Oxford University Press, 1989.

Laxer, Robert. *(Canada) Limited: The Political Economy of Dependency*. Toronto: McClelland and Stewart, 1973.

Lees, Sue. "Sex, Race and Culture: Feminism and the Limits of Cultural Pluralism." *Feminist Review*, vol. 17 (1986).

Locust, Carol. "Discrimination Against American Indian Families in Child Abuse Cases." *Indian Child Welfare Digest* (1990): 7-9.

Mandell, Nancy, and Ann Duffy. *Reconstructing the Canadian Family: Feminist Perspectives*. Toronto and Vancouver: Butterworths, 1988.

____. *Canadian Families: Diversity, Conflict and Change*. Toronto: Harcourt Brace, 1995.

Marks, Lynne. "The 'Hallelujah Lasses': Working-Class Women in the Salvation Army in English Canada, 1882-92." In *Gender Conflicts: New Essays in Women's History*, eds. Franca Iacovetta and Mariana Valverde. Toronto: University of Toronto Press, 1992.

McClintock, Anne. "Family Feuds: Gender, Nationalism and the Family." *Feminist Review*, vol. 44 (1993): 61-79.

____. *Imperial Leather: Race, Gender and Sexuality in the Colonial Conquest*. London: Routledge, 1995.

McLaren, Angus. *Our Own Master Race: Eugenics in Canada, 1885-1945*. Toronto: McClelland & Stewart, 1990.

Miles, Robert. *Racism*. London: Routledge, 1989.

Monture-Angus, Patricia. *Thunder in My Soul: A Mohawk Woman Speaks*. Halifax, Nova Scotia: Fernwood Publishing, 1995.

Naylor, Tom. *The History of Canadian Business, 1867-1914*. 2nd ed. Toronto: McClelland and Stewart, 1975.

Nicholson, Linda. "The Myth of the Traditional Family" In *Feminism and Families*, ed. Hilde L. Nelson. London: Routledge, 1997.

Okin, Susan. "Families and Feminist Theory: Some Past and Present Issues." In *Feminism and Families*, ed. Hilde L. Nelson. London: Routledge, 1997.

Parmar, Prathiba. "Gender, Race, and Class: Asian Women in Resistance." In *The Empire Strikes Back: Race and Racism in 70s Britain*. The Centre for Contemporary Studies. London: Hutchinson, 1985.

Ponting, Rick. *Arduous Journey: Canadian Indians and Decolonization*. Toronto: McClelland and Stewart, 1986.

Pupo, Norene. "Preserving Patriarchy: Women, the Family and the State." In *Reconstructing the Canadian Family: Feminist Perspectives*, eds. Nancy Mandell and Ann Duffy. Toronto: Butterworths, 1988.

Ramazunaglu, Caroline. "Ethnocentrism and Socialist Feminist Theory: A Response to Barrett and McIntosh." *Feminist Review*, vol. 22 (1986).

Roberts, Barbara. "'A Work of Empire': Canadian Reformers and British Female Immigration." In *A Not Unreasonable Claim: Women and Reform in Canada, 1880-1920*, ed. L. Kealey. Toronto: Women's Press, 1979.

Roy, Patricia. *White Canada Forever*. Vancouver: University of British Columbia Press, 1989.

Seccombe, Wally. "The Housewife and Her Labour Under Capitalism." *New Left Review*, vol. 83 (Jan.-Feb. 1974): 3-24.

Silvera, Makeda. *Silenced*. Toronto: Williams-Wallace, 1983.

Stebbins, Robert. "Men, Husbands, and Fathers: Beyond Patriarchal Relations." In *Reconstructing the Canadian Family: Feminist Perspectives*, eds. Nancy Mandell and Ann Duffy. Toronto: Butterworths, 1988.

Stoler, Ann Laura. *Race and the Education of Desire*. Durham: Duke University Press, 1995.

Stone, Lawrence. *The Family, Sex, and Marriage in England, 1500-1800*. London: Penguin, 1979.

Toronto Star. "High Spousal Sponsorship Rejection Rate Queried." May 12, 1996.

Trivedi, Parita. "To Deny Our Fullness: Asian Women in the Making of History." *Feminist Review*, vol. . 17 (1984): 37-48.

Turpel, Mary Ellen. "Aboriginal Peoples and the Canadian Charter: Interpretive Monopolies, Cultural Differences." *Canadian Human Rights Yearbook*, vol. 6, no. 3 (1989-1990): 3-45.

_____. "Women on the Rekindling of Spirit at the Wake for the Meech Lake Accord." *Queen's Law Journal*, no. 15 (nd): 345-59.

Ursel, Jane. *Private Lives, Public Policy*. Toronto: Women's Press, 1992.

Valverde, Mariana. "'When the Mother of the Race Is Free': Race, Reproduction, and Sexuality in First-Wave Feminism." In *Gender Conflicts*, eds. Franca Iacovetta and Mariana Valverde. Toronto: University of Toronto Press, 1992.

_____. *The Age of Light, Soap, and Water: Moral Reform in English Canada, 1885-1925*. Toronto: McClelland & Stewart, 1991.

_____. "'When the Mother of the Race is Free': Race, Reproduction, and Sexuality in First-Wave Feminism." In *Gender Conflicts: New Essays in Women's History*, eds. Franca Iacovetta and Mariana Valverde. Toronto: University of Toronto Press, 1992.

Ware, Vron. *Beyond the Pale: White Women, Racism and History*. London: Verso, 1992.

Yuval-Davis, Nira, and Floya Anthias, eds. *Women-Nation-State*. London: MacMillian Press, 1989.

Yuval-Davis, Nira. "Women and the Biological Reproduction of 'The Nation.'" *Women's Studies International Forum*, vol. 19, nos. 1/2 (1996): 17-24.

CHAPTER TEN

A Question of Silence

Reflections on Violence Against Women
in Communities of Colour

HIMANI BANNERJI

Calcutta, 15 November 1997

Dear Ena and Angela,
Breaking with scholarly protocols, I am writing this piece as a letter to you
because what I want to say needs an embodied reader. The topic is too close to
our everyday life and politics to come wrapped in a package of academic or
theoretical abstractions. Thank you for asking me to write, and for accepting a
piece that is more reflection than definitive research. Thank you also for being
my ideal readers through whom I can speak to others.

1.

Issues of patriarchy and violence against women are disturbing in general, but they become even more so when considered in relation to our so-called own communities. I am speaking of South Asian communities about which I know most, but what I have to say may apply to "other" Canadian communities which are non-white.[1] I know that violence against women is a pervasively present phenomenon among us, in spite of much talk about honour and respect for women, including deification of the feminine principle as claimed by the hindus. I also know that not only I, but large numbers of women, have been in a position to know of instances of violence of various degrees, and have not known what to do or where to speak about it. We have often spoken among ourselves in a private or personal capacity, and sometimes we have expressed our concerns publicly. I have been haunted by the story of a Sri Lankan woman who killed her two daughters and attempted suicide. These events are not, as far as I can understand, a matter of personal pathology — they have to be informed with a consideration of her migration, her isolation, her lack of economic and social support, an extremely abusive marriage, and a sexist and racist host society, where hospitals continue to neglect signs of violence against women. On a lesser scale, we worry about women who leave the temporary refuge of the shelters for their "homes," returning to the same partners whose violence drove them out in the first place. But in spite of our general concern and common knowledge, I have not read anything extensive or substantial on the phenomenon of violence against

261

women within their so-called communities — communities which are constituted by outside forces with (rather than by) "people of colour." Perhaps there is
writing coming out of the United Kingdom or United States, but it has not gained
enough prominence to attract public attention.

So, as things stand now, a direct critical assessment, social analysis, or political project on this issue has not been undertaken. We seem to have left this task
mainly to poets and fiction writers, whose business we think it is to deal with
experience. And as you know, as social scientists we have been taught to regard
experience with extreme suspicion as a source for reliable social knowledge. Even
though certain types of feminist theorists have sought to valorize experience, the
current discursivism of feminist theories has put a big question mark against
experience, against actual lives as they are lived by women. But rendered into
literary or cultural artifacts and relegated to the borderlands of fact and fiction,
what we know and say about community violence against women does not create
the same pressure for address or redress as it would if we had to admit that this
violence is a direct part of our diasporic reality. We would then have to speak to
and act on patriarchal violence within our homes, within the moral or social
regulation of the very modalities of constituting "the community." As things are,
we maintain a public silence, even if we know it only rebounds on us negatively.
We need to explore this silence, to ask what our investment in it might be. This is
precisely what I am trying to do in this letter, as well as to speak to the nature of
patriarchal violence within the terrain of our domestic lives.

We cannot even begin to plumb the depth of this silence unless we recognize
its complex character. As you know, silence is highly telling — it can mean anything from complicity to resistance. Its presence, in the shape of an absence in
public discourse about violence against women in South Asian or other non-
white communities, speaks volumes about our political and socio-cultural organization and stance. And even though this silence creates large holes in the fabric
of our public political culture, that which we have not addressed directly seeps
out, is displaced or slips into other concerns or issues. The repressed returns, as it
were, in court cases, in refugee and immigration hearings, in women's shelters,
changing individual and private instances into examples of public and collective
lives.

One of the reasons for this paradoxical silence may be that public utterance
puts us in a situation of responsibility — it makes us accountable to and for others
and ourselves. After all, what we say in print, in any public medium, is fixed in
form, content, and time. It becomes part of an acknowledged, even official reality,
liable to be seen as a distinct political position. We are no longer just overheard or
peeped into. The doors of the community open as we speak "out." So, obviously,
we are wary, not only about what we say in public, but where and how we say it.
We want to assess the location and reception of our public statements, our disclo-
sures and discussions in the arena of social communication. We are, if anything, overly sensitive towards the ideological strands or networks into which
they will be woven, how our statements will be received by those who are not

"us," particularly those "others" who consider us not as people, but as "ethnic communities." These are not unimportant considerations for those who hold not only "minority," but "visible minority," status in a white and christian majoritarian nation state. But then we are in a situation of double jeopardy, since speaking and not speaking both entail problems. In fact, we may be better off breaking this silence, since this articulation itself is a political act giving rise to other political possibilities. But going public in this matter requires that we are able to expose and critique the patriarchal constitution of our communities, which is the same as all other communities, without too much squeamishness about our dirty laundry.

2.

To put forward our critique regarding violence against women in our communities, we cannot begin by taking the concept of "community" for granted. We need to remember that it is a political and cultural-ideological formation reliant upon social relations which are the bases of social life, and not a spontaneous or natural association of people. This constructed and contingent nature of the concept of community is important to keep in mind, since it is becoming increasingly common in social sciences to treat this concept, along with a definite article or an adjective, as a natural, almost an instinctive, form of social and cultural association. Cultural anthropology, with its various types of relativism, seems to have been an important source for this practice of considering "community" as a self-contained and natural formation, a social given, which may be interchangeable with the concept of civil society.

But if, instead of naturalizing "community," we see it as a formation, an ideological, that is, cultural and political practice, it becomes possible for us to develop a critique of the social organization, social relations, and moral regulations which go into the making of it. We can then begin to see that a group of people with a language, a religion, or an interest in common may only become an identifiable and stable social and political structure — in spite of the presence of power relations among them — through a combination of internal and external factors. It is in their interaction of contradiction and convergence that a so-called community is formed. This community, as in the case of women and on issues of gender and patriarchy, can only hold itself together by maintaining a silence about issues of power. A community is also formed both on grounds of difference and commonness. The difference is obviously from those who lack features in common, and therefore are "others" to the collective "self" of the community, usually a smaller group marked out as different by the majority. This makes the community into a minoritarian concept, one whose political and social roots lie in being collectively marked out as different from the hegemonic group. It is not difficult to understand this process of community formation when we see the different ways in which the Canadian state and hegemonic common sense mark out their social "others." This othering implies racism, ethnicization (with a "race" component), and homogenization. People who are thus "othered" also bond together *vis a vis* these designatory processes in a defensive move, while being penned within a political and cultural boundary. Silence regarding malpractices within these stereotypically constructed and defensively self-constituted communities is therefore not unexpected.

Inscribed and instituted politically from the outside, the communities themselves also suppress internal sources of division and seek to present themselves, at least in their representational endeavours, as seamless realities. Silence, therefore, regarding class, gender, and other power relations, characterizes this voluntary aspect of community making as well. And as we shall see later, the technology for constructing difference relies on the concept of tradition, which is implicated in both aspects of community formation. This is what characterizes these communities as traditional, in contradistinction to the "modernity" of the "Canadians," the second half of this binary paradigm. This construction of traditionality is then fleshed out with the invention of particular traditions — relevant for different nationalities and cultural groups. Needless to say the notion of a traditional community rests explicitly on patriarchy and on severely gendered social organization and ideology. These are legitimated as an essence of the identity of these communities. This traditional (patriarchal) identity, then, is equally the result of an othering from powerful outside forces and an internalized Orientalism and a gendered class organization.

Keeping these processes of community formation in view — disputing its natural and synonymous status as and with civil society — we can begin our critique by invoking our general membership as women of these communities. We need to remember that we are the "others" of white women in the Canadian national imaginary, and this is connected with the fact that we are an integral part of the peoples who were brought as indentured workers, or migrated to Canada from former colonies under severe economic conditions created by post-colonial imperialism. Unlike European or white women, we present "Canada" with the problem of inassimilation. We are simultaneously essentialized into homogenized yet racialized and ethnicized subjects, whose actual differences are drowned in the multicultural discourse of diversity. We are worried, understandably, to speak of "our" brutalities and shortcomings, because of not being even minimally in control of the public and political domains of speech or ideological construction. The pre-existence of a colonial/racist/Orientalist perception and stereotypes of us, embedded in official and everyday structural and cultural practices and meanings, have been powerful sources of distortion and misrepresentation of our subjectivities and politics. This, of course, is not only true of Canada but of elsewhere in the West as well. This sexist-racist common sense, with its pervasive presence in the political economy and dominant culture of Canada, is rooted in a history of colonial conquests, genocides and ongoing projects of profit and rule. This is productive of an ethos of European or white supremacy which provides the political conscious or unconscious of Canada's nation state and political-cultural space. We are simultaneously present and absent in these spaces, and in the apparatus of the state. It is this paradox of presence and absence, of difference and sameness (as some sort of members of this Canadian nation), that multiculturalism both constructs and augments. Our political and social identities are contingent upon this. We might say that the reasons both for our presence in Canada and for the official discourse of multiculturalism are connected to our actual absence in and abdication of public space and speech regarding ourselves and our communities' horrendous treatment of women.

The situation is complicated. But how can it be any different, when we come from colonial and imperialist histories and presents and find ourselves in the midst of a white settler colony struggling to transform itself into a liberal democracy? Canada's participation in imperialism on the coat tails of the United States is not hidden from public view. Inhabiting this terrain, our refugee and immigrant statuses mark us as second-class citizens, if citizens at all. We stand, both men and women, uncertainly at the edge of "Canada," the nation. Comprehended in this political economy, a racialized class organization which is as much about whiteness as blackness, we step back in time. We are recolonized, directly — and that isn't just speaking metaphorically. Coming from countries which have seen anti-colonial struggles in one form or another and shaken off direct colonial rule, we put ourselves back into socio-political spaces closely resembling a colony — at least where we are concerned. Here we are marked by a difference which has less to say about us — our histories and cultures — than about a mode of socio-political interpretation within a pre-established symbolic and practical schema of a racialized or ethnicized colonial and slave-owning discourse.

It is at the receiving end of this proliferation of denigrating differences and homogenization that the incoming "others" go through their community formation. Of course, at the same time they are going through a process of class formation as well, which is creating a difference among themselves, as much as between them and "Canadians." But the discourse of community cannot and is not meant to express or accommodate that. In the ideological discourse of "the community" it was made to appear that when people migrated, they did so as communities, not as responses to national and international political economy.

We can say, therefore, that there is nothing natural about communities. In fact they are contested grounds of socio-cultural definitions and political agencies. Contradictory processes of creating "us" and "them" are at work in them, and we have here a situation of mini-hegemonies confronting and conforming to a national ideological hegemony. Form and content of communities reflect this, and we continue to be constructed and excluded by the same overarching hegemony. This becomes evident when we look at the discourse and workings of official multiculturalism, in which where we are from, as nationalities and cultures — Jamaica, Vietnam, or India — matters very little when we are being distinguished from "Canadians," while our specific differences provide the stepping stones for this general difference. We know very quickly that we are not "them" or "Canadians," while our "us" can cross national boundaries, and sometimes it does. Racism, Eurocentrism, or ethnocentrism, which impacts on all non-whites in this way, generates a space for a broader community among us, creating a ground for anti-racism. But this again is not a given or a foregone conclusion, since internalized racism or community boundaries generally help create a closed in socio-cultural space and a highly fragmented political agency. So while there is in this mechanism of mass exclusion, called multicultural community, room for the excluded to unite irrespective of their different regional and individual histories, languages, and religions, the unity in actuality has not been more than that of region, religion, and perhaps language. In fact, regional and linguistic communities seem to be in the process of fast alternation on the ground of religion — thus being "hindus" and "muslims" has currently become alarmingly relevant. This deepening of traditionality has not boded well for women among these communities.

So, possibilities for a community of the excluded notwithstanding, we have been docile with regard to the political economy of Canada. We have by and large uncritically inhabited the socio-economic zones, grids, or boxes created for us by Manpower and Immigration or Employment and Immigration Canada. We have been legally bonded and bounded. This boundary, invisible though inexorable, is the outer wall of the community — whatever that may be — and it not only keeps others "out," but us "in." From this point of view community is not only an ideological and social category, but also a category of the state. This becomes evident if we reflect on the role of this category in the mode of administering the civil society, for example, in electoral politics, in organizing the labour market, in social assistance or cultural funding.

You might at this point object to this non-cultural way of reading the sociogenetics of the concept of community, which goes against the grain of conventional use of the term. You might refer to the role that our own ethnocultural varieties and differences play in the making of communities. You might want to speak of religions, languages, social customs — the semiotic and moral constructions and regulations that we identify ourselves by. Are we not marked as communities in these terms, making "us" distinct from others? These would be, or should be, our questions if we were to read the "community" as an equivalent for the civil society. But as I have pointed out, communities are formed through the pressure of external forces far more than for reasons of cultural expression. There is no reason for the inhabitants of any region to engage in an exercise of collective self-identification unless there is the presence of a dominant group which is ascribing certain definitions and identity markers onto them. This process of complex and contradictory interactions between external and internal forces, which I have already spoken to, makes it evident that "community" is a very specific way of politicizing and organizing cultural particularities of social groups. In this it is no different from the use of the concept of caste or religion with which the colonial powers created administrative and ruling regimes in the colonies.

Questioning the status of the community as a natural, social formation does not automatically imply a dismissal of points of commonality among peoples of different regions, cultural habits, nationalities, and histories, or, for that matter, among religious groups from those regions. It is true that such people often tend to seek each other out, to speak the same language, eat the same food, or display fashions. Very often in the earlier part of their existence in Canada it is a survival necessity for learning the ropes in the new country, getting employment or business contacts, and so on. But if the Canadian society into which they come were non-threatening and non-exclusive, if racism were not a daily reality, this stage of cultural bonding would be short, and more fluid than it is at present. In that case cultural practices would not harden into "identities" or ethnic typologies, but temporary stages of social becoming, both at individual and collective levels. Such elective affinities or cultural associations cannot be called communities, which imply organization and institutionalization — a mechanism for a rigid cultural reproduction. Voluntary cultural associations are both temporary and much less organized, and often a very small part of the existence of people. This is evident if we observe the European or white immigrants who may live in ethnic networks, for example the Italians or Ukrainians, but who did not ossify into permanent communities with fixed and branded identities.

Things are different with us, that is, non-white immigrants — even if we are conversant in English or French, which people from South Asia, Africa, and the Caribbean generally are. With them the process is reversed, since they come as individual migrants and slowly harden into the institutional form of the community. The reason for this, I am afraid, is not what is inside of them, but rather in their skin. Their skin is written upon with colonial discourse — which is orientalist and racist. Thus memories, experiences, customs, languages, and religions of such peoples become interpreted into reificatory and often negative cultural types or identities. The political process of minoritization accompanies this interpretive exercise, and together they lead to the formation of communities. When we speak of "diversity" it is this set of reified and politicized differences that we are invoking, and they provide the basis for ethnocultural identity and politics of representation.

That communities are not simple self-projections of cultural groups, but rather, inherently political formations, is something we need to keep in mind. This is particularly important in the last two decades, when a discourse of community and cultural diversity has been engraved into the Canadian body politic. This is not just at the level of society at large, but in the official formulation and implementation of multiculturalism. Though it may strike one as curious that any "ism" can be made out of culture (we don't, after all, talk of "culturalism" as state policy), we do live in an era when political and ideological stances are created and institutionalized out of features of everyday life or cultures (especially of nonwhite people). Entire administrative apparatuses are alerted to cultural characteristics of non-white/non-European "others," extending from law and policing to mental health and labour. Such cultural "isms" and their practicalization in the context of ruling and administration cannot but need and create essentialist characteristics in the interests of stability and predictability. If the groups were not to be seen as homogeneous in terms of possessing these essential traits, no administration could be put in place. Difference and diversity would not then be effective categories for deployment in ruling, but indeed contrary to it.

We might ask at this point a question or two regarding the content of these putative differences and diversities. Is this content entirely invented? Are they simply baseless, imagined essentialities? The answer to this question points us towards the epistemology implied in the creation of all ideological categories, as elaborated by Marx, and best discussed in *The German Ideology*. It is not that ideology invents particular socio-cultural features, found among many, but rather it centres some and erases others which might contradict the centrality of the selected ones. These selected features do not exist as discrete or floating pieces, but rather assume a categorical status by an extraneous connection which is established among them, often in a causal or positive mode. In other words, a discursive mode is established which creates falsehood, we might say, by a particular arrangement of existing characteristics. It is the whole discursive organization that is distortive or untrue, not particular features as such, and it is in their establishment as "essential" that the harm is most palpable. This ideological activity of consciousness has been called power/knowledge when particularly annexed to the project of ruling. Critique of colonial discourse, now so frequently practised, provides us with more than ample examples of this. It is there we see that paradigms, such as that of civilization and savagery or tradition and modernity, offer the discursive terrain or interpretive schema for understanding or representing cultural traits of colonized or enslaved peoples. It is from this source that the content of difference and diversity of official multiculturalism evolves. This reduces non-Europeans the world over into pre-modern, traditional, or even downright savage peoples, while equating Europeans with modernity, progress, and civilization. The social ethos and cultural identities of the "others" of Europe are presumed to be religious, their conduct ritualistic, and their temperament emotional and unruly. They are at once civilizationally ancient (and therefore in decay) and primitive (therefore undeveloped). These are the ideological underpinnings of the not so benign discourse of multicultural diversity. This is difference and representation as constructed through historical and social relations of power, and it leads to the making of a selective constellation of cultural attributes and ideological packages which contour and control the multicultural community.

This, then, is the ascriptive or normative process through which multicultural communities come to life and into political play in relation to state repression and conditional or limited rewards. Furthermore, we have a situation here of double reification, which combines communitization from above (state and dominant ideology or hegemonic commonsense) and from below (from the subject populations themselves). These reified collectivities of difference create a situation of unofficial apartheid, a general culture of apartheid in the overall sociocultural terrain of the country. Essentialized cultural identities already in place are rigidly maintained, while the general culture of apartheid proliferates fragmented and enclosed cultural territories which are both officially and voluntarily maintained. Political participation of non-white immigrants or their political subjectivities or agencies are increasingly conceived and conducted on these bases.

The concept of community and its organization, then, provides the articulating basis between people and the state.[2]

3.

These complexities of community formation provide us the problematic within which patriarchal violence, in its various manifestations, has to be grounded. We must remind ourselves here of the pervasive presence of patriarchy and specific forms of gender organization in all societies of our present day world, and of their long historical presence. Both general social organization and specific forms of ruling, of creating hegemonies, require this gendering and patriarchy as ideological and moral regulation. Whether this patriarchy is intrinsic and biologically based or contingent need not detain us here. What is important is that they have been historically in place for a very long time. The incoming peoples about whom we have been speaking come from spaces as deeply patriarchal and gender organized as the social space they enter into in Canada. They do not learn patriarchal violence after coming here. They also come from a social organization and politics of class, from national hegemonic systems, all of which are organized by gender and patriarchy. Class and gender, seemingly two distinct systems of oppression, are only so in theory — in practice they constitute and mediate each other in a network of overall social relations of power. White or not, immigrants and "Canadians" all live in this gendered and classed social reality. So violence against women, latent or blatant, is not surprising among communities which have, like all other social groups, all the social conditions for this and other patriarchal forms of violence, such as homophobia. Misogyny, an extreme form of patriarchy, cannot be discussed here in detail — but it should suffice to point out that the homosexual male has long been feminized, and the lesbian seen as a masculinist, female aberration. The hatred for both contains, on the one hand a displaced hatred for women, and on the other an anger or even hatred for those who invert the patriarchal social norm of heterosexuality. Unlike the artificial divide instituted between the West and the rest, there is in fact a deep commonality between them in matters pertaining to these hegemonic norms, and regarding practices and ideologies of property and class. What, then, is the specificity of violence against women within the confines of the community?

The answer to this question refers us back to the point I made about recolonization, which occurs when people of former colonies return to direct white rule by coming to the West. Class and gender organization and normative behaviour undergo a peculiar twist in this situation. On the one hand the process of internalization of colonial values, such as of racism, is intensified and projected through self-hatred and anti-Black racism; on the other hand, this submission gesture is refuted or compensated by gestures of resistance. They revive and develop further a certain kind of nationalism, with some features in common with the nationalism of formerly colonized countries. This can happen very easily as these non-white, non-European communities function like mini-cultural nationalities in this recolonizing context. They seize upon the mainstream's and the

state's tendencies and rules to differentiate them, and adopt these cultural differences. They proclaim these differences to be substantive and inherent, and proclaim their cultural autonomy in the face of an ethics of assimilationism while
seeking to become political agents within the same framework of ideologies and
institutions. Their resistance, what there is of it, is mostly cultural, and typically
minority politics, which cannot and does not aspire to state formation, unlike anti-
colonial nationalisms. In this surrender-submission dialectic they rely mainly on
colonial discourse, especially as they are from "the East." The main idea that they
carry over with themselves and deepen on the Western soil is their self-characteri-
zation as "traditional." From this stance they engage in self-reification as a collective group, and develop logically their self-projection as religious, anti- and pre-
modern peoples. They evoke mythical pasts or histories to support their current
ideological stances, and create a politics internal to their definition of community
which relies extensively on patriarchal moral regulations. This invention of tradition legitimizes and institutionalizes them as clients of the state, while the essentialist logic of community formation homogenizes all into one, and a few can
represent the rest to the state and the world at large.

The community, as we can see, is a very modern formation, as is cultural
nationalism. Its appeal to tradition, i.e. religion and antiquity, are its passwords
into some limited space in the realms of power. To speak authoritatively in a
representational capacity it is therefore imperative to speak in moral terms. This
is most effectively done through a religious discourse and related practices of
moral regulation. It requires in particular an absolute subscription to feudal or
semi-feudal patriarchies, as well as the erasure of class, as this leads to social
conflicts. All this provides a situation of surplus repression for women, sexual
"others," as well as for people of lower class standing — all in the way of creating
communities. Hierarchy and patriarchy as natural or divinely ordained conduct
allows for a peculiar situation where class and gender power are both vindicated
and occluded at once. Domination of women, of sexual "others," and subordination of children take on here the character of duties that each male head of the
family and the male leaders of the community, who may also be religious heads,
must perform. Patriarchal social violence is thus daily and spiritually normalized
in these walled towns of communities or religious and cultural ghettoes.

What is put forward by the communities as assertion of difference, as resistance, often turns out to be colonial discourse with reversed valuations. In this
context, tradition is considered in a highly positive light, while modernity, ra-
tionalism, and social criticism are negatively valorized. Religious fundamentalism is considered a particularly authentic sign of our Easternness. This is mini-
cultural nationalism writ small, within a larger national imaginary, putting up its
barricades and political signs with a neo-colonial inflection. This situation is not
new. In the context of development of one strand of nationalism in India, among
the hindu petty bourgeoisie, we have already seen this situation on a much larger
scale. Many scholars and critics, feminists and others, have remarked on the
peculiar importance of the sign of woman, as mother in particular, and of the

feminization of the land or country as mother-goddess. These ideological manoeuvres have little to do with women, except to indicate their property or service role to the nation. The same could be said of the use of women and familial regulations pertaining to the ideological positioning of the community.

4.

The vested interests of upwardly mobile males, with religious patriarchal power in their hands, either in these types of communities or in nationalist projects, makes it difficult to question the imputed homogeneity or unity of the community. "Divisive" issues of gender and class, or for that matter of internalized colonial discourse or racism, cannot therefore be broached without enormous resistance and silencing from within. In formulating the interest of women and the causes of their oppression, no matter how aware of and informed with other social relations of power, we thus need to step back from the ideological and political schema of the community. Furthermore, we need to speak about patriarchy in inter- and intra-class terms, even at the risk of being misunderstood as separatist feminists, because it involves being "disloyal" to our so-called civilizations or national cultures.

If we do take this "disloyal" stance, which is the only real critical stance we can take, we can see that a cognizance of patriarchy and gender is also a cognizance of class and property relations in general. It is this that patriarchal or male perception cannot see or tolerate. Their resistance to colonial or national domination has never been questioning of either property or patriarchy. This is where their male and petty bourgeois or bourgeois class character is fully visible. This does not mean that mini-cultural nationalities or political collectives do not engage in class politics, but they do so, fully though implicitly, with the purpose of upward mobility rather than in the interest of social and economic equality. They are part of the phenomenon of class formation, and display the same characteristics as did the bourgeoisie in their earliest years of state formation, when they spoke in the name of all. It is then that they created theories of democracy and liberalism, which they were unable to actualize due to their class interests. In this commitment to an ethics of possession and politics of property, where property includes labour power and physical or reproductive capacities, the "others" of metropolitan capitalist democracies are in no way different from the mainstream, though their operational modalities may be highly situation specific.

In this erasure of class and gender, in protecting property and its proprieties, the "traditional" communities and the "modern" Canadian state show a remarkable similarity and practical convergence. Through the state's need to create an apparatus of political interpellation of "others," official multiculturalism came into being. This could then create political agencies through the various modalities of development of multiculturalism, whose ideology is refracted in the language and practices of diversity and implementation of institutional projects. Neither class nor gender, which are differences created through social relations of power, nor "race," another of these excruciating constructs of power, could be raised as issues within this discourse of diversity and redressed. In fact, what counted as difference were so-called cultural differences, and the project was aimed at preaching "tolerance" to the majority while leaving relations of power unchallenged either among them or among the objects of their tolerance. An intensification of class, gender, and patriarchy was encouraged through multicultural identifications, since the "others" were deemed "traditional" (i.e. patriarchal, hierarchical, and religious) and thus "natural" practitioners of these inequalities. Criticisms of abuse of women in the community, even when brought into the court, fell prey to "cultural" or "religious" legal arguments.

This continues to be the case. Definitional boundaries which are vital for legal and social jurisdiction of the Canadian state, which is as thoroughly "traditional" in these matters as the immigrants, rest on these essentialization gestures. It suits the Canadian state just as much as it suits the elite in the communities to leave intact these traditions and rituals of power. That the community is a political-ideological construct, particular to history and a politics, and therefore ignores the real diversities among people migrating from "other" countries, can have no place in this scheme of things. Progressive and critical people among these immigrants are thus dubbed atypical, Westernized, and inauthentic to their culture, both by the leading conservative elements among them and by their progenitor protector, the Canadian state. Violence against women or sexual "others," aggressive and hateful attitudes towards the religion of others, especially towards islam, become the bedrock of normal community identity. Oppression of women and feudal (rather than bourgeois) patriarchy thus become "our" social being, and such behaviour earns or maintains a colonial or racist contempt for us, while being treated permissively by the state. This deprives women of legal and political recourse and social assistance. On the other hand, the same type of characterization also deprives muslim males in Canada, particularly from Arab countries, of legal justice, since the community as a whole is tarred with the brush of fanaticism.

Communities, or the elite of these mini-nationalities, of course play their card of cultural difference according to dictates. They too, in spite of their anti-liberal stance, separate culture from all other social moments, such as that of economy. Equating "culture" with religion, and making a particularly elite brand of that religion the fountainhead of all ethical and customary values, they too assert the master script and make no fundamental socio-economic demands. Through the mask of pre-modernity and anti-materialism they participate most effectively in a capitalist state of a highly modern nature. In return for proclaiming a primordial traditionality they are left alone as rulers of their own communities, to rule over women, sexual "others," the economically dispossessed, and children. The social space of countries they migrate from or flee as refugees becomes a state of mind rather than a place in history. The political and cultural conflicts raging in South Asia, in Egypt or Algeria or Latin America, for example, where secularism and religious fundamentalism are in struggle, are altogether erased. A totalizing myth of tradition engrosses entire land masses, in fact two-thirds of the world, which foundationally rests on patriarchy. This is the imputed and self-proclaimed organic unity or wholeness of communities!

When we look at the status of women in the communities, we find it to be one of "property," of belonging to individual male heads of families as well as to the institutions called the family and the community. The morality of a collective organic nature seems to apply to them, whereas males are encouraged to individualism and entrepreneurialism in their very definition of masculinity. This control over women as a community's property, the object of patriarchal command, is not only traditional or god-given, but this sacred authority is actualized and reinforced by the secular construction and sanction of the Canadian state. The legal category of "the head of the family," with all the prerogatives and responsibilities pertaining to it, is entirely a category of state-delegated power to men. It is a category that extends from "immigrants" to "Canadians," and offers men who hold this position practically a life-and-death power over women and children. This has been discussed specially with regard to "sponsored immigrants," generally wives, who are held at the mercy of their husbands since they have no legal rights in Canada independent of their relationship with their husbands. The threat of deportation that hangs over their head — the loss of livelihood, displacement, separation from children, and social disgrace that might result from a breakdown of sponsorship — is a violent and volatile one. This is what makes innumerable women stay with their husbands in dangerous and humiliating situations, or to return to their so-called homes. Any challenge to the cultural identity of being "traditional," which means questioning religious and patriarchal injunctions, cannot be very effectively mounted from such a vulnerable socio-economic location. If this law were to have been amended, and wives of immigrating husbands could be seen as independent political and legal adults, not as their dependents, we might have seen something quite different from "traditional" behaviour. It is then that we would have known whether muslim women veil themselves because they want to, or because they are made to under conditions of subtle and overt duress. As it is we have no way of knowing their real will, since they are subject to what is called "multiple" but also converging patriarchies of the community male elite and the Canadian state. Facile anti-racism or cultural nationalism simply offers a window-dressing of legitimation.

To return to a theme introduced earlier, we might say that women's status as a "sign" or even a symbol for "our" cultural autonomy amounts to no more than being handmaidens of god, priest, and husband. This subordination or domination is mediated and regulated through the patriarchal family code, and anchored to the moral regulations of honour and shame. Any deviance from the domestic patriarchy of family (extended into wider kinship networks), from strict heterosexist codes, is a pathway to shame and punishment. This may range from censure to physical violence and social ostracism by the community. Women, and involved men, who help to bring about sexual disgrace may even be killed. The cases of killings of "deviant" women in Vancouver — for example, a woman who left her community by developing an emotional and sexual attachment outside of it —

may be extreme, but not out of line with this moral regulation. The irony, there-fore, of a situation where the most powerless member of the community is exalted to the status of goddess or an embodiment of honour of the community, should not be lost on anyone. In fact, if she were not powerless, she could not have been pushed into the mould of a symbol or disembodied into a metaphor. This meta-phoric or symbolic exaltation is simultaneously an objectification of women and of "our" difference from "the West." Disembodiment and objectification are the foundation of violence against women, which cannot happen without a material or social base of domination. It is not an accident that the honour of this symbolic investiture is not conferred upon men, and that women have no choice about being chosen as symbolic or significatory objects.

The dehumanization involved in converting a person, an embodied socio-historical being, into a sign or symbol implies much more than an epistemologi-cal violence. It is based on the same principles that enabled a physical, social, and symbolic violence to be visited upon jews in pogroms and the holocaust, on vari-ous indigenous peoples in colonial genocides, and on Africans in slavery. Thus patriarchy, anti-Semitism, or racism, with or without fusing into each other, pro-vide an overall social organization of relations of domination which extends from everyday-life repressions to extermination. The symbol is a formalization of ac-tual violent, social relations which organize the society as a whole. It is a way of encoding, naming, and perpetuating them. This reality is evident in widow im-molations in India, stoning of adulterous women in Pakistan, or female genital mutilation among some groups in Africa, to give a few examples. Discursivities entailed in these symbolic expressions mediate and stabilize violent social rela-tions through various forms of textualization. They make room for elite males to be exonerated from responsibility as perpetrators of such social violence.

The significational figurations of women have been used as objects of he-gemony by colonizers, nationalist elites and their analogues in Canada — the communities of non-white immigrants, and by the state. Women have become objects for creating history, but are given no role of their own to play in the making of it, except as victims of wars. The organization of societies in terms of gender has identified women with the private sphere, except at a symbolic level. This means an identification with "home," domesticity, and the family, which come into being through their activities and end up by being their enclosures.

The most prominent of the women signs in the contexts of nations and com-munities is that of the mother, the ultimate incarnation of the "good woman." The "goodness" of women in this extreme patriarchal incarnation, but in others as well, is manifested in a nurturing and sacrificing conduct at the service of the patriarchal family and equally patriarchal causes of larger collectivities, such as the nation or the community. Fear of disruption of this normative design comes chiefly from a fear of women's sexuality, which is, therefore, demonized and punished. The somewhat lesser disruptive source is the life of reason, which would put women in public spaces. Any move made by women in these direc-tions is therefore considered to be "Western," "white," or "colonial," that is, treasonable to the greater "national" or community causes. But it is also "abnormal," as it would upset the sign of difference with which "our" co-opted male elite make political deals in multicultural terms or create attempts at cultural national resistance. It is important to note that both female sexuality and interest in rationality or education become threatening because they confer on women active roles which transgress the normative public-private divide. Containment and control of women through the normative mechanism of femininity underpin both proscriptions. In situations where such fully religious fundamentalist conduct cannot be enjoined, the proscriptive moral regulations still hold in a somewhat compromised or "modernized" manner. But it is not an exaggeration to say that the more women belonging to the community could be forced into its organizing religio-patriarchal norms and forms, the more the community could proclaim its definitively authentic status. Straying from these laid-down paths would call for censures of betrayal of a nature similar to those extended towards white women by white supremacist groups for betraying the empire, the "race," or the nation through miscegenation.

When we examine issues of patriarchal violence against women, it becomes apparent that the traditional community's social organization does not serve the greater good of the collectivity. Neither women nor less privileged men have their interests represented in it. The real benefit that it confers on males of all classes is great power over women and children, even men who are excluded or marginalized by the host society. This is not unlike national governments which cannot face up to international financial powers, but rule as dictators within national boundaries. In fact, the international or the multicultural national state's approval of them is dependent upon how well they can control these internal forces and their potential for opposition.

By a perverted extension of this logic the men of these communities are excused, even by anti-racist or otherwise feminist activists, for their generally sexist or even violent misconduct against women. Racism and class discrimination are held responsible for the rage that men vent on women, children, or homosexual members of their communities. This tolerance can extend up to severe abuse or even murder. Locking up women without their clothes, severe beating, mutilation or burning them with cigarette stubs, are some of the violences we have heard of. It is extraordinary how infrequently it is noted, if at all, that women too are subjects of colonialism and racism, and these oppressions are intensified by sexism or gross forms of patriarchy. It is a known fact that non-white women mostly work at worse paying and more menial jobs than their husbands, keep a double day of work inside and outside the home, and suffer from particularly humiliating forms of sexual harassment. In spite of all this, a woman does not often take out her frustration on her husband and children, as a man does. And certainly her mistreatment of them is never explained in the same terms, nor extenuated by the community and others for the same reasons, with which even the Canadian justice system credits abusive men. Whereas compromised and reduced masculinity of such men is noted sympathetically by scholars of colonialism and slavery, the compromised humanity of women, their punishment through hyper-femininity, rarely draws equal attention. If anything, a woman who wants to go beyond such roles and ascriptions, who is critical of patriarchy within the community, is often blamed for aiding and abetting in the colonial project of emasculation. Meanwhile, police and other forms of state and daily racist, social violence are directed against non-white women. The police murder of the sons of black women (and men) is as much a violence against their mothers (and fathers) as is the shooting of Sophia Cook or the strip search of Audrey Smith.

5.

I have outlined so far, and quite extensively, some salient aspects of the social problematic and certain specificities regarding violence against women in the community. Obviously a lot more remains to be said. But this is an attempt to break the silence I referred to at the beginning of my letter. I have tried to point towards a politics which, I hope, addresses the multiple social relations of power which organize our society. I have tried to show that a simplistic binary politics of self and other, of essentialist identities pitted against each other in a politics of cultural nationalism, is not a viable option for women. This reflection of cultural nationalism, of so-called multicultural community politics, does not erase racism or colonial oppression. In fact, a real struggle against the socially hegemonic forces and their expression in the Canadian state requires the perspective that I have offered. We cannot allow ourselves to be blackmailed in the name of cultural authenticity, identity, and community, any more than we can be duped by the mythologies of social democracy proffered by a racist and imperialist bourgeois state.

What awaits us is the political task of forging a real anti-racist feminism informed by a class analysis, with a critique of imperialism exposing the hoax of globalization. This politics cannot be brought to life if we stop only at a critique of patriarchal and gendered social organization. Such a critique, without an aware-ness and theorization of women as historical and social agents, would fall into the trap of showing women as victims of men and society. We must remember, then, that because women are also subjects of colonialism, racism, and class organiza-tion, because they also inhabit the same social relations as men, they too are part of the dynamics of resistance and domination. They have the same political needs, rights, and potentials as men — to be full citizens or members of nation states and to become agents in revolutionary politics.

It will not serve women to look for enclosed and co-opted identities in the name of family, god, nation, or the multicultural state — to live for their approba-tion. Our politics will have to be indifferent to special pleadings of arguments of spurious difference, but concentrate instead on the workings of the construction of difference through social relations of power, on the instruments of ruling. De-veloping a critical perception of sexist-racist social and cultural common sense and of the apparatus of the state, questioning laws that position "immigrants" in vulnerable roles within the political economy, questioning "multiculturalism" which co-opts and distorts popular political agency — these are our immediate tasks. Obviously they are not easy tasks, nor are results to be achieved instantly. Nor can they be carried on within the locked doors of community or identity politics. We, non-white women, women of "communities," must claim various political movements in Canada as our own. This means the women's movement and movements of resistance against state and class power, against pervasive and insidious racism and homophobia. Though it may sound like a tall order, it is possible to enter our politics through the door of particular "women's issues," for example, and come into the arena of a general political resistance. It is only in doing this that one can shape one's politics in ways that are nuanced by other struggles, where what comes out is the convergence of various politics against oppression, and not their separate directions. I don't think we need to fear a loss of specificity, of our selves, in a vast sea of abstraction or generalities controlled by others. If we can frame our critique and create organizations that challenge patriarchy, heterosexism, class, and "race" with even a semblance of integrity, we will create the bases for an embodied, social revolution. Needless to say, in this process we will have to redefine our friends and enemies, our notions of insiders and outsiders, and to whom, when, how, and about what we can talk. This open letter about our silence is only a very small experiment at that talk.

With love and solidarity,
Himani

NOTES

1. I am aware that calling people "non-white" is a debatable practice. I would not do so if I were to use it as a term denoting identity — namely, as a signification for *who we are*. I use this term here as a political signifier, not an ontological one, to point out the hegemonic cause of our woes, namely racism. In this matter where we come from, our national cultures, are less significant than the fact that whoever is not "white" will fall within the purview of racialization and discrimination. For this purpose I prefer to use the expression "non-white," since the conventional terms "woman of colour," "immigrants," etc. do not always do the job at hand.
2. Here we might, following Althusser, speak of being interpellated by the ideological apparatuses of the state, the state being understood as both an institution and a general political body. The political subjectivities and agencies of communities constructed through these processes are both conditional and subcontracted to current hegemonies.

PART V

CANADIAN INSTITUTIONS:
Reproducing Marginalization

CHAPTER ELEVEN

R.D.S. v. Her Majesty The Queen

A Case About Home

SHERENE RAZACK

A *white police officer arrested a black 15-year-old who had allegedly in terfered with the arrest of another youth. The accused was charged with unlawfully assaulting a police officer, unlawfully assaulting a police officer with the intention of preventing an arrest, and unlawfully resisting a police officer in the lawful execution of his duty. The police officer and the accused were the only witnesses and their accounts differed widely. The Judge weighed the evidence and determined that the accused should be acquitted. While delivering her oral reasons, the Judge remarked, in response to a rhetorical question by the Crown, that police officers had been known to mislead the court in the past, that they had been known to overreact particularly with non-white groups, and that such behaviour would indicate a questionable state of mind. She also stated that her comments were not tied to the police officer testifying before the court. The Crown challenged these comments as raising a reasonable apprehension of bias. After the reasons had been given, and after an appeal to the Nova Scotia Supreme Court (Trial Division) had been filed by the Crown, the Judge issued supplementary reasons which outlined in greater detail her impressions of the credibility of both witnesses and the context in which her comments were made. The Crown's appeal was allowed and a new trial ordered on the basis that the Judge's remarks gave rise to a reasonable apprehension of bias. This judgment was upheld by a majority of the Nova Scotia Court of Appeal. At issue here is whether the Judge's comments in her reasons gave rise to a reasonable apprehension of bias.*

INTRODUCTION

Recently, meeting for the first time a white woman well acquainted with my family, I was drawn into a conversation about racism in the university. This young woman wanted to know about my experiences of racism, but this will to know, as it so often happens, was accompanied by anxiety. Her question, "Is there really racism in your work life?" seemed to me to be underpinned by another question: "There couldn't possibly be racism in your work life by people from my race, gender, and class, could there? What would you think of me, then?" In the face of this will *not* to know, I felt that I had only two choices; either one would cost me dearly. If I asserted with passion that there was indeed racism, I would most certainly spoil the pleasantness of the mood and the holiday setting in which the conversation occurred. I would be asked for proof and, as the proof would entail describing personal encounters with white people like herself, she would soon begin to feel implicated, if not accused. Few interracial encounters seem to bear the weight of the naming of racism. On the other hand, if I brushed off the question or even uttered a vague disclaimer, I would undermine my own sense of security that my social environment was a safe one, one, that is, where the realities of my life could be named and acknowledged. There is of course a gendered dimension to this story. As women we are schooled to keep the peace, to smooth feathers, to make things nice. There is also a race dimension. People of colour know from experience that there is usually a price to pay for making white people feel accused. And, there is also class. Well-mannered, middle-class girls learn quickly not to be rude by bringing up unpleasant things.

In white society, racism is a story that cannot be told without consequences. It cannot be told with ease in a hot tub on a holiday, in a classroom, or in a courtroom. The legal case that I discuss in this chapter, *R.D.S. v. Her Majesty the Queen*, illustrates this simple point in the context of the law. The courtroom is, of course, different from a hot tub, and the words of judges have different consequences than do the words of friends, family and acquaintances. While the will not to know is the same in each setting, in the courtroom, it cannot go unchallenged, as it might in interpersonal relations. Courtrooms are places where stories become official accounts of who we are as Canadians. They are places where the work of symbolic reproduction goes on. If the courts say there is no racism, it becomes exceptionally difficult to fight racist practices.

A trial is a moment of public education, a lesson in lines to be crossed and not crossed. Describing the O.J. Simpson trial as one such moment, Toni Morrison comments that such trials construct a national narrative, an agreed upon public truth. In the case of O.J., the official story, Morrison contends, is one of racial culpability. The trial teaches us about Blackness as deviance. Mr. Simpson is thrown into the role of standing in for the entire Black race.

> The official story has thrown Mr. Simpson into that representative role. He is not an individual who underwent and was acquitted from a murder trial. He has become the whole race needing correction, incarceration, censoring, silencing; the race that needs its civil rights disassembled; the race that is sign and symbol of domestic violence; the race that has made trial by jury a luxury rather than a right and placed affirmative action legislation in even greater jeopardy. This is the consequence and function of official stories: to impose the will of a dominant culture.[1]

I propose to read *R.D.S. v. Her Majesty the Queen* as a similar moment of public education in Canada, when an official story, an agreed-upon public truth, is told. This public truth is also about race. It is the story that race does not matter *except under highly specific and limited circumstances*. The heroes of this story are innocent, white subjects.

The power of official stories should not be underestimated, as Morrison also contends. She observes that after the O.J. trial,

> [M]any African Americans found themselves intimidated in the workplace, unwilling to voice even minor aspects of a counter-narrative lest they be accused of...what? showing race preference? It was easier to say nothing or agree.
>
> Women were especially intimidated — because to question the story amounted to approving of or dismissing domestic violence.[2]

April Burie, representing the Congress of Black women, an intervenor in *R.D.S.,* made a similar point about the impact of *R.D.S.* on people of colour. If the official story is that there is no racism in Canada, then those who insist otherwise do not belong. Ms. Burie began her address to the Supreme Court with a ringing statement that this case was really about home and belonging. What does it mean for a Black person, Ms. Burie asked, to live in a place where racism and the legacies of slavery are routinely denied? At home, people use "the word." The "racism" word. "How transformative is the power of the word," Ms. Burie observed. In places that are not home, its utterance has the power to bring down the full wrath of the justice system, to define who is reasonable and who is not, who is a good judge and who is not, and who belongs and who does not. Conversely, when it is acknowledged, the word "racism" has the power to make Canada home. It has the power to heal.[3]

While I would not claim that *R.D.S.* had the same kind of massive public educational impact on the lives of people of colour as the O.J. trial did, I do want to say that scars nonetheless remain. Lessons were taught and some of them were learned. Anyone of colour who is in a public role (and I count myself in this group), those few of us who are judges, lawyers, professors, teachers, politicians, in short, anyone of us working in the corporate, educational, judicial, or political elite, knows about the consequences of disputing the official story. We know now, if we didn't before, what happens when we dare to say that race matters. We have been warned. And this, no matter what the outcome of the decision itself, remains the enduring lesson of *R.D.S.*

It will surprise some that I begin so despondently, since the decision itself counts officially as a win. With Justices Lamer, Sopinka, and Major dissenting, six judges rendered a majority decision that Judge Sparks, a Black woman, did not exhibit a reasonable apprehension of racial bias when she observed that some police officers have been known to overreact when they come into contact with non-white groups. More than this, Justices L'Heureux-Dubé and McLachlin asserted unequivocally that the comments of Judge Sparks reflected "an entirely appropriate recognition of the facts in evidence in this case and of the context within which the case arose."[4] Judge Sparks' comments were not, as another member of the Court, Justice Cory, argued, "close to the line," unfortunate or unnecessary. Instead, they were entirely appropriate. So why don't I feel at home? Why is this acknowledgement of the significance of naming racism by a majority of the Supreme Court still not enough to convey to me, a woman of colour, that the *R* word no longer separates the citizens from the non-citizens?

My unease with the decision in *R.D.S.* stems from the powerful lessons this case (the processes leading up to the trials as well as the trials themselves) offers people of colour about "the line" we must not cross. This is the line that Justices Lamer, Major, and Sopinka all felt Judge Sparks crossed, the line that Justice Cory felt she came close to crossing, and the line that Justices L'Heureux-Dubé and McLachlin felt she did not cross. This line separates those who think race always matters from those who think it only matters, if at all, under highly limited circumstances involving specific individuals.

A commentator on the lower court trials, Richard Devlin, has offered what remains a useful beginning for thinking about the line and the claim that race matters.[5] Devlin suggests that the lower courts embraced a formalist position and rejected a realist one. In the case of the formalists, colour blindness holds sway and we are never to presume that racism is a factor to be taken into account, unless there are specific indicators that it is present. In the case of the realists, race matters and the possibility that racism has influenced how individuals think and act must always be considered. I suggest that colour blindness as revealed in the Supreme Court's responses to Judge Sparks' actions was more than simply a commitment to formal equality. I would describe colour blindness as a determined making of oneself as innocent, as outside of history, a wilful forgetting or what I described earlier as a will *not* to know. Further, with the exception of Justices L'Heureux-Dubé and McLachlin, the Supreme Court remained faithful to colour blindness. The question of whether people of colour can use the words of Justices L'Heureux-Dubé and McLachlin to name the bias of racist white judges arises. We can, but we should take note that colour blindness is always just around the corner waiting to reinstall innocent white subjects. And, the gains made towards taking race into account may not benefit racialized women because the paradigmatic form of racism that is acknowledged is the kind of racism directed at Black males.

PART ONE
Making Innocent Subjects

Both lower courts in Nova Scotia allowed the appeal of the Crown and in so doing found Judge Sparks to have exhibited bias. Commenting on these decisions, Richard Devlin argued that these lower court decisions represented the triumph of colour blindness over contextualized judging. Distinguishing between formalists, who embrace colour blindness and "the assumption ...that each person is an individual and that racial identity (in the sense of skin colour) is an irrelevant consideration, unless its specific relevance can be demonstrated," and realists, for whom race matters and "racialization (in the sense of hierarchical social relations on the basis of race) is still an extremely important social factor and, therefore, that legal decision-making should always be sensitive to the possibility that race is a variable," Devlin concluded that the formalists prevailed at the lower courts in *R.D.S.*[6]

Something different occurred in the Supreme Court. There, the realists apparently won the day. That is to say, the majority decision reveals some endorsement for contextualized judging and thus for the position that race matters. It is important, however, to consider what colour blindness and contextualized judging mean for this court. Colour blindness, I would contend, as exhibited by the dissenting judges as well as some of those who ultimately decided there was no evidence of bias, is much more than a position advocating formal equality. Rather, it is a determined pursuit of white innocence, marked by considerable anxiety about the real meaning of white and Black bodies. Some of this anxiety survives even in the advocates of contextualized judging (Justices L'Heureux-Dubé and McLachlin).

The colour blindness approach espoused by Justice Major in dissent, and supported by Justices Lamer and Sopinka, is the same one articulated by the lower courts: there was no evidence presented at the trial that this particular police officer was motivated by racism. In observing that white police officers sometimes overreact when dealing with non-white youth, Judge Sparks was stereotyping police officers.[7] "Life experience is not a substitute for evidence," Justice Major opined, and "you can't stereotype police officers any more than you can stereotype women, children and minorities."[8] It is noteworthy, of course, that Judge Sparks is being accused by analogy of a misdemeanour as reprehensible as the stereotyping of society's most disadvantaged groups — women, children, and minorities. Relying on the same chain of equivalences (dominant groups = subordinate groups), Chief Justice Lamer also complained during the trial that the defence appeared to be arguing that the policeman had "some kind of hill to climb to demonstrate he was not racist."[9] Such strict scrutiny of police officers was clearly unacceptable, the honourable judge argued, because everyone can claim to be unfairly stereotyped; people of colour have no monopoly on racial stereotyping. The chief justice reminded the defence that he, too, was a victim of intolerance as a French Canadian. More significantly, asserting that the Chinese were tremendous gamblers (a statement he later denied by claiming that it was a hypothetical example[10]), both in his day as a lawyer in Montreal and at the present time, the Chief Justice wondered if he ought to apply what *he* knows about the Chinese whenever a Chinese person appeared before him. Once down this "slippery slope" of personal knowledge, he warned, the unthinkable — the stereotyping of people of colour by white judges — will start to happen.[11] Judge Sparks, by implication, is really leading us straight to racism against people of colour when she suggests that white police officers have been known to overreact when dealing with non-white populations!

If we are to link the formal logic of colour blindness in the decision to what was said by the dissenting justices during the actual trial, colour blindness begins to look less like formal logic and more like a language to support deeply held beliefs that racism does not exist. An insistence on formal equality (a white,

French Canadian Supreme Court judge is the same as a Black youth in Halifax, Nova Scotia in an encounter with white police; Judge Sparks' knowledge of white police officers in Nova Scotia is the same as the Chief Justice's own knowledge of Chinese people's propensity for gambling), looks more like a *wilful* forgetting of social and historical context, not to mention of subject position. An uneasiness accompanies this heavy insistence on formal equality, an undertone of emotion, nothing empirically provable, but something that is present nonetheless in the frequent interruptions, analogies, and wild hypotheticals the dissenting judges put to the defence lawyers. Is this the unease that comes from knowing that once race is taken into account, and the stereotypes come tumbling down, what is left is the awesome fact of white supremacy? James Baldwin reminds white people: "If I am not who you think I am, then you are not who you think you are either. And that is the crisis."[12] Without gambling Chinese and emotional Black women partial to their own people and biased against white police officers, there would be no reasonable and impartial white men.

Not all members of the Supreme Court espoused colour blindness with the same degree of insistence as Chief Justice Antonio Lamer and Justice Major. However, even those who ended up voting to deny the Crown's appeal and who concluded that there was no apprehension of bias, still relied on some version of colour blindness and betrayed the same anxiety to establish that race does not matter, except under highly specific circumstances. Justice Cory, (concurring with Madame Justices L'Heureux-Dubé and McLachlin), made a distinction between references to social context based on expert evidence and tendered in a case like *Parks* (a case involving jury selection which I discuss below) and a case like *R.D.S.* where social context is being used to assist in determining credibility.[13] He concluded:

> In some circumstances it may be acceptable for a judge to acknowledge that racism in society might be, for example, the motive for the overreaction of a police officer. This may be necessary in order to refute a submission that invites the judge as trier of fact to presume truthfulness or untruthfulness of a category of witnesses, or to adopt some other form of stereotypical thinking. Yet it would not be acceptable for a judge to go further and suggest that all police officers should therefore not be believed or should be viewed with suspicion where they are dealing with accused persons who are members of a different race. Similarly, it is dangerous for a judge to suggest that a particular person overreacted because of racism unless there is evidence adduced to sustain this finding.[14]

For Justice Cory, if Judge Sparks is off the hook, it is largely because the Crown also generalized when it submitted that there was no reason to suspect a police officer might be lying. To suggest that police are somehow different from others and never lie was, for Justice Cory, also an example of unacceptable group stereotyping. In spite of his overall assessment that Judge Sparks made her decision based on the evidence before her, Justice Cory finds Judge Spark's comments "unfortunate,"[15] "troubling,"[16] "worrisome,"[17] "inappropriate,"[18] and "unnecessary."[19] Ultimately, concluding that the comments of Judge Sparks were "close to the line,"[20] Justice Cory is not far off from Justices Major, Lamer, and Sopinka in regarding race as irrelevant unless its relevance can be very specifically demonstrated.

To Justices L'Heureux-Dubé and McLachlin, race matters a good deal more than it does to their male colleagues. Instead of finding Judge Sparks' comments close to the line as did Justice Cory, they explicitly announce that the comments "reflect an appropriate recognition of the facts in evidence in this case and of the context within which the case arose — a context known to Judge Sparks and to any well-informed member of the community."[21] Relying on Jennifer Nedelsky's argument[22] that judging requires that we take the views of marginalised social groups into account, they proceed to elaborate that a reasonable person engaging in contextualized judging in this instance would have to take into account anti-black racism[23] and the Donald Marshall Inquiry which indicated that racism existed in the Nova Scotia Justice system.[24] In their reasons, Justices L'Heureux-Dubé and McLachlin write unequivocally that "a reasonable person is cognizant of the racial dynamics in the local community."[25] If this alone served as precedent, racial minorities would have gained a great deal.

If, however, these comments are then contextualized in terms of how the justices then go on to assess Judge Sparks, a little of their vigour is lost. Justices L'Heureux-Dubé and McLachlin advise us to remember that Judge Sparks delivered an oral judgment and that she was probably an overworked trial judge.[26] They note that she assessed the testimony[27] and the evidence[28] before her and that her comments were made in response to the Crown's submissions.[29] They clarify that Judge Sparks found a probable overreaction on the part of the police[30] but did not conclude that this overreaction was racially inspired.[31] While all of these paragraphs might be taken to weaken the central argument that race matters, in that they sound like the "mitigating circumstances" we ought to take into account to exonerate Judge Sparks, ultimately, their argument does return to a stronger position:

> While it seems clear that Judge Sparks *did not in fact* relate the officer's probable overreaction to the race of the appellant R.D.S., it should be noted that if Judge Sparks *had* chosen to attribute the behaviour of Constable Steinburg to the racial dynamics of the situation, she would not necessarily have erred. As a member of the community, it was open to her to take into account the well-known presence of racism in that community and to evaluate the evidence as to what occurred against that background.[32]

Agreeing with Appeal Court Judge Freeman (dissenting from the lower court's decision), Justices L'Heureux-Dubé and McLachlin repeat his words that this case was "racially charged" from the start on account of its location and the race of the key players.[33] While this does not declare that racism is always a factor in such contexts, it directs us to consider how it might be operating.

PART TWO
Calling White Judges to Account

What, then, is the wider application of a direction from the two female justices of the Supreme Court that comes astonishingly close to making Canada home? The force of colour blindness from the other members of the Court gives me pause. It is not easy to forget the wilfulness behind their impulse to treat us all as the same, as though history and context did not matter. Neither is it easy to ignore the high anxiety that accompanied this performance of strict logic during the trial. Here I want to briefly explore how the words of Justices L'Heureux-Dubé and McLachlin might apply in cases of reasonable apprehension of bias when the judge whose impartiality is in question is white, and when what is at issue is his bias against, rather than for, Black men. I then want to anticipate some of the issues when the "race" in question is the race of racialized women.

Accused Black Men and White Judges

On November 15, 1993, a white, male, trial judge began hearing the case of Dudley Laws and Lawrence Motley, both Black men accused of transporting illegal migrants across the Canadian/U.S. border. The trial was a highly publicized one involving a well-known Toronto Black activist, Dudley Laws. It had all the ingredients of the "racially charged" environment noted in *R.D.S.* Mr. Laws is well-known for his activism on the issue of police accountability for the shootings of Black men and the case involved police wiretaps and the possibility that the police had deliberately entrapped Mr. Laws, one of their most vociferous critics. Before the proceedings could even commence, Judge Whealy, the presiding judge, rather unceremoniously demanded that male spectators wearing hats take them off. One individual (who later was identified as the Imam for prisons) who was asked on the first day to take off his hat or leave, protested that he was wearing a head covering for religious reasons. The fracas in the court room led to a formal ruling by Judge Whealy two days later. In this ruling he made clear that "a presiding judge not only has the authority but also the duty to oversee the demeanour, solemnity and dignity which must prevail in a superior court of law."[34] The judge noted that any highly visible groups must be barred from the courtroom. Recognising that head coverings may be required in some religions, the judge was prepared to grant this right to major, recognized religions but warned that "self-proclaimed and unrecognized forms of religion or cults claiming to be religious" would receive limited protection under the Charter of Rights and Freedoms.[35] Subsequently, other men wearing the head covering were also banned. Since the religion in question was Islam (the world's largest religion), it is not difficult to see why the defence in this case would argue that the barring of Muslim men wearing headdress, all of whom were Black, indicates a reasonable apprehension of bias. On January 5, 1995, ruling again on the motion for an order for another judge, Judge Whealy again reiterated his position, denying the motion.[36] Michael Taylor, one of the men banned from the courtroom filed a complaint against the judge with the Canadian Judicial Council (an interesting parallel to the Halifax

Police Chief who complained to the Chief Justice of the Nova Scotia Trial decision about Judge Sparks). The Council decided that a single ruling by a judge was
insufficient evidence to call for Judge Whealy's dismissal. The Canadian Human
Rights Commission, with whom Taylor also filed a complaint, refused to hear the
case because of judicial immunity. Ultimately, Michael Taylor's lawyer went to
the Federal Court of Appeal to ask that the Commission be required to hear the
case. A lawyer for the Attorney General argued that Whealy's judicial immunity
was absolute and should not be subjected to a discrimination hearing by the commission. He further argued that Taylor could simply wait to resolve the issue at
the appeal of the Dudley Laws case, a point disputed by Taylor's lawyer on the
grounds that the appeal only concerns Law's rights as the accused and not Taylor's
rights as a spectator.[37]

What is immediately a difference in the case of Michael Taylor is that it has
not been possible to even air the issue of judicial bias given the great difficulty in
getting any single legal body to hear the complaint. This in itself is instructive.
Should the issue of Judge Whealy's bias ever be subjected to scrutiny, would it
then be possible to argue that in dismissing Islam as a fringe religion, and finding
one of its practices incompatible with dignity and decorum in a courtroom, Judge
Whealy showed himself to be biased against male, Black Muslims?[38] Further,
could it be argued that the judge brought to this case personal knowledge about
world religions that was in fact stereotypical and revealing of his bias towards
and limited knowledge of the religions practised by racial minorities? Could we
point to the racially charged atmosphere (Black/police issues in Toronto) and
say that Judge Whealy has a duty to acknowledge the racially charged nature of
the case, the more so when he considers his duty to ensure that justice is done and
is seen to be done? Barring Muslim skull caps from the courtroom can hardly
indicate his sensitivity to justice being seen to be done.

With the words of Justices L'Heureux-Dubé and McLachlin, I believe such
arguments can be raised with some chance of success when the cases involve
Black men in Halifax or Toronto, and when it involves Aboriginal men in the
West. They will not, however, be easy arguments to make. As the Laws and Motley trials indicate, the first problem is finding a place to make such arguments
when the complaint is made against white judges. Further, neither Chief Justice
Lamer nor Justice Allan McEachern of the BC Supreme Court faced censure
when complaints of racism were made about them. Indeed, in a situation of considerable irony, it was Justice McEachern who heard the complaint against Chief
Justice Lamer.

There has been greater success in naming racism when the issue is the
potential bias of jury members, although here again, lower courts have been
less than enthusiastic. In the precedent-setting case *R. v. Parks*,[39] the Supreme
Court concluded that in communities where racial bias was clearly extreme
against the group to which the accused belonged, it was permissible to interrogate potential jurors in order to establish whether or not they were biased.
Relying on *Parks,* in *R. v. Williams* Madame Justice McLachlin, writing for the

majority, concluded that an Aboriginal man accused of robbery and tried in British Columbia, did have the right to have potential jurors questioned about their attitudes to Aboriginal peoples. Overturning the lower courts, she wrote:

> ...there is an equation of being drunk, Indian and in prison. Like many stereotypes, this one has a dark underside. It reflects a view of native people as uncivilized, and without a coherent social and moral order. The stereotype prevents us from seeing native people as equals.
>
> There is evidence that this widespread racism has translated into systemic discrimination in the criminal justice system...Finally, as Esson C.J. noted, tensions between aboriginals and non-aboriginals have increased in recent years as a result of developments in such areas as land claims and fishing rights. These tensions increase the potential of racist jurors siding with the Crown as the perceived representative of the majority's interest.[40]

These statements are a clear acknowledgement that racism exists and can affect how juries think. It is important to note, however, that such ringing declarations that racism can and does exist rely on the accumulation of reports on systemic racism.[41] They also emerge after concerted efforts by anti-racist groups to name racism in the justice system.[42] Racialized women, for a number of reasons, generally have not been the focus of such texts and activities. One exception is the attention given to the murder of Helen Betty Osborne, an Aboriginal woman, by the commissioners of the Aboriginal Justice Inquiry of Manitoba. Here the commissioners note that Aboriginal women are the targets of sexual violence by white men in the remote Northern Manitoba community in which Osborne lived. They note too that Osborne's gender possibly contributed to the lack of outcry about her murder both from her own community and from the white community. Importantly, however, while the specific racism directed at Aboriginal women is noted, the commissioners do not then conclude that racism influenced the sixteen-year delay in bringing Osborne's murderers to justice.[43] When a case involves possible bias against racialized women, what would the Courts use to establish systemic racism and widespread community bias? The lack of "proof" of widespread racism against women of colour and Aboriginal women, in particular proof of the kind Courts prefer, namely statistics and "scientific" studies, remains a major barrier. It is to this aspect that I turn in the postscript.

POSTSCRIPT
Race in Scientific Dress

Throughout the writing of this comment, I repeatedly sought, and failed, to find a way to describe the subject position from which I experienced *R.D.S.* The personal knowledge of racism that I felt I brought to the case, knowledge acquired in my everyday life as a woman of colour who is an academic, could not be translated into the language this comment required. It seemed to have no place in scholarly argument. For instance, I was struck by two details more than any other and found them immensely believable and central, yet I could only weave them into the comment in a postscript. First, R.D.S. is a young, Black man and a cousin of the youth, N.R., who was being arrested by the white officer. In R.D.S.'s version of events, he was trying to get the details of his cousin's arrest in order to go and tell N.R.'s mother what was happening. A woman, in the crowd of mostly young people under twelve that gathered, attempted to get the phone number of R.D.S. in order to tell *his* mother what was happening, but the police officer held R.D.S. in a choke hold and he could not respond. In the end, the first youth being arrested, N.R., gave the woman the phone number.[44] Second, the police officer in this case complained to his union and the police chief about Judge Sparks' comments. The Halifax Police Chief then publicly complained to the Chief Family Court Judge. A local newspaper was contacted. The newspaper sought access to the tapes of the transcript but Judge Sparks refused to grant access on the grounds that the transcripts were protected under the *Young Offenders Act.*[45] The Crown pursued its appeal on the basis of apprehension of bias with what appeared to be unseemly vigour.[46]

Taken all together, these two aspects of *R.D.S.* (the behaviour of the Black people in the story and the behaviour of the white people in decision-making roles) push many buttons for me, as I imagine they do for other people of colour. The youth's story about trying to get a message home is entirely familiar. This act of communal solidarity underscores that people of colour must look out for each other in a racially hostile world, and it specifically recalls the need to have community strategies for dealing with racist police who are so often beyond accountability.[47] The machinery that swung into action against Judge Sparks for calling attention to the operation of racism — the media, the judiciary, the civil service, is also all too familiar. The power of the dominant group, and the speed at which that power is exerted to penalize people of colour who name racism, are elements of the everyday experiences of many people of colour.[48] Yet something makes it difficult for the fully contextualized, historical meaning of these features of life in a racist country to enter the courtroom as things we know to be relevant to the case. The same "something" makes it difficult for me to argue that they must enter this article as *scholarly* and not personal knowledge and must help us to read the decision. Having been through the exercise of reviewing both the videotape of the trial and the decision, I wondered what would actually facilitate the entry of everyday and elite racism as facts in the courtroom. Could we, for instance, call upon the studies of everyday racism[49] to support the credibility of the story of *R.D.S.* that he was only trying to get a message home? Could we use the studies of elite racism[50] to show how quickly and efficiently the elite swung into action to call Judge Sparks to account, a showing of white group consensus? How many more Marshall Inquiries and Commissions on Systemic Racism will suffice to make the case that Canadians are racist and carry specifically organised racist responses into the courtroom? Can we draw on psychologies of prejudice, as American litigators have done, to argue that white stereotyping of Blacks is near inevitable in a racist society?[51] I think we can, but not without considerable opposition. It is clear that the ideas that give colour blindness its force, ideas of innocent white subjects without histories or present day privilege, block the naming of racism at a deep emotional level. I cannot easily forget the *demeanour* of several members of the Supreme Court as they pushed and pulled at whatever argument they were offered to make it fit into the small space of colour blindness. Dressing race up in scientific garb seems a weak strategy at best in the face of such denial.

The problems associated with naming racism in the courtroom are already large enough but when we add gender to the pot, the small ray of light offered by Justices L'Heureux-Dubé and McLachlin begins to fade even more. How do we prove that communities are racist towards women of colour, Black women, and Aboriginal women? When I think of the specific forms of racism women face, I wonder how we might scientifically argue that white jurors or white judges possess a number of stereotypical perceptions of us. While racialized women encounter some of the same obstacles in naming their realities in a court of law as do racialized men, obstacles I have summed up as the will *not* to know on the part of white people, our problems are also gender specific. We will need to talk, for example, of the sexual violence that is so central to the racism directed against women of colour and Aboriginal women. Bringing gendered racism to a Court's attention begins with expanding the paradigm of what constitutes racism. But complicating the stories of what racism is, talking about how ethnicity, class, colour, sexuality, ability and gender operate to structure it, requires a repertoire of well-known images and signs. Racialized women have generally had to choose from the images in circulation about the oppression of Black men or white women and these images, it goes without saying, are a limited number to begin with. After Rodney King, it is hard to argue that racism has other faces beyond the image of white policemen beating Black men, especially when this very egregious form of racism is in itself routinely denied. When courts have shown themselves receptive to feminist narratives, the kinds of studies and experts on which they rely have not generally paid attention to how race structures a woman's experience of gender oppression as well as her responses to it. For example, sexual violence directed against racialized women is routinely minimized and acknowledged only when our cultures and the men of our communities can be marked as barbaric and blamed for the violence.[52]

To communicate gendered racism to the Court, we will need a language of interlocking oppression where we can describe how the racism we experience has a different structure to it because it depends upon how female, racialized bodies are perceived and treated in this society. We will also need some of those scientific studies and Royal Commissions that quantify the systemic racism directed at us. For example, a detailed study of racism in the health care professions would bring to the surface the plethora of racist perceptions and treatment of racial minority women as nurses and nurses aides. Such a study would also mark the structural features of this site of racism, where an entire segment of the labour market is virtually structured to restrict the opportunities of racialized women.

When a Black nurse gets to a courtroom to protest racism in employment, she is going to have to show that what happened to her happened to many other racialized women. If the experience of Judge Sparks teaches us anything, it is that we had better be prepared. Gendered racism is not an easy case to make to people who are so intent on taking themselves outside of history. The double legacy of *R.D.S.* for me is that while it offers a small ray of light that courts will acknowledge that race does matter, it also confirmed that to make it matter more often, we will need something more than a scientific study or two on the operation of racism in Canadian society. And racialized women will need even more.

NOTES

1. Toni Morrison, "The Official Story: Dead Man Golfing," in *Birth of a Nation 'hood*, eds. Toni Morrison and Claudia Brodsky Lacour (New York: Pantheon Books, 1997), xxviii.
2. Ibid., xx.
3. *R.D.S. v. Queen*, File no. 25063, 10 March 1997. All subsequent references to comments made during the Supreme Court's hearing of the case refer to this source, the videotaped trial prepared for television, hereafter *Videotape*.
4. *R.D.S. v. Her Majesty the Queen and The Women's Legal Education and Action Fund, the National Organisation of Immigrant and Visible Minority Women of Canada, the African Canadian Legal Clinic, the Afro-Canadian Caucus of Nova Scotia and the Congress of Black Women*, File no. 25063, 10 March 1997; 26 September 1997, paragraph 30.
5. Richard F. Devlin, "We Can't Go On Together with Suspicious Minds: Judicial Bias and Racialized Perspective in *R. v. R.D.S.*," *Dalhousie Law Journal*, vol.18, no.2 (1995):408.
6. *Ibid.*, 436.
7. *R.D.S., supra* note 4, para. 19.
8. *R.D.S., supra* note 4, paras. 13 and 18.
9. *Videotape, supra* note 3.
10. Dale Anne Freed, "Top Judge Accused of 'Stereotyping,'" *Toronto Star*, 4 November 1997, A25. Citing the comments of Lamer J. during the trial of *R.D.S.*, the Chinese Canadian National Council lodged a complaint with the Canadian Judicial Council in Ottawa. Lamer J. wrote to the *Toronto Star* one day later explaining that he was using the Chinese example as a hypothetical. See Nicolaas Van Rijn, "Chief Justice Denies Attack on Chinese," *Toronto Star*, 5 November 1997, A8. The judicial council investigating the complaint against Lamer made by the Chinese Canadian National Council concluded that judges must be free to use hypotheticals. Ironically, this decision was written by BC Chief Justice Allan McEachern, himself accused of racist remarks in his decision as the trial judge in the Gitksan and Wet'suwet'en lands claims case. "Top Judge Cleared of Misconduct — Judicial Council Acquits Lamer," *Vancouver Sun*, 24 January 1998, A7.
11. *Videotape, supra* note 3.
12. James Baldwin, "A Talk to Teachers" (1963), in *Graywolf Annual Five: Multicultural Literacy*, eds., Rick Simonson and Scott Walker (St. Paul: Graywolf Press, 1988), 8. Cited in Lucy Lippard, ed., "Introduction," *Partial Recall* (New York: The New York Press, 1992), 43.
13. *R.D.S., supra* note 4, para. 127.
14. *Ibid.*, para. 132.
15. *Ibid.*, para. 150.
16. *Ibid.*, para. 151.
17. *Ibid.*, para. 152.
18. *Ibid.*, para. 153.
19. *Ibid.*, para. 158.
20. *Ibid.*, para. 152.
21. *Ibid.*, para. 30.
22. Jennifer Nedelsky, "Embodied Diversity and the Challenges to Law," *McGill Law Journal*, vol. 42, no. 91 (1997).
23. *R.D.S., supra* note 4, para. 46.
24. *Ibid.*, para. 47.
25. *Ibid.*, para. 48.
26. *Ibid.*, para. 50.
27. *Ibid.*, para. 51.

28. *Ibid.*, para. 52.
29. *Ibid.*, para. 53.
30. *Ibid.*, para. 54.
31. *Ibid.*, para. 55.
32. *Ibid.*, para. 56.
33. *Ibid.*, para. 58.
34. Her Majesty the Queen and Dudley Laws, *Ruling*, Ontario Court of Justice, Whealy, J., 22 November 1993, p. 1, para.. 10.
35. *Ibid.*, p. 5, para. 30 and p. 6, para. 5.
36. Her Majesty the Queen and Dudley Laws, Ontario Court of Justice, *Ruling*, Whealy J., 5 January 1994.
37. Canadian Press, "Make Judge Go before Rights Panel Court Told," *Toronto Star*, 8 December 1997, A6.
38 Women wearing headdress were permitted to stay. The reasoning was that most civilized peoples believed that men must take off their hats as a mark of respect.
39. *R. v. Parks* (1993), 84 C.C.C. (3d) 353.
40. *R. v. Williams*, File no. 25375, 4 June 1998.
41. These include various Royal Commissions on Aboriginal Peoples, the Donald Marshall Inquiry and the Report of the Commission on Systemic Racism.
42. For example the African Canadian Legal Clinic, Aboriginal Legal Services of Toronto and the Urban Alliance on Race Relations.
43 *Report of the Aboriginal Justice Inquiry of Manitoba, vol. 2: The Deaths of Helen Betty Osborne and John Joseph Harper*. Commissioners A.C. Hamilton and C.M. Sinclair. (Winnipeg: Queen's Printer, 1991), 1-107.
44. *R.D.S.*, *supra* note 4, para.67.
45. Devlin, *supra* note 5, p. 411.
46. *Ibid.*, 429.
47. While writing this case comment, the *Toronto Star* ran a three part series detailing cases where the police assaulted mostly poor people and people of colour and faced no disciplinary measures. See John Duncanson and Jim Rankin, "Above the Law," *Toronto Star*, 30 November 1997, A1, A14. As well, Bill 105, the *Ontario Police Services Amendments Act* was passed which abolished the Police Complaints Commission and any other avenue of complaint to an external, civilian authority about police practices. Rosie Dimanno, "New Era for complaints against police," *Toronto Star*, 8 December 1997, E1.
48. In her study of everyday racism, Philomena Essed documented the stories of over fifty women of colour. Many of these women made statements about the refusal of white people to hear stories of racism and their often hostile responses to those who told such stories. See *Everyday Racism* Translated from the Dutch by Cynthia Jaffe. (Claremont, California: Hunter House Inc., 1990). It is also noteworthy that the naming of whites as a group with power has often produced a near hysterical denial in the courtroom. For an example of this, see the reaction of Judge Allan McEachern to the suggestion that whites as a group have been dominant in the history of white/ Aboriginal relations in British Columbia. Reported by Dara Culhane in *The Pleasure of the Crown* (Burnaby, British Columbia: Talon Books, 1998), 136-7.
49. Philomena Essed, *Understanding Everyday Racism* (Newbury Park, Ca.: Sage Publications, 1993).
50. Teun van Dijk, *Elite Racism* (Newbury Park, Ca.: Sage Publications, 1993).
51. Cynthia Kwei Yung Lee, "Race and Self-Defence: Toward a Normative Conception of Reasonableness," *Minnesota Law Journal*, vol. 81, no.2, (December 1996): 462. Richard Devlin also discusses the sociological and psychological research that would support the notion that race is frequently conflated with criminality. Devlin, *supra* note 5, p. 432.
52. See Sherene Razack, *Looking White People in the Eye: Gender, Race and Culture in Courtrooms and Classrooms* (Toronto: University of Toronto Press, 1998), chaps. 3 and 5.

CHAPTER TWELVE

Racism, Women's Health, and Reproductive Freedom

CAROLYN EGAN AND LINDA GARDNER

Of all the forms of inequality, injustice in health is the most shocking and inhumane.

Martin Luther King, Jr.

Unfortunately there has been very little written on racism and women's health in Canada. We hope that this chapter will be a useful contribution to the body of knowledge available, and will lead to more work being done on the topic. In the article we intend to firstly review the findings of the research that is available that deals with the experiences of women of colour in the healthcare system, and examine the intersection of race, class, and gender. We will then analyze how one organization, the Ontario Coalition for Abortion Clinics, tried to relate to the health care needs of women of colour in its organizing for reproductive rights.

Racism has long been present in health care in this country. In Alberta between 1928 and 1972, 2844 people were forcibly sterilized through the province's sexual sterilization act. Under this legislation a eugenics board approved the operation, if reproduction involved the risk of "hereditary taint." Sixty-four percent of those sterilized were women, 20 percent were less than sixteen years old. They were for the most part poor and working class. The racism of its application is obvious. First Nations and Metis people represented 2.5 percent of the population, but accounted for 25 percent of the sterilizations in the law's later years.[1] Both Alberta and British Columbia had such laws in effect, and it is believed that hundreds of such operations were carried out in Ontario as well.

We believe that racism still permeates every facet of Canadian society, and medical services are no exception. A recent study, "Immigrant, Refugee and Racial Minority Women and Health Care Needs," carried out by the Women's Bureau of the Ontario Ministry of Health documents the health care experiences of minority women in Ontario. Researchers interviewed both individuals and groups of women in six regions: Ottawa, Thunder Bay, London, Windsor, Sudbury, and Toronto. These women outlined the situations they faced and the racism they experienced. The document concludes, "The most critical finding of this community consultation process was that immigrant, racial minority, and refugee women are discriminated against by the Ontario health care system."[2]

There are well over one million women who could be defined as immigrant, refugee, or racial minority in Ontario, at least one quarter of the female population of the province. There is, of course, an enormous range of difference in class, language abilities, racial, and ethnic backgrounds among these women, and therefore care has to be taken when making generalizations. The document does not differentiate between women of colour, and other immigrant and refugee women, which is unfortunate for our purposes. We know that the majority of immigrants to Canada today are from non-European countries.

You will see from the comments of the women themselves, that they perceive their health is being jeopardized because of the racism and discrimination they face. Racial barriers were clearly identified in the study. Many of the respondents observed that those who are racially different are seen as inferior by white, Canadian health care providers. Women spoke of how they were treated disrespectfully and in a discriminatory manner. Structural barriers were outlined by the women, including the lack of access to language training and ghettoization in low paying jobs, which restricts the time to access health services. Racism, limited language and literacy levels, combined with a lack of economic opportunities inhibited the ability of respondents to use medical services, which has a huge impact on women's health.

Through no fault of their own, there is a lack of knowledge among immigrant and refugee women of health care practices that are available such as pap tests or breast screening. Very little effort is made in Ontario to make this information accessible in a racially sensitive manner, or in languages other than English or French. There is a lack of adequate translation and interpreter services, which creates real barriers and can greatly increase a sense of anxiety, alienation, and isolation. This can prevent women from using available services, and ensures that their needs remain unaddressed.

In Thunder Bay participants talked directly about their experience with racial discrimination and stereotyping by health care providers. Public health units were seen to be having a difficult time relating to them. Little effort had been made to develop programs and outreach initiatives, which were appropriate and responsive to minority women's needs. They spoke of how childbirth education programs were not reaching women. Concerns were also raised about the high number of Cesarean births and the over-medication of women involved in the study.

In Ottawa, women described a "softer but more pervasive" form of discrimination. Women spoke of a lack of understanding about their reality and the situations they were describing, as they spoke to health care providers. They felt very reticent to express concerns or feelings about their health, which contributed to stress and mental health problems. Health professionals were often dismissive, treating women as though they were stupid. The women spoke of a lack of trust, and felt no confidentiality in their interactions with health care providers. They felt that their experiences were devalued by the health care system.

In Sudbury women identified a particular need for information on gynecological care, pre- and postnatal services. Women underutilized pap tests and breast exams, because of the lack of outreach to their communities. They were being denied basic health services because of who they are. Many physicians were not aware of conditions such as sickle cell anemia, which can have devastating effects on women of colour.

The authors of the study told us that women's reactions ranged from "polite disappointment to outright anger." The report documented that immigrant, refugee, and racial minority women have obvious health care needs, but they make use of health care services at a significantly lower rate than other women. This is clearly due to the barriers they encounter, which are not only the biases of individual providers, but systemic barriers integrated into the health care delivery system itself. As the study states, "This contradiction is due in large measure to...racial, linguistic, gender and class barriers embedded within the system, their needs are not being met by existing programs and services...many areas of the health care delivery system are simply inappropriate for or insensitive to the needs of minority women."[3] Unfortunately we were not provided with a breakdown on the racial backgrounds of the women interviewed, how long they have been in Canada, or differences among the cities targeted. But the interviews make it clear that immigrant women and refugees, the majority of whom today are women of colour, experience the health care system differently than white women, because of the racism embedded within it.

An earlier study by the Immigrant Women's Health Centre (IWHC) in Toronto showed similar findings. The centre was established in 1975 and provides medical and educational services to women from a variety of communities. It also organizes around the health needs of immigrant women and women of colour. It is a multilingual, multiracial collective with a central focus on sexual health. The counsellors are members of the communities, which the centre serves. They deal with birth control, pregnancy, childbirth, abortion, sexually transmitted diseases, and other gynecological issues, as well as stress management, nutrition, and patient's rights. The centre was started because of the racism that women encounter in mainstream health services, and the need for health care geared to meet their needs. It established specific outreach services, such as the Black Youth Hotline, a mobile unit, and has responded to the needs of the Tamil community and other recent immigrants to Toronto.

The IWHC conducted a study with the women who were using its mobile health unit, which visited work sites between January 1984 and August 1985. The study focused on working women between the ages of twenty-five and forty-five including women from the West Indian, Vietnamese, Chinese, and Spanish communities. Many of the women spoke very little English, did not have previous Canadian job experience, and were forced to work in low paying jobs, often with unhealthy working conditions. They were often not able to find medical services that they could access and that were sensitive to their needs.

In the study, a health care worker at the IWHC said, "They...are often taken advantage of without knowing what recourse to take. The implications for reproductive health, let alone reproductive rights, are limited. Unattended gynecological ailments, such as STD's, vaginal infections, information on breast examination, pap tests, and stress-related infections are seen at the Centre. The women are prey to poor quality health services because of their economic, cultural, and political status in society."[4] Mainstream health care did not provide for these women, and this put their health at serious risk.

We don't have data on the numbers of women from each community that participated in the study, we do know that today the majority of the women who are seen at the IWHC clinics are women of colour. The study reached 1500 working women at twelve workplaces. Using information gathered in a 1983 community health survey, done by the city of Toronto health department, they compared the preventative health practices of women in the IWHC target group, to those of other women in the city. They were asked questions about pap tests, breast examination by physician, and breast self-examination. The findings showed that only 43 percent of women in the IWHC target group had a pap test in the year prior to the interview, compared to 65 percent of other women. It was also found that women were even less likely to have had a pap test if they worked in semi-skilled or unskilled occupations. "The overall pattern suggests that women in the communities served by the IWHC, who worked in semi-skilled and unskilled jobs are at more risk of having undetected cervical dysplasia than women in any other groups."[5] In terms of breast examination by a physician, a similar pattern emerged in both number and percentage of women who had this performed in the year prior to the interviews. This was the case, not because the women had no concern about their health care needs, but because they had difficulty accessing services because of racism and systemic barriers.

The women seen by the IWHC tend to be concentrated in jobs where they work in assembly or product fabrication, as dishwashers, cleaners, cafeteria workers, waitresses, or domestic workers. The work makes women unable to take time off for routine health care. Treatable health problems, such as cervical or breast cancer, go undetected, jeopardizing chances of survival. Other health problems also go undiagnosed. For example, a woman with untreated high blood pressure is four times more likely to develop kidney disease. Women of colour face discrimination in employment, which makes it more likely that they will work in low-paying jobs, which do not allow easy access to medical services. They are denied health care that white, middle-class women take for granted.

In terms of reproductive issues, the study states, "women face a lack of options on family planning due to their economic condition and this has a direct relation to the measure of control they have or they don't have over their bodies. All of these must be taken into account; how the issue of birth control, pregnancy, abortion, etc., really affect women who work two jobs, who lack a facility in English, or who encounter racism in the society.... Women often seek abortions...because their material conditions, i.e. housing, employment, lack of daycare, low salary jobs, have dictated to them how many children they may have at any given time in their reproductive life."[6] The intersection of race, class, and gender is very clear in the lives of the women interviewed in this study, and strongly impacts on how they experience health care in this country.

The racism that women of colour confront in the health care system is not confined to Ontario. In a study that specifically deals with the Chinese community in Vancouver, British Columbia the rate of cervical cancer was also found to be much higher.[7] A significant number of Chinese women in their late forties through late sixties were being diagnosed with cervical cancer in a province that was said to be leading the world in pap test screening. This was significantly higher than the general population. We do not know the class background of the women, but it is likely that they are poor or working class. Again it was a question of systemic racism, and the lack of appropriate community programs. Many Chinese women also found it unacceptable to be examined by male doctors, and this was not being taken into account by health providers.

There were a number of structural barriers. Pap screening was a provincial responsibility, but there was a very real absence of creative thinking or support for changes in the program that would make it more accessible to specific communities. Also, the Ministry of Health lacked a funding mechanism to allow for more accessible programs.

Women from the Chinese community took up the issue themselves. A pap smear campaign was highlighted in the Chinese media, featured at community health fairs, and training was provided for volunteers and health professionals from the community. An evening program was launched providing women with information and services in their own language and women doctors from their own community. Chinese women developed their own solutions to a critical problem, which was being ignored by the medical community.

Interestingly Statistics Canada reported in 1996 that recent immigrants report less health problems of a chronic nature than people born in Canada, but the longer they are resident the greater the incidence of chronic health problems. "The difference is particularly marked for recent immigrants from non-European regions, who now account for most of the immigration flow.... The evidence suggests that health status of immigrants weakens the longer they stay in Canada," said Edward Ng, an analyst for Statistics Canada.[8] The health status of people of colour deteriorates at a greater rate than white immigrants the longer they are in the country.

It is clear that government cutbacks are having an impact on the health care of the most vulnerable in Canadian society. Insufficient nutrition, emotional stress, isolation, poverty, and job or family pressures are contributing factors to the situation. Women of colour, because of the systemic racism that exists in the delivery of health care, and the class position that many of them occupy are even more at risk.

We want to mention one last study that gives a national overview. At the fourth conference and biennial general meeting of the National Organization of Immigrant and Visible Minority Women, a document entitled "Political Participation for Change: Immigrant and Visible Minority Women in Action" was produced which examined a number of important issues confronting minority women. Health care was one of the concerns addressed. The document states, "The biological makeup of women and their role in society as child-bearers, mothers, nurturers, wives and sexual partners is an important component of life and calls for unique health care needs...immigrant women with linguistic and cultural barriers are often denied and deprived of information and access to various options on reproductive health care services." This document identified sexually transmitted diseases, infertility, and unintended pregnancies as areas that had to be addressed. "With the advancement in reproductive technologies, women have options to control pregnancy with a variety of birth control measures or even to terminate their pregnancies. Even though these options are relatively accessible through mainstream health care services, immigrant and visible minority women's access to information on birth control options, information regarding their right to access these birth control options, and their awareness of making informed decisions in controlling pregnancy is severely limited because of language and cultural barriers. Other barriers also exist that prevent immigrant and visible minority women from accessing appropriate birth control options. These include cultural insensitivity, lack of cross cultural awareness or even racism."[9] This indicates that the conclusions of the Ontario study cited earlier in this article, that women of colour face racial barriers in the health care system, appear to be applicable nationally.

In response to the fact that women of colour experience racism in the Canadian health system, they have tried to gain control over their health care. They have established centres that particularly meet their needs such as the Immigrant Women's Health Centre, and have developed community-based programs as did Chinese women in British Columbia. We believe that it is not only the role of women of colour to take up these concerns. Racism must be addressed by all organizations that work in health care.

The studies we reviewed deal with reproductive health. We are now going to examine the work of the Ontario Coalition for Abortion Clinics (OCAC), a reproductive rights organization, and how it attempted to meet the needs of women of colour in its organizing. We both worked for many years in the coalition, and are speaking from our own experience.

OCAC was formed in 1982. Women health care workers from the Immigrant Women's Heath Centre, Hassle Free Clinic, and the Birth Control and VD Information Centre in Toronto, felt they must challenge a system which was denying access to abortion to working-class women and women of colour. OCAC began as a grassroots, broad-based activist organization. Its immediate goals were to overturn the federal law, which restricted access to abortion, and to legalize freestanding clinics providing medically insured abortions. This campaign was one of the most hotly contested struggles between the Canadian women's movement and the state. OCAC worked with Dr. Henry Morgentaler and opened a clinic to challenge the criminal code restrictions on abortion. In 1983 the clinic was raided by the police, and the doctors were arrested. The clinic became a symbol of women's resistance to an unjust law, and a long campaign against two levels of government and an organized right wing movement began.

There was access to abortion in Canada at that time, but it was a very privileged access. In 1969 a federal law had been introduced which allowed an abortion to be performed, if it took place in an approved or accredited hospital with the approval of a therapeutic abortion committee. In practice, this resulted in access for middle-class women, primarily white, who could afford a private gynecologist or travel to the U.S. or Montreal. First Nation women, women of colour, and many working-class women did not have access to abortion services. In spite of claims that Canada had universal access to health care, in practice there was a two-tiered health system. The federal law was racist and class biased in its application.

Organizations such as the Immigrant Women's Health Centre and Women Working with Immigrant Women worked with OCAC and had a profound influence on its organizing. Women such as Linda Gardner a Chinese-Canadian activist, Sherona Hall a long-time organizer in the Black community, Yuki Hayashi, leader of Students for Choice were very active in the campaign. Today Rhonda Roffey, a First Nations woman, and Brenda Lee, from the Chinese community, are in the leadership. A broad reproductive rights perspective was fought for in the organization, and was won.

While OCAC organized a struggle with a very specific focus it did not mean that it was a single-issue group. The demand for abortion access was never seen in isolation, but as one of a number of interdependent struggles. OCAC found this reproductive rights perspective to be vital, not only because it reflects the reality of women's lives, but because it explicitly deals with class and race. In linking various struggles it was able to build a broad movement through demonstrations, marches, and rallies in which thousands of women could participate. Community leaders such as Judy Vashti Persad of the Cross Cultural Communications Centre, Salome Lucas of Women Working with Immigrant Women, and Joan Grant-Cummings of the Women's Health and Women's Hands clinic spoke at many of OCAC's events about the needs of women of colour, the racism they encountered in seeking abortions, and the need for the movement to address these issues.

OCAC tried to make it clear in its organizing that it is a fundamental right for women to make the decision to terminate a pregnancy, but the pro-choice movement needed an analysis that went much further. It believed, that it is equally important that women have the right to bear the children they choose to bear. It broadened the definition of "Choice," beyond an individual right. For all women to truly have choices in our society regardless of race, class, sexuality, or ability, they require: safe and effective birth control with information and services in their own languages, and in their own communities, decent jobs, paid parental leave, free childcare, the right to live freely and openly as lesbians, an end to forced or coerced sterilization, employment equity, an end to sexual and racial harassment, and, of course, the right to full access to free abortion. All of these must be fought for in order for women to have reproductive freedom. It was argued that this must be more than simply a statement of principles. There had to be active involvement in and support for these interrelated struggles.

OCAC was very much aware of the limits of the notion of "choice." Full access to free abortion, as significant an advance as that would be, does not guarantee that all women have real choices over their lives or over having and raising children. It tried to show these limits concretely by stressing that the choice to have a child can never be free in a racist, sexist society in which women earn so much less than men, in which quality daycare and affordable housing are not available and where racism is systemic. OCAC actively supported these related struggles and believed that the alliance building, coalition work, and the concrete linking of these struggles strengthened each.

Its organizing included the fight against extra billing by doctors, supporting First Nations people at Oka, walking picket lines with striking workers, and marching against police violence in the Black community. OCAC always tried to engage in movement building. Its first outreach activities were to broaden and strengthen the involvement of working-class women in trade unions, and immigrant women and women of colour organizations in the campaign. It worked to directly address the reproductive health issues and concerns of women of colour and working-class women. It fought for the provision of abortion services in clinics that served women of colour such as Women's Health and Women's Hands. It joined with First Nations women in demanding an end to abusive treatment and the lack of anesthetic during abortion procedures in a Yellowknife hospital.

To win demands from a racist and sexist government that was actively denying women reproductive freedom, a movement had to be built that included trade unions, people of colour organizations, lesbian and gay groups, and all of those who believe in the liberation of women. Without active involvement and broad support for its demands, no change would occur in the balance of forces in this country, and this was necessary to overturn the federal abortion law and increase access for every woman, regardless of race or class.

The lack of abortion rights impacts on women of colour in a different way than it would on a middle-class, white woman, and this had to be acknowledged. For example, OCAC challenged the coerced sterilization that women of colour were forced to undergo by therapeutic abortion committees. It fought the extra billing that gynecologists were imposing on their abortion patients which denied access to poor and working-class women. As the campaign continued, OCAC sponsored forums bringing together women with disabilities, lesbians, First Nations women, and women of colour to speak for themselves of their particular struggles for sexual and reproductive control and to support each other. The goal was to build a visible, mass movement, which spoke to a broad reproductive rights agenda. The full message was often lost in the media presentations of our campaign where more attention was given to the single issue and demand for abortion than to the broader context, and that was a problem.

Achieving the best balance between short- and long-term objectives, between the polemical value of the choice slogan and the constraints of such arguments, and between abortion and the broader struggle for reproductive freedom was difficult. There were many debates. Such strategic complexities and dilemmas were made no easier in a movement that was constantly under direct attack from the state and the conservative right. Nonetheless, it was clear that these complex questions could not be left until after short-term objectives had been won. For example, do we put our limited energy or resources in an election campaign or do we fight anti-choice harassment at the clinics, when we know its targets are most frequently women of colour? Do we prioritize the lobbying of politicians or building mass actions with the active involvement of women of colour organizations putting forward their views and which give everyone an opportunity to be actively engaged in the struggle against a new law? Do we structure ourselves in a traditional manner with a board of directors or have general biweekly meetings open to anyone? We openly debated these questions and always tried to chose the activity, which would involve the broadest and most representative number of people. At strategic junctures in the campaign, we advertised open public strategy meetings to involve the largest number possible in determining our direction. Many people who could not commit themselves to the organization in an ongoing way attended.

OCAC tried to be inclusive. For example, coerced sterilization could not be seen separately from the struggle for abortion rights. Prior to the overturning of the federal abortion law, the therapeutic abortion committees also functioned as a primary mechanism for coerced sterilization. Doctors denied women abortions unless they agreed to be sterilized. The Immigrant Women's Health Centre and the Birth Control and VD Information Centre had spoken to women who were subject to this coercion. It particularly affected women of colour, First Nations women, and women with disabilities. Strategically, OCAC believed that by fighting the federal abortion law, and winning free abortion, it would reduce the numbers of coerced sterilization in this country. This was made clear in our organizing.

OCAC also supported the Supreme Court case which stopped the practice of sterilization of women with disabilities without their consent. As Angus McLaren pointed out in his book, *Our Own Master Race,* the eugenic idea of "race betterment," legitimized state intervention to protect Canada from "degenerates."[10] As already stated, the governments of Alberta and British Columbia passed legislation, which allowed for sterilization of those deemed to be "unfit." Prior to the Second World War, this ideology impacted immigration laws, birth control, family allowance, and a range of social policies. Determining the extent of the abuse in northern communities was difficult. In the 1970s, 23 percent of women of the Inuit community Igloolek between the ages of 30 and 50 had been sterilized by government health services. Inuit women had been quoted as saying "if we had known exactly what the operation we were made to undergo meant, we would never have accepted it."[11] When the New Democratic Party raised a question in the House of Commons concerning a series of sterilization operations performed on Inuit women on Holman Island, regulations were changed clarifying the permanence of the procedure and translating the consent forms into Inuktitut. OCAC believed that it was important to outline the abuse, which had taken place in this country. It initiated forums with First Nations women in Ottawa, Toronto, and Montreal to bring attention to and broaden awareness of the problem.

In 1991, during the Toronto mayoralty campaign, OCAC along with the Ontario Coalition Against Poverty (OCAP), raised the fact that candidate June Rowlands, who later became mayor, had twenty years earlier called for the sterilization of low income men on welfare. OCAC and OCAP called a press conference. Groups including the Black Action Defense Committee, the Coalition of Visible Minority Women, Women Working with Immigrant Women, and the Labour Council of Metropolitan Toronto and York region demanded that she retract her statement and clarify her current position. It was important to oppose this perspective whenever it appeared. AIDS activists often spoke at our rallies, outlining the pressures on HIV-positive women to have abortions and sterilizations, and why this must be opposed.

In 1992, the government of Saskatchewan was considering de-funding hospital abortions, giving in to anti- choice pressure through cutbacks to health care. In 1995, the Alberta Conservative government tried to do the same. In the U.S., the government denies poor women funding for abortions, but it still pays 90 percent of the cost of sterilizations. Angela Davis has said that when abortion is denied and sterilization is available this constitutes coerced sterilization.[12] These government actions were fought by pro-choice groups in the provinces affected, as well as by organizations such as OCAC. If these changes had been successful, it would have forced poor and working-class women to make the decision to be sterilized, since they would no longer have access to abortion.

When the Supreme Court overturned the existing abortion law in January of 1988, it was through the strength of a broad-based movement with the active participation of working-class women and women of colour. It was a collective victory. Tens of thousands of supporters across the country played an active role. The fact that OCAC understood that the state was not neutral, that it was racist and class biased, and that it was actively working against our interests, was critical to our campaign. Only a mass movement could change the balance of forces in the interests of all women.

The Conservative government in Ottawa began the process of introducing new legislation recriminalizing abortion. The campaign against a new law gained wide support from groups such as the National Organization of Immigrant and Visible Minority Women, the Canadian Labour Congress, the National Council of Jewish Women, the Federation des Femmes du Quebec, the Canadian Medical Association, the United Church of Canada, and a range of local labour and anti-racist groups. This broad support created the political pressure to defeat the legislation in the Senate in 1991, after it narrowly passed in the House of Commons.

At the same time, OCAC was also pressuring the provincial government to expand access in Ontario. It was quite difficult for the organization to do both, but we felt the struggle for the legal right could not be separated from the fight for full and free access, if we were to remain true to our principles. We were committed to eradicating race and class barriers for all women. In the end, the law was defeated and the Ontario NDP government announced that four free-standing clinics would be fully funded. It also established a Task Force on Abortion Access, which was to develop a strategic plan to expand access across the province.

As WWIW said in a statement released when the law was defeated: "Today, we applaud the death of Bill C43 acknowledging that collective visible actions by many different constituencies led to its defeat. We strongly support OCAC's position that the legal right to choose, as important as it is, is meaningless unless fully funded services exist to give every woman the opportunity to make that choice in her own language and her own community. WWIW will continue to work with OCAC to put pressure on the federal government to implement the Canada Heath Act to ensure that every province provides full access to free abortion and to insist that the provinces provide this critical service with all the other demands that will ensure real choices in our lives...."[13]

During the campaign against the new law and for increased access, anti-choice activists began another assault. "Operation Rescue," as they called it, started in Toronto, during the fall of 1988. Hundreds of anti-choice protesters blockaded the entrance of the Morgentaler Clinic. They physically and verbally assaulted women seeking abortion services. OCAC organized a defence of the clinics, rejecting the argument that it should be left to the police to protect the facilities. Many of the women using the clinics did not view the police as a friendly force. Women from working-class communities and communities of colour had seen the role of the police during strikes and in violent incidents with members of their communities. The police had previously raided the clinic, arrested the doctors, followed and harassed patents. They also made it clear by their actions that they were in no hurry to remove the blockades, often viewing pro-choice activists as more problematic that the anti-choice vigilantes.

Supporters would link arms chanting, "Racist, sexist, anti-gay, born-again bigots go away," "Campaign Life, your name's a lie, you don't care if women die" — chants which reflected the politics of the campaign. It would not be unusual to see women and men from the United Steelworkers, the Black Women's Coalition, Canadian Auto Workers, AIDS Action Now!, Women Working with Immigrant Women, the Immigrant Women's Health Centre, and Eco-media standing shoulder to shoulder to defend the clinics. Because of the strong mobilization and community support, "Operation Rescue" was stopped. This speaks to the strength of the movement-building strategy, and the active alliance building. Those who defended women's access believed that the clinic was legal as a result of their collective struggle and were committed to defending it.

OCAC recognized that women's lives are such that not all women are able to actively participate in the day-to-day campaign. It is difficult to know how representative our organizing is, and we are sure more could have been done, but we try to be accountable to the groups with whom we work. Building strong alliances and working in coalition with organizations of women of colour and working-class women must always be key priorities in order to ensure their active involvement and a representative politic.

According to a recent poll 77 percent of people in Canada believe that an abortion is a decision that should be made between a woman and her doctor. There is no federal law on abortion. Today, in Ontario, abortion is fully covered in hospitals, and in five free-standing clinics due to the struggle in this province. However, it is still a very fragile system of abortion services. Northern Ontario is very poorly served. In northwestern Ontario, First Nations women must make three trips off the reserve to obtain the procedure, which is a totally unnecessary burden and destroys any confidentiality. Anti-choice harassment has forced some doctors to stop providing these services. In 1992, the fire bombing of the Morgentaler Clinic in Toronto, shows the extremes that anti-choice sympathizers take. In 1994, 1995, and 1997 doctors were shot in Vancouver, Ancaster, Ontario, and Winnipeg because they were providing abortions.

There are now thirty free-standing clinics offering abortions to women across the country, and access is much wider then in the early 1980s when the campaign began. In provinces other than Ontario, British Columbia, Alberta, Newfoundland and Quebec (Quebec is not fully covered), governments are still refusing to pay the costs of clinic abortions. Abortion is entirely unavailable in Prince Edward Island and quite limited in the Atlantic provinces in general. In rural areas throughout the country access is still very difficult. The fight for the maintenance of universal health care which is presently under attack through cutbacks, hospital closures, and reduction of services, particularly affecting working-class women and women of colour, and must continue.

While the overall strategic situation has changed, and will always change, the lessons of this campaign will remain relevant. Issues of race and class must be prioritized in their organizing if movements are to speak to the realities of all women's lives. These are the principles and strategies that created a broad-based campaign to overturn the oppressive federal law, and create a network of abortion clinics in most provinces. Initial and partial victories certainly, but still major gains for women's reproductive freedom, and these are the principles that can continue to push the struggle forward.

It is only through the ongoing development of an anti-racist, class perspective, with the participation and leadership of women of colour and working-class women, that the possibility exists to eradicate racism and class bias from the health care system, and win full reproductive freedom for all women.

NOTES

1. Janice Tibbets, *The Ottawa Citizen*, June 12, 1995.
2. *Immigrant, Refugee and Racial Minority Women and Heath Care Needs: Report of Community Consultations*, Women's Health Bureau, Ontario Ministry of Health (August 1993), 17.
3. *Immigrant, Refugee and Racial Minority Women and Health Care Needs: Report of Community Consultations*, Women's Heath Bureau, Ontario Ministry of Health (August 1993), iii.
4. *Immigrant Women's Health Centre, Annual Report* (1986), 8.
5. *Immigrant Women's Health Centre: Mobile Health Unit Project. Preventative Health Care for Immigrant Women* (September 1995), 6.
6. *Immigrant Women's Health Centre: Mobile Health Unit Project. Preventative Health Care for Immigrant Women* (September 1995), 7.
7. *What Women Prescribe: Report and Recommendations,* from the National Symposium, Women in Partnership: Working Toward Inclusive, Gender-sensitive Health Policies, Canadian Advisory Council on the Status of Women (May 1995), 68-9.
8. Edward Ng, "Immigrants Healthier than People Born Here," *Toronto Star* (April 2, 1996).
9. *Political Participation for Change: Immigrant and Visible Minority Women in Action,* Fourth National Conference and Biennial General Meeting of the National Organization of Immigrant and Visible Minority Women of Canada (March 1995), 38.
10. Angus McLaren, *Our Own Master Race* (Toronto: McClelland and Stewart, 1990).
11. Robert Lechat, "Intensive Sterilization for the Inuit." *Eskimo* (Fall/Winter 1976): 57.
12. Angela Y. Davis, *Women, Race and Class.* (New York: Random House, 1981).
13. Women Working with Immigrant Women. Statement issued on the defeat of Bill C 43 (1991).

CHAPTER THIRTEEN

Continuing on the Ground

Feminists of Colour Discuss Organizing

ANGELA ROBERTSON

Anti-racist thought has a rich history in Canada, but that thinking has been dispersed across the country and rarely brought together. Nor has how women of colour experience race and gender in Canada been highlighted in the literature. This collection has taken on addressing these absences. To further these ends, in the summer of 1998, collection co-editor Angela Robertson brought together a number of women of colour who have worked as front-line activists to look at how women of colour have organized and to talk about the achievements and lack thereof in progressive anti-racist change.

Issues on the table for discussion included what is happening and has happened to feminist organizing by women of colour during the recent change in political climate, as well as visions for organizing in the context of political backlash. Discussion aimed to look at the history of how feminists of colour have organized, at the limitations of some actions taken and at what's still missing. Vital questions, like the differences between mainstream and feminist organizing and what tensions exist when women of colour organize ourselves, either amongst ourselves or within mainstream feminist organizing, were open for discussion.

One major focus was globalization — what's happening on a global scale and how that affects women of colour and feminist organizing, nationally and globally. What do global changes mean for how organizing is envisioned? What do they mean for the agenda of organizing issues? And what are some of the ways in which organizing needs to look different?

The discussion was moderated by collection co-editor, *Enakshi Dua*, who teaches sociology at Queen's University. The participants were: *Pramilla Aggarwal* who teaches at George Brown College; *Deena Ladd* who worked for six years with the International Ladies Garment Workers Union and has been involved with a number of different coalitions and organizations — the Toronto Committee Against Racism, the Coalition Against Racist Police Violence, the Women's March Against Poverty, and Desh Pardesh; *Beverly Bain*, in the anti-violence movement for 17 years, a part-time college instructor in the Assaulted Women's and Children's Counsellors Advocacy program and a facilitator/trainer working with women's groups in the anti-violence movement; collection co-editor *Angela Robertson*, active in anti-racist feminist organizing through the Black Women's

Collective and integration of women of colour's issues within feminist publishing in Canada, at the Ontario Women's Directorate during the NDP government reign and now executive director of Sistering, a drop-in centre for homeless and marginalized women in Toronto; and *Carol Ann Wright*, executive director of the North End Health Centre in Halifax, part-time teacher in an adult education program through Dalhousie University, and a Nova Scotia regional representative for National Action Committee on the Status of Women (NAC).

The discussion began with the last ten years, then moved into exploring current and future challenges, and old and new strategies. Participants were asked to begin with an assessment of what they thought had been achieved in anti-racist feminist organizing in the last decade.

ORGANIZING OVER THE LAST DECADE

Beverly: The last ten years have really fluctuated in terms of achievements from an anti-racist perspective. And I want to be clear on an anti-racist *perspective*, because I am not convinced that we have actually managed to come up with an anti-racist framework in its entirety. We have touched the periphery, in terms of an idea of what anti-racist organizing should look like or would look like — how an organization is made up in terms of identity, issues of identity, issues of social grouping, social location, and an equity policy.

When we talk about anti-racism, for me, what we have achieved is a focus on equity, a struggle around equity. In Ontario that actually worked for a while, until employment equity was taken away under the present Conservative government. At the federal level employment equity is a joke.

Anti-racism has worked in the format of equity and addressing issues of equity, but it has not been the kind of perspective we need. We need an integrated perspective which includes looking at women of colour in all of our dimensions. Looking at how intersections of race, sex orientation, class, issues of age and issues of ability actually work to locate women. An anti-racist framework would mean being able to re-address how privilege gets reproduced in organizations. That's been the struggle throughout feminist organizations. Whenever we have addressed issues around power and privilege, and tried to work with concepts like inclusion and representation (the concepts we have worked with in the anti-racism movement and the way of addressed inequity), privilege has somehow been reintroduced or reproduced. We haven't figured out how to struggle around that.

We've seen some really solid work. That has been the result of women of colour communities struggling around readdressing how power is manifested in the women's movement. In Toronto, one of the biggest was IWD 1986 — From Toronto to South Africa — where there was a real struggle within the International Women's Day Committee. A challenge was put forward, particularly by the Black Women's Collective and First Nation women, in terms of how women of colour have been isolated, and how the work of women of colour and of First Nation women historically has always gone unnoticed, and how we work around ensuring that the women's movement recognizes that work. So we have seen a lot of that progress.

In the past 10 years, I've seen various points where we have seen gains in terms of our struggles as women of colour through our hard work at the grass-roots level and the challenges we've posed to the white women's community. To restructure this whole concept of feminism, from meaning only in opposition to men, to feminism being about power relationships that do exist and the need to recognize that feminism, for women of colour, is an intersectional reality.

Deena: Ten years ago I moved to this country from England. I was 17 and got involved with the Ryerson Women's Centre. Ten years spans my political involvement and activism, and I would probably use "roller coaster" to describe it. There's been some incredible highs, but there's also been moments where I've felt sick.

My first four years were at Ryerson and I saw real gains there. When I first started, you'd have security guards secretly coming down to the women's centre saying, "Oh well, there's been a sexual assault in the library but it's being hushed up." By the time I left — after the Montreal shooting at l'ecole polytechnique by Marc Lepine — the whole space on campus opened for us to really bring out issues of date rape, violence against women, sexual assault, incest, to make the links with racism, start up gay and lesbian student groups on campus, and try to get an integrated approach.

After that explosion happened on campus — for employment equity, educational equity, challenging curriculums, trying to get an anti-racist approach, a feminist approach, an integrative perspective — we started to experience backlash, not only from right-wing student groups, but from a very right-wing administration. With the funding to universities closing down, just as a lot of things were changing, it was shut down again.

Within labour, I work primarily with low-income, immigrant women in the garment industry who faced incredible devastation in their lives with the passing of the free trade agreement and NAFTA. Seeing the effects of that and working for the past six years in a predominantly female union, an immigrant workers' union with a predominantly female staff, trying to bring in a feminist perspective and an anti-racist perspective in labour issues has, again, had incredible highs. The highs came in dealing with the effects of free trade and global restructuring, looking at creative organizing with home-based workers, trying to grapple with new ways of organizing and new models of challenging employers, to take on restructuring. But now I see that slipping away again. Labour has become incredibly protective of itself in terms of the white, male, unionized workforce losing their jobs. The gains that we pushed for around community unionism and an anti-racist approach within the labour movement are closing down again. As the movement becomes quite protectionist, I feel quite discouraged.

Pramilla: In the last ten years, a fair amount of good quality academic work has hit the press and developed some sensible frameworks in the Canadian context. Work which is quite unique, which had not happened before. Some of the books generated are very good and are now in the general discussion. They are not hidden, marginal, as Black women's voices used to be. So, there is some sense that, at least politically, a contribution is being recognized in the academic world.

There has been good work around analytic framework in the education sector from George Dei at the Ontario Institute for Studies in Education (OISE) and people associated with him, good quality work, not dogmatic or separating Black and white but really looking at the power situation and at class. These books all contribute to feminism, analytic feminism, through progress in academic discourse.

I don't think the anti-racist feminist movement has become a social movement, which I was hoping it would. That is why we think of the fluctuations as a roller coaster ride, because it's not sustaining itself. It gets organized, it takes on issues, and then it runs aground every now and then.

I also find that in community-based organizations the representation in the agencies and on boards of agencies is still very white. In the power structure, where I would have hoped revolutionary change could have happened in the last 15 or 20 years, change has not really occurred. In the front-line staff we have some Black women, but mostly all decision-making power in all the mainstream institutions, as well as in non-mainstream institutions, has not changed. It is still white, and that is disheartening. There are no Native people there, there are no Black people. What the heck is going on? Where is the movement in terms of change?

Equity has not happened in mainstream institutions. No hiring has happened which would demonstrate that there is equity on the minds of unions. I come from a unionized workforce and I don't see any issues around equity or anti-racism. In the educational institutions there is either complete absence of discussion about racism or, at best, it appears in the form of diversity training, which has completely watered down everything. If you talk about equity hiring, the union is up there against it, because pay is all based of course on a very objective principle of seniority.

I find that throughout my work, both in the community and in the college where I teach, equity has only been given lip service. I'm not feeling very encouraged. After a lot of struggle in small pockets, we have not made a big dent. I'm hoping I'm wrong.

An Organizing Roller Coaster

Angela: It has been a roller coaster. Fast-paced progress and then the snail state, the molasses state. And, within the last five years, a rapid regression. Between 1988 and 1993, I saw real momentum around anti-racist and feminist organizing, workers of colour organizing within labour and talking about labour needing to put anti-racism on labour's agenda. I saw progress in academia, in government.

Government from a policy perspective beginning to talk about equity, not anti-racism, but equity, which I would hope would lead to anti-racism if it progressed.

Employment equity had momentum, not because government thought they should have equity principles, but because of the community mobilizing work that happened prior to 1988 that demanded government action on systemic racism and systemic discrimination. The change in government and in social policy did not happen because policymakers thought it should happen, but because of women and women activists. Primarily, on the anti-racism issues, it was women of colour who were saying these issues are not on your agenda and we're demanding they be put here.

Also, within the first five years of the 1990s, there was a real push from within by anti-racist feminists, women of colour specifically, pushing mainstream feminist organizing. We saw real shifts in NAC, and in women's studies programs, from the push for the politics in feminism to be broad and inclusive, and not broad and inclusive in the lip service way, but with a real integrated analysis.

Somehow the state began co-opting these equity principles. A political debate around anti-racism became watered down, now argued around equity principles. And equity was becoming really broad and fluid and meaning anything and everything and everybody. As activists, when we talked about anti-racist feminism and anti-racism, we were getting lost in a morass of equity that became really undefined in terms of state policy, government policy. What we were beginning to get out of employment equity wasn't what we wanted in the first place. We weren't sure how we would be able to hold anyone accountable for implementation.

We pushed for real inclusion, not always asking for inclusion but placing ourselves at the table. What we got, in the last five years, has been a real backlash. How is it that now that women of colour have become front-and-centre in mainstream feminist organizing, feminist organizing has again become marginalized? And we women of colour have become marginalized as merely single issue, only concerned around race, while we have been demanding an inclusive agenda around race, gender and class, that cuts across issues of labour, issues of unemployment and issues of police violence. We've been really pigeon-holed and beaten up as only concerned about special interests, and what we've been arguing for as an inclusive anti-racist politics has been labelled special interest. Now we're running away from "special interest," which means some people are running away from active anti-racist politics.

After the high of the struggles and achievements, the last five years have become a real disappointment. As organizers, it has become much more difficult for us as women colour to actively engage as we had years prior. I want to hear more about that, because it has become so increasingly difficult for us to organize.

Changing Leadership at NAC

Carol Ann: My first point is that over the last ten years, anti-racism has created a lucrative industry for anti-racist practitioners. I think that has done a lot of damage. The larger struggle has been co-opted, we participated in that to some degree, those of us who have been anti-racist practitioners are those who have done it. People have gotten away with a lot in terms of co-opting the language and watering down policies. The bottom line of this discussion should be are Black women and women of colour struggling any less? We're struggling more on issues of anti-racism.

From a Nova Scotia perspective, particularly coming here from Ontario, the racism is much clearer here. You can defend Ontario if you want to, but I find it so convoluted. People have gotten really sophisticated on the language, but it's really hard to get an identification of issues, people have intellectualized them. Here it's very clear. I much prefer the enemy that I can clearly see, know exactly what they're doing, and to hit the target straight on. It's a very different thing. For me it's been very disappointing over the ten years. When I look at the 1960s in terms the history of Nova Scotia, in terms what was happening here — the segregation, the racism — the 1960s was a much more productive era, much more progressive than the last while. And for me that's scary. What is happening now?

In terms of NAC, we've gone from reaction to change in leadership. From Sunera Thobani to Joan Grant-Cummings, there has been a whole lot of stuff around anti-racism. As women of colour on the executive, we have stopped trying to make it easier for people, trying to placate people on the executive. I'm not even talking about the external work of NAC, I'm talking about the executive, the inner workings, which was a real internal struggle for a long period of time. People just had to get used to it. We were the majority on the executive. People had to get used to understanding the roles of Black women in leadership positions, and what that meant, the impact on the organization and on the membership, and why this organization needed to be representative. Because people began to try make us feel guilty for the organization's change in leadership. Like you know you are responsible for NAC now not being representative, you are responsible for NAC now not getting funding. This is the kind of backlash that's still present now, and these are the things that I find really, really disappointing.

On a personal note, having hit forty this year I have a different approach to this question. I am no longer interested in the education piece. There has been ten years of education. We have struggled with this, we have constantly raised issues with the women's community, the white women's community. And we're belabouring the point. I reached the end of the line in constantly explaining why Black women are in this place, what the agenda is. The explanations are over, it's just continual action and taking our space where we need to take it.

In NAC, we've had two women of colour presidents in succession and that was a really important change for NAC. That's been a really important position for NAC to be in. It has made women underground, grassroots women, become aware of NAC and start asking the important questions. For us, as women of colour, that's the most important thing, that women start coming to the organization recognizing the national and international ramifications of supporting the organization, and the political challenges that go with that, and the political impact of women understanding the collective agenda.

In terms of the executive, it meant that being an executive member included having those really honest discussions on the executive without people having confrontophobia and thinking that the world's going to fall apart if we disagree. Having Sunera and then Joan has been a really important catalyst for NAC both on a national and an international level.

Angela: We've been successful in getting some broad achievements within the feminist movement, not specifically the anti-racist and feminist movement, some achievements around pay equity. As a women's movement we've achieved some pieces around pay equity but that has had minimal impact for women of colour. And as anti-racists and feminists we've demanded employment equity and the achievements have been good, but they have not been felt by us because of where women of colour are located within the labour force.

One of the other achievements is some significant presence as a feminist voice offering challenges and alternatives for feminism, and women's organizing. We have a presence. Women of colour who come from activist bases have put some significant writing on the table. I'm not sure if the impact has been widespread beyond the confines of academic institutions, but certainly we have had presence as a voice offering alternatives and challenging how feminism has been and needs to be constructed in Canada.

The other piece that I would say we have been successful in — and again it's a double-edged sword — is in terms of our representation. When we look at NAC as a national organization, having Sunera and Joan as presidents of this national women's organization has been significant. It has been talked about as representation and people have linked it to the activism of women of colour. While we grapple around what we're not getting from NAC as a national organization as presently constituted, the fact is that there has been some significant shift in the leadership of NAC. How we use that in the next ten years is the challenge.

As women of colour organizing in community-specific organizations we have seen the creation of some much-needed community-specific — women of colour community-specific — programs in not-for-profit community agencies. These are right now being destroyed left, right, and centre. The question arises then, to what extent, as women of colour who organize for direct service, can we rely on state funding? Is that secure? If those programs must be or should be state-funded, what are some of the mechanisms that we need to have in place so that they remain accountable to provide that funding? What we've seen, with NAC as a national organization, and other women's and service organizations is that governments are moving from core to project dollars. Nobody is talking about sustaining services for women of colour.

Poverty, Economics, and Organizing

Pramilla: I cannot think of things as successes which in my own little lifetime are already gone. In Ontario, in the last ten years we have had two governments. For all it's problems, with the NDP in power, some of our friends like Carol Ann and Angela and many others, were in government, which made me a little bit more confident that reason could be heard. That had a lot to do with some of the success, with feeling like there was merit in putting a lot of energy in getting organized. In terms of success, the larger political situation has a lot to do with success being possible or not being possible. I wish it did not depend on such outside forces, but that is where we are.

Deena and I worked on a couple of very exciting projects — hard work, actually — which were not looking for any money from anybody. They were self-sustaining, self-supporting kinds of organizations, but even those fell by the wayside. Six or seven of us formed the Foundation Workers' Collective. We had a very lofty agenda and blueprint of how it would change the face of work for unionized and non-unionized workers of colour in Ontario at least, if not internationally. We kept it alive for about a year and a half, trying to get it on the labour agenda, which was a very, very critical step.

One of the things that keeps on getting in the way is class. We keep on putting most of our emphasis on gender, second on race and then maybe class. The anti-poverty struggle is just mentioned, as is Black people's poverty, people of colour's poverty, whether it is homelessness, or women on welfare or Family Benefits Allowance. We don't see anti-racist feminist organizing in the forefront of everyday issues of Black people's poverty. Organizing around that piece is absolutely essential.

Carol Ann: The Ontario Conservative government has been really the most regressive government I've seen in terms of poverty issues. In terms of strategies for dealing with that government, people have almost run out of ideas. What do you do with a government that has no heart and doesn't care? It's been really difficult to strategize in Ontario around the anti-poverty movement. I've seen a real downturn.

In Nova Scotia, the movements here really fluctuate in terms of success and failures and getting government to move on really reactive policies. Nova Scotia is not as bad as the Harris government, but just as reactionary and regressive. Nova Scotians have had to deal with the same kind of regressive workfare policies. It's very divided here, there's no integrated, anti-racist, anti-poverty approach to how we deal with these things. For me that's what creates the problems. These have to be integrated before we'll be successful at any one of them.

Pramilla: The *Employment Standards Act* was something I got really attached to emotionally. At heart, even in a very magical sort of way — even though it only protects about 60 percent of the working population — it is a basis of protecting working people in terms of minimum standards legislation. There were a couple of things which we had fought for a very long time with the NDP government to include in it. An employment standards act applies to the kind of people we have worked with, people who are underemployed — severely, grossly underemployed — in restaurants, in the garment industry, in those sectors where our representation is. And that *Act* was one of the things which I fought for and I was a little bit encouraged during the NDP regime, that there would be some kind of justice for people who were being shortchanged.

But the whole employment standards branch has been decimated in the last four years, it is almost not to be seen. The government reduced its workforce by 40 percent. That was the first branch of the government slashed by the Conservatives, and then there were no checks on employers, in terms of wages. There's not even a reception area. They don't have an office where you can go and meet anybody. The enforcement process has become nonexistent.

The government has frozen the minimum wage for ten years which has never happened in the history of employment standards. Even though it was never a living wage, the minimum wage did increase by three to six percent every year. This is very symbolic. They have actually given this message to the world, to Ontario employers. Even though some of the changes which they have introduced have not been legislated, the message is very clear that we are employer friendly and we will not even slap your wrist if you are in violation of the *Act*. And the Conservatives have completely dissolved the wage protection fines, so there is no way to actually fine anyone anymore.

This all has a very disproportionate effect on poor workers and on women of colour. Who else would it effect? The poor, the most poorly paid, the most marginal, those people are women of colour. It needs to be said again and again that organizations which are fighting in the interests of women of colour need to renew a position on these matters.

My big problem with feminism is they're not taking on issues of economics. That's the basis of living in the capitalist world. How else can you make a living other than being a wage worker? Everybody can't become a shopkeeper. And then you have bankruptcies coming like glory. No bank is going to give a woman of colour a $10,000 loan to start a vending machine business when they don't own anything else. We are in a capitalist economy with wage workers. We need good labour practices.

Deena: I wholeheartedly agree. The women's movement has missed a huge organizing potential in not dealing with the issues of working-class women and poor women. There is such an incredible void here, just an incredible loss of connection. Look at some of the key issues, especially in Ontario in the last three years. Absolute fundamental dismantling of our healthcare system and our educational system. If there are two issues you can talk to every single person in this country about and get a point of connection, a fundamental connection with them and their families where they're living and what they're dealing with, those would the two issues, and then work. Such a missed opportunity. It's something that we can still do something about, but what do we face in terms of how we organize? If I look at the last ten years and the success that I thought that I was involved with, those do not exist at this moment.

I have not ever really been formally involved with NAC. I've never been to a general meeting, I've never been a representative. However, I was involved with the Women's March Against Poverty. When I think back to really incredibly positive moments of organizing, that has to be one of them. I think that is directly connected to the fact that Sunera Thobani was in the NAC leadership at that point. That Winnie Ng was the southern Ontario regional representative. Winnie Ng dragged us in, kicking and screaming, because she wanted us involved. It provided access points for women who are working on the grassroots who have never been involved in these organizations. I think that Winnie Ng made sure that women who would be organizing in Toronto would be women of colour, women with disabilities, young women, immigrant women.

I was dragged into the Women's March on Poverty even though I was incredibly overworked at the union where I worked. It became an incredible project because we did incredible outreach. For the first time in a long time you were having 60 and 70 women at meetings, immigrant women. And everybody was working their asses off. We had a very strict deadline, but obviously you never have enough time. We had six or seven weeks to organize this march. I saw women I'd never met before, never been involved with politically, and it was an incredibly exciting time. Women just took on the organizing in their own communities. We had posters in seventeen languages and it wasn't just seventeen languages for the sake of seventeen languages, it was women who were involved in the organizing who translated the posters. We did the outreach in their communities. We barely had any money for any of this stuff, for translators or any of the grassroots work. What was done was done on practically no budget. We can talk about why we lost an opportunity there, but the kind of inclusion of women with disabilities, women of colour, and immigrant women at the March itself, and in the organizing committee was one of the most successful things that I've been involved in and a really positive experience.

I want to talk about why that is a challenge. I think we've really lost those women. I think it will take a lot to build that trust again in terms of getting them involved again because those women were saying "We want this to continue, we want to be involved, we want a women's movement. This has been one of the most exciting things we've been involved with, we've never been able to do anything like this before." And we missed that opportunity because nothing happened. There was no follow-up. I have the phone list from those things and I'm waiting, but it's been a lost opportunity. But I still am optimistic.

Another success was at the International Ladies Garment Workers Union (ILGWU). When I look back at where we were and the reason why it was a success, in 1990 to 1991 we started to create a real analysis around what was happening in the garment industry, what was happening to immigrant workers in those industries and the incredible destruction of work and of women's lives. The union was at a crisis point. It had nowhere else to go. It had lost 60 percent of its membership. It wasn't going anywhere unless it came up with a creative strategy. They did community outreach, they had no choice but to do outreach, to understand how to organize immigrant women and who to bring in to do that organizing. Its whole operating policy had to change, it knew that it had to grapple with the situation. Those who were involved at that point used the opportunity to try to do the kind of outreach and organizing we had to do.

You saw things happen for the first time, like an associate membership where we managed to outreach to home workers, home-based workers, immigrant women working in the home. It provided a space to do outreach with garment workers who had lost their jobs. Previously, the union had no interest in connecting with them after they'd lost their work. But they were forced to look at restructuring in the industry and to know that women who were in those low-income jobs were constantly moving from various forms of precarious work. We had to have an analysis that would integrate anti-racist, feminist, and class perspectives. You had to organize in the whole continuum of precarious work to grapple with the restructuring happening in the industry.

Now other sectors and other unions are facing the same kind of restructuring and devastation that we faced in the garment industry at that point. And they have learnt from those lessons. I don't want this to happen with the rest of the women's movement, but you reach such a crisis point you have nowhere else to go. I do think that element is here, that maybe we are at a critical point, where there is such a void in the anti-racist grassroots movement, in identity politics, in the women's movement and the labour movement that we have to force ourselves to look at the alternatives.

Coalition Building

Deena: A huge shaping of my political experience was the formation of the Toronto Coalition Against Racism (TCAR). It was incredible, it had incredible moments of success. Again, the organization has folded, no organizing is happening in coalition work against racist police violence, which we see no end of at this point.

TCAR was, in 1993, a spontaneous coming together of immigrant communities, of people of colour, of young people, people who had never really been involved in institutionalized forms of organizing or had any connection with any organizations but came together because of the racist attacks in the Black community. TCAR was very issue focused. It had a very tangible goal — saying we have the right to walk on the streets without racist attacks and death.

What was wonderful was a real sense of coming together of many communities that were isolated and alienated, including immigrant communities that were very recent immigrant communities and really ostracized and targeted. The Somali community in particular. Remember Liberal leader Lynn McCleod targeted Somali women as financing the war and the warlords in Somalia through state abuse and social service abuse.

What brought people together was saying we need mass protests on the streets, we need to have a mass movement. Yes, we need petitions, we need that kind of lobbying but there needs to be a grassroots, community-based response. There were problems around organizing in terms of making sure women were represented. But, in trying to bring together people of colour and immigrant communities and young activists there was an incredible energy and excitement which embraced not only looking at racist police violence but at immigrants and refugees, at systemic racism in a very broad, inclusive perspective.

Pramilla: I want to really reiterate the importance of TCAR in my life. That was one of the most exciting pieces of organizing in terms of breadth and depth. I'm very sorry about its demise. I had my students research it. I said go talk to TCAR, do research on TCAR as an organizing piece and why it folded and how it could have sustained itself, because I think that is the question. How do you sustain something which sustains both outsiders and insiders really doing good work? And really, energy was there.

Deena: It's a very good question. How do we do coalition building? A million dollar question.

Framing and Reframing

Beverly: I see the successes as a combination of the struggle of women of colour at the grassroots and of state construction. The state provided openings for us to enter. By that I mean that a lot of what we actively struggled for hasn't been what we actively got. And I think we need to be very clear.

Employment equity benefitted the movement of white women as opposed to women of colour and people of colour. Our people were the last on the list. We need to talk about how representation has been constructed for us. Representation was really constructed within the context of political parties, of how women can be represented in the political system. This is the struggle of white women in the feminist movement. In government, we have been struggling around the issue of representation and that's been just women to men. That doesn't challenge the hierarchical and patriarchal structure, if anything, it enforces it.

We were given access to the process of representation, this is why we're able to have women of colour in leadership at NAC, for example, as we have. But the trouble with that is the challenge to the structure of how privilege is entrenched in our organization and continues to work against women of colour who are in those positions. We get marginalized and isolated as "single issue." For Sunera, every time she was in an argument it was always about race, even if she was talking about economics or anything else. It always got contextualized in the context of race because that is the entry point at which the larger society is going to see you — as not male, not white. And that also was the situation in the feminist community, in terms of how they wanted us to be in those positions. We become marginalized in those positions, isolated and undermined in the work we're trying to do.

We also got access in terms of support to work around anti-violence specifically in our community as women of colour. The state was really concerned about how violence manifested in the Black community, the South Asian community, the South East Asian community, because violence is viewed as unique to those particular communities. How do we get "those people" to work with each other, to work through issues of violence? So we were given that particular space. But we were given the space in a voyeuristic way, where the state looks in on us, diagnosing the community as having specific kinds of issues which then isolate it from the larger picture.

A major thing is to see the connections, how the system works on all levels. That we have not been allowed to make those connections has been a real problem for us. Because we are constantly struggling, we enter at those given access points exhausted, in some cases very much alone, and with no opportunity to actually have worked through the issues. Even though we struggle in context — everyone has talked about all the struggling we have done — even though we pull and struggle and come together, somehow what happens at the end is everything gets dissipated. And we don't see how that takes place.

It's all controlled by a larger force, the state. The state designed it for us and we work around that design. I'm not even sure that I would say that feminism has missed anything. Feminism hasn't been contextualized in a way that brings all the issues together. I don't think feminism is just about gender issues. That's feminism stuck in a very white frame. Feminism is about gender, about economics, about race, about class, about every social, political, and economic piece. Because feminism hasn't brought those pieces together, a lot of the other pieces have been left out.

In terms of talking about gains, the struggle is to see that gains have been about a combination of our work and the access that we have been given. At present, those access points have been taken away. And they have been taken away because the larger total context decided to move on. Those gains are not working for them anymore. That's gone, and all we are left with is what we have started with — our bodies on the ground without the frame. We are back to square one, trying to build a new frame. The frame that we need to build, in my mind, is integrative feminist anti-racist and anti-oppression frame. That's something I don't think we have and I think it's a piece we can put together.

FUTURE STRATEGIES AND CHALLENGES

Carol Ann: I still find that we're trying to do two things. We're trying to organize and trying to educate within the grassroots movement across different sectors, as well as trying to impact on government policy. That creates a really schizophrenic role.

Right now, I am really happy to work within my own community, which is in the Black community. I know that sounds very problematic and very marginalizing, but it's been very important for me to come home. I don't have to pretend that I know everything about everything. I know about my community, I know what the issues are. Within the Black communities things like economics need to be addressed. Black communities here do not make a separation between economy and race, it is a very natural intersection.

There is no expectation that I'm going to educate a movement on the issues of anti-racism. I'm not saying that I shouldn't, I'm saying that right now I'm very comfortable not having to do that. What that means is that I put steam and energy in the community behind a specific issue — like landfill going in Black communities and the health impact — and have some impact on an issue for the community and see some immediate change. When you try to intersect everything and try to cover all the bases sometimes it loses steam by the time of impact. We really have to look at the challenge in how we start organizing from now on and into the millennium.

Pramilla: On one hand it is a very sensible idea to focus and work within a community because you understand it and we need to work at that level all the time, absolutely. And in this Canadian context, I can't visualize a social movement based on anti-racism myself at this time. If I want to make a picture of it or see it in my head — what would it look like? What would it take on? And who will be in it on a continual basis? I have difficulty conceptualizing it.

This piece on race is constantly on my mind, because I became raced when I came here. The issue of racism is as present now as it has ever been. It just keeps on taking different contours, different languages, different shapes, but the impact of racism on people is exactly the same if not worse. The only difference is that five or ten years ago, it became a part of the discourse. People talked about racism. Now that has gone too. There's a real kind of "No, no, no, racism is not a category anymore" attitude that's really disturbing. As if it has been taken care of. "Let's talk about committee building, development, let's talk..." as if race has been taken care of. As if women have become equal to men. Gender is gone, race is gone. There's an emptiness I'm struggling with.

It's related to the global forces of transnational corporations and the havoc they create completely unbridled in their search of power and profit. It completely boggles my mind. I can't even think about the kinds of struggles of people in India, people in the Philippines, because I find that all those buzzing bees in the elephant's nostrils are really being squished by the elephant constantly. In some ways for me, like you, it is saner and safer and more productive to work on smaller pieces than larger pieces of work. I'm really torn in terms of how to do both because I think small pieces do not lead to big revolution. Different kinds of struggles make bigger things, and small things remain small. That is my very common sense of analysis of social movements. Maybe six years from now we'll look back and say, "No, this was actually a social movement, which led to very interesting history."

Angela: In terms of challenges — when I look at what we face in a national context, we are beginning to talk as if our policy makers or the state somehow manages the issue of racism, the issue of systemic discrimination. Like managing equity. So these things have been managed and now, what do we need to put in place to make Canada work smoothly? But when I look at what is currently happening, police violence and racism is still very prevalent. When we look at welfare reform, who are the people who are going to be severely impacted by these regressive welfare reforms? We need to look at stereotyping around eligibility requirements, we need to look at support for sole-support parents and housing allowances, shelter allowance. All those things have been cut. Who is impacted? Primarily communities of colour, who already have been marginalized.

There isn't a broad social movement making challenges to those issues. We have sporadic activism by activists, who come from a history of social activism, raising questions but not supported by a broad social movement. So nothing seems to be moving or shifting. We seem to be talking to ourselves.

When we look at immigration reform and what the federal government has been proposing in the last three years, we don't see challenges. We don't see a social movement saying these kinds of regressive changes come from a place that says our labour and our presence here in this national space called Canada is no longer needed. We're no longer valuable to the Canadian economy, we're no longer essential, so therefore there is no onus for any support programs, no basis on which the state needs to offer us anything any longer, to either placate us to keep us for our labour. We are longer needed. With the globalization of the economy we can stay where we are and work for Canada and Canada does not have to have any social responsibility to us as citizens or as workers.

I really underline the lack of a social movement. Whatever brought us together as women of colour and anti-racist feminists is no longer there. Where there were signals that could make building a social movement possible, they got reduced to mere representation because they weren't tied to a larger politic around our issues as women of colour. Instead, we got focused on mere representation, focused around single issues and pigeon-holed in the cycle of "We're only interested in race" and dismissed by that. For me, the challenge that keeps resonating is the real lack of a space for building social movement.

Carol Ann: There's also, as far as I'm concerned, a lack of debate on the left or whatever's left for people like myself. What we are doing is reacting to the right. I go back to the history of the Black Panther party. There was an agenda, there was a ten point program. Movements had programs. They had agendas that they wanted to fulfil and they never strayed from that. That is what we're critically lacking, an agenda, to do our checks and balances against. We fervently reacted to what the right is saying or what the government is saying, instead of having a clear agenda so we don't stray, don't get off track and they don't surprise us.

In terms of the women's movement specifically, I still feel that the premise to the women's movement is very flawed. I've been in NAC way too long. It hasn't changed, even though the leadership has changed. We work very hard on the executive, and the executive — I think is a majority women of colour now — has changed the way committees have worked. But the essence of it is still very white. Some of the context still comes from America, it doesn't even reflect the reality of Canadian women at times. That needs to change for us to be successful in the women's movement. We need to reflect that global women's movement as well. We can no longer speak in the North American context of what the women's movement is about. We're connected as women of colour to other countries of women. Those two things are very, very critical.

Building an Anti-Racist, Feminist Social Movement

Beverly: A social movement provides a framework to get our issues addressed. But as far as some type of organizing happening here in Ontario, as women of colour, we are no longer there.

There is this whole thing that racism no longer exists, that gender no longer exists. "We all stand to lose our jobs. We all stand to lose our gains," and therefore "I don't want to hear about women of colour." What this is about is the middle class now seeing themselves as victims of social and economic policies. We need to realize that this is what we are up against. Women of colour who were already facing backlash are facing further backlash, and that disappears from the entire debate.

Deena: In terms of the struggles and challenges that face us, it fundamentally comes down to the way we do organizing — organizing on many levels, organizing to build a broader movement. Organizing is going to be taking place within the different movements, that can come together. One of the fundamental challenges is how to come to grips with the incredible alienation that people are facing, but also to have people understand that they can affect change, they can get involved and make a difference. This is sort of cliché but I do think that optimism, to be able to affect changes, to be able to be involved and engaged on so many different levels, is something we have to come to grips with.

There is this incredible opposition that you come up against when you are trying to organize within the more mainstream, broader movement. One example was the Days of Action in Toronto against the Ontario PC government, where there was an instituted Community Labour Committee supposedly nominated to organize in the Toronto area. The lack of representation was incredible. There was such a void. Joan Grant-Cummings had a position, an Aboriginal representative, Gordon Peters, had his position. But aside from those, there was no representation of women of colour, of immigrant communities, of people who are actually doing the organizing. What ended up happening was so much of our energies were used fighting to include representation — fighting to get bits of funding to try and provide translation and argue how to do organizing — we should have just said, "Screw it. We are going to do our own organizing, in our own communities." From that base of pressure, whatever happens, that momentum will change things. Instead of trying to fight for scraps.

One of the challenges is how to do that organizing which, as women of colour, as activists or organizers, gives us a strength to continue in our own work, organizing which nourishes us in our work and provides opportunity to participate in and organize within the broader movements.

A lot of my work has been in the labour movement. One of the major challenges that faces the labour movement right now is to organize in a way that can tackle the restructuring happening with work. Women's work, women of colour's work, and immigrant women's work, that is the wave of the future for work. You are looking at the service sector, you are looking at contracting jobs, at part-time, seasonal, contract work. That is the world of work that we're facing and that is the indoctrination we are getting, even from the federal government — that this is the future of work.

You need to survive, so don't cry about the fact that you don't have a full-time job, just get on with it. If you can't somehow find three part-time jobs, or if you somehow can't sustain yourself and the family, then you're to blame. Part of the struggle for the labour movement is how to organize low-income workers, workers of colour, women of colour. And to change their whole attitude of just recruiting on the basis of trying to supplement their declining membership. They are losing their members and getting protectionist. They are trying to organize new members within the labour movement but not in a way that fuels a dynamic labour movement that can take on the state. It's definitely a labour movement that is basically trying to survive. That is a fundamental challenge they face.

What a lot of the women were saying to me was that it's time for us to be able to have a group of women to take the space and to influence the debate, because that is not happening. Because we have become so discouraged and bruised by the struggles we have been in the past ten years, there is a tendency to go inside and be protective of ourselves. I needed to take time in the past year to think about how to take care of myself, and I think now is the time to take space where we direct and influence the way the movement goes. Because it certainly isn't coming from anyone else. We have all talked about the void there is. Many people are having informal discussions and thinking, "Where is the women's movement? Where's the anti-racism movement? What is going on with the labour movement?" It's as if people are waiting for something to happen but nothing is happening. That's a real challenge.

Beyond Co-optation

Angela: I think our advocacy has become fragmented and almost bureaucratized by the state in the large context. Looking specifically at Ontario, in 1988 and prior, what I was seeing was on-the-street activism, on-the-street mobilizing, public mobilizing to build mass support. And what happened, ironically, is with a left-leaning government — NDP — we moved into consultations. Our protests became bureaucratized, they were no longer public and that only benefitted a privileged few who became part of the consulted. Many of us benefitted from the privatization of anti-racism as an industry. It's not even that people aren't making challenges to regressive changes. But it is happening in these very bureaucratized ways, in these things called state consultations.

Beverly: That goes back to the whole thing about mainstreaming the work that we have done at the grassroots level. It has now become co-opted by the state, and we no longer have those points of entry anymore. The reason why we are looking for somebody else to do it is because we have become so oriented to those mechanisms which were set up for us. "Who's going to call us? Who's going to tell us that there is another mechanism set up?" We got caught up with all these bureaucratic mechanisms set up by the state. And now that they have taken all that away we are lost, waiting to be called again.

Deena: This is an incredibly important discussion that we are having, because that leads to the whole sense of alienation. These processes are totally alienating. You have to write briefs. You have to go to these meetings. There are rules, this sense of how you behave and how you speak and how well you speak and how well you can write a brief. I find it an incredibly intimidating process to work through. And so I really think that there needs to be a discussion of going back to: when something happens we take the space and organize.

How can we start mobilizing in our different neighbourhoods? A school facing a crisis around lack of funding or being under-funded is a way of mobilizing community members. A single issue mobilizes people. How do we take that and integrate it as a sustaining force in the neighbourhoods, communities, movements? That is a challenge. How do we do that education through that process? To say, "Yes, you know the mainly refugee communities that live in these apartment buildings in your neighbourhood are also facing these issues. We need to be active in supporting them, they are involved in the struggles too, right?" That integrated, grassroots perspective is really needed.

Angela: The thing that I still find hopeful is that there is still a presence, not just on the part of activists who have been doing the work since whenever, but I still get the sense that there is some energy for anti-racist, feminist organizing. I still get that sense of a commitment to do some work. People are wanting to see who's going to start it. Something still resonates with the people about the inequities that exist and they want to change that.

Beverly: One of the things we had in the last ten years that doesn't exist now is a real hunger for this kind of debate and commitment. Ten years ago there was a way of transmitting historical struggle and experiences. That isn't happening anymore. In the last five to seven years it is because of the falling apart of the social struggle, and earlier through the collapse of the socialist and communist movements.

Despite the problems within these larger struggles, they provided a historical basis for us to struggle, as feminists of colour, in particular. They also provided some type of continuum in terms of struggle for all of us, and some ways of mobilizing that no longer exist. Now people across generations are organizing in isolation from each other without any kind of history or historical reference point, which is critical. Because of the global economic restructuring and because of the backlash, we have lost that piece that has given us some basis for a social movement.

Playing the Party Politics Game

Beverly: The Liberal government nationally is a government carrying out the "global agenda" against all the progressive gains that we have made as feminists, as workers, as unemployed.

Angela: Political parties are not a place I would look for direction, but I think they're a place that can be utilized by social movements. What happened around the NDP government in Ontario and around labour as a social movement, is that labour became the party. Then, we were not in a space where we could, as a social movement, hold the political party, the politics, and the policies, accountable. We were too much part and parcel of what the government was putting forward. Where political parties are signalling that there are spaces for them to placate or support us with progressive policies, we need to take advantage of that. But we should not give them our social movements, or become the social movements for political parties.

Deena: I'm like many activists who have had no history with being involved with any political parties, and it is something that I feel very alienated from. A lot of my experience has been working in different movements and working on a grassroots level. I always said I feel very much like a socialist without a home, because I would actually like a political party that would bring together those sections of my life, the people that I work with and the activism that I do.

Beverly: My argument is not that there isn't struggle or benefits in terms of organizing around parties. A lot of women of colour and people of colour have been involved in party politics. Especially in the era of the NDP, people who didn't usually go out to vote, went out to vote. If anything, there were more people involved in party politics around that particular time. But one thing that happens in party politics and especially around the NDP, is disappointment and the backlash, particularly for women of colour who backed the NDP. We work on contract, we lost employment equity, we lost our jobs. And we lost any opportunity of gaining any jobs, that we thought we could have had. There has been a recognition of the importance of party politics, because it's as a result of those parties that we gained access. I am not saying there isn't room to work with parties but, parties need a push from the social movement.

Linking Beyond National Boundaries

Angela: How is it that we organize ourselves within anti-racist feminist organizations, create our own organizations? How is it that we do that? We talk an inclusive politic about our strategies with regard to state challenges, in terms of global factors and how it impacts on our lives as women of colour, First Nation women, but what is it that we don't do internally to sustain our organization? One of the ways our organizations become fragmented is by how we actually do our organizing. What makes it difficult sometimes to sustain our organizing? How inclusive are we in how we actually organize to do the work? To build a social movement?

We are sometimes not that inclusive. One of the issues around our anti-racist, feminist organizing is how is it that we talk about gender, race, and class? Do we talk about sexual orientation? How do we integrate sexuality in how we organize? How do we maintain the inclusivity in the discussions? What is it that we need to do in order to sustain healthy organizations?

When we build our social movements, we need to build them beyond our national boundaries. One of the things that was started some time ago, but never really sustained, is international linkages. Capital has internationalized itself. Canada does not necessarily need to import women of colours' labour to Canada to utilize it. Therefore one of the key things that we need to ensure within our organizing is to go beyond our national boundaries. The thread that binds us together crosses national boundaries.

Deena: I agree that we need to organize to sustain the struggles. We need to be able to acknowledge our weaknesses in terms of the way we do organizing and have a very critical analysis of who we aren't reaching within our own respective communities. That is a really critical piece.

Sometimes we are only organizing with other activists, or other people who have had the opportunities to have education, or be involved in some way. We really need to go back into the communities we're from, the neighbourhoods that we live in, the struggles that are around us, and get involved in that. We need to share the power and be able to facilitate the leadership of people who have never been involved before. We need to open up that space for women and facilitate leadership. We have to be able to work in a way that is participatory and democratic, and be able to facilitate an organizing approach that provides that strength and space to develop the leadership abilities of people to take on various struggles in their own communities. To look at ways of linking various issues and different movements is a very important challenge.

In the garment industry, we've seen international campaigns take place around supporting workers in various countries — in Central America, for example — through links with retailers and corporations that buy clothing and sell it here. Those international campaigns that link to women who do the work in different countries is critical, and it is critical to facilitate those exchanges. That leadership, that ability to communicate and to do campaigns, to be able to take on corporations in various states, is an incredible challenge that faces us in North

America. Incredible strength can come from that mobilization. We've seen that in a number of different struggles. The challenge is to continue and to make sure that the people who are doing the work and the ones being affected by the policies, are the ones that are leading the struggles in the various movements. That point has to reiterated again and again. We need to be self-critical of all movements and the way we work.

Beverly: Building international and global links with the women's struggle is key. What's really important is developing this, having spaces where we come together as women of colour and women from all various social locations and do some critical, constructive analysis, in terms of our work, in terms of where we go from here.

There's a hunger for discussion around how to build a social movement in terms of doing anti-racist, feminist work. There has to be a place for constructive, critical analysis and the development of an integrated anti-racist, feminist analysis that brings all of those pieces together. We need talk about our struggles in the context of what's happening globally, what's happening internationally, what's happening locally, and how that impacts on every aspect of our work.

We may seem fragmented because we are, we may seem lost. But, we are working. We have not stopped working and we have not stopped struggling. The priority is to figure out how to make gains for the fights and the struggles that are still continuing on the ground.

Contributors

Sedef Arat-Koc teaches women's studies and sociology at Trent University, Peterborough, Ontario. Her research is in the areas of Canadian immigration policy and its implications for women; feminist and Muslim discourses in Turkey; and transnational feminism. She is the co-author of *Through the Kitchen Window: The Politics of Home and Family* and the co-editor of *Maid in the Market: Women's Paid Domestic Work*.

Himani Bannerji teaches in the Department of Sociology at York University in the areas of anti-racist feminism, Marxist cultural theories, gender, colonialism, and imperialism. Her recent publications include *The Mirror of Class: Essays on Bengali Theatre* (1998), *Thinking Through: Essays on Feminism, Marxism and Anti-Racism* (1995), *The Writing on the Wall: Essays on Culture and Politics* (1993) and the edited anthology *Returning the Gaze: Essays on Racism, Feminism and Politics* (1993). She has also published two books of poetry, *A Separate Sky* and *Doing Time*, and is involved in anti-racist and feminist activism.

Dionne Brand was born in Trinidad and has lived in Canada since 1970. A renowned writer, she has written two collections of poetry, *No Language is Neutral* (shortlisted for the Governor General's Award in 1990) and *Land to Light On* (winner of the Governor General's Award for Poetry in 1997). Her novels, *In Another Place, Not Here* (1996) and *At the Full and Change of the Moon* (1999) have been published to acclaim. Her many contributions to anti-racist feminist work include co-founding Toronto's Black Women's Collective and producing the film *Sisters in Struggle* documenting black women's activism.

Linda Carty is Associate Professor of sociology and also teaches in the Women's and Gender Studies Program at the University of Michigan-Flint.

Enakshi Dua is Assistant Professor in the Department of Sociology at Queen's University. She works on race, class, and gender as well as Third World development. She is currently working on a research project that explores the discursive construction of the category "South Asian" women in the Canadian context. Her critical articles on South Asian women in Canada have appeared in *Canadian Woman Studies* and *Resources for Feminist Research*, as well as in edited anthologies. She has been active in the anti-racist feminist movement in Toronto and Kingston.

Christina Gabriel is a Post Doctoral Fellow in the Department of Political Science at the University of Alberta. Her current research interests include immigration and citizenship, gender, transnational politics, and globalization.

Tania Das Gupta is Associate Professor in the Sociology Department of Atkinson College at York University. She is the author of several publications including *Racism and Paid Work* (1996) and *Learning From Our History: Community Development By Immigrant Women in Ontario* (1986). She has been researching racism, sexism, and class issues as they are experienced in workplaces. In addition, she has been involved in anti-racist, feminist activities in Toronto.

Carolyn Egan is a healthcare worker, board member of the Immigrant Women's Health Centre and Women Working with Immigrant Women, President of the United Steel-workers' Local 8300, and member of the Ontario Coalition for Abortion Clinics.

Linda Gardner is a health care worker, a member of AIDS Action Now!, a board member of the Community AIDS Treatment Information Exchange, and a member of the Ontario Coalition for Abortion Clinics.

Ronnie Joy Leah is a sociologist, educator, and activist who specializes in critical anti-racism, women's studies, labour studies and social transformation. Ronnie has a Ph.D. in Sociology in Education (University of Toronto, 1986), was Assistant Professor of Sociology at Queen's University and University of Lethbridge, and Associate Member of Women's Studies and Industrial Relations. Ronnie currently works as a popular educator; through her consulting company Circle of Learning, she facilitates "Honouring Our Stories" workshops on racism and cultural identity, and "Act for Change" interactive theatre workshops. She works extensively with women's groups, unions, First Nations and anti-racism groups. Ronnie's publications include: "Anti-Racism Studies: An Integrative Perspective," "Aboriginal Women and Everyday Racism in Southern Alberta," "Black Women Speak Out: Racism and Unions," "Linking the Struggles: Racism, Sexism and the Union Movement."

Sharon Donna McIvor is currently completing her Doctor of Laws thesis at the School of Graduate Studies and Research, University of Ottawa Faculty of Law. She is also the Academic Dean of Indigenous Studies at Nicola Valley Institute of Technology, in Merritt, BC. Countless hours of historical research and published papers are among her accomplishments. She devotes most of her spare time to her grandchildren, read-ing, and travelling.

Sherene Razack is Professor of Sociology and Equity Studies in Education, at the Ontario Institute for Studies in Education, University of Toronto. Her books include *Looking White People in the Eye: Gender, Race, and Culture in Courtrooms and Class-rooms* (Toronto: University of Toronto Press, 1998) and *Canadian Feminism and the Law: The Women's Legal and Education Fund and the Pursuit of Equality* (Toronto: Second Story Press, 1991). She has also published articles on race, space, and prostitu-tion; the race to innocence and hierarchical relations among women; Canadian na-tional mythologies and immigration policies of the 1990s, and the Somalia affair.

Angela Robertson is the Executive Director of Sistering, a centre for homeless and marginalized women in Toronto. She has been active in the anti-racist feminist movement in Toronto for more than ten years. She has worked as Co-managing Editor of Women's Press and was a member of the Black Women's Collective.

Winona Stevenson is a member of the Fisher River Cree First Nation, Koostatak, Manitoba. She is an Associate Professor and Head of the Indian Studies Depart-ment at the Saskatchewan Indian Federated College, and has published articles on various aspects of First Nation histories.

Index